Name Kelsey Date

Uses of Numbers

You can use **ordinal numbers** to show position.

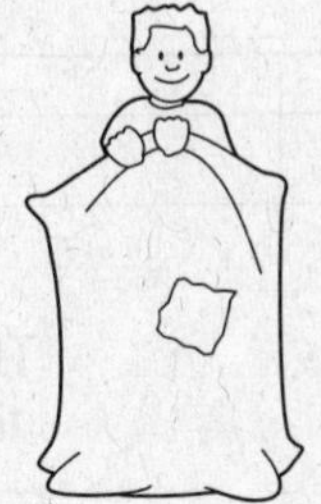

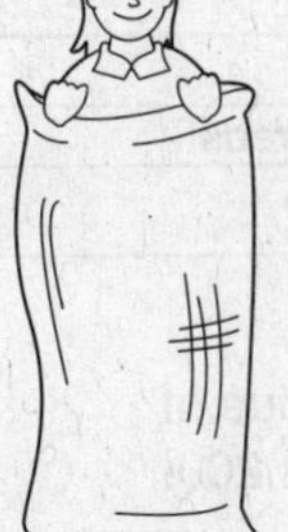

First Place Second Place Third Place Fourth Place

The teacher finished the sack race in third place.

You can use numbers to count.

There are 4 runners in the sack race.

You can use numbers to measure.

The sack is 2 feet wide.

You can use numbers to label.

Sack Race
Start Time: 11:00

The race starts at 11:00.

Tell how each number is used. Write *position, count, measure,* or *label* for each.

1. 16 cats ________
2. 20 pounds ________
3. second in line ________

Complete.

4. third, fourth, ______, sixth
5. first, second, ______, fourth
6. seventh, eighth, ninth, ______

Problem Solving

7. Beth is first in the talent show. Luis is next. In what place is Luis?

____

Use with text pages 4–5.

Name ____________________ Date ____________

Homework 1.2

Place Value: Ones, Tens, and Hundreds

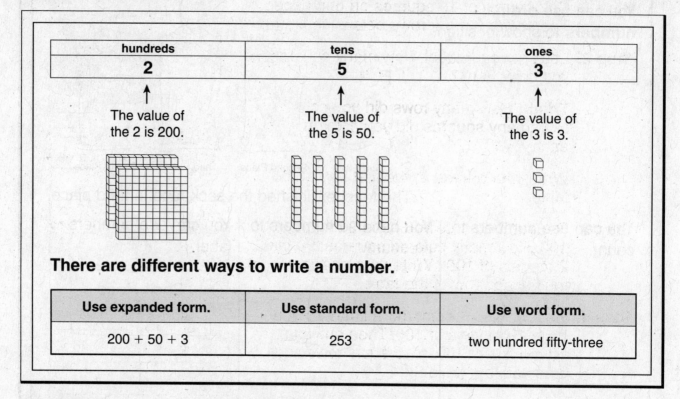

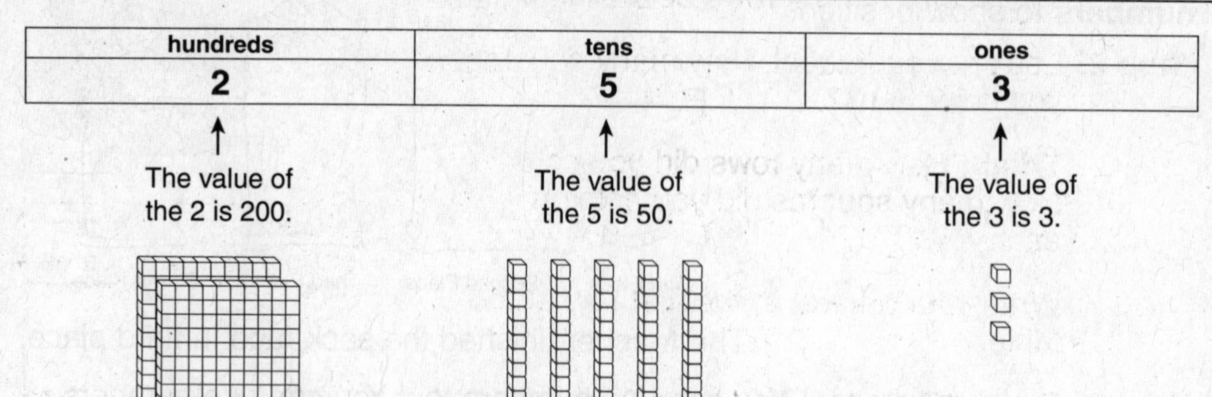

There are different ways to write a number.

Use expanded form.	Use standard form.	Use word form.
200 + 50 + 3	253	two hundred fifty-three

Write each number in standard form.

1. ______

2. 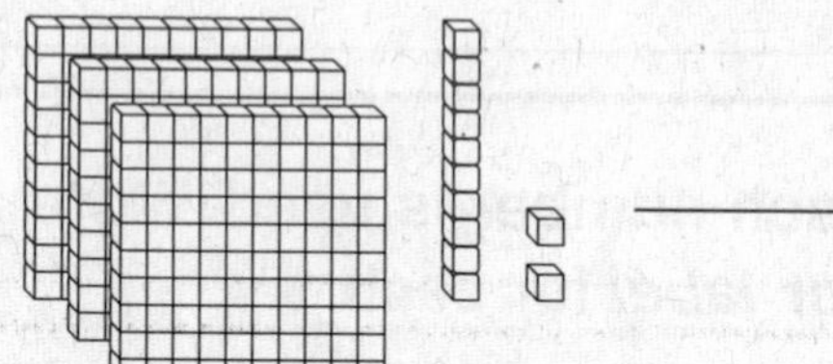 ______

Write the place of the underlined digit. Then write its value.

3. <u>7</u>16

____

4. 9<u>3</u>8

____

Problem Solving

5. Students collected 405 cans for the canned food drive. What is the number of cans written in expanded form?

____

Use with text pages 6–7.

Name ______________________ Date ____________

Homework 1.3

How Big Is One Thousand?

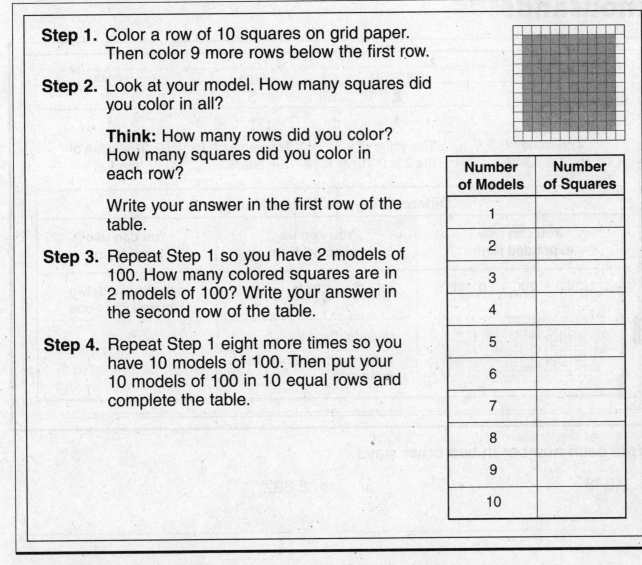

Step 1. Color a row of 10 squares on grid paper. Then color 9 more rows below the first row.

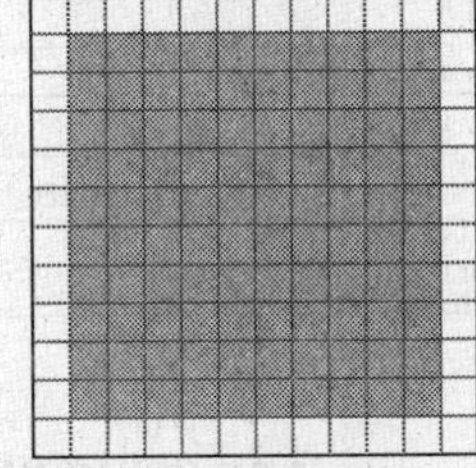

Step 2. Look at your model. How many squares did you color in all?

Think: How many rows did you color? How many squares did you color in each row?

Write your answer in the first row of the table.

Step 3. Repeat Step 1 so you have 2 models of 100. How many colored squares are in 2 models of 100? Write your answer in the second row of the table.

Step 4. Repeat Step 1 eight more times so you have 10 models of 100. Then put your 10 models of 100 in 10 equal rows and complete the table.

Number of Models	Number of Squares
1	
2	
3	
4	
5	
6	
7	
8	
9	
10	

Tell if each is *greater than, less than,* or *equal to* 1,000.

1. 10 boxes of 10 envelopes ______________
2. 10 bags of 100 push pins ______________
3. 8 bags of 100 buttons ______________
4. 1 pack of 1,000 sheets of paper ______________

Problem Solving

5. Inez needs 1,000 straws for the school party. How many boxes of 100 straws should she buy?

Use with text pages 8–9.

Name ______________________ Date ____________

Homework 1.4

Place Value Through Thousands

thousands	hundreds	tens	ones
1	2	3	1
↑ The value of the 1 is 1,000.	↑ The value of the 2 is 200.	↑ The value of the 3 is 30.	↑ The value of the 1 is 1.

Different Ways to Write a Number		
You can use expanded form.	**You can use standard form.**	**You can use word form.**
1,000 + 200 + 30 + 1	1,231 ↑ A comma is used to separate thousands and hundreds.	one thousand, two hundred thirty-one

Write each number in two other ways.

1. 2,846

____

____

2. 8,392

____

____

3. 7,000 + 400 + 50

____

____

4. five thousand, four hundred seven

____

____

Problem Solving

5. The Golden Gate Bridge in San Francisco spans 1,280 meters. Write this number in expanded form.

____

Use with text pages 10–12.

Name ______________________ Date ______________

Homework 1.5

Problem-Solving Strategy: Find a Number Pattern

Suppose the first four building numbers on a street are 215, 225, 235, 245.

If the number pattern continues, what are the numbers on the next two buildings likely to be?

UNDERSTAND

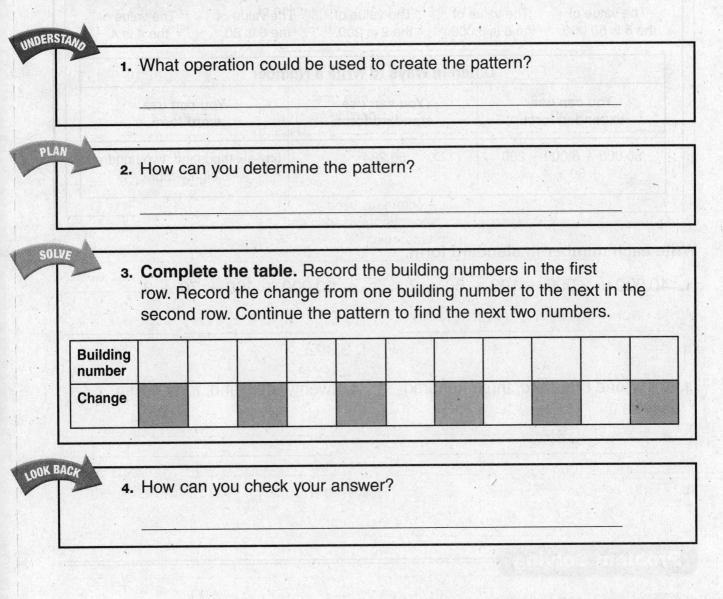

1. What operation could be used to create the pattern?

____

PLAN

2. How can you determine the pattern?

____

SOLVE

3. **Complete the table.** Record the building numbers in the first row. Record the change from one building number to the next in the second row. Continue the pattern to find the next two numbers.

Building number											
Change											

LOOK BACK

4. How can you check your answer?

____

Name ______________________ Date ______________

Homework 1.6

Place Value Through Ten Thousands

ten thousands	thousands	hundreds	tens	ones
5	6	2	8	4
↑ The value of the 5 is 50,000.	↑ The value of the 6 is 6,000.	↑ The value of the 2 is 200.	↑ The value of the 8 is 80.	↑ The value of the 4 is 4.

Different Ways to Write a Number

You can use expanded form.	You can use standard form.	You can use word form.
50,000 + 6,000 + 200 + 80 + 4	56,284	fifty-six thousand, two hundred eighty-four

Write each number in standard form.

1. 40,000 + 3,000 + 100 + 60 + 2 ______________
2. 90,000 + 400 + 70 + 3 ______________
3. thirty-one thousand, three hundred twelve ______________
4. twenty thousand, forty-seven ______________

Problem Solving

5. The average depth of the Pacific Ocean is 12,925 feet. Write this number in expanded form.

____

Use with text pages 18–19.

Name ______________________ Date ____________

Homework 1.7

Place Value Through Hundred Thousands

hundred thousands	ten thousands	thousands	hundreds	tens	ones
3	0	4	9	5	2

Different Ways to Write a Number		
You can use expanded form.	**You can use standard form.**	**You can use word form.**
300,000 + 4,000 + 900 + 50 + 2	304,952	three hundred four thousand, nine hundred fifty-two

Write each number in standard form.

1. 600,000 + 50,000 + 200 + 40 + 9

____

2. 80,000 + 700 + 40

____

3. four hundred thousand, five hundred four

____

4. two hundred three thousand, seventy-one

____

Write the place of the underlined digit. Then write its value.

5. 317,<u>9</u>24

____

6. 147,8<u>2</u>6

____

Problem Solving

7. The Bering Sea has an area of 873,000 square miles. What is the value of the digit 3?

____

Name ____________________ Date ____________

Homework 2.1

Compare Numbers

Compare. Write >, <, or = for each ○.

253 ○ 273

Use a place-value chart.

hundreds	tens	ones
2	5	3
2	7	3

same — 5 tens < 7 tens

When you compare the digits in the tens place, 5 tens < 7 tens.

So, 253 < 273.

1. 37 ○ 32
2. 48 ○ 78
3. 93 ○ 93
4. 8 ○ 80
5. 167 ○ 57
6. 145 ○ 145
7. 174 ○ 178
8. 197 ○ 217
9. 129 ○ 93
10. 1,645 ○ 1,643
11. 705 ○ 792
12. 1,586 ○ 1,986

Algebra • Symbols
Write = or ≠ for each ○.

13. 12 + 4 ○ 18
14. 15 + 4 ○ 19
15. 20 + 3 ○ 23
16. 40 + 6 ○ 64
17. 100 + 40 ○ 130
18. 200 + 3 ○ 230

Problem Solving

19. Jamal is studying the Great Lakes. He found that Lake Michigan is 307 miles long and Lake Superior is 350 miles long. Which lake is longer?

____

20. Jamal is studying Baykal Lake in Asia and Lake Superior in North America. He found that Baykal Lake is 395 miles long and Lake Superior is 350 miles long. Which lake is longer?

____

Use with text pages 28–29.

Name ______________________ Date __________

Homework 2.2

Order Numbers

Wendy found the length of three lakes. She found that Kariba Lake is 175 miles long, Lake Erie is 241 miles long, and Great Bear Lake is 192 miles long. Which lake is the shortest?

hundreds	tens	ones
1	7	5
2	4	1
1	9	2

1 hundred $<$ 2 hundreds, so 241 is the greatest number

7 tens $<$ 9 tens, so 175 is the least number.

The order of the numbers from least to greatest is: 175 192 241.

Solution: The shortest lake is Kariba Lake.

Write the numbers in order from least to greatest.

1. 18 23 14 ____________

2. 127 98 125 ____________

3. 2,367 2,514 1,879 ____________

4. 89 879 409 ____________

5. 115 521 512 ____________

6. 6,495 6,395 6,459 ____________

Write the numbers in order from greatest to least.

7. 73 71 80 ____________

8. 497 492 536 ____________

9. 972 1,583 1,246 ____________

10. 185 105 1,058 ____________

11. 237 1,717 1,770 ____________

12. 9,999 9,799 998 ____________

Problem Solving

13. Lake Onega is 145 miles long. Lake Ladoga is 124 miles long. Lake Athabasca is 208 miles long. Which lake is the shortest?

____

14. Lake Tanganyika is 420 miles long. Lake Michigan is 307 miles long. Lake Superior is 350 miles long. Which lake is the longest?

____

Use with text pages 30–31.

Name ______________________ Date ______________

Homework 2.3

Round Two-Digit and Three-Digit Numbers

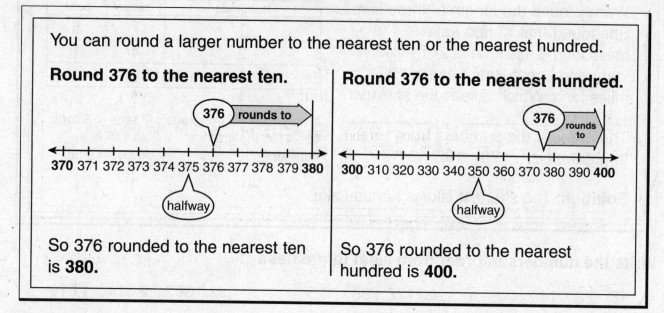

You can round a larger number to the nearest ten or the nearest hundred.

Round 376 to the nearest ten.

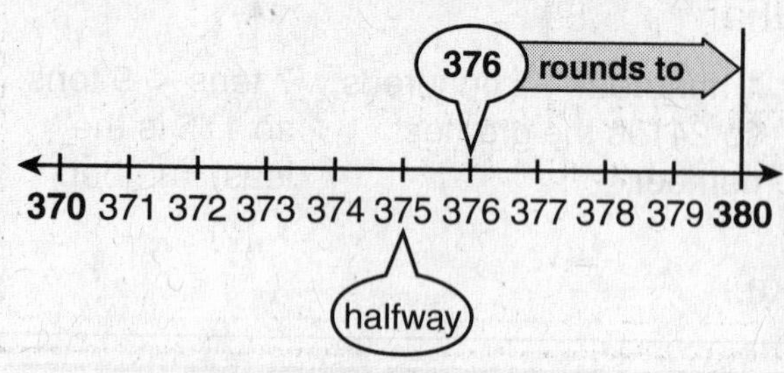

So 376 rounded to the nearest ten is **380.**

Round 376 to the nearest hundred.

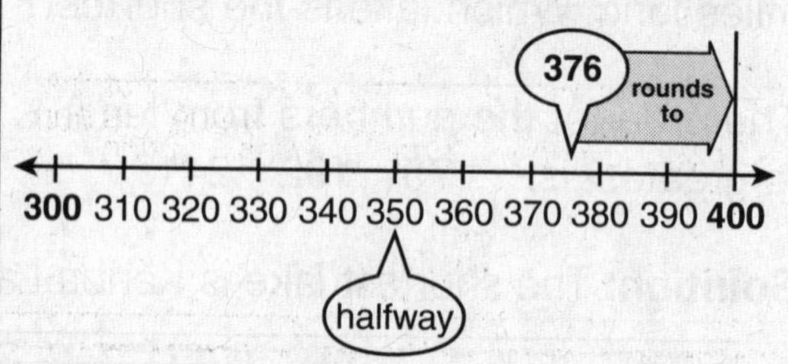

So 376 rounded to the nearest hundred is **400.**

For each number, write the 2 tens the number is between. Then round to the nearest ten.

1. 21 ________ ________
2. 76 ________ ________
3. 483 ________ ________
4. 625 ________ ________
5. 402 ________ ________

For each number, write the 2 hundreds the number is between. Then round to the nearest hundred.

6. 361 ________ ________
7. 537 ________ ________
8. 258 ________ ________
9. 709 ________ ________
10. 455 ________ ________

Problem Solving

11. Esther has 36 plants. Rounded to the nearest ten, how many plants does Esther have?

____

12. Omar has 318 marbles. Rounded to the nearest hundred, how many marbles does Omar have?

____

Use with text pages 32–34.

Name ______________________ Date ____________

Round Four-Digit Numbers

Round to the place of the underlined digit.

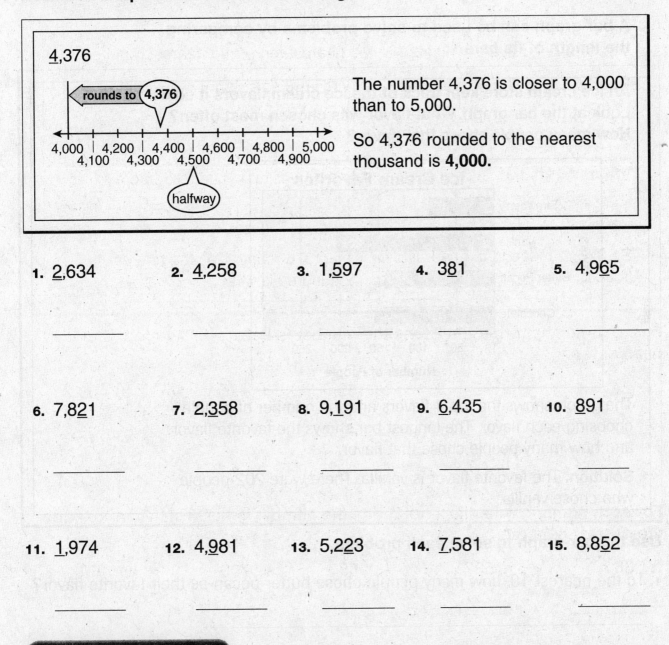

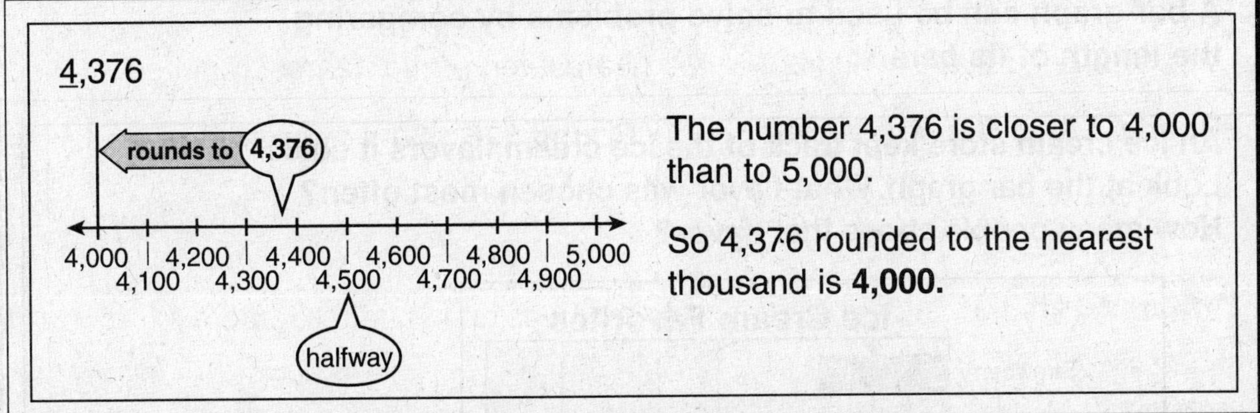

The number 4,376 is closer to 4,000 than to 5,000.

So 4,376 rounded to the nearest thousand is **4,000.**

1. 2,634 ________

2. 4,258 ________

3. 1,597 ________

4. 381 ________

5. 4,965 ________

6. 7,821 ________

7. 2,358 ________

8. 9,191 ________

9. 6,435 ________

10. 891 ________

11. 1,974 ________

12. 4,981 ________

13. 5,223 ________

14. 7,581 ________

15. 8,852 ________

Problem Solving

16. A train traveled 2,317 miles. Rounded to the nearest thousand, how many miles did the train travel?

____

17. The distance between Atlanta and San Francisco is 2,496 miles. Rounded to the nearest hundred, how many miles is it between the two cities?

____

Use with text pages 36–37.

Name ______________________ Date ____________

Homework 2.5

Problem-Solving Application: Use a Bar Graph

A bar graph can be used to solve problems by comparing the length of its bars.

An ice cream store kept track of the ice cream flavors it sold. Look at the bar graph. What flavor was chosen most often? How many people chose that flavor?

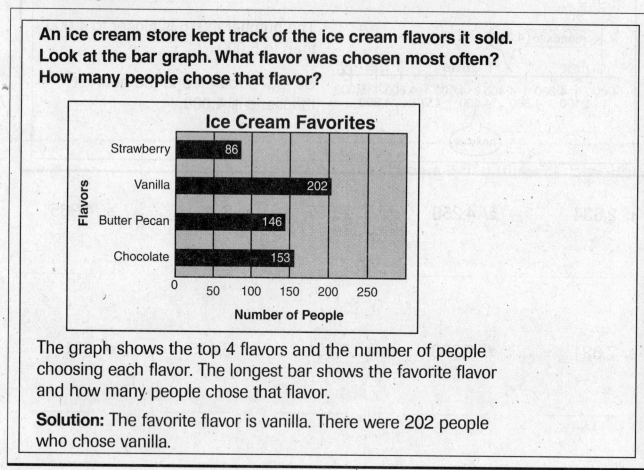

The graph shows the top 4 flavors and the number of people choosing each flavor. The longest bar shows the favorite flavor and how many people chose that flavor.

Solution: The favorite flavor is vanilla. There were 202 people who chose vanilla.

Use the bar graph to solve each problem.

1. To the nearest 10, how many people chose butter pecan as their favorite flavor?

____

2. Which flavor was chosen by the least number of people? How many people chose that flavor?

____

3. Which two flavors were chosen by about the same number of people?

____

Use with text pages 38–40.

Name ________________________ Date ____________

Homework 3.1

Value of Money

A dollar, a dime, and a penny have different values.
Their values can be shown using places.

1 dollar
100 cents
100¢

1 dime
10 cents
10¢

1 penny
1 cent
1¢

Dollars	Dimes	Pennies
1	1	1

one dollar and eleven cents

$1.11

dollar sign ↑ ↑ decimal point

Write each amount using a dollar sign and a decimal point.

1. 

____

2. 

____

3. 

____

4. 

____

5. 

____

6. 

____

Problem Solving

7. Tamara has $4.35 in her bank. How much will she have if she adds 1 dollar, 4 dimes, and 4 pennies?

____

Use with text pages 46–47.

Name ______________________ Date ______________

Homework 3.2

Count Coins and Bills

Write each amount using a dollar sign and a decimal point.

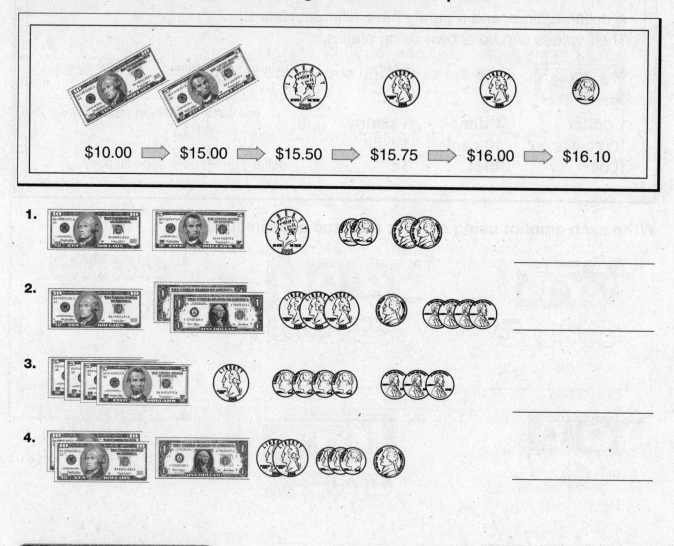

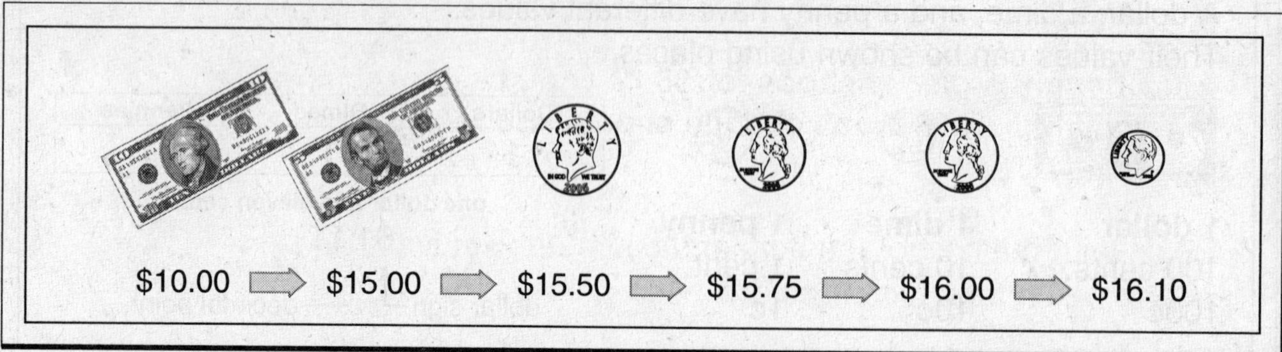

1.  ______________

2. ______________

3. ______________

4. ______________

Problem Solving

5. Harry has 1 half-dollar, 2 dimes, and 3 nickels. Using a dollar sign and a decimal point, write the amount of money he has.

____

6. Mara gets 1 ten-dollar bill, three quarters, and 1 nickel for each pie that she sells. How much money does she get for selling a pie?

____

Use with text pages 48–49.

Name ______________________ Date ____________

Homework 3.3

Problem-Solving Application: Make Change

Alisa bought a pair of shoes for $8.79 and paid for them with a ten-dollar bill. How much change should she receive?

Begin with the cost of the item and count up with coins and bills to reach the amount paid.

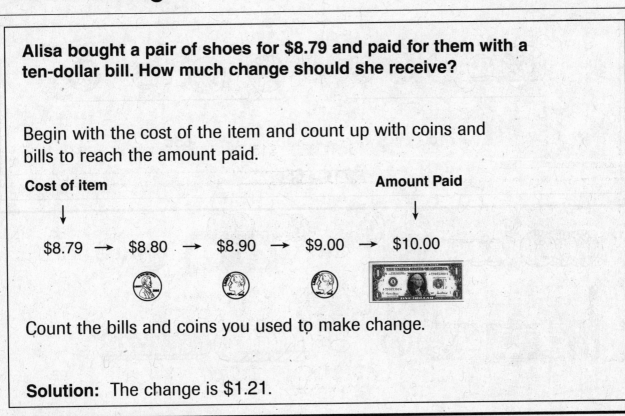

Cost of item ↓ **Amount Paid** ↓

$8.79 → $8.80 → $8.90 → $9.00 → $10.00

Count the bills and coins you used to make change.

Solution: The change is $1.21.

Solve each problem.

1. Maria pays for a $0.38 candy bar with $1.00. How much change should she receive?

 ____

2. Juan bought a DVD for $7.99. How much change should he receive if he pays for it with a ten-dollar bill?

 ____

3. Darren paid for a $1.65 drink with a five-dollar bill. How much change should he receive? List the coins and bills he might receive as change.

 ____

 ____

Use with text pages 50–51.

Name ______________________ Date ____________

Homework 3.4

Compare Money Amounts

Compare. Write >, <, or = for each ◯.

71¢ ◯ **65¢**

71¢ > 65¢

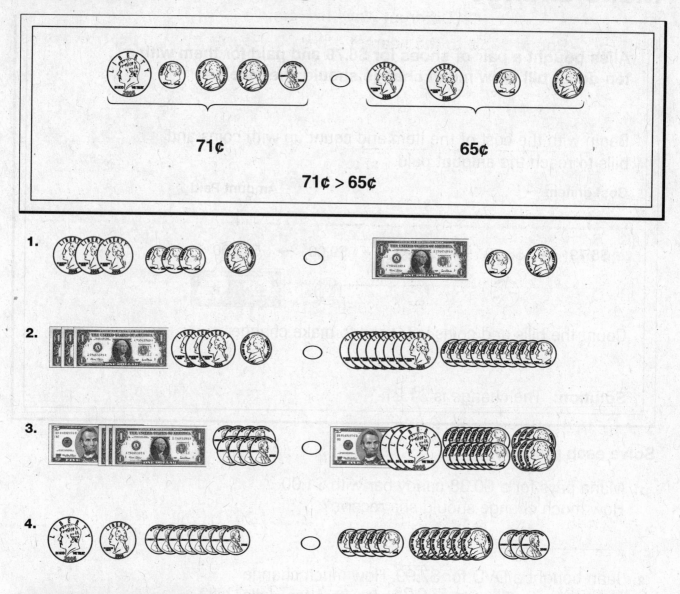

1. ◯

2. ◯

3. ◯

4. ◯

Problem Solving

5. Patty saved some money this week. She saved some money last week. Which group of money has the greater value? Use >, <, or = to compare.

◯

Use with text pages 52–54.

Name ________________________ Date ____________

Homework 3.5

Round Money

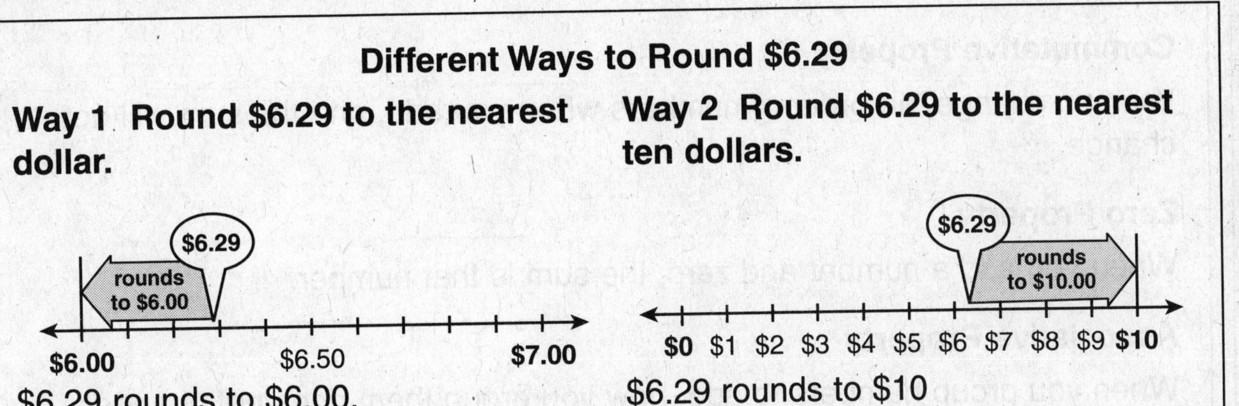

Different Ways to Round $6.29
Way 1 Round $6.29 to the nearest dollar.
$6.29
rounds to $6.00
$6.00
$6.50
$7.00
$6.29 rounds to $6.00.
Way 2 Round $6.29 to the nearest ten dollars.
$6.29
rounds to $10.00
$0 $1 $2 $3 $4 $5 $6 $7 $8 $9 $10
$6.29 rounds to $10

Round to the nearest dollar.

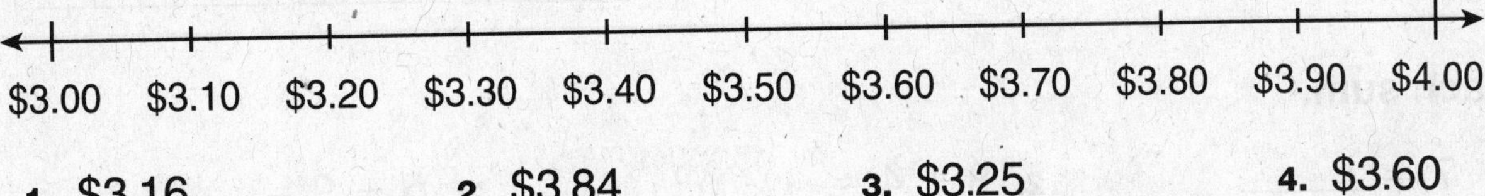

1. $3.16 ______

2. $3.84 ______

3. $3.25 ______

4. $3.60 ______

Round to the nearest ten dollars.

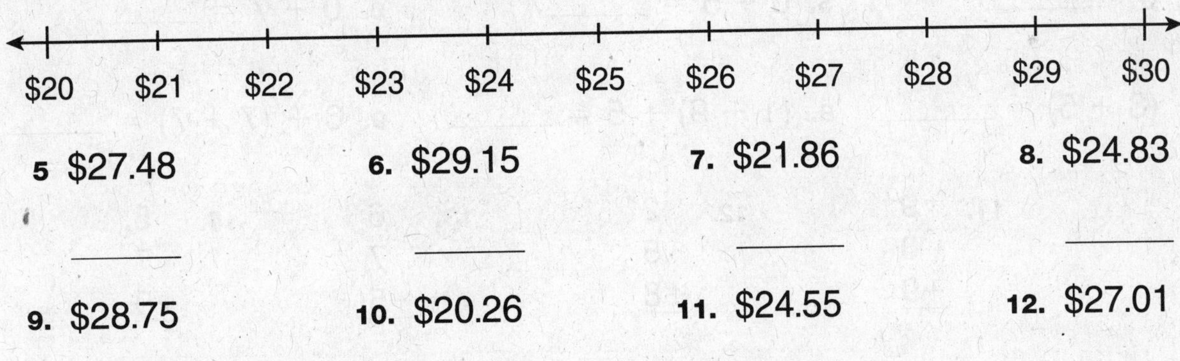

5 $27.48 ______

6. $29.15 ______

7. $21.86 ______

8. $24.83 ______

9. $28.75 ______

10. $20.26 ______

11. $24.55 ______

12. $27.01 ______

Problem Solving

13. Joanna paid $3.65 for a jade plant. About how much did she pay for the plant, rounded to the nearest dollar?

______

14. Warren paid $5.71 for a paint brush. About how much did he pay for the paint brush, rounded to the nearest ten dollars?

______

Use with text pages 56–58.

Name ______________________ Date ____________

Homework 4.1

Addition Properties

Commutative Property

You can change the order of numbers when you add, and the sum will not change.

Zero Property

When you add a number and zero, the sum is that number.

Associative Property

When you group numbers to add, how you group them does not change the sum.

$(3 + 5) + 2$ $\quad$ $3 + (5 + 2)$

$8 + 2 = 10$ $\quad$ $3 + 7 = 10$

Find each sum.

1. $3 + 7 =$ ______
   $7 + 3 =$ ______
2. $8 + 4 =$ ______
   $4 + 8 =$ ______
3. $5 + 9 =$ ______
   $9 + 5 =$ ______
4. $2 + 0 =$ ______
5. $0 + 5 =$ ______
6. $0 + 7 =$ ______
7. $4 + (8 + 5) =$ ______
8. $(1 + 9) + 5 =$ ______
9. $6 + (7 + 7) =$ ______

10.	11.	12.	13.	14.
3	9	2	6	5
4	0	5	7	7
+7	+9	+8	+5	+9

Problem Solving

15. Anna has 4 science books, 9 sports books, and 1 mystery book. How many books does Anna have in all?

____

Use with text pages 76–77.

Name ______________________ Date ____________

Homework 4.2

Estimate Sums

On Thursday 276 people came to the school concert. On Friday 138 people came to the concert. About how many people came to the concert in all?

To estimate a sum, you can round the addends.

Estimate 276 + 138.

Round each number to the greatest place. Then add.

276	rounds to	300
+ 138	rounds to	+ 100
		400

Solution: *About* 400 people came to the concert.

Round each number to the greatest place. Then add.

1. 231 + 194

2. 326 + 207

3. 374 + 469

4. 85 + 64

5. \$7.92 + 8.06

Tell what compatible numbers you would use. Then add.

6. \$2.55 + \$1.34

7. 419 + 263

8. 227 + 781

9. 67 + 119

Problem Solving

10. Tara bought a ticket to the concert for \$2.75. She bought flowers for \$5.35. About how much is the total cost of the ticket and flowers?

Use with text pages 78–80.

Name ______________________________ Date ______________

Homework 4.3

Regroup Ones

Rosa's class made 127 programs for the class play. The class also made 149 programs for music night. How many programs did the class make in all?

You can add numbers by using columns. First add the ones, then the tens, then the hundreds.

Add.

If the sum of the digits in the ones place is 10 or greater, regroup 10 ones as 1 ten. Then add the tens.

$$\begin{array}{r} {}^{1} \\ 127 \\ +149 \\ \hline 276 \end{array}$$

Solution: The class made 276 programs in all.

Find each sum.

1. $\begin{array}{r} 175 \\ +118 \\ \hline \end{array}$
2. $\begin{array}{r} 329 \\ +164 \\ \hline \end{array}$
3. $\begin{array}{r} \$2.57 \\ +\ 1.24 \\ \hline \end{array}$
4. $\begin{array}{r} 36 \\ +49 \\ \hline \end{array}$
5. $\begin{array}{r} 408 \\ +387 \\ \hline \end{array}$
6. $\begin{array}{r} 127 \\ +236 \\ \hline \end{array}$
7. $\begin{array}{r} 28 \\ +59 \\ \hline \end{array}$
8. $\begin{array}{r} 308 \\ +246 \\ \hline \end{array}$
9. $\begin{array}{r} 165 \\ +417 \\ \hline \end{array}$
10. $\begin{array}{r} 249 \\ +439 \\ \hline \end{array}$

Problem Solving

11. There are 159 students in the school chorus and 134 students in the school band. How many students are in the chorus and band altogether?

____

Use with text pages 82–84.

Name ______________________ Date ______________

Homework 4.4

Regroup Ones and Tens

264 people rode bicycles last year to raise money. This year, 359 people rode bicycles. How many people rode bicycles to raise money in two years?

Find 264 + 359 = ■.

$$\begin{array}{r} {}^{1\,1} \\ 264 \\ +359 \\ \hline 623 \end{array}$$

Solution: In two years, 623 people rode bikes to raise money.

Add. Check by adding upward.

1. 153 + 269
2. 284 + 367
3. \$5.98 + 1.75
4. 453 + 267
5. 258 + 679
6. 408 + 567
7. 276 + 287
8. 347 + 489
9. 176 + 796
10. \$2.19 + 3.94
11. 195 + 326
12. 483 + 117
13. 946 + 85
14. \$1.24 + 3.76
15. 338 + 475

Problem Solving

16. On Thursday, 165 cars parked in the lot at the train station. On Friday, 247 cars parked in the lot. How many cars parked in the lot on Thursday and Friday?

____

Use with text pages 86–88.

Name ______________________ Date ______________

Homework 4.5

Problem-Solving Strategy: Guess and Check

Joe is 3 years older than Phillip. Together their ages total 27. How old is each boy?

Facts you know: Their ages add up to 27. Joe is 3 years older than Phillip.

Guess. Think of 2 numbers that have a difference of 3 and then check to see if they add up to 27.

Guess	Check
13 − 10 = 3	13 + 10 = 23 (Guess higher.)
17 − 14 = 3	17 + 14 = 31 (Guess lower.)
15 − 12 = 3	15 + 12 = 27 (Correct.)

Solution: Joe is 15 and Phillip is 12 years old.

Use guess and check to solve each problem.

1. Emily and Kaitlin together have 35 stuffed animals. Emily has 7 more stuffed animals than Kaitlin. How many stuffed animals does each girl have?

____

____

2. Noah has a total of 45 toy cars and trucks. He has 5 more toy cars than toy trucks. How many toy trucks does he have?

____

3. Leo has 8 more markers than colored pencils. He has a total of 32 markers and colored pencils. How many of each kind does he have?

____

____

Use with text pages 90–92.

Name ______________________ Date ____________

Homework 4.6

Column Addition

The auditorium has 214 seats on the first level, 59 seats on the second level, and 76 seats on the third level. How many seats does the auditorium have?

Find 214 + 59 + 76 = ■.

$$\begin{array}{r} {}^{1\,1} \\ 214 \\ 59 \\ +\ 76 \\ \hline 349 \end{array}$$

Solution: The auditorium has 349 seats.

Find each sum.

1. 125 + 64 + 37
2. 82 + 29 + 53
3. \$2.17 + 1.38 + 3.72
4. 316 + 57 + 34
5. 35 + 97 + 503
6. 498 + 67 + 213
7. 79 + 344 + 476
8. 194 + 604 + 96
9. 203 + 57 + 578
10. \$1.80 + 4.06 + 1.94
11. 589 + 207 + 46
12. 415 + 501 + 34
13. 129 + 899 + 542
14. \$4.15 + 7.99 + 8.50
15. \$1.89 + 0.49 + 7.05

Problem Solving

16. The auditorium has 174 seats on the right side, 168 seats on the left side, and 35 seats in the center. How many seats does the auditorium have in all?

____

Use with text pages 94–96.

Name ______________________ Date ____________

Homework 4.7

Add Greater Numbers

In the town of Harville, there are 2,348 people. In the town of Oakdale, there are 1,976 people. How many people are there in both towns combined?

Add. 2,348 + 1,976 = ■.

For each place, you should regroup if the sum of the digits in the column is 10 or greater.

$$\begin{array}{r} {}^{1\,1\,1}\\ 2,348 \\ +1,976 \\ \hline 4,324 \end{array}$$

Solution: There are 4,324 people in both towns combined.

Find each sum. Estimate to check.

1. 2,356 + 1,968
2. 1,872 + 3,569
3. \$24.96 + 18.57
4. 3,079 + 2,975
5. 6,589 + 2,434
6. \$56.38 + 16.07
7. 4,897 + 3,844
8. 2,796 + 5,895
9. \$55.27 + 49.25
10. 1,480 + 2,320
11. 8,961 + 3,425
12. \$15.56 + 63.45

Problem Solving

13. A shirt costs \$23.87. A book costs \$16.99. What is the total cost of the shirt and the book?

____

Use with text pages 98–99.

Name ______________________ Date __________

Homework 4.8

Choose a Method

Kevin's town held a parade. There were 345 people who walked in the parade. There were 400 volunteers who worked at the parade. Another 1,578 people attended the parade.

How many people walked in, worked at, or attended the parade altogether?

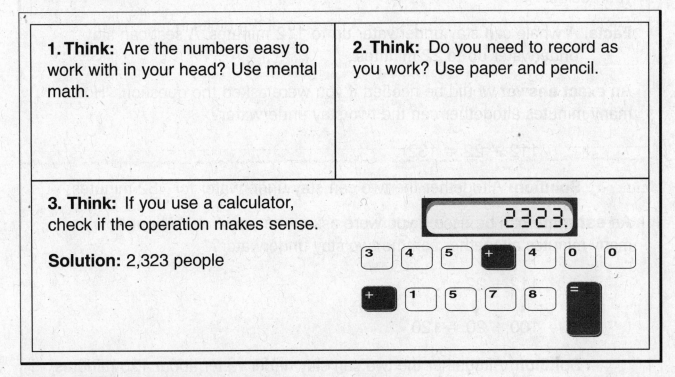

1. Think: Are the numbers easy to work with in your head? Use mental math.

2. Think: Do you need to record as you work? Use paper and pencil.

3. Think: If you use a calculator, check if the operation makes sense.

Solution: 2,323 people

Add. Choose mental math, paper and pencil, or calculator. Explain your choice.

On Thursday 219 people visited the art museum. On Friday 650 people visited, and on Saturday 1,286 people visited.

1. How many people visited the museum on Thursday and Friday altogether?

____

____

____

2. How many people visited the museum on all three days?

____

____

____

Use with text pages 100–101.

Name ______________________ Date ____________

Homework 4.9

Problem-Solving Decision: Estimate or Exact Answer

Before solving a problem, you must decide if you need to find an exact answer or an estimate. Looking for certain words in the problem can help you decide.

Facts. A whale can stay underwater up to 112 minutes. A seal can stay underwater up to 22 minutes.

An **exact answer** would be needed if you were asked the question, "How many minutes altogether can the two stay underwater?

$112 + 22 = 132$

Solution: Altogether the two can stay underwater for 132 minutes.

An **estimate** can be used if you were asked the question, "About how many minutes altogether can the two stay underwater?"

$112 + 22$

↓ ↓

$100 + 20 = 120$

Solution: Altogether the two can stay under water about 120 minutes.

Solve. Tell whether you need and exact answer or an estimate.

1. An elephant in the wild eats 449 pounds of food each day and an elephant in a zoo eats 153 pounds of food each day. About how many pounds of food do the two together eat in a day?

____

2. A tiger is 87 inches longer than a housecat. A housecat is 38 inches long. How long is the tiger?

____

Use with text page 102.

Name ________________________ Date ______________

Homework 5.1

Subtraction Rules

Subtract. Use subtraction rules when you can.

Subtracting Zero	Subtracting a Number From Itself
When you subtract zero from a number, the difference is that number.	When you subtract a number from itself, the difference is zero.
$\begin{array}{r} 16 \\ -\ 0 \\ \hline 16 \end{array}$	$\begin{array}{r} 37 \\ -37 \\ \hline 0 \end{array}$

1. $\begin{array}{r} 68 \\ -68 \\ \hline \end{array}$
2. $\begin{array}{r} 12 \\ -\ 2 \\ \hline \end{array}$
3. $\begin{array}{r} 15 \\ -\ 0 \\ \hline \end{array}$
4. $\begin{array}{r} 33 \\ -33 \\ \hline \end{array}$
5. $\begin{array}{r} 28 \\ -\ 5 \\ \hline \end{array}$
6. $\begin{array}{r} 12 \\ -12 \\ \hline \end{array}$
7. $\begin{array}{r} 47 \\ -\ 0 \\ \hline \end{array}$
8. $\begin{array}{r} 41 \\ -41 \\ \hline \end{array}$
9. $\begin{array}{r} 56 \\ -\ 0 \\ \hline \end{array}$
10. $\begin{array}{r} 18 \\ -\ 7 \\ \hline \end{array}$

11. 52 − 52 ______
12. 18 − 18 ______
13. 18 − 5 ______
14. 24 − 4 ______
15. 10 − 0 ______

Algebra • Properties **Find each missing number.**

16. 15 − ■ = 15
17. ■ − 6 = 0
18. 0 = 20 − ■
19. 22 − 22 = ■
20. ■ − 14 = 0
21. 0 = ■ − 26
22. 28 − ■ = 28
23. 58 − 58 = ■

Problem Solving

24. Mark had a basket of carrots. He counted 29 carrots in the basket. He fed the rabbits 29 carrots. How many carrots did Mark have left?

____

Use with text pages 108–109.

Name ______________________________ Date ______________

Homework 5.2

Relate Addition and Subtraction

Fact Family for 2, 6, and 8
2 + 6 = 8
6 + 2 = 8
8 − 6 = 2
8 − 2 = 6

Use counters to find each missing number.

1. 6 + 3 = 9
9 − 3 = ■

2. 9 + 9 = 18
18 − 9 = ■

3. 8 + 3 = 11
11 − ■ = 8

4. 7 + ■ = 12
12 − 7 = 5

Complete each fact family.

5. 4 + 6 = 10
6 + ■ = 10
10 − 6 = ■
10 − ■ = 6

6. 3 + 9 = 12
■ + 3 = 12
12 − 9 = ■
■ − 3 = 9

7. 7 + 4 = 11
4 + 7 = ■
11 − ■ = 4
11 − 4 = ■

8. 8 + 6 = 14
6 + 8 = ■
■ − 8 = 6
14 − ■ = 8

Problem Solving

9. Tim has 8 goldfish and 16 guppies in his fish tank. How many fish does he have in all?

____

Use with text pages 110–111.

Name ______________________ Date ____________

Homework 5.3

Estimate Differences

Round each number to the greatest place. Then subtract.

88 − 71

88	rounds to	90
−71	rounds to	−70
		20

88 − 71 is about 20.

1. 72 − 27

2. 94 − 13

3. 69 − 29

4. 84 − 78

5. 51 − 36

6. 92 − 43

7. 370 − 114

8. 563 − 175

9. 776 − 171

10. 657 − 438

11. 78 − 26

12. 94 − 22

13. 198 − 196

14. $3.75 − $1.19

15. $57 − $32

16. $6.99 − $4.87

17. 842 − 172

18. $398 − $255

Problem Solving

19. Marisa's family is traveling 528 miles to visit her aunt. If they travel 364 miles the first day, about how far do they have to travel the second day to complete the trip?

____

Use with text pages 112–114.

Name ______________________ Date ____________

Homework 5.4

Regroup Tens

Find each difference. Estimate to check.

654 − 238

$$\begin{array}{r} 6\overset{4}{\cancel{5}}\overset{14}{\cancel{4}} \\ -238 \\ \hline 416 \end{array}$$

Check: 654 rounds to 700
−238 rounds to −200
500

654 − 238 = 416

1. 33 − 17
2. 72 − 25
3. \$60 − \$15
4. 33 − 18
5. 81 − 68
6. 434 − 118
7. 225 − 118
8. 150 − 82
9. \$392 − \$149
10. 745 − 318
11. 94 − 57 ______
12. \$671 − \$216 ______
13. 843 − 527 ______
14. \$391 − \$119 ______

Problem Solving

15. Ms. Pierce has 36 art students in her third-grade class. She has 19 students in her fourth-grade class. How many more students are in her third-grade class?

____

Name ______________________ Date ____________

Homework 5.5

Regroup Tens and Hundreds

Subtract. Check by adding.

438 − 289

$$\begin{array}{r} \overset{3}{\cancel{4}}\overset{\overset{12}{\cancel{2}}}{\cancel{3}}\overset{18}{\cancel{8}} \\ -289 \\ \hline 149 \end{array}$$

Check:

$$\begin{array}{r} 289 \\ +149 \\ \hline 438 \end{array}$$

438 − 289 = 149

1. $\begin{array}{r} 734 \\ -488 \\ \hline \end{array}$

2. $\begin{array}{r} 854 \\ -285 \\ \hline \end{array}$

3. $\begin{array}{r} 932 \\ -345 \\ \hline \end{array}$

4. $\begin{array}{r} 746 \\ -459 \\ \hline \end{array}$

5. $\begin{array}{r} 856 \\ -687 \\ \hline \end{array}$

6. $\begin{array}{r} 345 \\ -268 \\ \hline \end{array}$

7. $\begin{array}{r} \$9.62 \\ -\$5.74 \\ \hline \end{array}$

8. $\begin{array}{r} 636 \\ -258 \\ \hline \end{array}$

9. $\begin{array}{r} 857 \\ -489 \\ \hline \end{array}$

10. $\begin{array}{r} 753 \\ -265 \\ \hline \end{array}$

11. $7.46 − $5.64 ______

12. 416 − 148 ______

13. 726 − 549 ______

14. 343 − 188 ______

15. 905 − 178 ______

16. $8.73 − $6.74 ______

17. 415 − 347 ______

18. 798 − 209 ______

Problem Solving

19. Heather is putting a 525-piece puzzle together. So far, she has 359 pieces in place. How many more pieces does she need to place?

____

Use with text pages 120–122.

Name ______________________ Date ____________

Homework 5.6

Subtract Greater Numbers

Find each difference. Check by adding or estimating.

3,523 − 1,486

```
  4 11 13
3,5̸2̸3̸          Check:    1 1
−1,486                   2,037
------                  +1,486
 2,037                  ------
                         3,523
```

3,523 − 1,486 = 2,037

1. 5,293 − 2,716

2. 4,200 − 3,100

3. 7,454 − 4,215

4. 8,760 − 7,386

5. 3,549 − 2,750

6. $2,177 − $1,153

7. 5,524 − 1,603

8. 7,243 − 4,537

9. 1,558 − 1,362

10. 4,292 − 1,728

11. 6,352 − 3,236 ________

12. 2,476 − 1,685 ________

13. 5,688 − 3,865 ________

14. 4,371 − 3,356 ________

Problem Solving

15. The attendance at the hockey game was 5,329 people. The attendance at the basketball game was 3,278. How many more people attended the hockey game?

____

Use with text pages 124–126.

Name ______________________ Date ____________

Homework 5.7

Subtract Across Zeros

Subtract. Check by adding or estimating.

700 − 324
Regroup from greater places as needed.

```
   9
 6 10 10
 7  0  0
− 3  2  4
  3  7  6
```

Check

```
  1 1
  376
+ 324
  700
```

1. 406 − 157

2. 905 − 453

3. 600 − 353

4. 803 − 626

5. 7,009 − 3,974

6. 703 − 214

7. 306 − 148

8. 500 − 337

9. 800 − 246

10. 3,060 − 1,436

11. 470 − 202 ______

12. 207 − 173 ______

13. 800 − 438 ______

14. 5,520 − 2,359 ______

Problem Solving

15. Jeffrey's ant farm has 400 ants. Jamal's ant farm has 265 ants. How many more ants are there in Jeffrey's ant farm?

____

Use with text pages 128–129.

Name ______________________ Date ______________

Homework 5.8

Problem-Solving Decision: Explain Your Answer

Solve. Explain how you solved each problem.

There are 317 crayons in the art room. A class borrowed 188 for a project. How many crayons are left in the room?

```
   10
 2 0̸17
 3̸1̸7̸
−188
 129
```

I subtracted 188 from 317.

I regrouped 1 ten as 10 ones. Then I subtracted the ones.

I regrouped 1 hundred as 10 tens. Then I subtracted the tens.

Last, I subtracted the hundreds.

So, 129 crayons are left in the room.

Show your work.

1. A company built 526 cars. It painted 245 of them. How many cars are left to paint?

   ____

2. The book James is reading has 300 pages. He has read 122 pages so far. How many pages does James have left?

   ____

3. Helen has 704 pennies in her bank. Richard has 365 pennies in his bank. How many more pennies does Helen have in her bank?

   ____

Use with text page 130.

Name ____________________ Date ____________

Homework 6.1

Collect and Organize Data

Use the tally chart below to answer Questions 1–2.

How many students have brown eyes?

Count the tally marks.
Remember that 卌 stands for 5.

5 + 5 + 2 = 12

Twelve students have brown eyes.

Students' Eye Color		
Color	**Tally**	**Number**
blue	卌	
brown	卌 卌 II	
green	卌	
hazel	III	

1. How many students have either blue eyes or green eyes?

   ____

2. How many more students have brown eyes than green eyes?

   ____

Ask each member of your family what color eyes they have. Record the results on the tally chart. Use the tally chart to answer Questions 3–4.

Family Members' Eye Color		
Color	**Tally**	**Number**

3. How many people were surveyed?

   ____

4. How many members of your family have brown eyes?

   ____

Problem Solving

5. Miss Hooks recorded the eye color of each student in her class. She found that 6 students had blue eyes, 7 students had brown eyes, 3 students had green eyes, and 8 students had hazel eyes. How many students are in Miss Hooks' class?

   ____

Use with text pages 148–149.

Name _______________________ Date _______________

Homework 6.2

Explore Range, Median, Mode, and Mean

Joel listed the number of hours he watched TV for 5 days: 2, 5, 2, 4, 2. From this data list, he can find the following information.

Range is the difference between the greatest and least number in a data set. 5 − 2 = 3 Range is 3.	**Median** is the middle number when data numbers are listed in order from least to greatest. 2, 2, **2**, 4, 5 Median, middle number, is 2.
Mode is the number that occurs often in the ordered list.	**2**, **2**, **2**, 4, 5 2 occurs three times, so most it is the mode.
Mean is the number of items if the total of the data were divided equally into as many groups as shown in data.	Use 15 counters to represent the total number of hours of TV watched. Separate the 15 counters into 5 equal groups. Each group contains 3 counters, so the mean is 3.

The table below shows the number of pairs of shoes John's friends said they owned. Use beans to help you answer these questions.

Friends	Number of Pairs of Shoes
James	4
Cassie	7
Brooke	6
Evan	2
Carlos	6

1. What is the range of the data?

____

2. What is the median of the data?

____

3. What is the mode of the data?

____

4. What is the mean of the data?

____

Use with text pages 150–152.

Name ______________________ Date ____________

Homework 6.3

Line Plots

What is the mode of the data?

Look for the number with the most X's.

The number 0 has the most X's.

The mode of the data is 0.

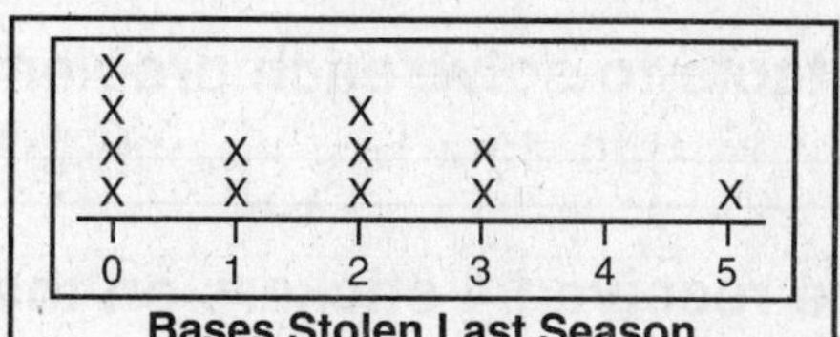

Use the data in the table to make a line plot on a separate sheet of paper. Use the line plot to answer Questions 1–5.

Touchdowns Scored Last Season			
John	3	Bill	2
Samantha	0	Jason	4
Charles	3	Denzell	3
Jack	4	Rachel	2
Timothy	1	Jessica	0
Michelle	6	David	3
Patricia	5	Juan	5

1. How many players scored exactly 2 touchdowns?

____

2. How many players scored more than 3 touchdowns?

____

3. How many players scored fewer than 3 touchdowns?

____

4. What is the range of the data? ____________

5. What is the mode of the data? ____________

Problem Solving

6. What is the median of the data below? Explain how you found your answer. 4, 8, 0, 1, 6

____

____

____

____

Use with text pages 154–156.

Name ______________________ Date ____________

Homework 6.4

Problem-Solving Strategy: Make a Table

Make a table to solve each problem.

Brice received 4 stickers on the first day of school. Each day after that, he received 2 more stickers than the day before. How many stickers will he receive on Day 5?

Make a table. Each day is 2 more than the day before.

Day 1	Day 2	Day 3	Day 4	Day 5
4	6	8	10	12

Brice will receive 12 stickers on Day 5.

Show your work.

1. Miss Ruiz's class collected canned goods for one week. On Monday, they collected 30 canned goods. Each day, they collected 15 more canned goods than the day before. How many canned goods did they collect on Friday?

____

2. Donovan gets 25 cents each week for his allowance. If he saves his allowance for 5 weeks, how much money will he have?

____

3. Greg is waiting to catch the bus that passes his bus stop at 8:33 A.M. The first bus passes at 8:13 A.M. The second bus passes ten minutes later. The third bus passes ten minutes later than the second bus. Which bus will Greg catch?

____

Use with text pages 158–160.

Name ______________________ Date ____________

Homework 6.5

Make a Pictograph

How many votes were there for handstands?

Each 🚶 stands for 2 votes.

There are $2\frac{1}{2}$ 🚶.

$2 + 2 + 1 = 5$

There were 5 votes for handstands.

Favorite Floor Exercises

Splits	🚶🚶🚶🚶🚶
Flips	🚶🚶🚶
Cartwheels	🚶🚶
Handstands	🚶🚶½

Each 🚶 stands for 2 votes.

Use the data in the table to make a pictograph on a separate sheet of paper. Use the key:

Each ♦ stands for 4 participants.

Use the pictograph to answer questions 1–4.

Field Day Participants

Grade	Number
First	12
Second	20
Third	24
Fourth	8
Fifth	16

1. How many ♦ did you draw for first grade?

____

2. How many ♦ did you draw for fourth grade?

____

3. Which grade had the greatest number of participants?

____

Problem Solving

4. If 12 more fourth grade students participated, how many ♦ would there be for fourth grade in all?

____

Use with text pages 162–163.

Name ______________________ Date ______________

Homework 6.6

Make a Bar Graph

How many more medals did Greece win than Denmark?

Find the value of the bar for Greece and the bar for Denmark.

The bar for Greece reaches to 8.
The bar for Denmark reaches to 6.
8 − 6 = 2

Greece won 2 more medals than Denmark.

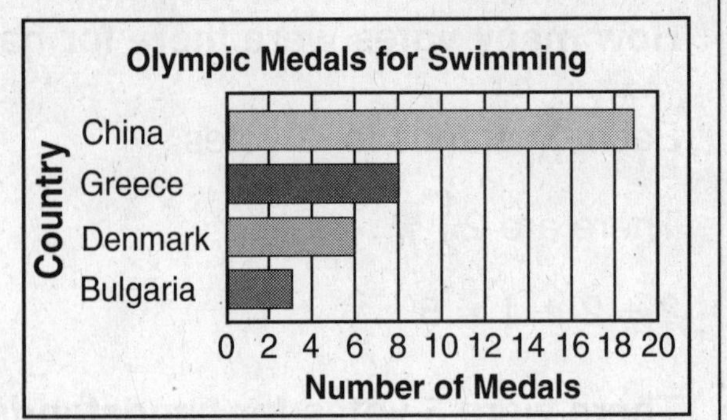

Use the data in the table to make a bar graph. Use the bar graph to answer questions 1–4.

Bats Joey Saw	
Type of Bat	**Number**
Fruit Bat	15
Vampire Bat	6
Long-Nosed Bat	13
Brown Bat	9

1. What is the graph about?

____

____

____

2. What is the scale on the graph?

____

3. Which bat did Joey see the least number of?

____

Problem Solving

4. Which type of bat did Joey see about twice as many of as the number of vampire bats he saw? Explain how you found your answer.

____

____

Use with text pages 164–166.

Name ______________________ Date ____________

Homework 6.7

Read Graphs with Ordered Pairs

Use the grid below. Write the ordered pair for each point.

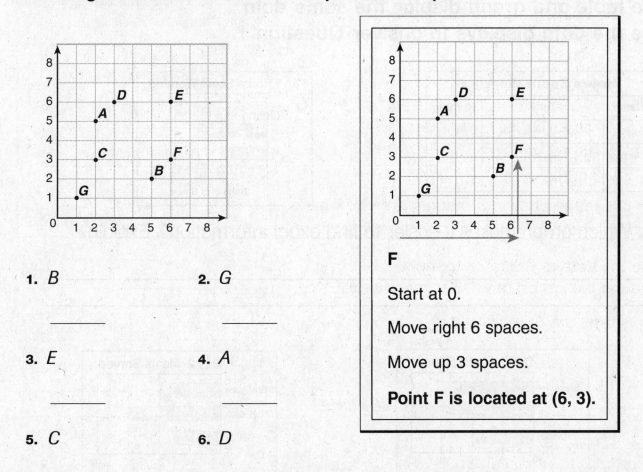

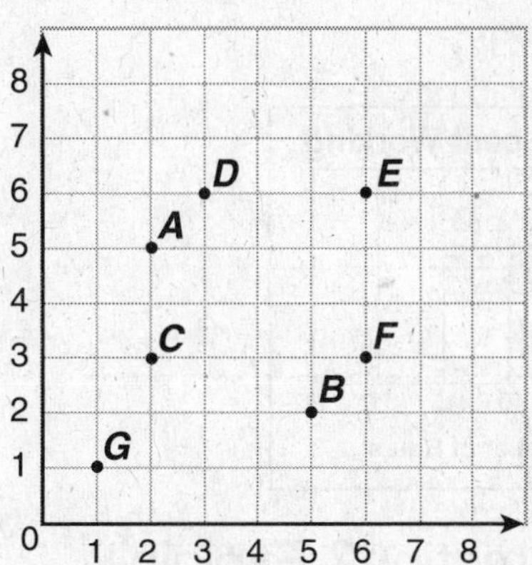

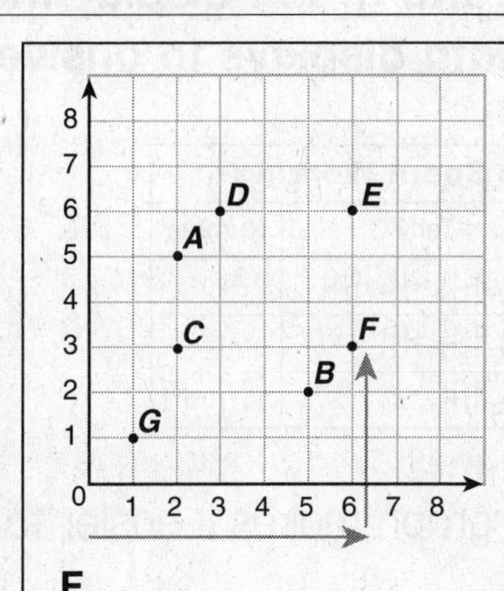

F

Start at 0.

Move right 6 spaces.

Move up 3 spaces.

Point F is located at (6, 3).

1. *B* ________

2. *G* ________

3. *E* ________

4. *A* ________

5. *C* ________

6. *D* ________

Place each point on the grid.

7. point *S* at (1, 5)

8. point *T* at (1, 1)

9. point *U* at (4, 1)

10. point *V* at (4, 5)

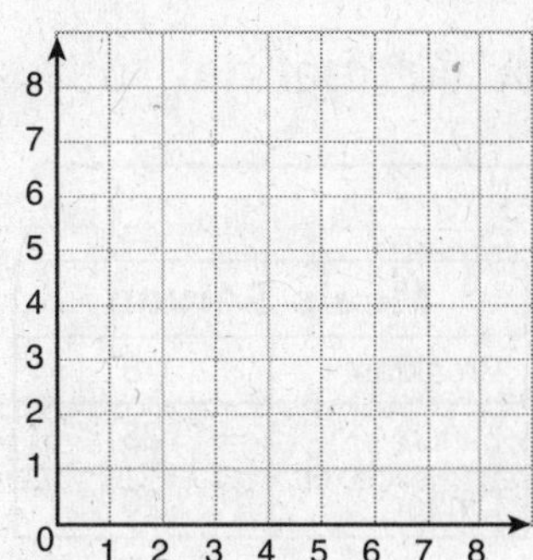

Problem Solving

11. Connect points *S*, *T*, *U*, and *V*. What shape did you make?

____

Name ______________________ Date ____________

Homework 7.1

Understand Data

The table and graph display the same data.
Use the data displays to answer Question 1.

Hours Spent Working		
Name	**Tally**	**Number**
Juan	卌 卌 卌 卌	20
Mitch	卌 卌 卌	15
Li	卌 卌	10

1. Which graph makes it easier to find exact information? Explain.

____

____

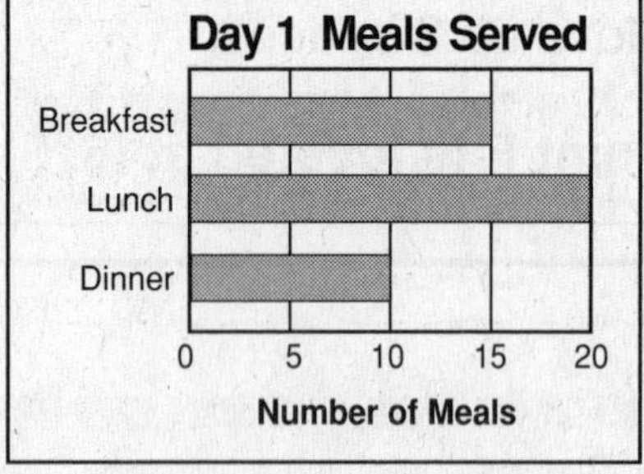

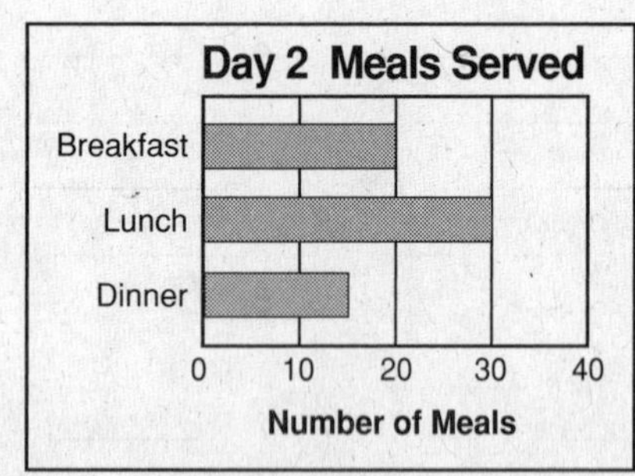

2. Which table shows the same data?

____

3. Which table shows the same data?

____

A.

Meals Served	
Breakfast	15
Lunch	25
Dinner	20

B.

Meals Served	
Breakfast	20
Lunch	30
Dinner	15

C.

Meals Served	
Breakfast	15
Lunch	20
Dinner	10

Problem Solving

4. How does a bar graph make it easier to compare information?

____

Use with text pages 176–177.

Name ______________________ Date ______________

Rounding Numbers on Graphs

Round the numbers in this table to the nearest hundred.

Building Heights	
Building	**Height (meters)**
Venus Center	233
Mercury Building	384
Mars Tower	265

1. About how tall is the Venus Center?

____

2. About how tall is the Mercury Building?

____

3. About how tall is the Mars Tower?

____

Round the numbers in this bar graph to the nearest ten.

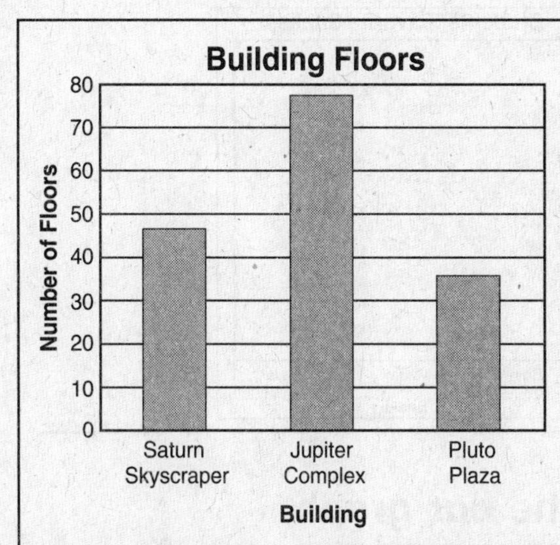

4. Which building has the most floors?

____

5. Which building has about half as many floors as the Jupiter Complex?

____

6. About how many floors do the Saturn Skyscraper and the Pluto Plaza have in all?

____

Problem Solving

7. What's Wrong Your friend asks you to round the numbers in the bar graph above to the nearest hundred. Is this a reasonable thing to do? Explain.

____

____

____

Show your work.

Use with text pages 178–181.

Name ______________________ Date ____________

Homework 7.3

Represent Data

Ilana surveyed students at her school to find their favorite reptile. The table and graph below show the results of her survey.

Students' Favorite Reptiles	
Reptile	**Number of Students**
Crocodile	200
Snake	350
Turtle	100

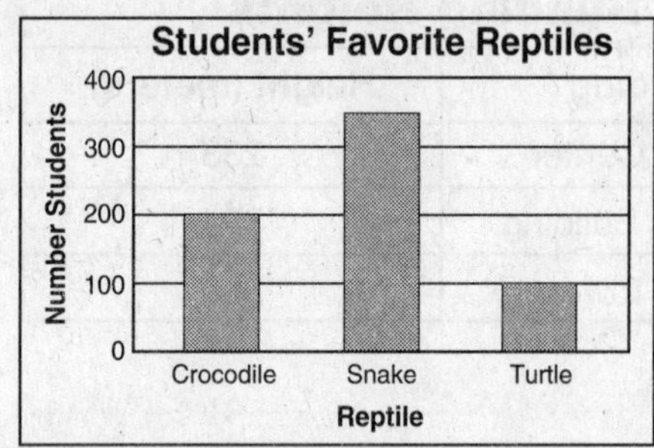

1. Is the scale on the bar graph appropriate for the data? Explain why or why not.

____

Use the data in the table to complete the bar graph.

Students' Favorite Snakes	
Snake	**Number of Students**
Boa Constrictor	15
Python	24
Anaconda	30

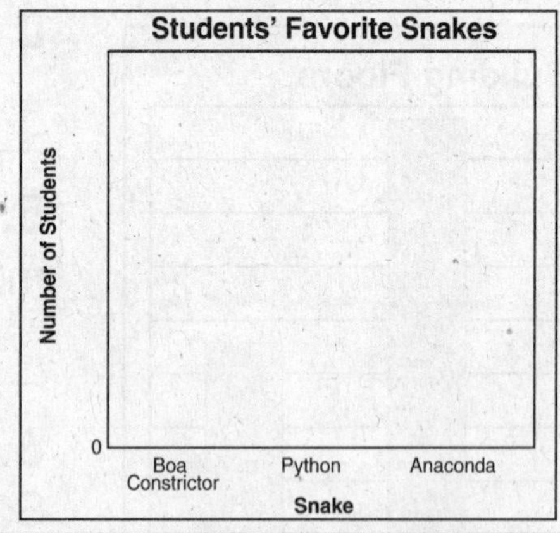

2. Explain how you chose the scale for your bar graph.

____

Use the data in the table to complete the bar graph.

Students' Favorite Turtles	
Turtle	**Number of Students**
Sea Turtle	35
Box Turtle	60
Snapping Turtle	47

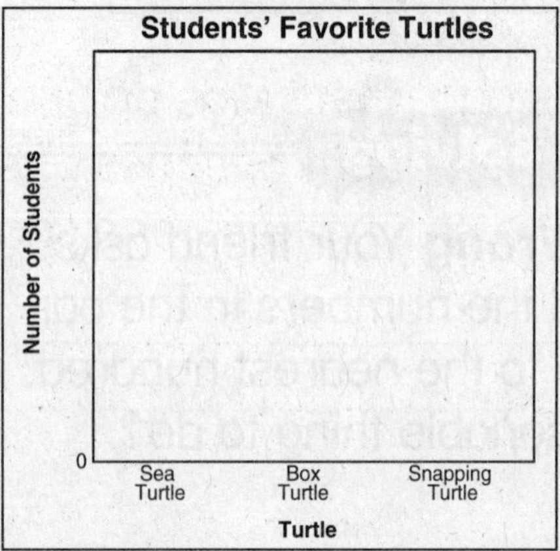

3. Explain how you chose the scale for your bar graph.

____

Use with text pages 182–183.

Name ______________________ Date ____________

Homework 7.4

Make Predictions

1. The bar graph shows the attendance for a movie over 5 days. Read the statement below. Is it reasonable based on the data? Explain why or why not.

Attendance has slowed down during the last two days. We should stop showing the movie.

____

____

Use the bar graph below to answer Question 2.

2. Rita's family is planning to hike Winter Mountain. They want to hike the mountain when there is no snow.
Predict: During which months is it unlikely to snow?

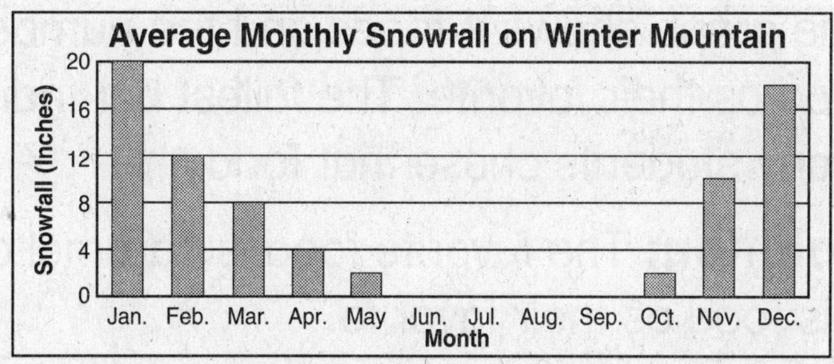

____

____

Problem Solving

3. Six years ago, there was an unusual snow storm in June on Winter Mountain. It left about 5 inches of snow on the mountain. Does this mean that the graph of average snowfall amounts is incorrect? Explain.

____

____

Name ______________________ Date ____________

Homework 7.5

Problem-Solving Application: Use A Graph

A bar graph can be used to solve problems.

Erin took a survey of students' favorite carnival foods. She displayed her results in a bar graph.

Look at the bar graph. Which food is the students' favorite? How many students chose that food?

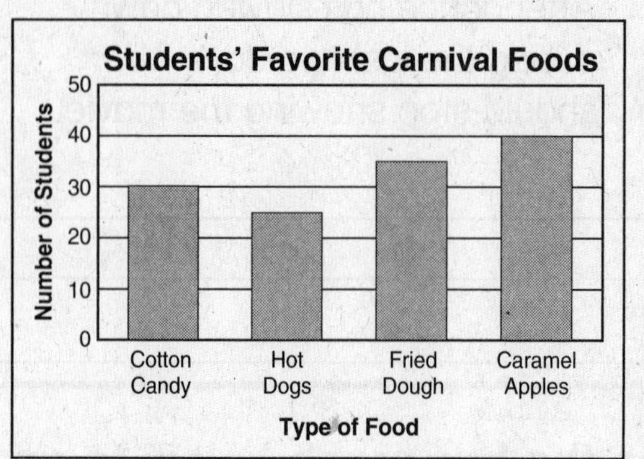

The graph shows 4 foods and the number of students who chose each food as their favorite. The tallest bar indicates the favorite food and how many students chose that food.

Solution: The favorite food is caramel apples. Forty students chose this food as their favorite.

Use the bar graph to solve Questions 1–3.

Show your work.

1. How many more students chose caramel apples than cotton candy?

____

2. Which food was chosen by the fewest students? How many students chose that food?

____

3. How many students took part in Erin's survey?

____

Use with text pages 188–189.

Name ______________________ Date __________

Homework 8.1

Model Multiplication as Repeated Addition

Model each set with counters. Then write an addition sentence and a multiplication sentence for each.

5 groups of 4

●●●●
●●●●
●●●●
●●●●
●●●●

$4 + 4 + 4 + 4 + 4 = 20$
$5 \times 4 = 20$

1. 2 groups of 7

____

____

2. 6 groups of 5

____

____

3. 7 groups of 3

____

____

4. 4 groups of 6

____

____

Write a multiplication sentence for each.

5. $6 + 6 + 6 + 6 = 24$

____

6. $3 + 3 + 3 + 3 + 3 = 15$

____

7. $2 + 2 + 2 + 2 + 2 = 10$

____

8. $4 + 4 + 4 = 12$

____

Problem Solving

9. Debra has 5 rows of marbles with 3 marbles in each row. How many marbles does Debra have?

____

Use with text pages 206–207.

Name ______________________ Date ____________

Homework 8.2

Arrays and Multiplication

Write a multiplication sentence for each array.

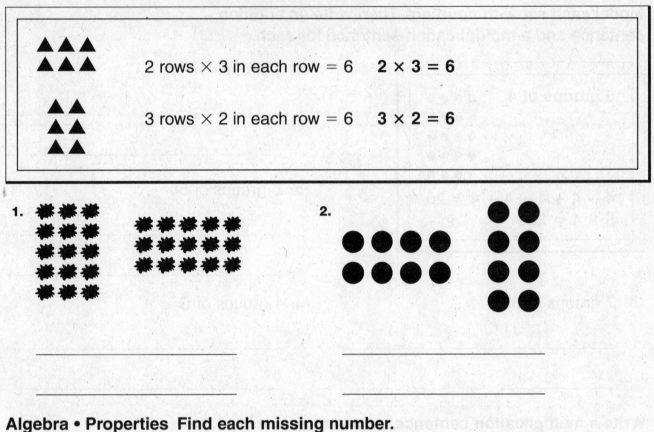

2 rows × 3 in each row = 6 **2 × 3 = 6**

3 rows × 2 in each row = 6 **3 × 2 = 6**

1.

____

____

2.

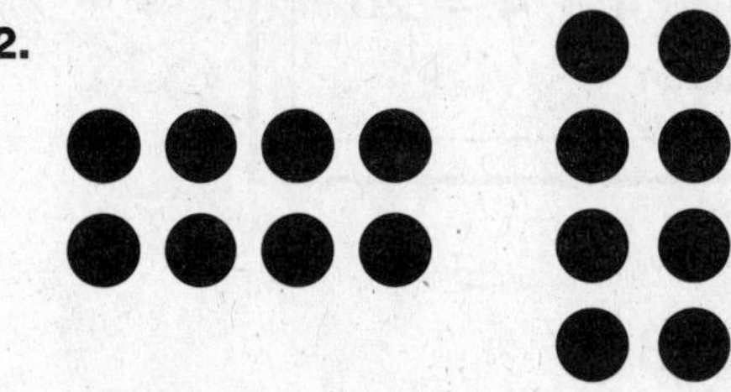

____

____

Algebra • Properties Find each missing number.

3. 8 × 4 = 32
4 × ■ = 32

4. 9 × 2 = 18
■ × 9 = 18

5. 10 × 2 = 20
2 × 10 = ■

6. 24 = 6 × 4
24 = 4 × ■

7. 5 × 6 = 30
6 × ■ = 30

8. 9 × 4 = 36
4 × 9 = ■

9. 7 × 9 = 63
■ × 7 = 63

10. 72 = 8 × 9
72 = 9 × ■

Problem Solving

11. Keesha has a sticker sheet. There are 6 rows of stickers. Each row has 6 stickers. How many stickers does Keesha have?

____

Use with text pages 208–209.

Name ____________________ Date ____________

Homework 8.3

Multiply With 2

Write a multiplication sentence for each picture.

There are 3 groups of 2 each.
3 groups × 2 in each group = 6
3 × 2 = 6

1. 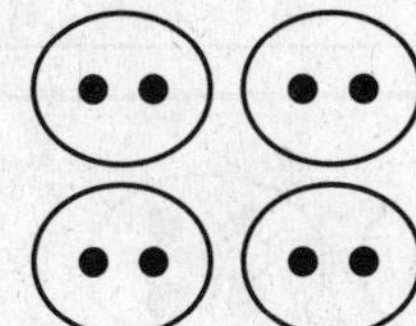
____

2. 
____

3. 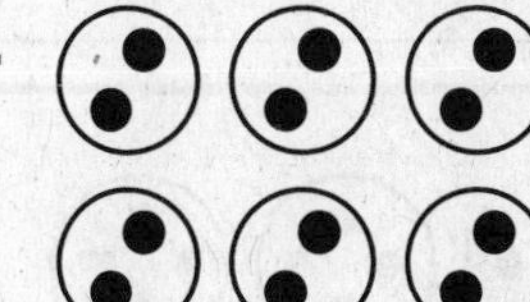
____

Multiply.

4. 2×2

5. 2×4

6. 7×2

7. 2×9

8. 8×2

9. 3×2

10. 9×2

11. 8×2

12. 2×5

13. 10×2

14. 6×2

15. 1×2

16. 3 × 2 ______

17. 5 × 2 ______

18. 2 × 7 ______

19. 2 × 4 ______

20. 2 × 6 ______

Problem Solving

21. The Art Club is making toy dolls. Each doll has 2 google eyes. The club made 7 dolls. How many google eyes did they use?

____

Use with text pages 210–211.

Name ______________________ Date ______________

Homework 8.4

Multiply With 4

Write a multiplication sentence for each picture.

There are 5 groups of 4 each.
5 groups × 4 in each group = 20
5 × 4 = 20

1. 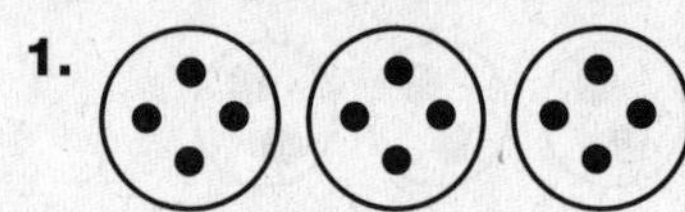

____

2. 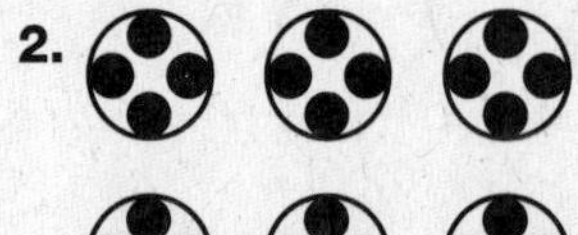

____

3. 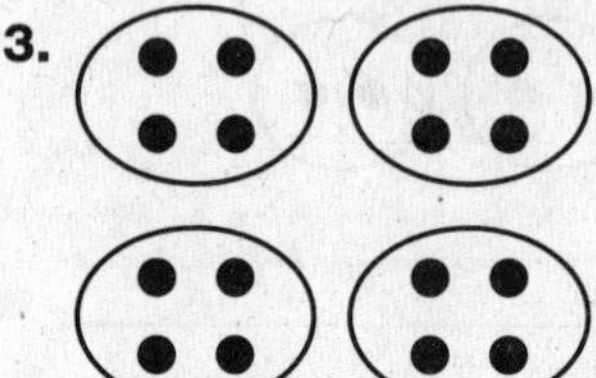

____

Multiply.

4. $\begin{array}{r} 1 \\ \times 4 \\ \hline \end{array}$

5. $\begin{array}{r} 4 \\ \times 4 \\ \hline \end{array}$

6. $\begin{array}{r} 4 \\ \times 7 \\ \hline \end{array}$

7. $\begin{array}{r} 8 \\ \times 4 \\ \hline \end{array}$

8. $\begin{array}{r} 4 \\ \times 5 \\ \hline \end{array}$

9. $\begin{array}{r} 2 \\ \times 4 \\ \hline \end{array}$

Algebra • Properties Find each missing number.

10. 7 × 4 = 28
    4 × ■ = 28

11. 36 = 9 × 4
    36 = 4 × ■

12. 4 × 3 = 12
    3 × 4 = ■

Problem Solving

13. A fly has 6 eyes. How many eyes are on 4 flies?

____

Use with text pages 212–214.

Name ______________________ Date __________

Homework 8.5

Multiply With 5

Find each product.

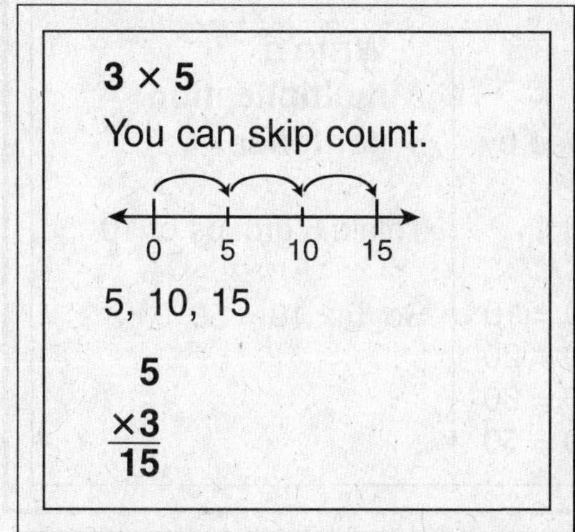

3 × 5
You can skip count.
0
5
10
15
5, 10, 15
5
×3
15

1. $\begin{array}{r} 5 \\ \times 8 \\ \hline \end{array}$

2. $\begin{array}{r} 5 \\ \times 1 \\ \hline \end{array}$

3. $\begin{array}{r} 6 \\ \times 5 \\ \hline \end{array}$

4. $\begin{array}{r} 3 \\ \times 5 \\ \hline \end{array}$

5. $\begin{array}{r} 5 \\ \times 9 \\ \hline \end{array}$

6. $\begin{array}{r} 7 \\ \times 5 \\ \hline \end{array}$

7. $\begin{array}{r} 2 \\ \times 5 \\ \hline \end{array}$

8. $\begin{array}{r} 10 \\ \times\ 5 \\ \hline \end{array}$

9. $\begin{array}{r} 4 \\ \times 5 \\ \hline \end{array}$

10. $\begin{array}{r} 5 \\ \times 2 \\ \hline \end{array}$

11. $\begin{array}{r} 5 \\ \times 5 \\ \hline \end{array}$

12. $\begin{array}{r} 8 \\ \times 5 \\ \hline \end{array}$

13. 3×5 ______

14. 5×5 ______

15. 5×6 ______

16. 9×5 ______

17. 2×5 ______

Algebra • Equations Find each missing factor.

18. $5 \times ■ = 5$

19. $■ \times 5 = 20$

20. $40 = 5 \times ■$

21. $35 = ■ \times 5$

Problem Solving

22. Vance planted 6 rows of flowers. He planted 5 flowers in each row. How many flowers did Vance plant?

____

Use with text pages 216–217.

Name ______________________ Date ____________

Homework 8.6

Multiply With 10

You can use different ways to find 5 x 10.

Skip count.	**Use a pattern.**	**Write a multiplication sentence.**
Say: 10, 20, 30, 40, 50 So, 5 x 10 = 50	When a number is multiplied by 10, write a zero after the number to show the product. Think: 1 x 1 = 1, so 1 x 10 = 10 1 x 2 = 2, so 2 x 10 = 20 3 x 2 = 3, so 3 x 10 = 30 5 x 2 = 5, so 5 x 10 = 50	Think: 5 groups of 10 So, 5 x 10 = 50

Find each product.

1. $\begin{array}{r} 10 \\ \times\ 8 \\ \hline \end{array}$

2. $\begin{array}{r} 10 \\ \times\ 6 \\ \hline \end{array}$

3. $\begin{array}{r} 10 \\ \times\ 4 \\ \hline \end{array}$

4. $\begin{array}{r} 10 \\ \times\ 3 \\ \hline \end{array}$

5. 2×10 ______

6. 10×9 ______

7. 10×6 ______

8. 8×10 ______

Algebra • Functions **Complete each table by following the rule.**

	Rule: Multiply by 2	
	Input	**Output**
9.	4	
10.		12
11.	9	

	Rule: Multiply by 5	
	Input	**Output**
12.	3	
13.		30
14.	8	

	Rule: Multiply by 10	
	Input	**Output**
15.	5	
16.		70
17.	3	

Problem Solving

18. Miss Henry bought crayons for her class. There were 10 crayons in each box. She bought 9 boxes. How many crayons did she buy?

____

Use with text pages 218–219.

Name ______________________________ Date ______________

Homework 8.7

Problem-Solving Strategy: Make an Organized List

Make an organized list to solve each problem.

John is baking cakes. He makes either a chocolate or yellow cake with a choice of chocolate, cream cheese, or coconut icing. How many different combinations of cake and icing can he make?

Start with one flavor of cake. Make all the possible combinations with each icing. Then move to the next flavor of cake. Count the number of combinations.

John can make 6 different cake and icing combinations.

Possible Combinations		
chocolate	→	chocolate
chocolate	→	cream cheese
chocolate	→	coconut
yellow	→	chocolate
yellow	→	cream cheese
yellow	→	coconut

Show your work.

1. Paula has a blue, a beige, and a red shirt. She has brown, black, and gray pants. How many combinations of shirts and pants can Paula wear?

____

2. Yvette is buying an ice cream sundae. She can choose chocolate, vanilla, strawberry, or mint ice cream. She can choose marshmallow, fudge, or butterscotch topping. How many combinations of ice cream and toppings are there for Yvette to choose from?

____

Use with text pages 220-223.

Name ______________________ Date ____________

Homework 8.8

Multiply with 1 and 0

Multiply.

The **Property of One** states that when 1 is a factor, the product is always equal to the other factor.	The **Zero Property** states that when 0 is a factor, the product is always zero.
$1 \times 8 = 8$	$9 \times 0 = 0$

1. 9×1
2. 4×0
3. 6×1
4. 1×7
5. 10×0
6. 3×0
7. 1×3
8. 5×1
9. 3×0
10. 8×1
11. 10×1 ______
12. 2×1 ______
13. 6×1 ______
14. 6×0 ______

Algebra • Properties Find each missing factor.

15. $8 \times 1 = 1 \times$ ■
16. $9 \times 1 = 1 \times$ ■
17. ■ $\times 3 = 0$
18. $10 \times$ ■ $= 0$
19. $3 \times 2 =$ ■ $\times 1$
20. $4 \times 2 =$ ■ $\times 8$

Problem Solving

21. Jenna gave one sticker to every classmate. She has 20 classmates. How many stickers did she give out?

____

Name ____________________ Date __________

Homework 9.1

Use a Multiplication Table

Use the multiplication table to answer each question.

What pattern do you see in the column for 3?

Look at the column for 3. What numbers do you see?

0, 3, 6, 9, 12, 15, 18, 21, 24, 27, and 30

The number increases by 3 each time.

The pattern in the column for 3 is add 3, or skip count by 3.

×	0	1	2	3	4	5	6	7	8	9	10
0	0	0	0	0	0	0	0	0	0	0	0
1	0	1	2	3	4	5	6	7	8	9	10
2	0	2	4	6	8	10	12	14	16	18	20
3	0	3	6	9	12	15	18	21	24	27	30
4	0	4	8	12	16	20	24	28	32	36	40
5	0	5	10	15	20	25	30	35	40	45	50
6	0	6	12	18	24	30	36	42	48	54	60
7	0	7	14	21	28	35	42	49	56	63	70
8	0	8	16	24	32	40	48	56	64	72	80
9	0	9	18	27	36	45	54	63	72	81	90
10	0	10	20	30	40	50	60	70	80	90	100

1. What do all the products in the column for 5 have in common?

____

____

2. Which rows and columns have products that are all even numbers?

____

____

Below are parts of a multiplication table. In which row or column is each part found?

3.

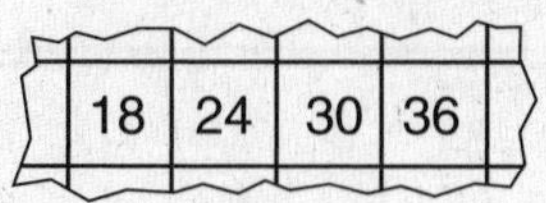

____

4.

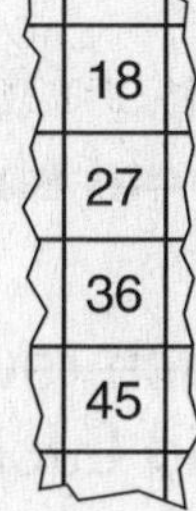

____

5.

____

Name ______________________ Date ____________

Homework 9.2

Multiply With 3

You can use different ways to find 6 x 3.

Skip count by 3s.

Say: 3, 6, 9, 12, 15, 18

So, 6 x 3 = 18

Draw a Picture.

Draw a picture.
Then use repeated addition.

3 + 3 + 3 + 3 + 3 + 3 = 18

Draw an array.

6 rows of 3 is 18

Find each product.

1. 3×6
2. 2×3
3. 3×7
4. 4×3
5. 3×0
6. 3×9
7. 3×5
8. 1×3
9. 8×3
10. 3×3

11. 7 × 3 = ______
12. 3 × 8 = ______
13. 3 × 5 = ______
14. 3 × 10 = ______
15. 1 × 3 = ______
16. 3 × 2 = ______

Problem Solving

17. Lucia planted 3 rows of lettuce. Each row has 4 lettuce plants. How many lettuce plants did Lucia plant?

____

Name ______________________ Date ____________

Homework 9.3

Multiply With 6

Multiply.

6 × 5

You can use doubling.
6 × 5 is double 3 × 5.

3 × 5   3 × 5

6 × 5

3 × 5 = 15
15 + 15 = 30
6 × 5 = 30

1. 6×3

2. 6×6

3. 10×6

4. 8×6

5. 5×6

6. 6×1

7. 6×7

8. 6×4

9. 2×6

10. 9×6

11. 6 × 8 = ______

12. 6 × 0 = ______

13. 2 × 6 = ______

14. 9 × 6 = ______

15. 4 × 6 = ______

16. 6 × 7 = ______

Problem Solving

17. There are 6 players on a volleyball team. How many players are in a game with 2 teams?

____

Use with text pages 236–239.

Name ______________________ Date ______________

Homework 9.4

Multiply With 7

Multiply.

> **3 × 7**
>
> **You can use a fact you know.**
>
> Remember that numbers can be multiplied in any order.
>
> You know that $7 \times 3 = 21$, so $3 \times 7 = 21$.
>
> **3 × 7 = 21**

1. 7×0 = ____

2. 6×7 = ____

3. 1×7 = ____

4. 7×8 = ____

5. 10×7 = ____

6. 7×4 = ____

7. 7×5 = ____

8. 7×2 = ____

9. 7×7 = ____

10. 3×7 = ____

11. $5 \times 7 =$ ______

12. $7 \times 7 =$ ______

13. $3 \times 7 =$ ______

14. $7 \times 2 =$ ______

15. $7 \times 6 =$ ______

16. $7 \times 9 =$ ______

Problem Solving

17. Tom's birthday is 4 weeks away. How many days away is Tom's birthday? Hint: Think about the number of days in one week.

____

Name ______________________ Date ____________

Homework 9.5

Multiply With 8

Multiply.

4 × 8

You can use doubling.

4 × 8 is double 4 × 4.

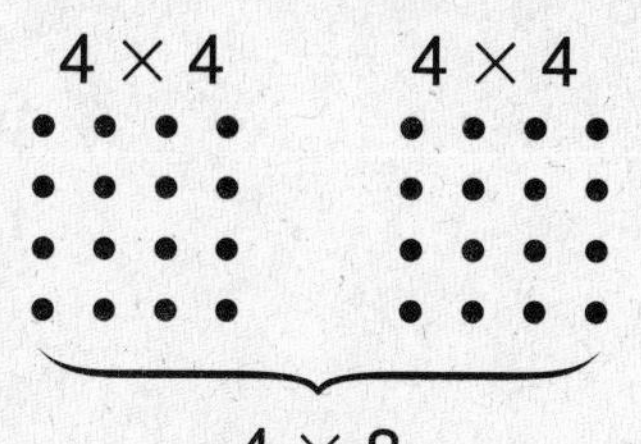

4 × 4 = 16

16 + 16 = 32

4 × 8 = 32

1. $\begin{array}{r} 8 \\ \times 2 \\ \hline \end{array}$

2. $\begin{array}{r} 5 \\ \times 8 \\ \hline \end{array}$

3. $\begin{array}{r} 8 \\ \times 8 \\ \hline \end{array}$

4. $\begin{array}{r} 8 \\ \times 9 \\ \hline \end{array}$

5. $\begin{array}{r} 8 \\ \times 1 \\ \hline \end{array}$

6. $\begin{array}{r} 8 \\ \times 4 \\ \hline \end{array}$

7. $\begin{array}{r} 7 \\ \times 8 \\ \hline \end{array}$

8. $\begin{array}{r} 8 \\ \times 3 \\ \hline \end{array}$

9. $\begin{array}{r} 6 \\ \times 8 \\ \hline \end{array}$

10. $\begin{array}{r} 8 \\ \times 0 \\ \hline \end{array}$

11. 7 × 8 = ______

12. 8 × 3 = ______

13. 8 × 8 = ______

14. 0 × 8 = ______

15. 6 × 8 = ______

16. 10 × 8 = ______

Problem Solving

17. Spiders have 8 legs. How many legs do 5 spiders have?

____

Use with text pages 242–244.

Name ______________________ Date ______________

Homework 9.6

Multiply With 9

Multiply.

9 × 9

You can use patterns to find 9s facts.

Think: The tens digit will be 1 less than the factor you are multiplying by 9.

9 − 1 = 8

So 9 × 9 = **8**_

Think: The sum of the digits in the product will be 9.

8 + 1 = 9

So **9 × 9 = 81.**

1. $\begin{array}{r} 9 \\ \times 3 \\ \hline \end{array}$

2. $\begin{array}{r} 1 \\ \times 9 \\ \hline \end{array}$

3. $\begin{array}{r} 8 \\ \times 9 \\ \hline \end{array}$

4. $\begin{array}{r} 9 \\ \times 9 \\ \hline \end{array}$

5. $\begin{array}{r} 9 \\ \times 4 \\ \hline \end{array}$

6. $\begin{array}{r} 6 \\ \times 9 \\ \hline \end{array}$

7. $\begin{array}{r} 7 \\ \times 9 \\ \hline \end{array}$

8. $\begin{array}{r} 9 \\ \times 0 \\ \hline \end{array}$

9. 9 × 5 = ______

10. 9 × 0 = ______

11. 2 × 9 = ______

12. 10 × 9 = ______

13. 4 × 9 = ______

14. 7 × 9 = ______

Problem Solving

15. There are 9 players on a baseball team. How many players are on 8 baseball teams?

____

Name ______________________ Date ____________

Homework 9.7

Patterns on a Multiplication Table

Write true or false for each statement. Give an example to support each answer.

Any multiple of 6 is also a multiple of 2.

Use the multiplication table to help.

List the multiples of 2:
2, 4, **6,** 8, 10, **12,** 14, 16, **18,** 20, 22, **24...**

List the multiples of 6:
6, 12, 18, 24, 30, 36, 42, 48, 54, 60...

Compare the lists. If the multiples of 2 were continued, all the multiples of 6 would be listed.

The statement is true.

×	0	1	2	3	4	5	6	7	8	9	10
0	0	0	0	0	0	0	0	0	0	0	0
1	0	1	2	3	4	5	6	7	8	9	10
2	0	2	4	6	8	10	12	14	16	18	20
3	0	3	6	9	12	15	18	21	24	27	30
4	0	4	8	12	16	20	24	28	32	36	40
5	0	5	10	15	20	25	30	35	40	45	50
6	0	6	12	18	24	30	36	42	48	54	60
7	0	7	14	21	28	35	42	49	56	63	70
8	0	8	16	24	32	40	48	56	64	72	80
9	0	9	18	27	36	45	54	63	72	81	90
10	0	10	20	30	40	50	60	70	80	90	100

1. Any multiple of 5 is also a multiple of 2.

____

____

Write whether each array shows a square number. If not, find the fewest counters that could be added to make it show a square number.

2. ● ● ● ● ●
● ● ● ● ●
● ● ● ● ●
● ● ● ● ●
● ● ● ● ●

____

3. ● ● ●

____

4. ● ● ● ● ● ●
● ● ● ● ● ●

____

Problem Solving

5. Is 24 a multiple of 5? Explain. __________

__________ __________

Use with text pages 250–251.

Name ______________________ Date ____________

Homework 9.8

Multiply Three Numbers

Find each product. Multiply factors in parentheses first.

Find the product of 4 x 2 x 5.

Use the Associative Property of Multiplication.

The way factors are grouped does not change the product. (Remember to multiply factors in parentheses first.)

You can multiply 4 x 2 first.	**You can multiply 2 x 5 first.**
(4 x 2) x 5 = 8 x 5 = 40	4 x (2 x 5) = 4 x 10 = 40

No matter which two factors are multiplied first, the product will be the same.

1. 7 × (3 × 2) = ______

2. 4 × (2 × 3) = ______

3. 8 × (0 × 3) = ______

4. 7 × (2 × 2) = ______

Use the Associative Property to help you. Find each missing factor.

5. (_____ × 2) × 5 = 50

6. (3 × 3) × _____ = 54

7. _____ × (3 × 2) = 36

8. (2 × _____) × 7 = 28

9. (7 × 3) × _____ = 0

10. _____ × (6 × 2) = 36

Problem Solving

11. Anna, Ben, and Inez each used 2 packs of poster paper. Each pack has 4 sheets of paper. How many sheets of paper did they use?

____

____

Use with text pages 252–253.

Name ______________________ Date ____________

Homework 9.9

Problem-Solving Decision: Multistep Problems

Solve each problem.

Henry has 8 model trucks. He has three times as many model cars. How many model trucks and model cars does Henry have in all?

Step 1. Find the number of model cars Henry has.
Think: Henry has 3 times as many model cars as model trucks.

$$8 \times 3 = 24$$

Henry has 24 model cars.

Step 2. Add the number of model cars to the number of model trucks to find the total.

$$24 + 8 = 32$$

Henry has 32 model trucks and model cars in all.

1. Frank receives $3 each week for washing the dishes and $2 each week for vacuuming. How much does Frank receive in 6 weeks?

____

2. Bonnie has 4 nonfiction books. She has four times as many fiction books. How many more fiction books does Bonnie have than nonfiction books?

____

3. Samantha collected 5 seashells. Ryan collected three times as many seashells. How many seashells did Samantha and Ryan collect in all?

____

Use with text pages 254–255.

Name ________________ Date ________

Homework 10.1

The Meaning of Division

Use counters to find the number in each equal group. Then complete each division sentence.

	Number of Counters	Number of Equal Groups	Number in Each Group	Division Sentence
	10	2	5	10 ÷ 2 = 5
1.	8	2	____	8 ÷ 2 = ____
2.	9	3	____	9 ÷ 3 = ____
3.	12	4	____	12 ÷ 4 = ____

Use counters to find the number of equal groups. Then complete each division sentence.

	Number of Counters	Number of Equal Groups	Number in Each Group	Division Sentence
4.	15	____	3	15 ÷ 3 = ____
5.	12	____	2	12 ÷ 2 = ____
6.	20	____	5	20 ÷ 5 = ____

Problem Solving

Show your work.

7. Fourteen people are seated at 2 tables. There are an equal number of people at each table. How many people are at each table?

____

Use with text pages 260–261.

Name ______________________ Date ____________

Homework 10.2

Model Division as Repeated Subtraction

Use repeated subtraction to find each quotient.

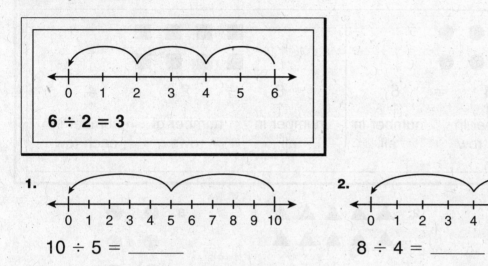

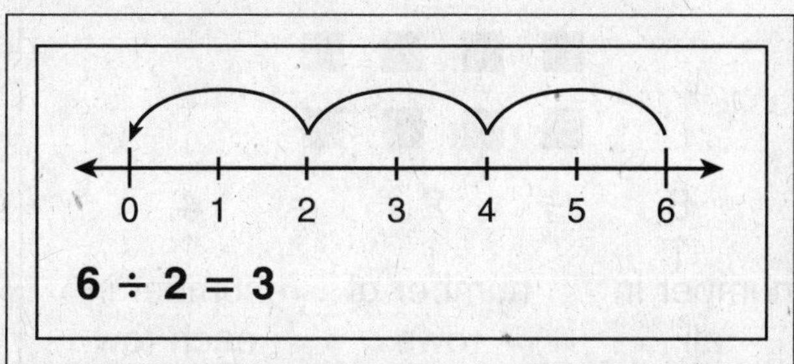

1. 0 1 2 3 4 5 6 7 8 9 10

10 ÷ 5 = ______

2.

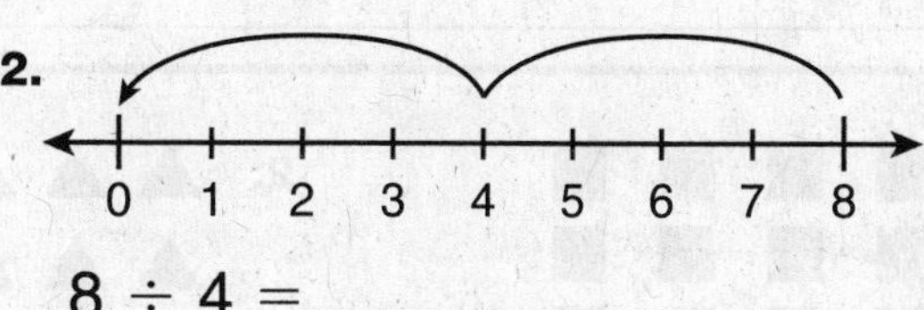

8 ÷ 4 = ______

Match each number line with the correct division sentence. Solve.

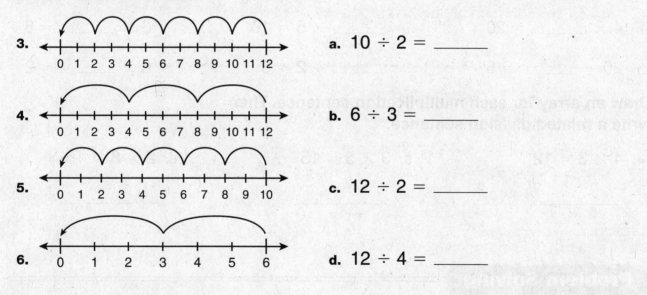

3.

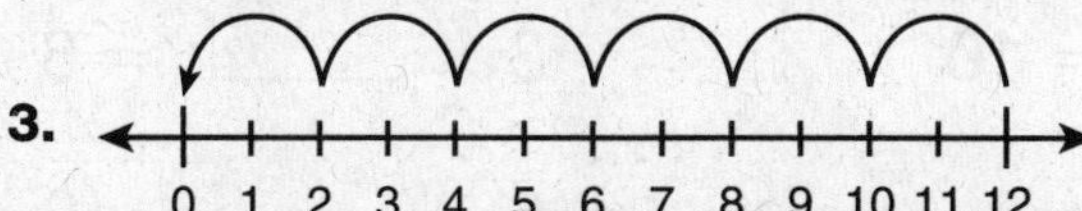

a. 10 ÷ 2 = ______

4.

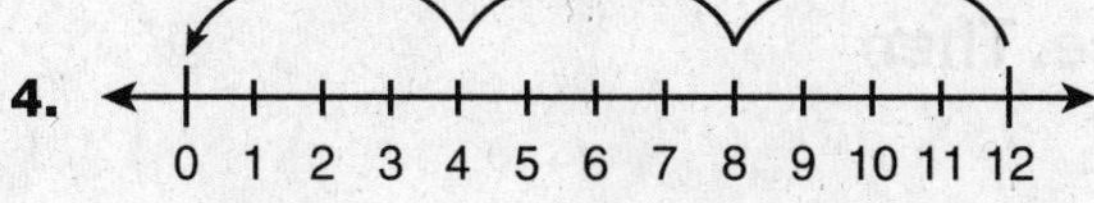

b. 6 ÷ 3 = ______

5.

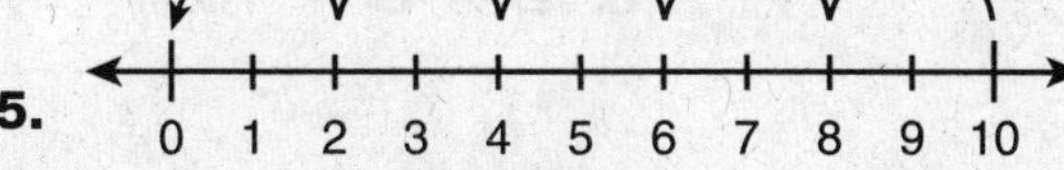

c. 12 ÷ 2 = ______

6. 0 1 2 3 4 5 6

d. 12 ÷ 4 = ______

Problem Solving

7. There are 12 eggs in bird nests. Three eggs are in each nest. How many bird nests are there?

____

Use with text pages 262–263.

Name ______________________ Date ____________

Relate Multiplication and Division

Use the array to complete each number sentence.

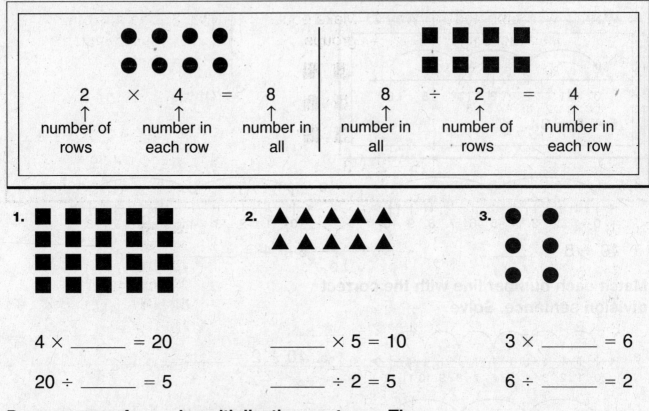

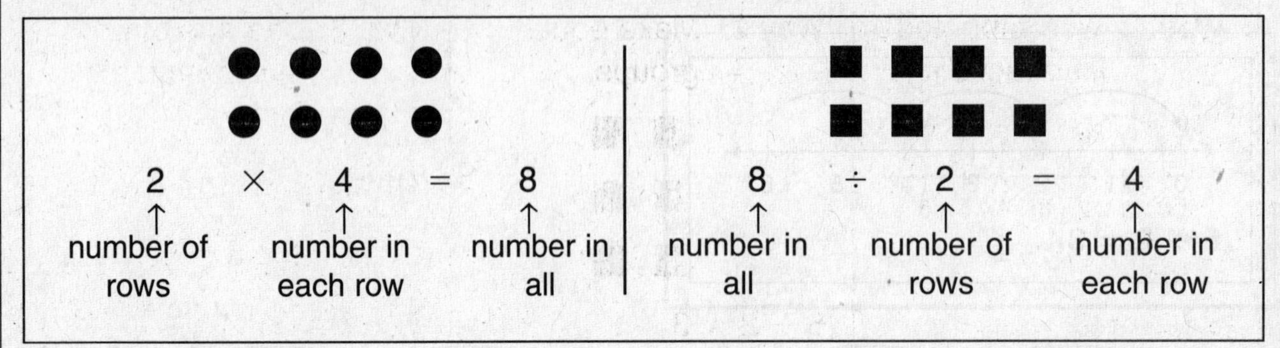

1. 4 × ______ = 20

   20 ÷ ______ = 5

2. ______ × 5 = 10

   ______ ÷ 2 = 5

3. 3 × ______ = 6

   6 ÷ ______ = 2

Draw an array for each multiplication sentence. Then write a related division sentence.

4. 4 × 3 = 12

   ____

5. 3 × 5 = 15

   ____

6. 2 × 8 = 16

   ____

Problem Solving

Show your work.

7. The school flag has 16 stars arranged in rows. There are 4 stars in each row. How many rows of stars are on the flag?

   ____

Use with text pages 264–265.

Name ______________________ Date ____________

Homework 10.4

Divide by 2

Use the pictures or the multiplication facts to find each quotient.

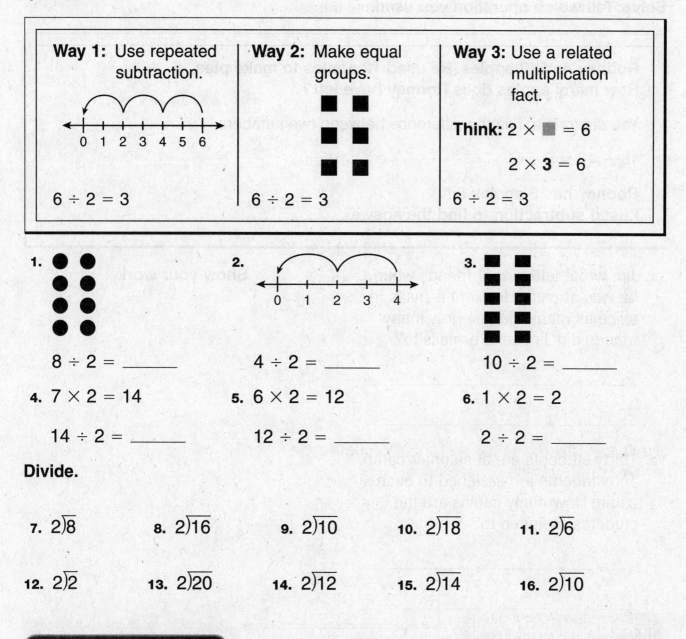

Way 1: Use repeated subtraction.	**Way 2:** Make equal groups.	**Way 3:** Use a related multiplication fact.
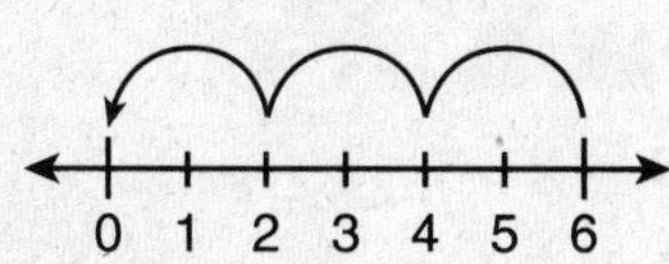		**Think:** 2 × ■ = 6 2 × **3** = 6
6 ÷ 2 = 3	6 ÷ 2 = 3	6 ÷ 2 = 3

1. 
   8 ÷ 2 = ______

2. 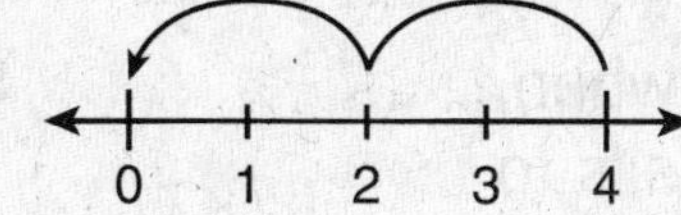
   4 ÷ 2 = ______

3. 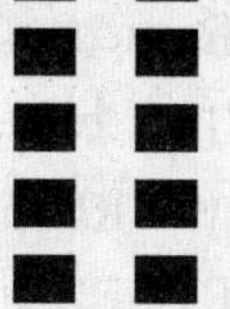
   10 ÷ 2 = ______

4. 7 × 2 = 14
   14 ÷ 2 = ______

5. 6 × 2 = 12
   12 ÷ 2 = ______

6. 1 × 2 = 2
   2 ÷ 2 = ______

Divide.

7. $2\overline{)8}$ 8. $2\overline{)16}$ 9. $2\overline{)10}$ 10. $2\overline{)18}$ 11. $2\overline{)6}$

12. $2\overline{)2}$ 13. $2\overline{)20}$ 14. $2\overline{)12}$ 15. $2\overline{)14}$ 16. $2\overline{)10}$

Problem Solving

17. There are 8 majorettes in the band. Two majorettes are in each row. How many rows of majorettes are in the band?

____

Use with text pages 266–267.

Name ______________________ Date ____________

Homework 10.5

Problem-Solving Decision: Choose the Operation

Solve. Tell which operation you used.

Rodney had 18 apples. He used 12 apples to make pies. How many apples does Rodney have left?

You *subtract* to find the difference between two numbers.

$18 - 12 = 6$

Rodney has 6 apples left.
I used subtraction to find the answer.

Show your work.

1. Jim wrote letters to 4 friends when he was at camp. He sent e-mails to twice as many friends. How many friends did Jim send e-mails to?

____

____

2. Thirty students are at summer camp. Ten students are assigned to each cabin. How many cabins are the students assigned to?

____

____

3. Maria brought 6 carrot sticks on a picnic. Her friend brought 8 carrot sticks. How many do they have in all?

____

____

Use with text page 268.

Name ______________________ Date ____________

Homework 10.6

Divide by 5

Use the array to help you find each quotient.

10 ÷ 5 = ______

There are 2 rows with 5 squares in each row.

10 ÷ 5 = 2

1. 20 ÷ 5 = ______

2. 15 ÷ 5 = ______

3. 5 ÷ 5 = ______

Divide.

4. 40 ÷ 5 = ______

5. 25 ÷ 5 = ______

6. 35 ÷ 5 = ______

7. $5\overline{)15}$

8. $5\overline{)45}$

9. $5\overline{)50}$

10. $5\overline{)30}$

11. $5\overline{)20}$

12. $5\overline{)5}$

13. $5\overline{)10}$

14. $5\overline{)40}$

Problem Solving

15. Mrs. Scott's class has 25 students. She wants to make 5 equal rows of desks for her students. How many desks will be in each row?

____

Use with text pages 270–271.

Name ______________________ Date ____________

Homework 10.7

Divide by 10

Find each quotient.

50 ÷ 10

Way 1: Use repeated subtraction.

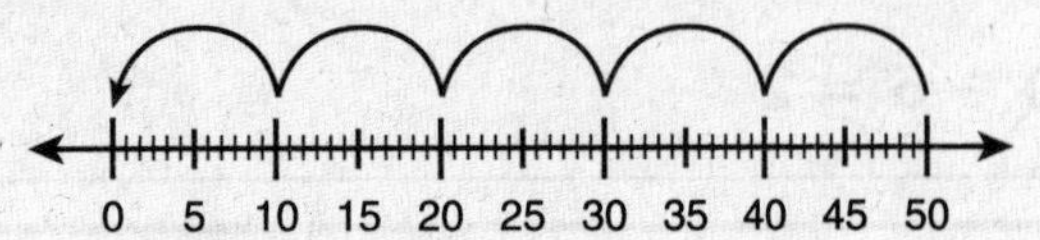

50 ÷ 10 = 5

Way 2: Use a related multiplication fact.

Think: 10 × ■ = 50

10 × 5 = 50

50 ÷ 10 = 5

1. $10\overline{)30}$ **2.** $10\overline{)60}$ **3.** $10\overline{)20}$ **4.** $10\overline{)80}$ **5.** $10\overline{)100}$

6. $10\overline{)50}$ **7.** $10\overline{)10}$ **8.** $10\overline{)90}$ **9.** $10\overline{)40}$ **10.** $10\overline{)70}$

11. 80 ÷ 10 ______ **12.** 20 ÷ 10 ______ **13.** 100 ÷ 10 ______ **14.** 30 ÷ 10 ______

Find each missing number.

15. 8 = ■ ÷ 10 **16.** 5 × ■ = 35 **17.** 2 = 10 ÷ ■ **18.** 16 ÷ ■ = 2

Problem Solving

19. Ben packed 60 oranges in 10 boxes. He put the same number of oranges in each box. How many oranges did he put in each box?

____

Use with text pages 272–273.

Name ______________________ Date ____________

Homework 10.8

Problem-Solving Strategy: Write a Number Sentence

Cassie has 30 books. She puts the same number of books on each shelf of a bookcase. If she puts 10 books on a shelf, how many shelves are in the bookcase?

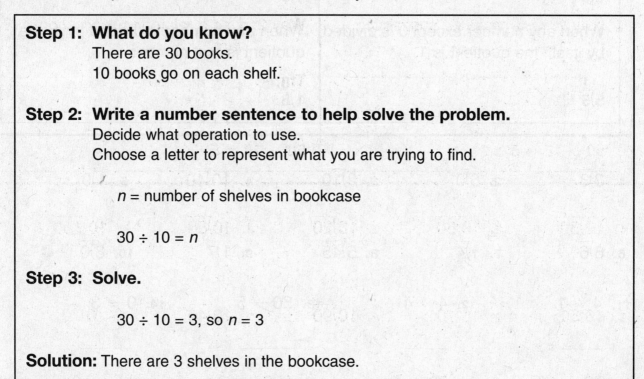

Step 1: What do you know?
There are 30 books.
10 books go on each shelf.

Step 2: Write a number sentence to help solve the problem.
Decide what operation to use.
Choose a letter to represent what you are trying to find.

n = number of shelves in bookcase

$30 \div 10 = n$

Step 3: Solve.

$30 \div 10 = 3$, so $n = 3$

Solution: There are 3 shelves in the bookcase.

Write a number sentence to solve each problem.

Show your work.

1. Jessie rode his bike 3 miles on Monday, 5 miles on Wednesday and 2 miles on Friday. How many miles did he ride in all?

____

2. Katie baked 35 cookies. She puts them into bags so that each bag contains 5 cookies. How many bags of cookies will she have?

____

3. Matt's soccer league team has 7 players on it. How many players would be on 6 teams in Matt's soccer league?

____

Use with text pages 274–277.

Name ______________________ Date ______________

Homework 10.9

Algebra: Division Rules

Divide.

$5\overline{)5}$ When any number except 0 is divided by itself, the quotient is 1. **$5\overline{)5}$ = 1**	**$1\overline{)8}$** When any number is divided by 1, the quotient is that number. **$1\overline{)8}$ = 8**

1. $3\overline{)3}$ **2.** $6\overline{)0}$ **3.** $2\overline{)10}$ **4.** $10\overline{)40}$ **5.** $1\overline{)9}$

6. $6\overline{)6}$ **7.** $1\overline{)4}$ **8.** $5\overline{)45}$ **9.** $1\overline{)7}$ **10.** $8\overline{)0}$

11. $4 \div 1$ ______ **12.** $4 \div 4$ ______ **13.** $50 \div 5$ ______ **14.** $0 \div 3$ ______

15. $0 \div 5$ ______ **16.** $18 \div 2$ ______ **17.** $10 \div 10$ ______ **18.** $7 \div 1$ ______

19. $0 \div 2$ ______ **20.** $12 \div 2$ ______ **21.** $7 \div 7$ ______ **22.** $9 \div 1$ ______

Problem Solving

23. Dan planted 10 flowers in 10 pots. He planted the same number of flowers in each pot. How many flowers did Dan plant in each pot?

____

Use with text pages 278–281.

Name ______________________ Date ____________

Homework 11.1

Divide Using a Multiplication Table

Complete the chart. Use the multiplication table to help you.

×	0	1	2	3	4	5	6	7	8	9	10
0	0	0	0	0	0	0	0	0	0	0	0
1	0	1	2	3	4	5	6	7	8	9	10
2	0	2	4	6	8	10	12	14	16	18	20
3	0	3	6	9	12	15	18	21	24	27	30
4	0	4	8	12	16	20	24	28	32	36	40
5	0	5	10	15	20	25	30	35	40	45	50
6	0	6	12	18	24	30	36	42	48	54	60
7	0	7	14	21	28	35	42	49	56	63	70
8	0	8	16	24	32	40	48	56	64	72	80
9	0	9	18	27	36	45	54	63	72	81	90
10	0	10	20	30	40	50	60	70	80	90	100

		Divisor	Dividend	Quotient
	42 ÷ 6	Find the row marked 6.	Move across this row to the column that shows 42.	Look at the number at the top of this column. It is 7. 42 ÷ 6 = 7
1.	40 ÷ 5			
2.	49 ÷ 7			
3.	36 ÷ 4			
4.	30 ÷ 3			

Use the multiplication table to find each quotient.

5. 16 ÷ 2 = ____ **6.** 27 ÷ 9 = ____ **7.** 56 ÷ 8 = ____ **8.** 6 ÷ 1 = ____

9. 12 ÷ 3 = ____ **10.** 20 ÷ 2 = ____ **11.** 6 ÷ 6 = ____ **12.** 25 ÷ 5 = ____

Problem Solving

Show your work.

13. Doug bought 48 baseball cards. The cards came in packs of 8. How many packs of baseball cards did Doug buy?

____

Use with text pages 286–287.

Name ______________________ Date ____________

Homework 11.2

Algebra: Fact Families

Complete each fact family.

5 × 6 = 30	5 rows × 6 in each row= 30 (total)	**5 × 6 = 30**
6 × ____ = 30	6 in each row × 5 rows = 30 (total)	**6 × 5 = 30**
30 ÷ 6 = ____	30 (total) ÷ 6 in each row= 5 rows	**30 ÷ 6 = 5**
30 ÷ ____ = 6	30 (total) ÷ 5 rows= 6 in each row	**30 ÷ 5 = 6**

1. 4 × 4 = 16

16 ÷ 4 = ____

2. 1 × 8 = 8

8 × 1 = ____

8 ÷ ____ = 8

8 ÷ 8 = ____

3. 4 × 7 = 28

7 × ____ = 28

28 ÷ 7 = ____

28 ÷ ____ = 7

4. 9 × 3 = 27

____ × 9 = 27

____ ÷ 9 = 3

27 ÷ 3 = ____

Write a fact family for each set of numbers.

5. 2, 10, 20

6. 5, 8, 40

7. 7, 6, 42

8. 9, 9, 81

Problem Solving

9. Jenna wants to arrange her button collection in a display case. She has 45 buttons. Write two multiplication sentences to describe two different ways she could display her buttons in equal rows.

____

Use with text pages 288–289.

Name ____________________ Date ______________

Homework 11.3

Divide by 3

Find each quotient.

$3\overline{)12}$

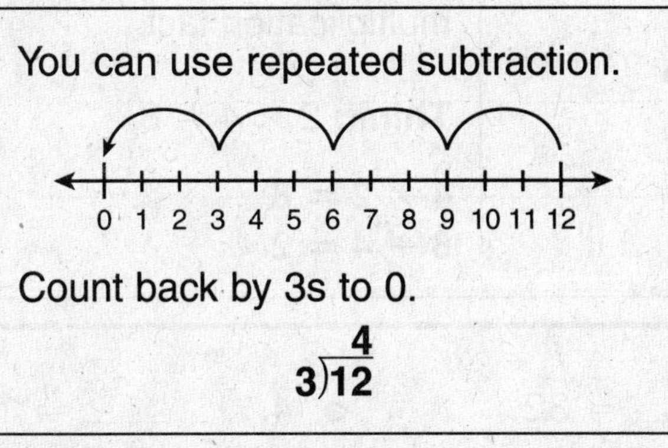

You can use repeated subtraction.
0 1 2 3 4 5 6 7 8 9 10 11 12
Count back by 3s to 0.
4
3)12

1. $3\overline{)9}$
2. $3\overline{)18}$
3. $3\overline{)3}$
4. $3\overline{)24}$
5. $3\overline{)15}$
6. $3\overline{)30}$
7. $3\overline{)6}$
8. $3\overline{)12}$
9. $3\overline{)0}$
10. $3\overline{)21}$
11. $27 \div 3$ ______
12. $15 \div 3$ ______
13. $9 \div 3$ ______
14. $24 \div 3$ ______
15. $18 \div 3$ ______
16. $0 \div 3$ ______
17. $30 \div 3$ ______
18. $12 \div 3$ ______

Algebra • Symbols Write >, <, or = for each ○.

19. 5×2 ○ $10 \div 5$
20. 8×3 ○ $8 + 3$
21. $50 \div 5$ ○ $50 - 5$
22. 7×3 ○ $12 \div 2$
23. $15 - 6$ ○ 3×3
24. $20 \div 10$ ○ $20 - 10$

Problem Solving

Show your work.

25. Walter sold 3 CDs at a yard sale for \$15. Each CD sold for the same price. What was the price of each CD?

____

Use with text pages 290–291.

Name ______________________ Date ____________

Homework 11.4

Divide by 4

Find each factor and quotient.

4 × ______ = 8 **8 ÷ 4 = ______**	You can make equal groups. ● ● ● ● ● ● ● ● **4 × 2 = 8** **8 ÷ 4 = 2**	You can use a related multiplication fact. **Think:** 2 × 4 = 8 **4 × 2 = 8** **8 ÷ 4 = 2**

1. 4 × ______ = 20

20 ÷ 4 = ______

2. 4 × ______ = 32

32 ÷ 4 = ______

3. 4 × ______ = 16

16 ÷ 4 = ______

4. 4 × ______ = 36

36 ÷ 4 = ______

5. 4 × ______ = 0

0 ÷ 4 = ______

6. 4 × ______ = 28

28 ÷ 4 = ______

Find the quotient.

7. $4\overline{)16}$ **8.** $4\overline{)20}$ **9.** $4\overline{)24}$ **10.** $4\overline{)0}$ **11.** $4\overline{)36}$

12. 12 ÷ 4 ______

13. 40 ÷ 4 ______

14. 4 ÷ 4 ______

15. 8 ÷ 4 ______

Problem Solving

16. Thirty-two students are on teams at a swimming meet. Four students are on each team. How many teams are at the swimming meet?

____

Use with text pages 292–294.

Name ______________________ Date ____________

Homework 11.5

Divide by 6

Divide.

$6\overline{)18}$

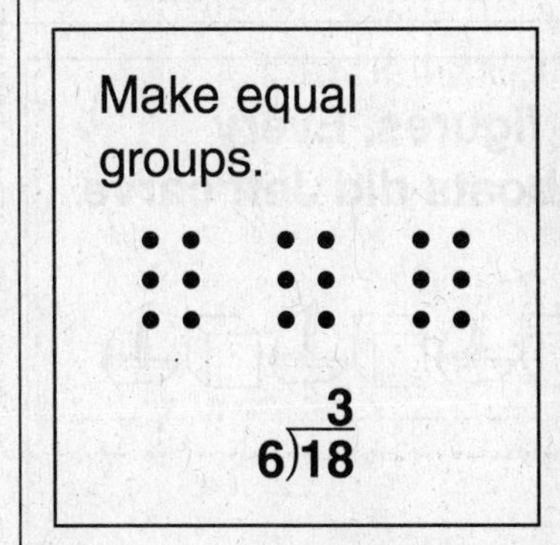

1. $6\overline{)12}$ 2. $6\overline{)30}$ 3. $6\overline{)42}$

4. $6\overline{)6}$ 5. $6\overline{)24}$ 6. $6\overline{)0}$

7. $6\overline{)18}$ 8. $6\overline{)36}$ 9. $6\overline{)48}$ 10. $6\overline{)60}$

11. $42 \div 6$ ______ 12. $54 \div 6$ ______ 13. $24 \div 6$ ______ 14. $30 \div 6$ ______

15. $6 \div 6$ ______ 16. $48 \div 6$ ______ 17. $60 \div 6$ ______ 18. $18 \div 6$ ______

Algebra • Symbols Write >, <, or = for each ◯.

19. $36 \div 6$ ◯ 4 20. 9 ◯ $27 \div 3$ 21. $32 \div 4$ ◯ 4×9

Problem Solving

Show your work.

22. Thirty gardening books are on 6 shelves in the library. The same number of books are on each shelf. How many gardening books are on each shelf?

____

Use with text pages 296–297.

Name ______________________ Date ______________

Homework 11.6

Problem-Solving Strategy: Draw a Picture

Draw a picture to solve each problem.

Jeff carves figures from wood. One day he carved 10 figures. Every other figure he carved was a sailboat. How many sailboats did Jeff carve that day?

Draw a picture.

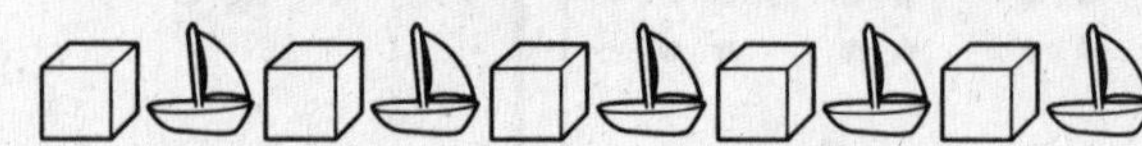

How many of the figures are sailboats?

Jeff carved 5 sailboats.

1. Wendy cut a ribbon into 11 pieces to make bows. How many cuts did she make?

   ____

2. Betty cut a 24-inch wooden board into 4 equal pieces. Then she cut each piece into 2 equal pieces. How many pieces of wood did Betty have? How long was each piece?

   ____

   ____

3. Henry is frosting cookies with blue, red, or green icing. He has 27 cookies to frost. If he frosts an equal number of cookies with each color, how many cookies will have blue icing?

   ____

Use with text pages 300–303.

Name ________________________ Date ____________

Homework 11.7

Divide by 7

Find each quotient.

$7\overline{)35}$

You can use a related multiplication fact.

Think: $7 \times 5 = 35$

$$\begin{array}{r} \mathbf{5} \\ 7\overline{)\mathbf{35}} \end{array}$$

1. $7\overline{)21}$
2. $7\overline{)49}$
3. $7\overline{)0}$
4. $7\overline{)28}$
5. $7\overline{)56}$
6. $7\overline{)14}$
7. $7\overline{)42}$
8. $7\overline{)35}$
9. $7\overline{)7}$
10. $7\overline{)70}$
11. $63 \div 7$ ______
12. $28 \div 7$ ______
13. $0 \div 7$ ______
14. $42 \div 7$ ______

Algebra • Symbols Write +, −, ×, or ÷ for each ○.

15. 49 ○ 7 = 7
16. 8 ○ 6 = 48
17. 30 ○ 6 = 24
18. 6 ○ 6 = 1
19. 70 ○ 7 = 10
20. 40 ○ 8 = 48

Problem Solving

21. Annie walked 14 miles in 7 days. She walked the same number of miles each day. How many miles did Annie walk each day?

____

Name ______________________ Date ______________

Divide by 8

Divide.

$8\overline{)40}$

> You can use a related division fact.
>
> **Think:** 40 ÷ 5 = 8
>
> $\begin{array}{r} 5 \\ 8\overline{)40} \end{array}$

1. $8\overline{)0}$
2. $8\overline{)24}$
3. $8\overline{)48}$
4. $8\overline{)16}$
5. $8\overline{)64}$
6. $8\overline{)56}$
7. $8\overline{)32}$
8. $8\overline{)80}$
9. $8\overline{)40}$
10. $8\overline{)8}$
11. 64 ÷ 8 ______
12. 72 ÷ 8 ______
13. 32 ÷ 8 ______
14. 48 ÷ 8 ______
15. 0 ÷ 8 ______
16. 24 ÷ 8 ______
17. 16 ÷ 8 ______
18. 56 ÷ 8 ______

Find each missing number.

19. $42 \div 6 = n$

    $n =$ ______

20. $8 \times b = 32$

    $b =$ ______

21. $a \div 7 = 4$

    $a =$ ______

Problem Solving

Show your work.

22. Sponges come in packages of 8. Jeremy bought 16 sponges. How many packages did he buy?

    ____

Use with text pages 306–309.

Name ______________________ Date ____________

Homework 11.9

Divide by 9

Find each factor and quotient.

9 × ______ = 27 **27 ÷ 9 = ______**	You can use a related multiplication fact. **Think:** 3 × 9 = 27 **9 × 3 = 27** **27 ÷ 9 = 3**	You can use a related division fact. **Think:** 27 ÷ 3 = 9 **9 × 3 = 27** **27 ÷ 9 = 3**

1. 9 × ______ = 36

36 ÷ 9 = ______

2. 9 × ______ = 81

81 ÷ 9 = ______

3. 9 × ______ = 0

0 ÷ 9 = ______

4. 9 × ______ = 72

72 ÷ 9 = ______

5. 9 × ______ = 18

18 ÷ 9 = ______

6. 9 × ______ = 45

45 ÷ 9 = ______

Divide.

7. $9\overline{)81}$ **8.** $9\overline{)27}$ **9.** $9\overline{)63}$ **10.** $9\overline{)90}$ **11.** $9\overline{)36}$

12. 9 ÷ 9 ______

13. 90 ÷ 9 ______

14. 54 ÷ 9 ______

15. 63 ÷ 9 ______

Problem Solving

Show your work.

16. Chet builds 9 birdhouses every day. How long will it take him to build 45 birdhouses?

____

Use with text pages 310–313.

Name ______________________ Date ____________

Homework 12.1

Hour, Half-Hour, Quarter-Hour

Describe each time in at least two ways.

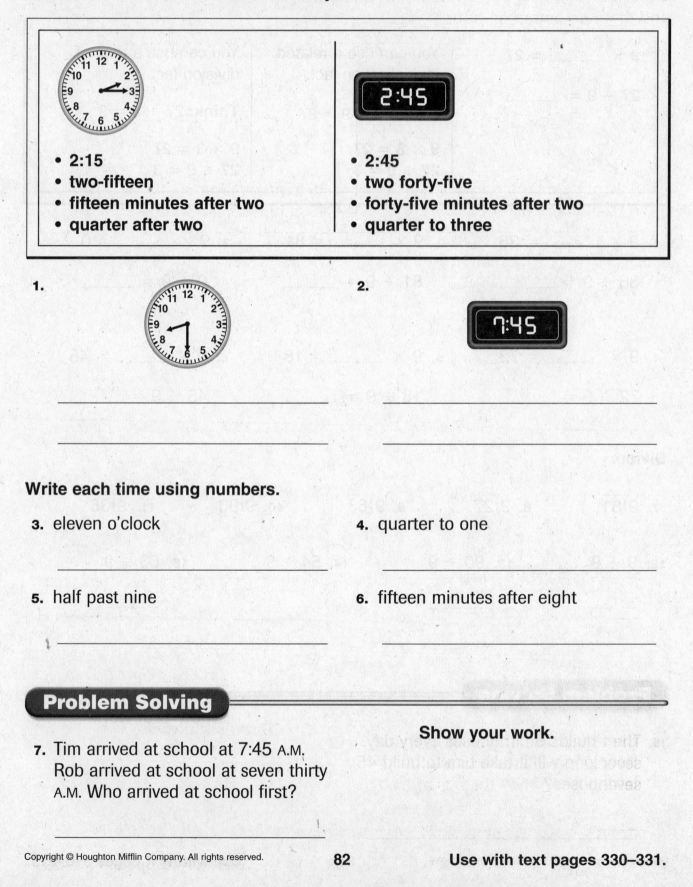

- **2:15**
- **two-fifteen**
- **fifteen minutes after two**
- **quarter after two**

- **2:45**
- **two forty-five**
- **forty-five minutes after two**
- **quarter to three**

1.

____

____

2.

____

____

Write each time using numbers.

3. eleven o'clock

____

4. quarter to one

____

5. half past nine

____

6. fifteen minutes after eight

____

Problem Solving

Show your work.

7. Tim arrived at school at 7:45 A.M. Rob arrived at school at seven thirty A.M. Who arrived at school first?

____

Use with text pages 330–331.

Name ______________________ Date ____________

Homework 12.2

Time to Five Minutes

Describe each time as minutes after an hour and minutes before an hour.

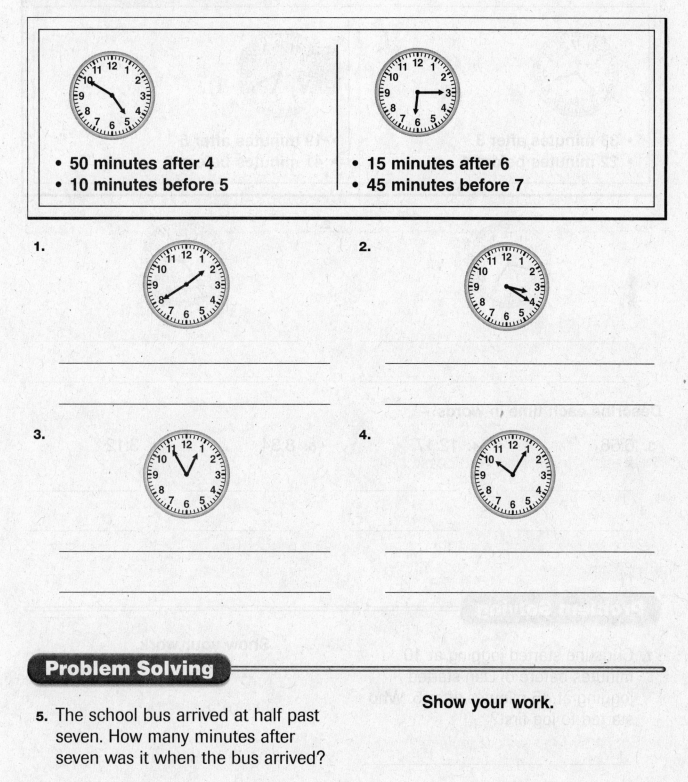

- **50 minutes after 4**
- **10 minutes before 5**

- **15 minutes after 6**
- **45 minutes before 7**

1.

____

____

2.

____

____

3.

____

____

4.

____

____

Problem Solving

5. The school bus arrived at half past seven. How many minutes after seven was it when the bus arrived?

____

Show your work.

Use with text pages 332–333.

Name ______________________ Date ______________

Homework 12.3

Time to the Minute

Describe each time two ways.

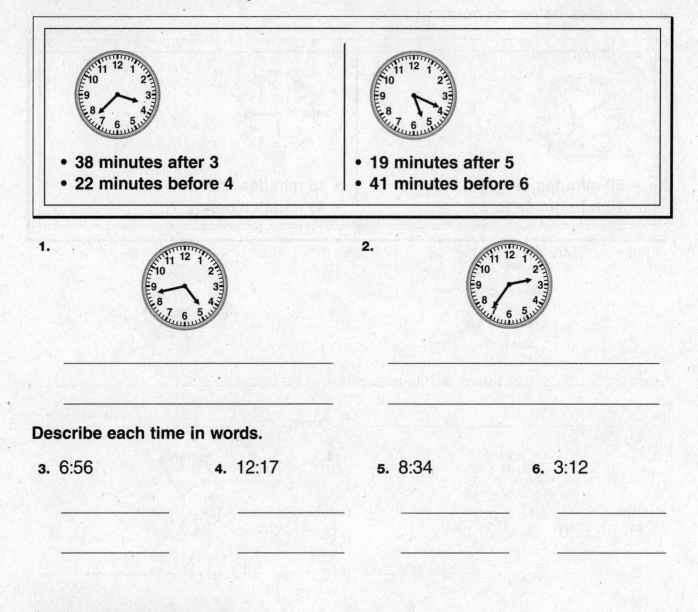

- **38 minutes after 3**
- **22 minutes before 4**

- **19 minutes after 5**
- **41 minutes before 6**

1.

____

____

2.

____

____

Describe each time in words.

3. 6:56

____

____

4. 12:17

____

____

5. 8:34

____

____

6. 3:12

____

____

Problem Solving

7. Christine started jogging at 10 minutes before 6. Dan started jogging at 45 minutes after 5. Who started to jog first?

____

Show your work.

Name ______________________ Date ____________

Elapsed Time

Tell what time it will be.

in 22 minutes

In 22 minutes, it will be 7:27.

Start at 7:05.

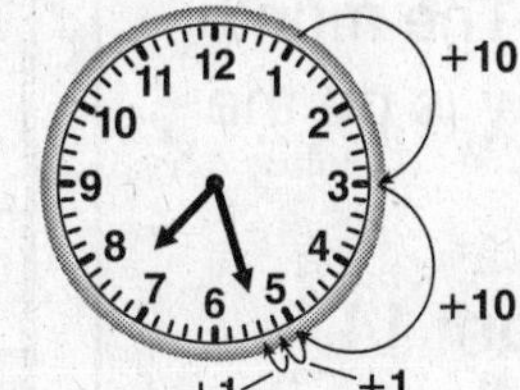

Count ahead 22 minutes.

1. in 25 minutes

______

2. in 4 hours

______

Look at each pair of times. Write how much time has passed.

3. Start: 5:10 A.M.
End: 5:25 A.M.

____

4. Start: 1:20 P.M.
End: 1:45 P.M.

____

5. Start: 9:40 A.M.
End: 11:40 A.M.

____

6. Start: 8:15 P.M.
End: 9:29 P.M.

____

Problem Solving

7. Chuck practiced the saxophone from 3:30 P.M. until 4:05 P.M. How long did Chuck practice?

____

Use with text pages 336–338.

Name ____________________ Date ____________

Homework 12.5

Use a Calendar

Use the calendar to solve each problem.

What date is the craft show?

Look at the calendar. The month is April. The craft show is on the space for 14.

The craft show is April 14.

April						
SUN	**MON**	**TUE**	**WED**	**THU**	**FRI**	**SAT**
						1
2	3	4	5	6	7	8
9	10	11	12	13	Craft Show 14	15
16	17	18	19	20	21	22
23	24	25	26	27	28	29
30						

1. What day of the week is April 12? ____________
2. What is the date of the third Thursday? ____________

Name the month that is 2 months after each month.

3. January ____________
4. September ____________
5. November ____________

Name the month that is 3 months before each month.

6. March ____________
7. July ____________
8. October ____________

Problem Solving

Use the calendar above.

9. Cindy's family is taking a two-week trip to the mountains. They are leaving on April 10. What date will they return?

____

Name ______________________ Date ____________

Homework 12.6

Problem-Solving Application: Use a Schedule

The Vanhoy family is spending the 4th of July attending events in their town. Use the schedule to help them plan their day.

They want to attend an event that starts at 1:00 P.M. and lasts less than 2 hours. Which event should they choose?

Find the events that start at 1:00 P.M.

- Air show
- Musical acts
- Baseball game

Now look at the ending times.

- Air show ends at 2:30 P.M.
- Musical acts end at 3:30 P.M.
- Baseball game ends at 4:00 P.M.

The air show starts at 1:00 and lasts for less than 2 hours, so the Vanhoy family can attend that event.

4th of July

Events	Starting Time	Ending Time
Parade	9:00 A.M.	11:45 A.M.
Car show	12:30 P.M.	5:30 P.M.
Air show	1:00 P.M.	2:30 P.M.
Musical acts	1:00 P.M.	3:30 P.M.
Baseball game	1:00 P.M.	4:00 P.M.
Band concert	7:30 P.M.	9:00 P.M.
Fireworks	9:15 P.M.	10:30 P.M.

Use the schedule above for Problems 1–3.

1. How long does the band concert last?

____

2. Could someone see all of the musical acts and all of the baseball game?

____

3. How much time is there between the end of the parade and the beginning of the baseball game?

____

Use with text pages 344–345.

Name ______________________ Date ____________

Homework 12.7

Temperature: Degrees Fahrenheit and Celsius

Write each temperature using °F or °C. Then write *hot*, *warm*, *cool*, or *cold* to describe the temperature of the air.

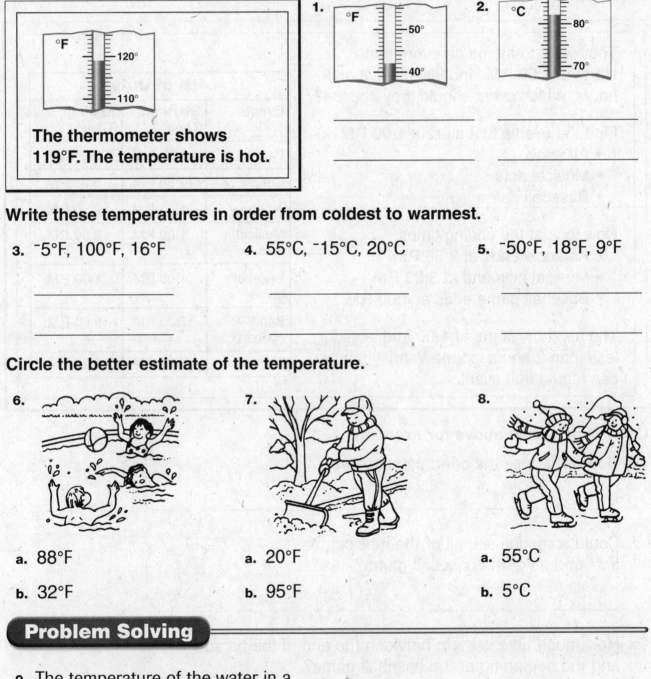

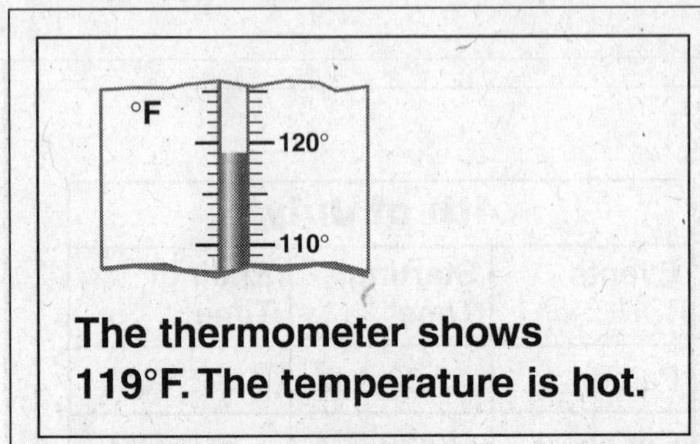

The thermometer shows 119°F. The temperature is hot.

1. 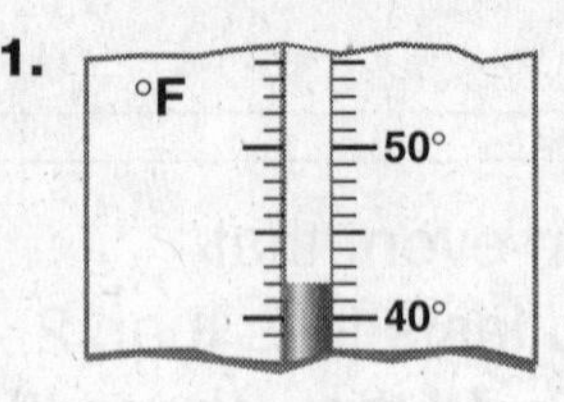

____

____

2. 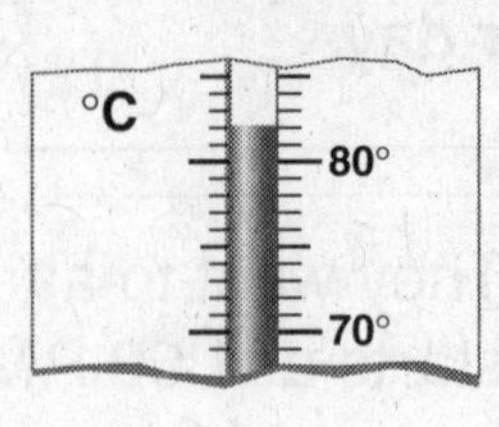

____

____

Write these temperatures in order from coldest to warmest.

3. ⁻5°F, 100°F, 16°F

____

____

4. 55°C, ⁻15°C, 20°C

____

____

5. ⁻50°F, 18°F, 9°F

____

____

Circle the better estimate of the temperature.

6. 

a. 88°F

b. 32°F

7. 

a. 20°F

b. 95°F

8. 

a. 55°C

b. 5°C

Problem Solving

9. The temperature of the water in a pond is 7° C. Is the temperature above or below freezing?

____

Use with text pages 346–348.

Name ______________________ Date ____________

Homework 13.1

Measure to the Nearest Inch

Estimate and then measure each object below to the nearest inch.

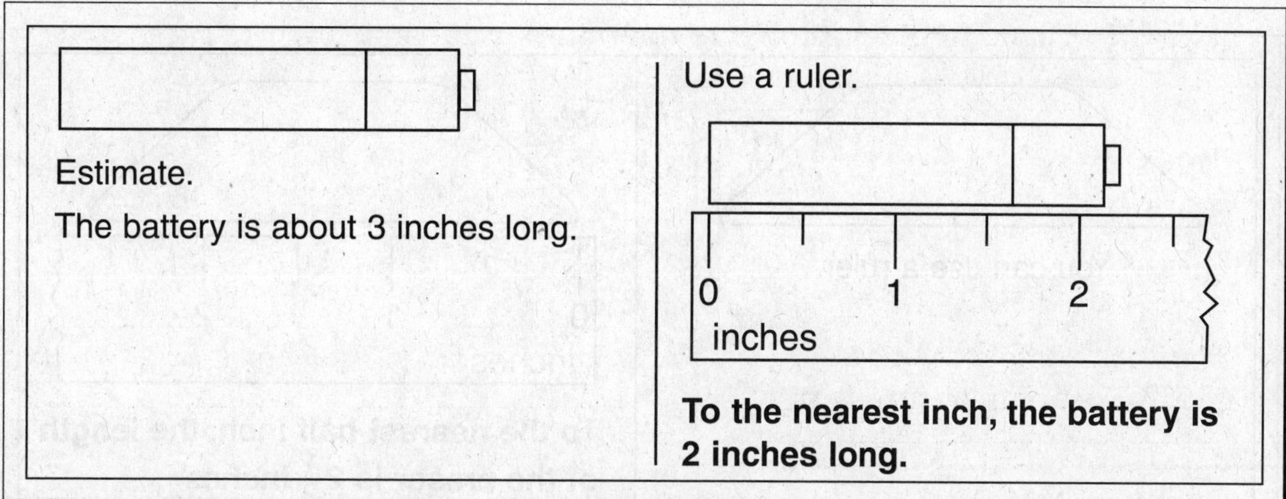

Estimate.
The battery is about 3 inches long.
Use a ruler.
0
1
2
inches
To the nearest inch, the battery is 2 inches long.

1. 

Estimate: ______

Measurement: __________

2. 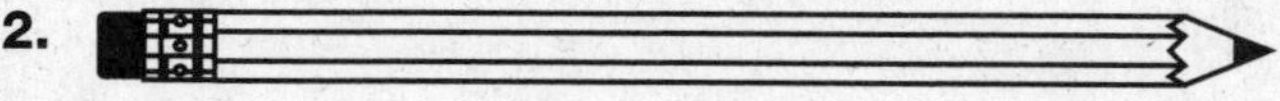

Estimate: ______

Measurement: __________

Use a ruler. Draw a line of each length.

3. 2 inches

4. 3 inches

5. 5 inches

Problem Solving

6. Maria's pencil measures a little less than 5 inches long. What is the length of Maria's pencil to the nearest inch?

____

Use with text pages 354–357.

Name ______________________ Date ______________

Homework 13.2

Measure to the Nearest Half Inch

Measure each to the nearest half inch.

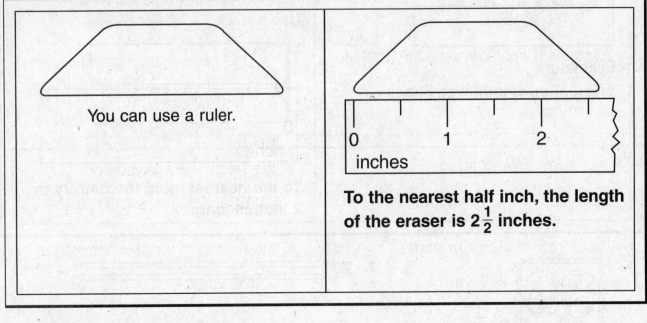

You can use a ruler.

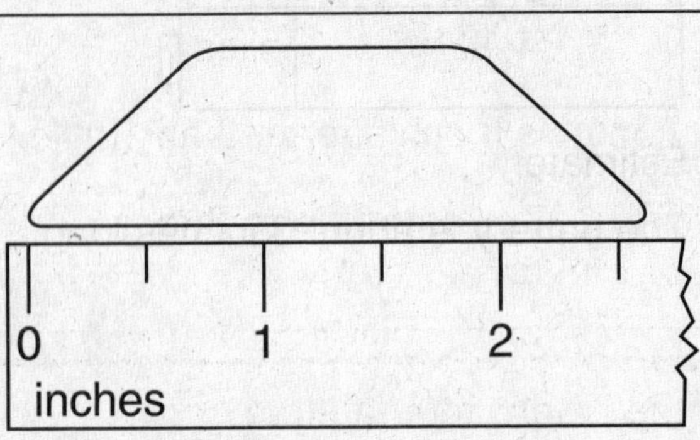

To the nearest half inch, the length of the eraser is $2\frac{1}{2}$ inches.

1.

2.

____

Use an inch ruler. Draw a line of each length.

3. $3\frac{1}{2}$ in.

4. 4 in.

5. $6\frac{1}{2}$ in.

Problem Solving

6. One piece of train track measures $5\frac{1}{2}$ inches long. Between which two inch marks does the right end of the track lie?

____

Name ______________________________ Date ______________

Homework 13.3

Customary Units of Length

Choose the better estimate.

the height of a man

a. 6 feet **b.** 6 miles

A man is much shorter than 1 mile.

The better estimate is 6 feet or choice a.

Customary Units of Length
1 foot = 12 inches
1 yard = 3 feet
1 yard = 36 inches
1 mile = 1,760 yards
1 mile = 5,280 feet

1. the height of a tall tree

a. 50 feet **b.** 50 inches

2. the height of a skyscraper

a. 200 miles **b.** 200 yards

3. the length of a pair of pants

a. 1 inch **b.** 1 yard

4. the length of a roll of kite string

a. 300 yards **b.** 300 miles

Complete.

5. 3 ft = ______ in.

6. 4 yd = ______ ft

7. 2 yd = ______ in.

8. 24 in. = ______ ft

9. 9 ft = ______ yd

10. 2 ft = ______ in.

Compare. Write >, <, or = for each ◯.

11. 6 yd ◯ 6 ft

12. 12 in. ◯ 1 ft

13. 1 mi ◯ 500 in.

Problem Solving

14. Becky and Ned made banners. Becky's banner is 3 yards long. Ned's banner is 6 feet long. Who made the longer banner?

Show your work.

____

Use with text pages 360–362.

Name ______________________ Date ______________

Homework 13.4

Problem-Solving Strategy: Use Logical Reasoning

Joel, Amber, and Stacy are in line according to their heights. Amber is 54 inches tall. Joel is 6 inches shorter than Amber. Stacey is 4 inches taller than Joel. How tall is Stacy?

Use logical reasoning to help you solve the problem. Start with what you know.

- Amber is 54 inches tall.
- Joel is 6 inches shorter than Amber.
  Subtract. 54 in. – 6 in. = 48 in.
  Joel is 48 inches tall.
- Stacey is 4 inches taller than Joel.
  Add. 48 in. + 4 in. = 52 in.

Solution: Stacey is 52 inches tall.

Use logical reasoning to solve each problem. **Show your work.**

1. Carlos, Maria, Anna, and Ricky bought a book. The books cost $3, $6, $9, and $13. Maria paid $3 for her book. Ricky paid three times as much as Maria for his. Carlos paid $10 more than Maria. Anna paid $3 less than Ricky. How much did each of them pay for their book?

____

2. John has 6 more baseball cards than Matt. Ian has 8 less cards than Matt. The boys have 12, 20 and 26 cards in their collections. How many cards are in each boy's collection?

____

Use with text pages 364–366.

Name ______________________ Date ______________

Homework 13.5

Estimate and Measure Capacity

Use the chart to find the missing measure.

2 pt = ____ c

There are 2 cups in each pint.

2 pints = 2 × 2 cups

2 pt = 4 c

1 pint (pt) = 2 cups (c)
1 quart (qt) = 2 pints
1 gallon (gal) = 4 quarts

1. 1 qt = ____ pt

2. 1 gal = ____ qt

3. 1 qt = ____ c

4. 1 gal = ____ pt

5. 2 gal = ____ pt

6. 2 pt = ____ c

7. 2 gal = ____ qt

8. 2 qt = ____ pt

9. 3 qt = ____ c

10. 4 pt = ____ c

11. 3 gal = ____ qt

Problem Solving

12. A punch bowl has a capacity of 8 quarts. How many 1-cup servings can the punch bowl hold?

____

Show your work.

Use with text pages 368–369.

Name ______________________ Date ____________

Homework 13.6

Customary Units of Capacity

A mug could not hold a pint, a quart, or a gallon.

The best unit to measure the capacity of the mug is *cup*.

1 pint = 2 cups
1 quart = 2 pints
1 gallon = 4 quarts

Choose the unit you would use. Write *cup, pint, quart,* or *gallon*.

1. 

____

2. 

____

Choose the better estimate.

3. tea pot

a. 1 cup **b.** 1 pint

4. paint can

a. 1 gallon **b.** 1 cup

5. bucket

a. 2 cups **b.** 2 gallons

6. gravy ladle

a. 1 cup **b.** 1 quart

Complete.

7. 6 c = _____ pt

8. 2 gal = _____ qt

9. 16 pt = _____ gal

Problem Solving

10. Tanisha bought 3 one-quart cans of red paint and 1 one-gallon can of blue paint. Did she buy more red or blue paint?

Show your work.

____

Use with text pages 370–371.

Name ______________________ Date ____________

Homework 13.7

Customary Units of Weight

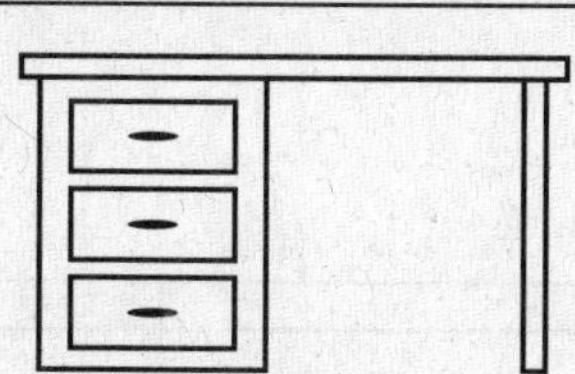

The best unit to measure the weight of the desk is *pounds.*

Ounces would be too light.

1 pound = 16 ounces

Choose the unit you would use to measure the weight. Write *ounce* or *pound.*

1. 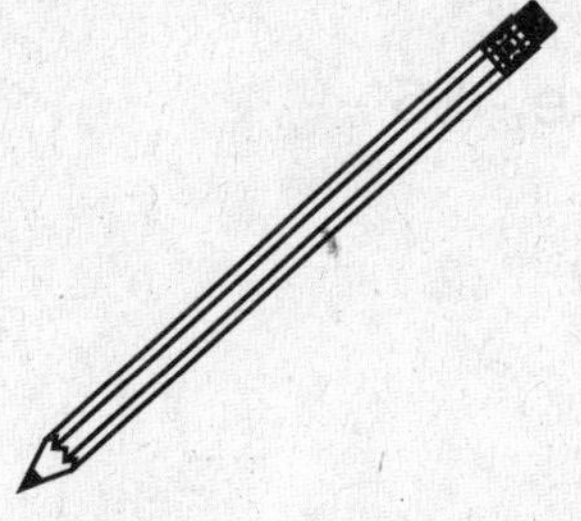
____

2. 
____

Choose the better estimate.

3. a lemon
   a. 4 ounces b. 4 pounds

4. a cat
   a. 10 ounces b. 10 pounds

5. a bicycle
   a. 17 pounds b. 170 pounds

6. a shoe
   a. 5 ounces b. 500 ounces

Write in order from the least weight to the greatest weight.

7. 12 ounces 18 ounces 1 pound
____

8. 24 ounces 2 pounds 36 ounces
____

Problem Solving

9. A large box of raisins weighs 1 pound. A small box weighs 4 ounces. Which is heavier, a large box or 3 small boxes? How much heaver?

Show your work.

____

Use with text pages 372–374.

Name ______________________ Date ____________

Homework 13.8

Problem-Solving Decision: Too Much or Too Little Information

Ellie bought 2 loaves of bread. How much did she spend? What facts do you need to solve the problem? **You need to know the price of each loaf of bread.** Is enough information given? **No; there are 2 different prices for loaves of bread.** What information is not given or not needed? **You need to know the size of each loaf of bread Ellie bought.**	**Bakery Prices** roll - 10¢ large loaf of bread - $3 small loaf of bread - $2 pie - $4 cake - $5

Solve. If you can't solve the problem, tell what information you need.

Show your work.

1. Kevin bought 2 small loaves of bread. He pays for them with a $5 bill. How much did he spend?

____

2. How much would it cost to buy 2 doughnuts and a pie?

____

3. How much more does a large loaf of bread weigh than a small loaf of bread?

____

Use with text page 376.

Name ______________________ Date ____________

Homework 14.1

Centimeter and Millimeter

Which is the better estimate for the length of a shoe? 2 cm or 2 dm

The tack is 1 centimeter long.	The crayon 1 decimeter long.
1 cm	**1 dm**

The better estimate for the length of a shoe is 2 dm.

Estimate. Then measure to the nearest centimeter.

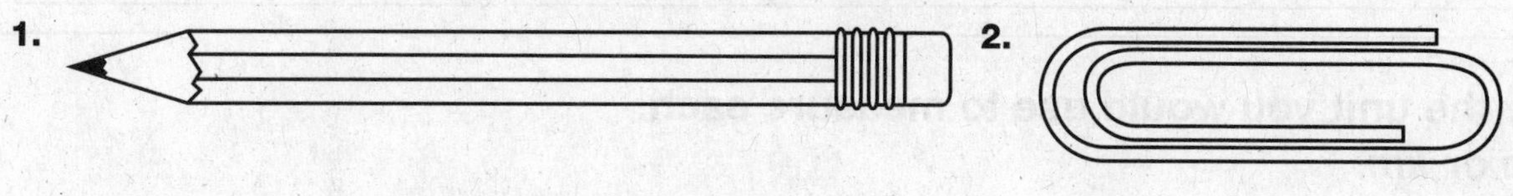

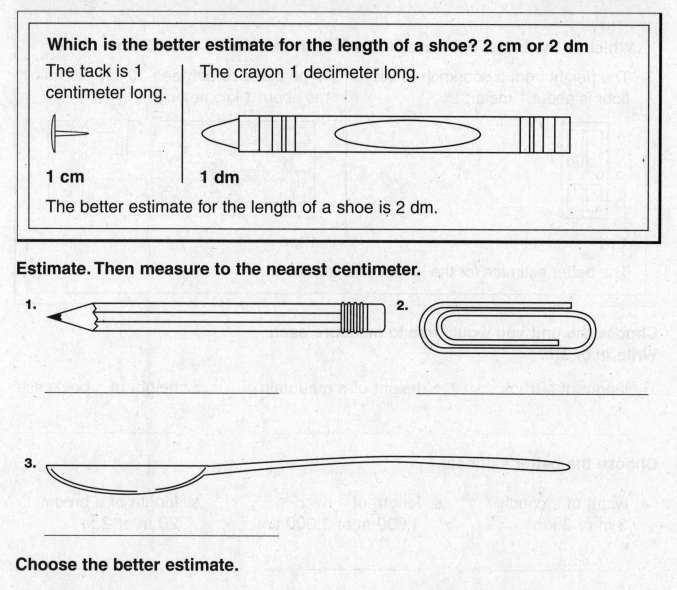

1. ____________

2. ____________

3. ____________

Choose the better estimate.

4. length of a marker
   5 cm or 15 cm
   ____

5. length of a CD case
   14 cm   4 mm
   ____

Problem Solving

6. Elsa wants to measure the length of a pen. Which is the better estimate of the length of the pen, 3 centimeters, 40 millimeters, or 13 centimeters?
   ____

Use with text pages 382–383.

Name ______________________ Date ____________

Homework 14.2

Meter and Kilometer

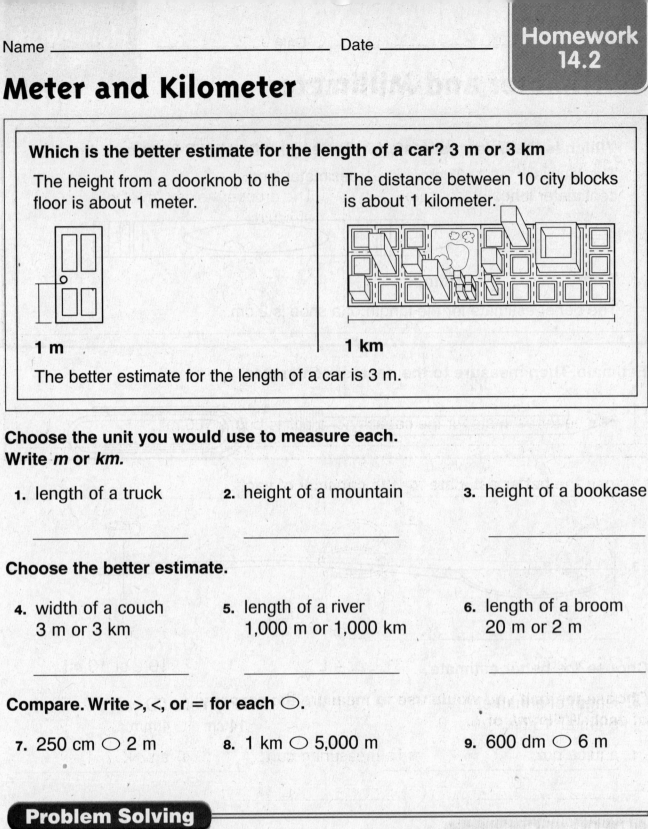

Which is the better estimate for the length of a car? 3 m or 3 km

The height from a doorknob to the floor is about 1 meter.

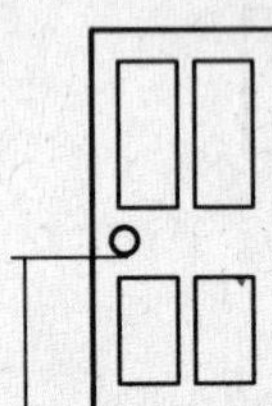

1 m

The distance between 10 city blocks is about 1 kilometer.

1 km

The better estimate for the length of a car is 3 m.

Choose the unit you would use to measure each. Write *m* or *km*.

1. length of a truck ____________
2. height of a mountain ____________
3. height of a bookcase ____________

Choose the better estimate.

4. width of a couch
   3 m or 3 km ____________
5. length of a river
   1,000 m or 1,000 km ____________
6. length of a broom
   20 m or 2 m ____________

Compare. Write >, <, or = for each ◯.

7. 250 cm ◯ 2 m
8. 1 km ◯ 5,000 m
9. 600 dm ◯ 6 m

Problem Solving

Show your work.

10. Mr. Diaz measured the length of the garden. It measured 9 meters long. How many centimeters long was the garden?

____

Use with text pages 384–385.

Name ______________________ Date ____________

Metric Units of Capacity

Which is the better estimate for the capacity of a coffee cup? 100 mL or 100 L

This water bottle holds 1 liter of water.

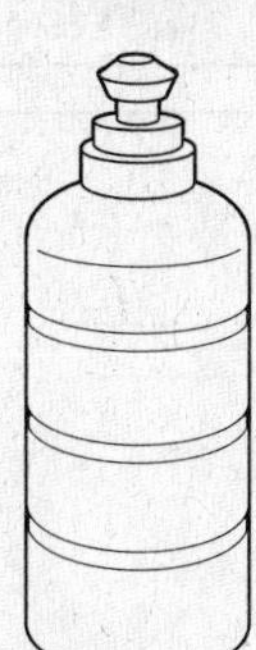

The dropper holds 1 milliliter of liquid.

The better estimate for the capacity of a coffee cup is 100 mL.

Choose the better estimate for the capacity of each.

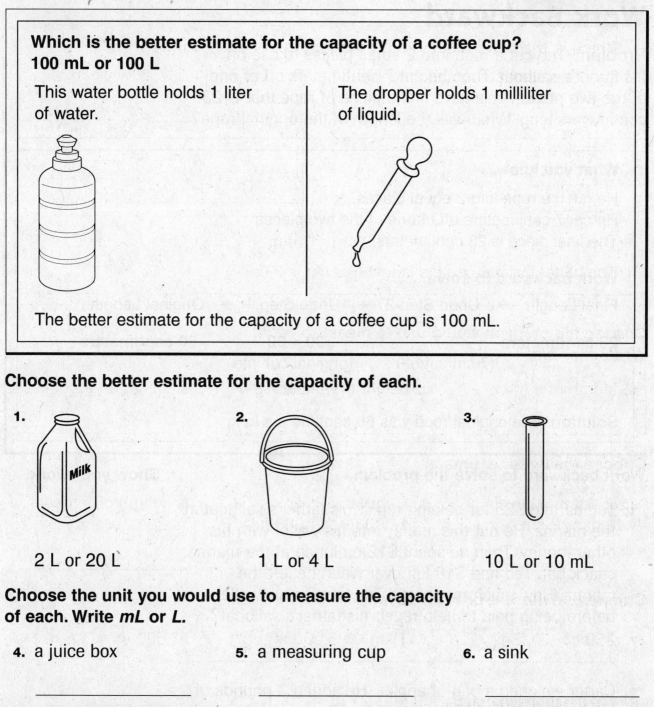

1. 

2 L or 20 L

2. 

1 L or 4 L

3. 

10 L or 10 mL

Choose the unit you would use to measure the capacity of each. Write *mL* or *L*.

4. a juice box ______________

5. a measuring cup ______________

6. a sink ______________

Problem Solving

Show your work.

7. Janice poured 4 liters of water into the pot. How many milliliters of water did she pour into the pot?

____

Name ______________________ Date ______________

Homework 14.4

Problem-Solving Strategy: Work Backward

Problem Ted cut a rope into 2 equal pieces to use on his father's sailboat. Then he cut 7 centimeters off of one of the two pieces. This gave him a piece of rope that is 23 centimeters long. What was the length of the original rope?

What you know.

He cut the rope into 2 equal pieces.
He cut 7 centimeters off of one of the two pieces.
The final piece is 23 centimeters.

Work backward to solve.

Final Length →	Undo Step 2 →	Undo Step 1 →	Original Length
23 centimeters	**+ 7** (7 cm cut off)	**30 + 30** (original cut into 2 equal pieces)	**60 centimeters**

Solution: The original rope was 60 centimeters long.

Work backward to solve the problem. **Show your work.**

1. Ted earned $25 for helping repair his father's sailboat at the marina. He put this money into his wallet with his other money. Then he spent $12 on lunch at the marina snack bar. Ted had $18 left over when he left the marina. How much money did Ted have in his wallet before being paid to help repair his father's sailboat?

____

2. Carter weighed a bag of apples. He added 3 pounds of apples to the bag. After he took out 6 pounds of apples, the bag weighed 12 pounds. How much did the bag weigh in the beginning?

____

Use with text pages 390–392.

Name ______________________ Date ____________

Homework 14.5

Metric Units of Mass

Which is the better estimate for the mass of a CD? 1 g or 1 kg

A peanut has a mass of about 1 gram.

A baking potato has a mass of about 300 grams.

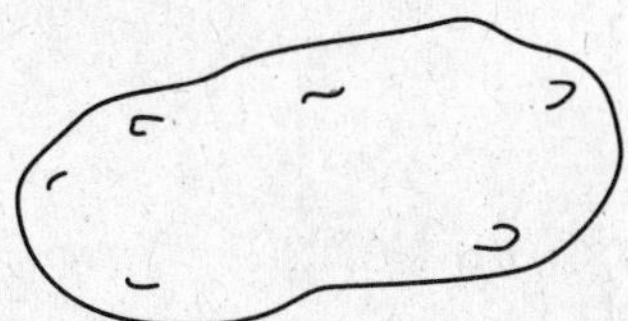

A cauliflower head has a mass of about 1 kilogram.

1 kilogram = 1,000 grams

The better estimate for the mass of a CD is 1 g.

Choose the unit you would use to measure the mass of each. Write *g* or *kg*.

1. a pen ________
2. a couch ________
3. an orange ________

Complete.

4. 4 kg = ________ g
5. 9 kg = ________ g
6. 2,000 g = ________ kg

Compare. Use >, <, or = for each ○.

7. 3,000 g ○ 3 kg
8. 100 kg ○ 10 g
9. 2,000 g ○ 5 kg

Problem Solving

10. Andy works at the bakery. He measured some flour onto a scale. It measured 2 kilograms. How many grams of flour did Andy measure onto the scale?

Show your work.

____

Use with text pages 394–396.

Name ______________________ Date ____________

Homework 15.1

Lines, Line Segments, Rays, and Angles

Write whether each figure is a *line, line segment,* or *ray*.

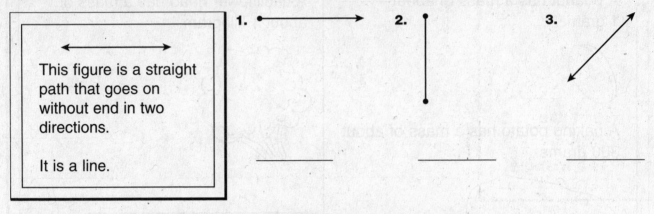

> This figure is a straight path that goes on without end in two directions.
>
> It is a line.

1. ____________

2. ____________

3. ____________

Tell whether each figure is a *right angle, less than a right angle,* or *greater than a right angle.*

4. 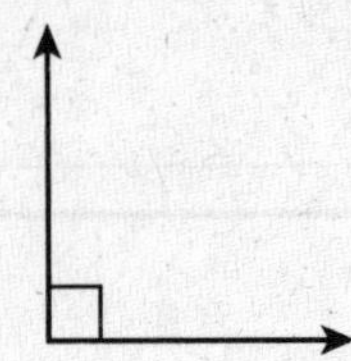 ____________

5. 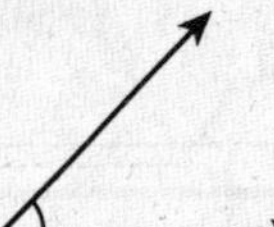 ____________

6. 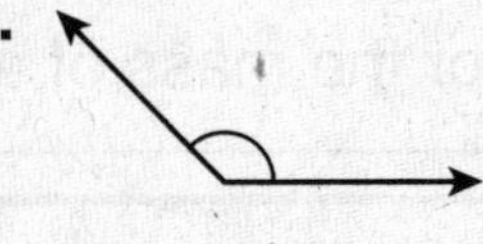 ____________

7. 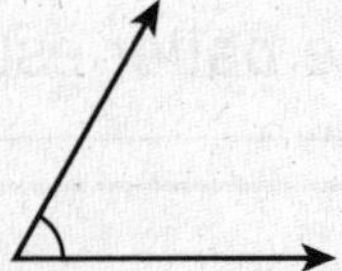 ____________

Tell whether each pair of lines is *parallel, intersecting,* or *perpendicular.*

8. 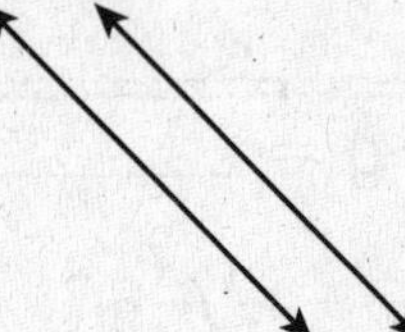 ____________

9. 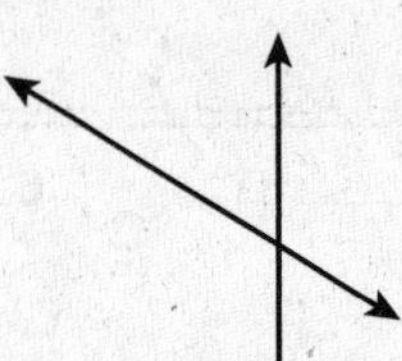 ____________

10. 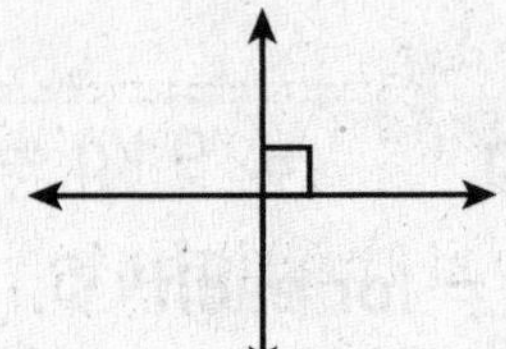 ____________

11. 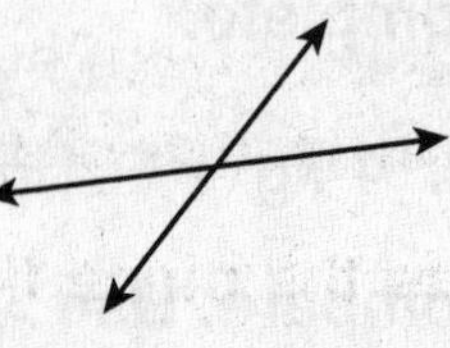 ____________

Problem Solving

12. Chen drew the letter E. What kind of angles do you see in the letter?

____

Use with text pages 414–417.

Name ______________________ Date ____________

Homework 15.2

Classify Plane Figures

Tell whether each figure is a polygon. If it is, write its name.

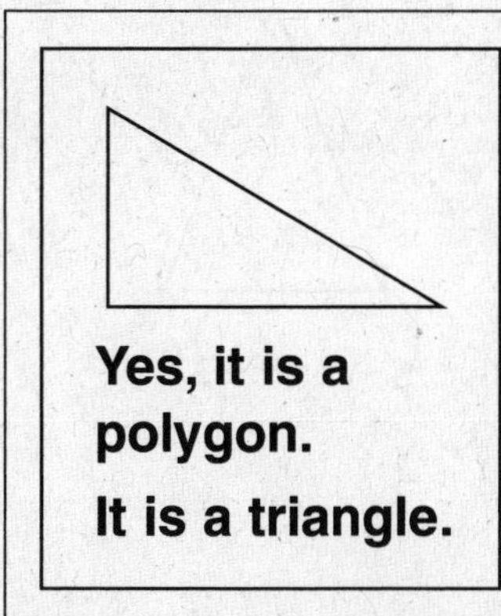

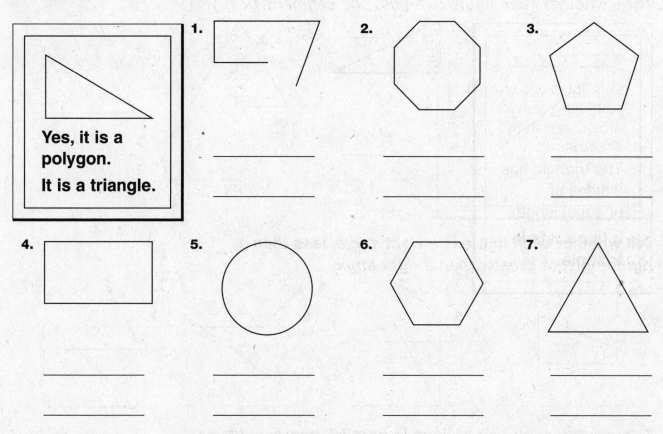

Yes, it is a polygon.
It is a triangle.

1.

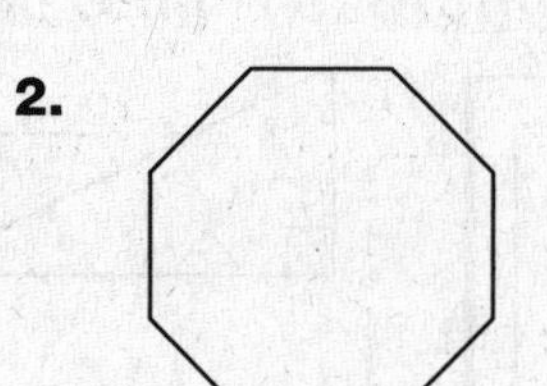

____

____

2.

____

____

3.

____

____

4.

____

____

5.

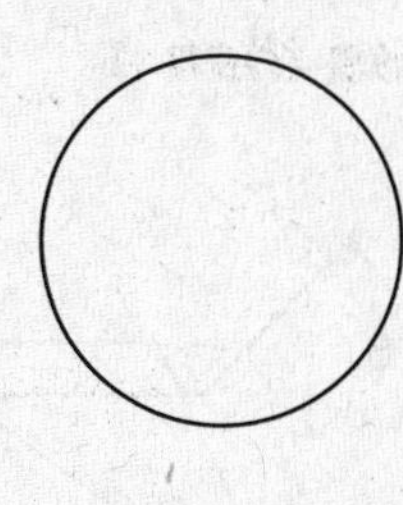

____

____

6.

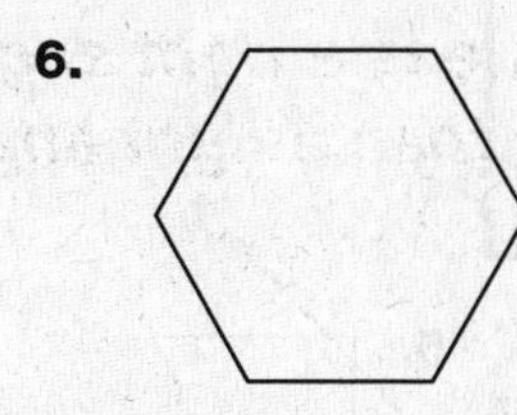

____

____

7.

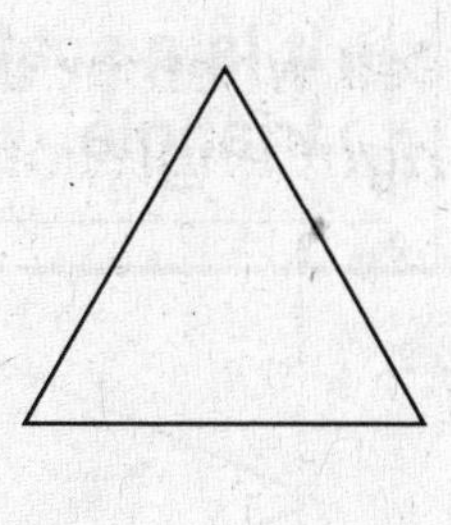

____

____

Problem Solving

Use the plane figures at the right to answer each question.

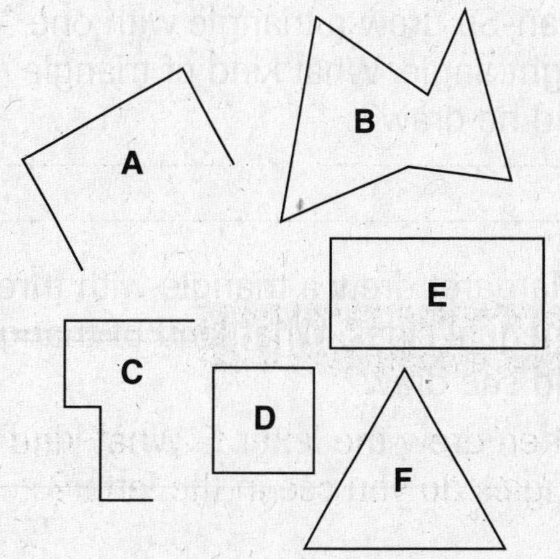

8. Which of the figures are polygons?

____

9. Which of the figures are irregular polygons?

____

Use with text pages 418–421.

Name ______________________ Date ____________

Classify Triangles

Name the kind of triangle shown. Write *equilateral, isosceles, right,* or *scalene.*

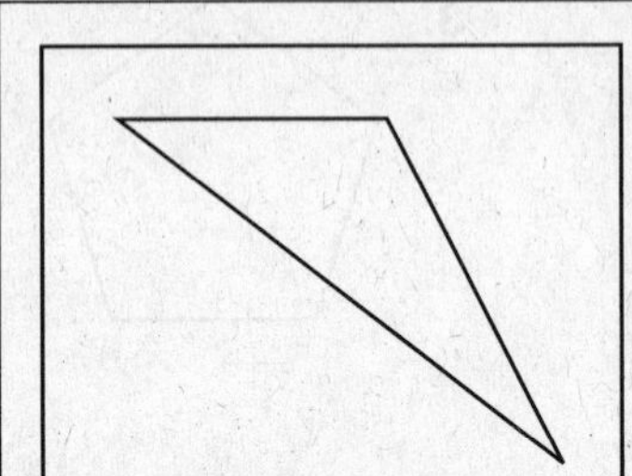

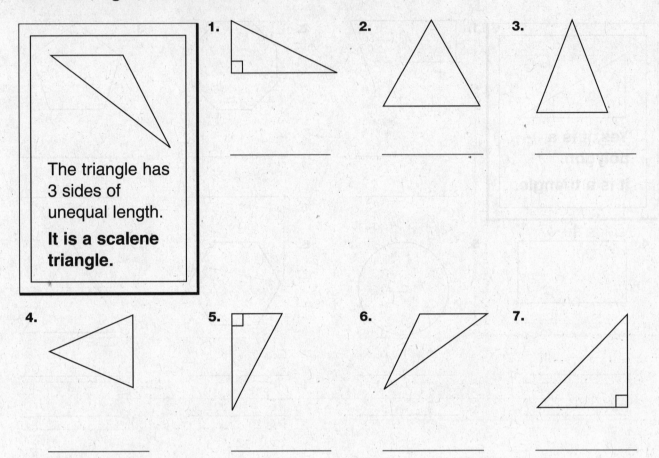

The triangle has 3 sides of unequal length.

It is a scalene triangle.

1. 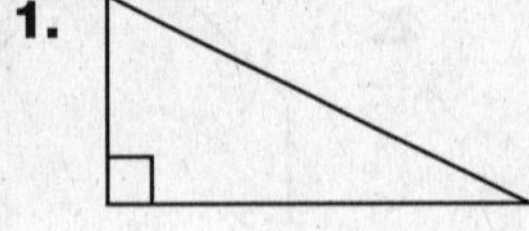

____

2. 

____

3. 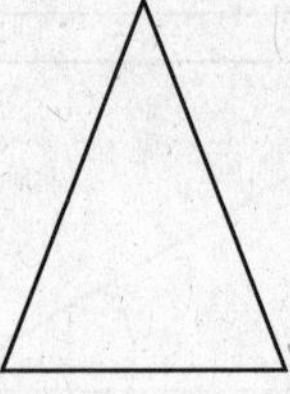

____

4. 

____

5. 

____

6. 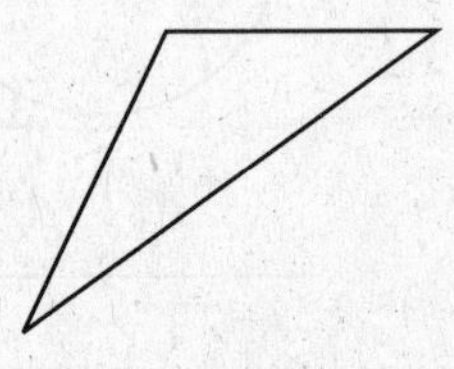

____

7. 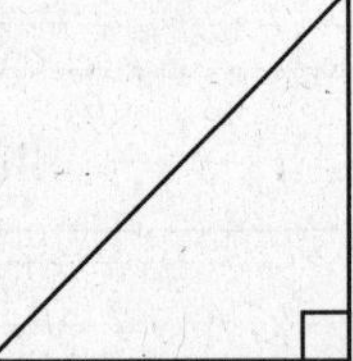

____

Problem Solving

8. Han-Su drew a triangle with one right angle. What kind of triangle did he draw?

____

9. Margaret drew a triangle with three unequal sides. What kind of triangle did she draw?

____

Use with text pages 422–423.

Name ______________________ Date ____________

Homework 15.4

Classify Quadrilaterals

Tell whether the figure is a quadrilateral. If it has a special name, write it.

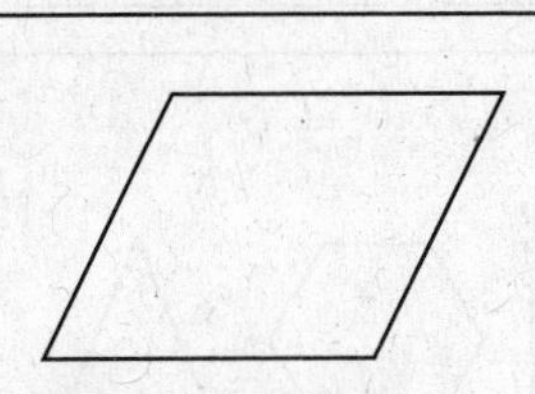

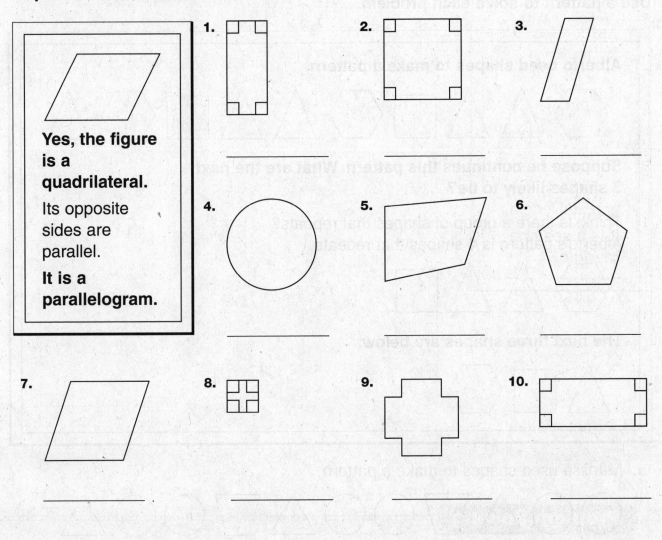

Yes, the figure is a quadrilateral.

Its opposite sides are parallel.

It is a parallelogram.

1. 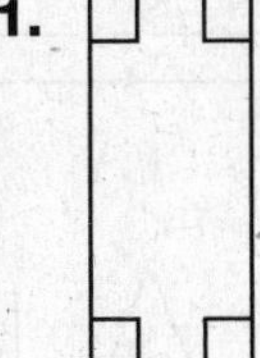

____

2. 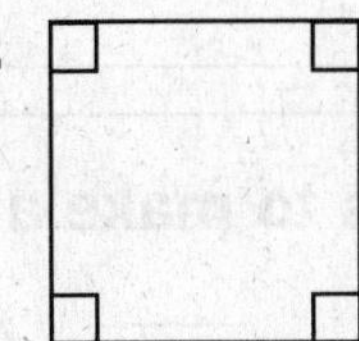

____

3. 

____

4. 

____

5. 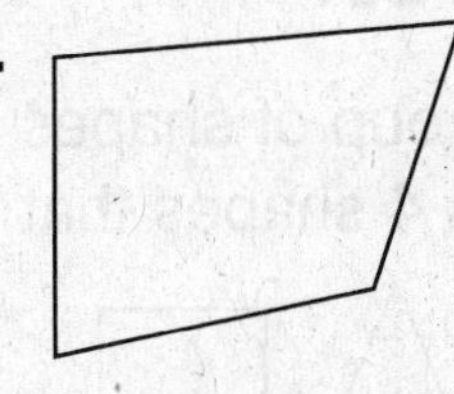

____

6. 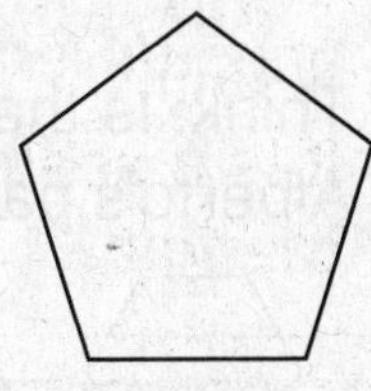

____

7. 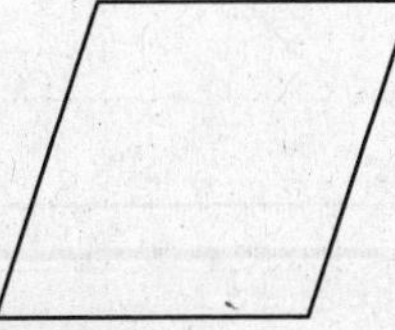

____

8. 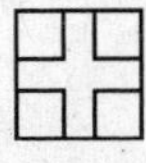

____

9. 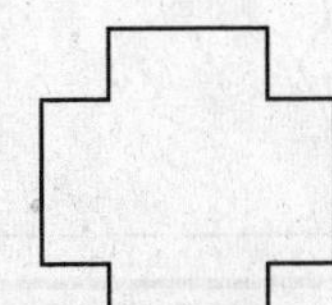

____

10. 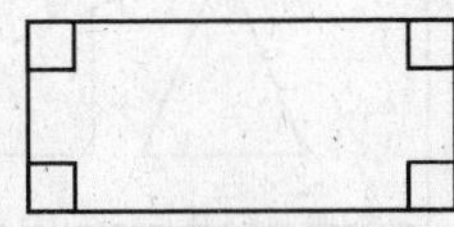

____

Problem Solving

11. Emilio drew a square and a rectangle that is not a square. How is the rectangle different from the square that Emilio drew?

____

____

____

Use with text pages 424–426.

Name ______________________ Date ______________

Homework 15.5

Problem-Solving Strategy: Find a Pattern

Use a pattern to solve each problem.

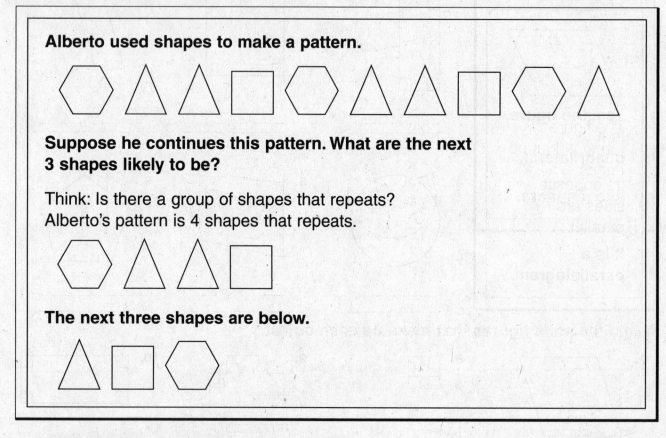

Alberto used shapes to make a pattern.

Suppose he continues this pattern. What are the next 3 shapes likely to be?

Think: Is there a group of shapes that repeats?
Alberto's pattern is 4 shapes that repeats.

The next three shapes are below.

1. Marissa used shapes to make a pattern.

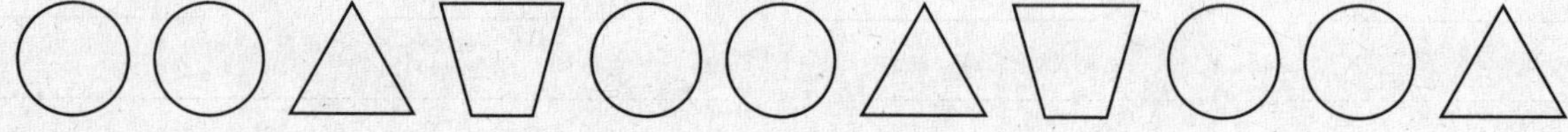

Suppose she continues her pattern. What are the next 3 shapes likely to be? Draw them.

2. Chet made a banner using strips of cloth. He used 12 strips in all. He used this pattern: blue, white, green, blue, white, green, blue, white, green. How many blue strips were in Chet's banner?

____

Use with text pages 428–430.

Name ______________________ Date ____________

Homework 15.6

Solid Figures

Name the solid figure that each object looks like.

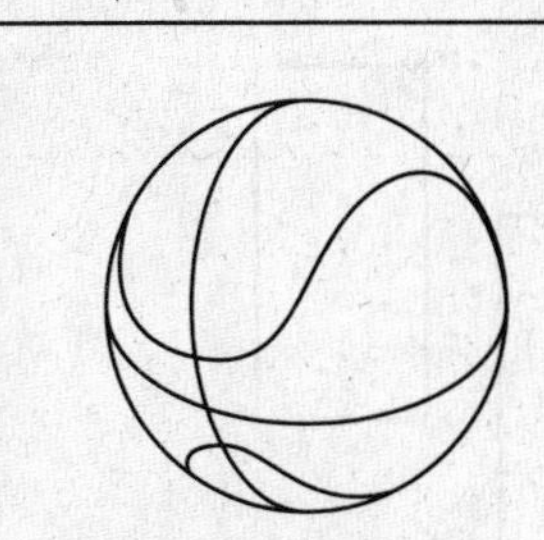

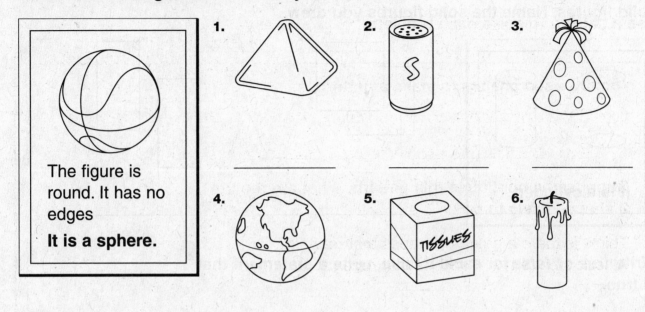

The figure is round. It has no edges

It is a sphere.

1.  ____________

2. 

____

3.  ____________

4.  ____________

5. 

____

6.  ____________

Name the solid figures that make up each object.

7.  ____________

8. 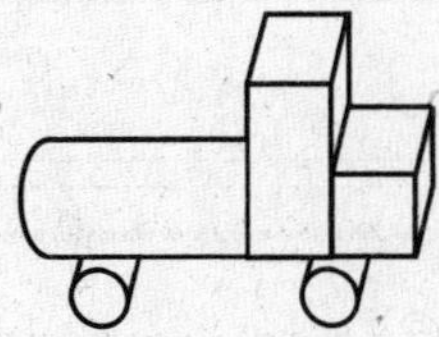 ____________

Problem Solving

9. Name 3 objects in your home that are rectangular prisms. Name 3 objects in your home that are spheres.

____

Use with text pages 432–433.

Name ______________________ Date ____________

Homework 15.7

Explore Solid Figures

Connect the plane figures with line segments to make solid figures. Name the solid figures you drew.

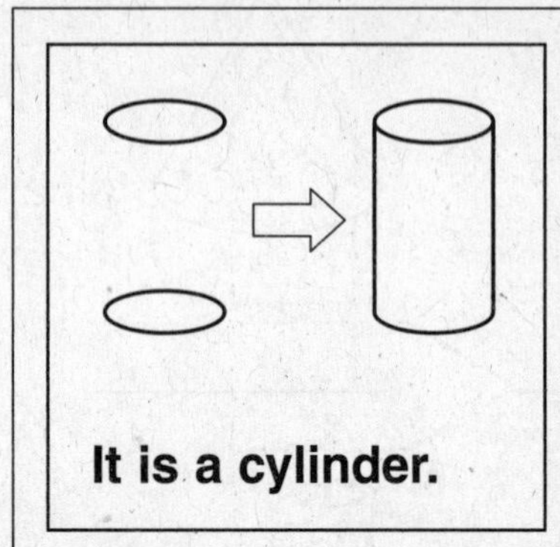

1.

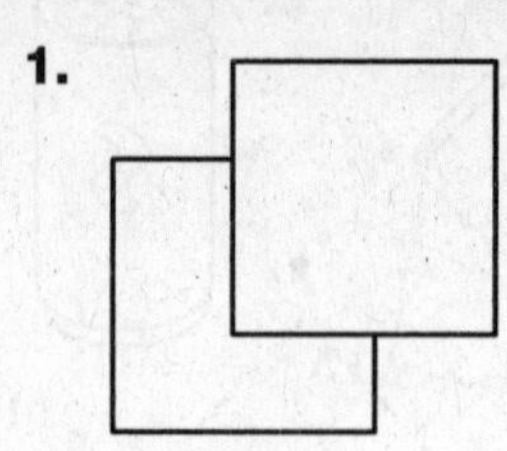

____

2.

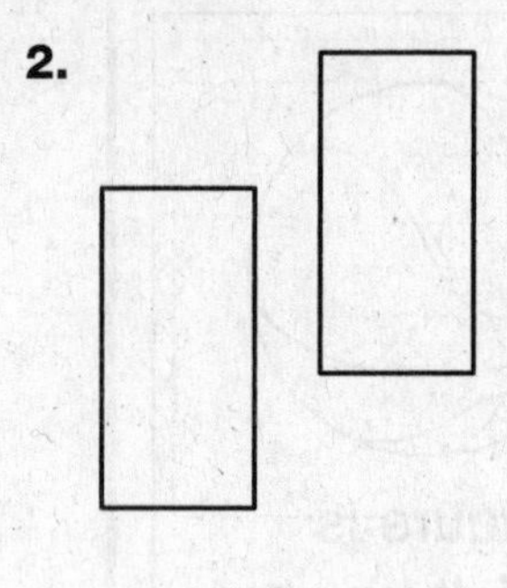

____

Write *true* or *false* for each. If false, write a statement that is true.

3. A cube has 6 faces.

____

____

____

4. A baseball looks like a cone.

____

____

____

Problem Solving

5. Shelly is holding an object. It has 12 edges and its faces are rectangles and squares. What is it?

____

Use with text pages 434–436.

Name ______________________________ Date ____________

Homework 16.1

Congruent Figures

Trace one of the two figures. Place the traced figure on top of the other figure. Are the figures in each pair congruent?

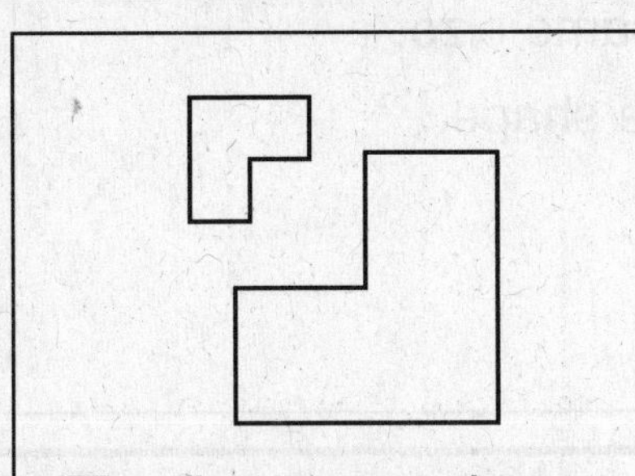

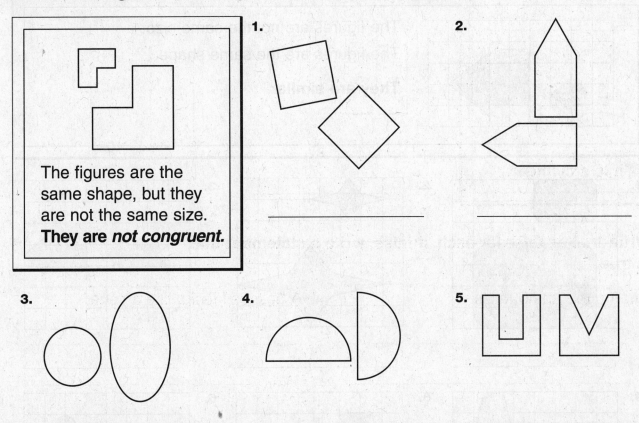

The figures are the same shape, but they are not the same size. **They are *not congruent.***

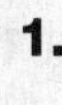

1.

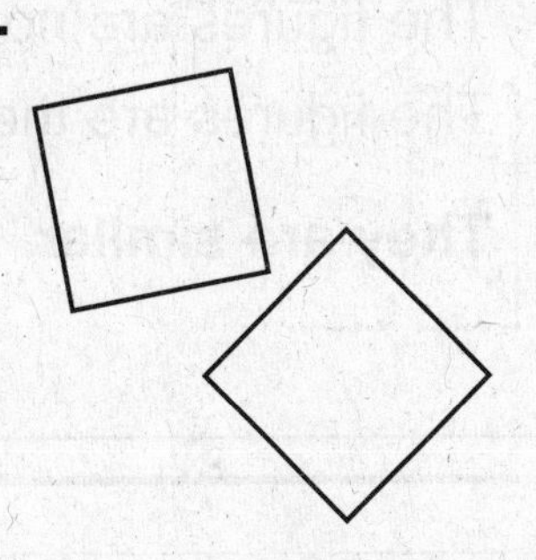

____

2.

____

3.

____

4.

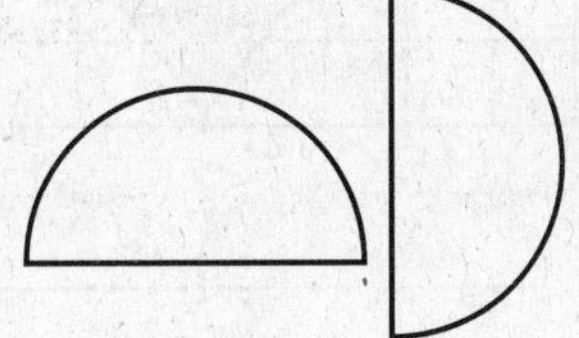

____

5.

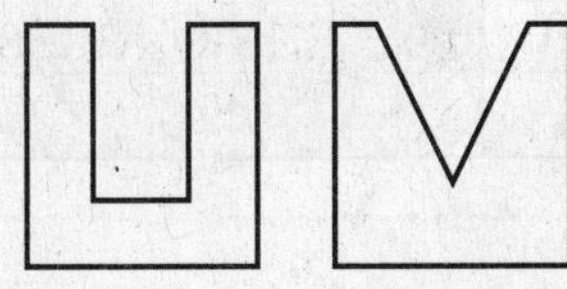

____

Trace the first figure. Place the traced figure on top of the other figures. Then choose the figure that is congruent to it.

6.

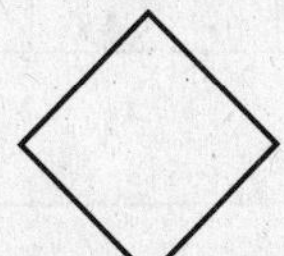

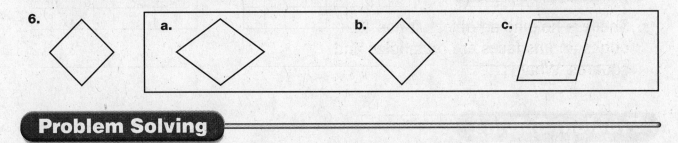

a.

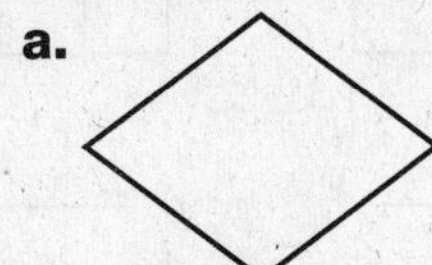

b.

c.

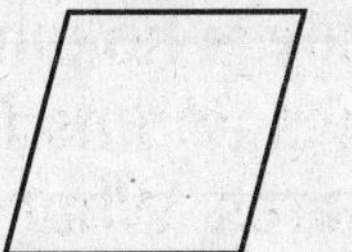

Problem Solving

7. Jessica drew some squares in different sizes. She says they are all the same shape. She says they are not all congruent. Do you agree? Explain.

____

____

Use with text pages 442–443.

Name ______________________ Date ____________

Homework 16.2

Similar Figures

Tell whether the two figures in each exercise are similar.

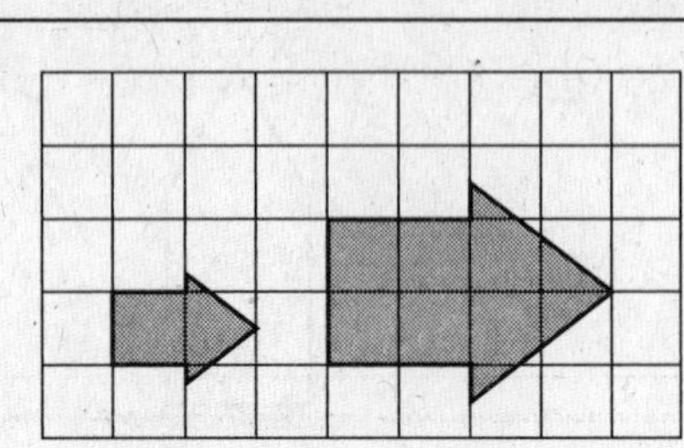

The figures are not the same size.
The figures are the same shape.

They are similar.

1.

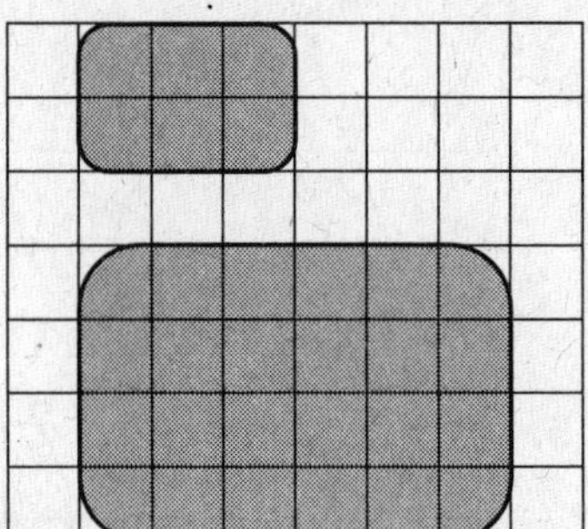

____

2.

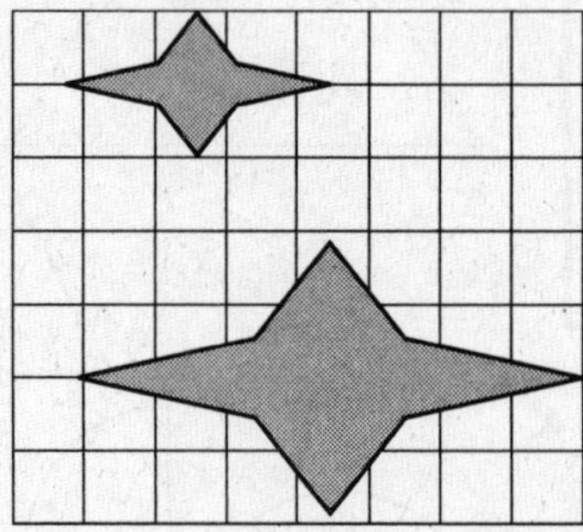

____

3.

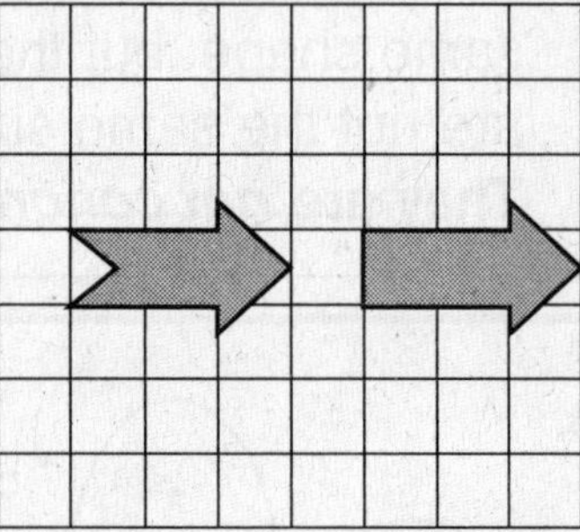

____

4.

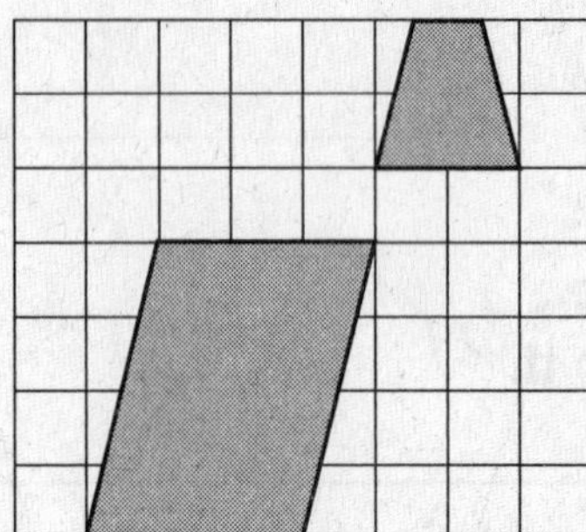

____

5.

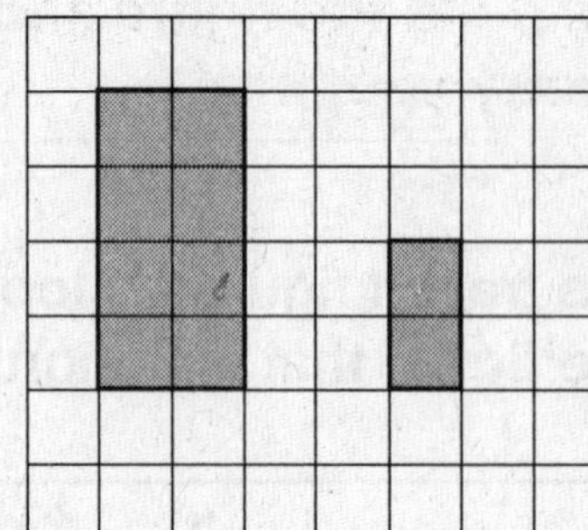

____

6.

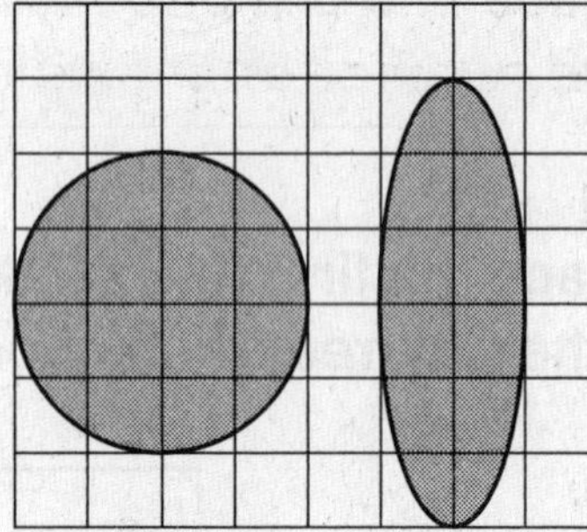

____

Problem Solving

7. Connor drew a circle. Then he drew another circle. Conner says that the circles are similar. Is he correct? Explain how you know.

____

____

Use with text pages 444–446.

Name ____________________ Date ____________

Homework 16.3

Line of Symmetry

Tell whether each line appears to be a line of symmetry.

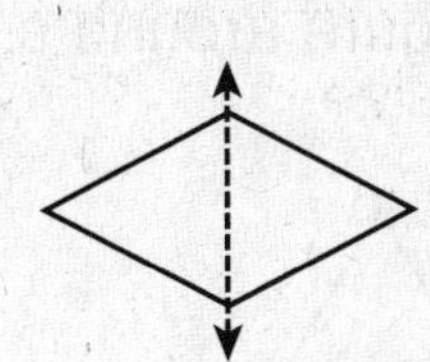

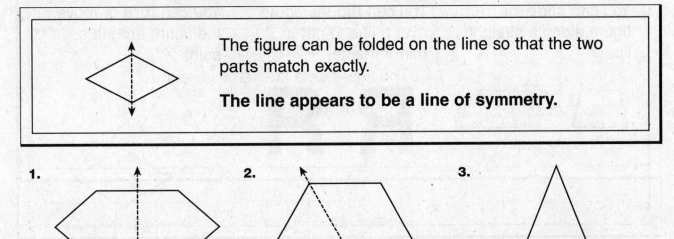

The figure can be folded on the line so that the two parts match exactly.

The line appears to be a line of symmetry.

1.

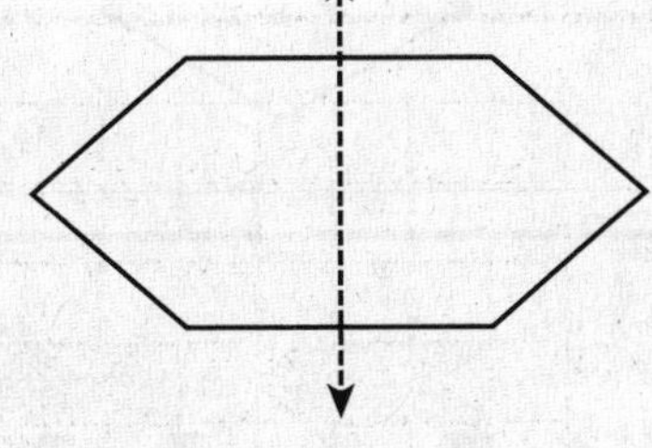

____

2.

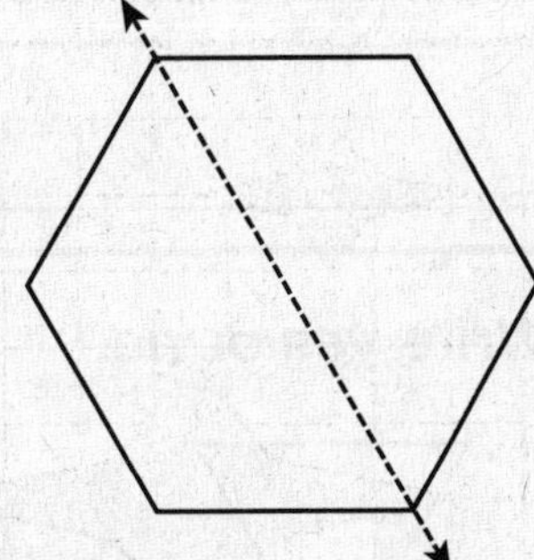

____

3.

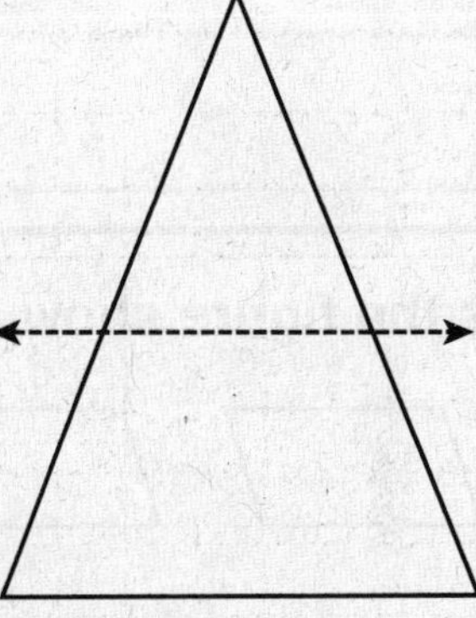

____

Trace and cut out each figure. Fold the figure and record the number of lines of symmetry you find.

4.

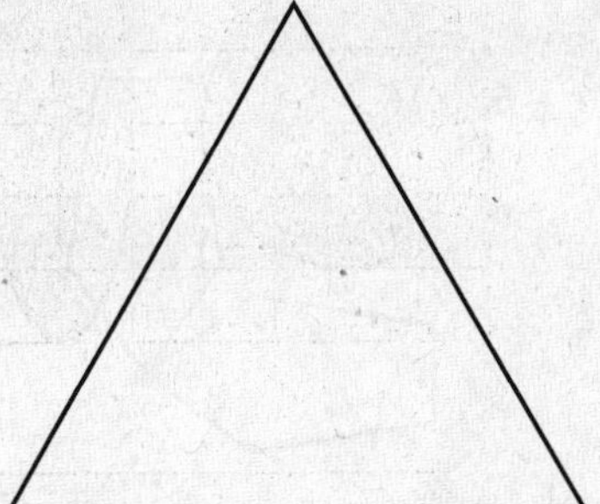

____

5.

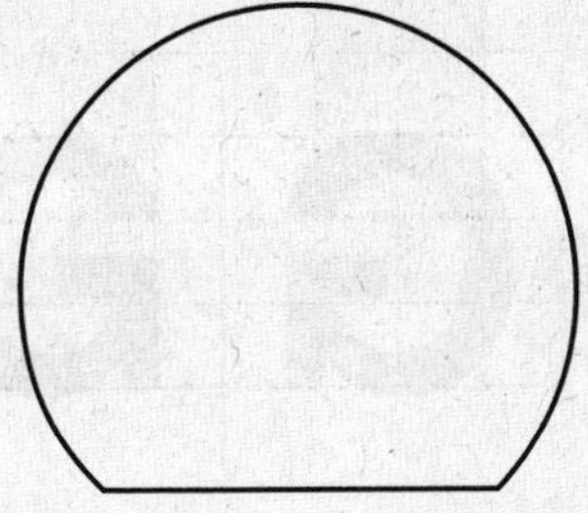

____

6.

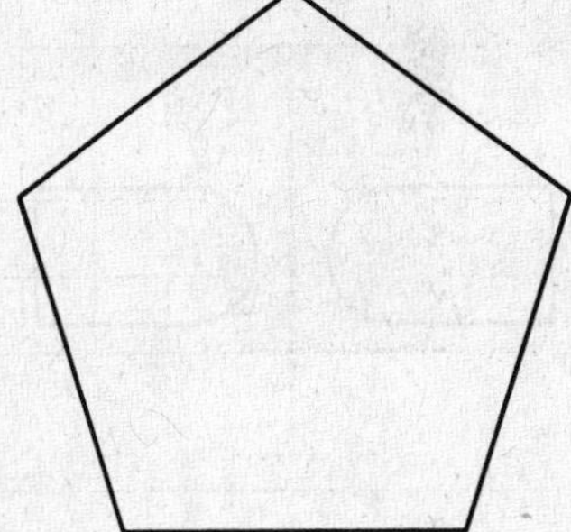

____

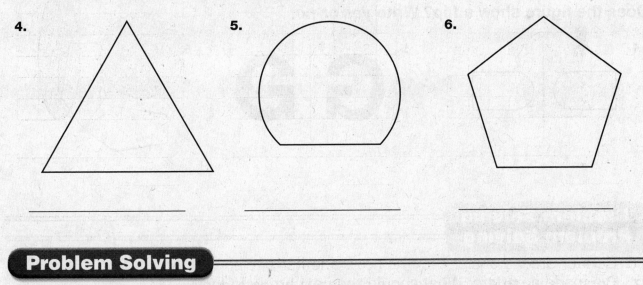

Problem Solving

7. Ming drew a rectangle. He drew 2 lines of symmetry. Draw a rectangle with 2 lines of symmetry.

Use with text pages 448–449.

Name ______________________ Date ____________

Homework 16.4

Transformations

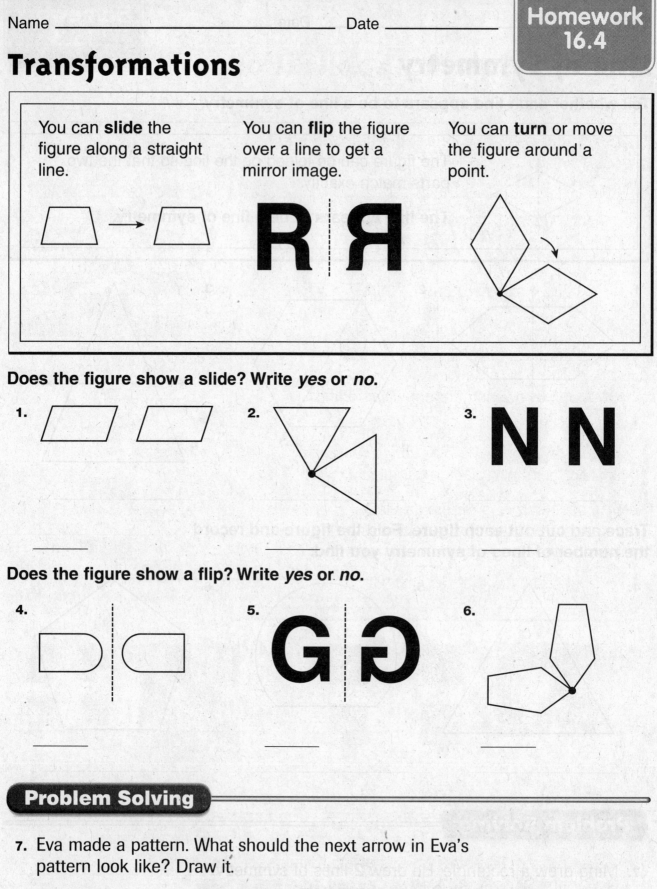

You can **slide** the figure along a straight line.

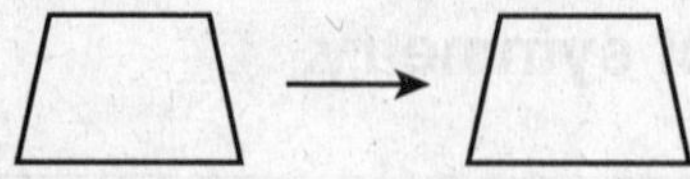

You can **flip** the figure over a line to get a mirror image.

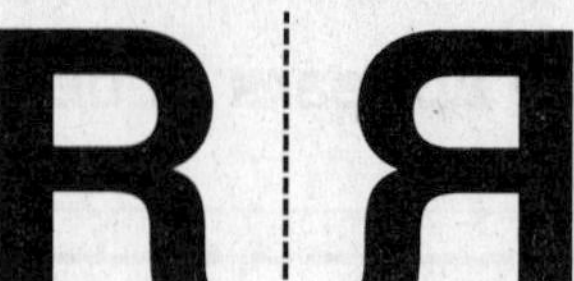

You can **turn** or move the figure around a point.

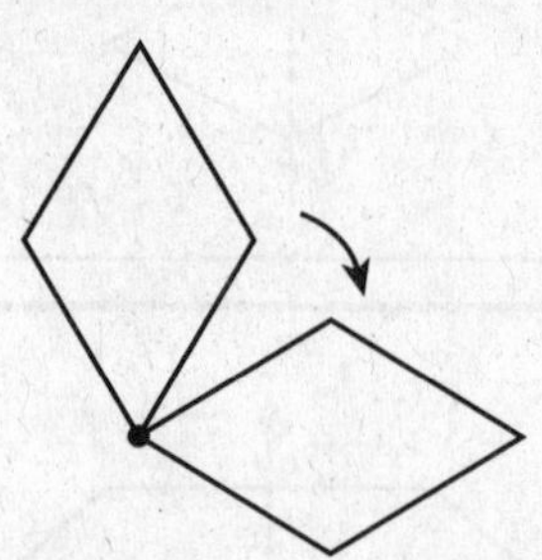

Does the figure show a slide? Write *yes* or *no*.

1. 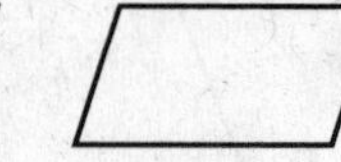

____

2. 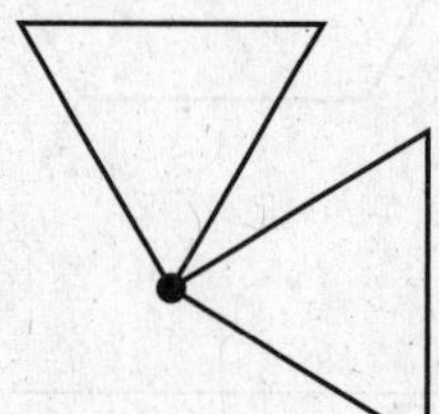

____

3. N N

____

Does the figure show a flip? Write *yes* or *no*.

4. 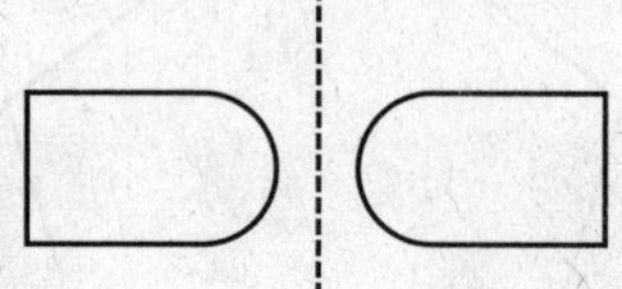

____

5. 

____

6. 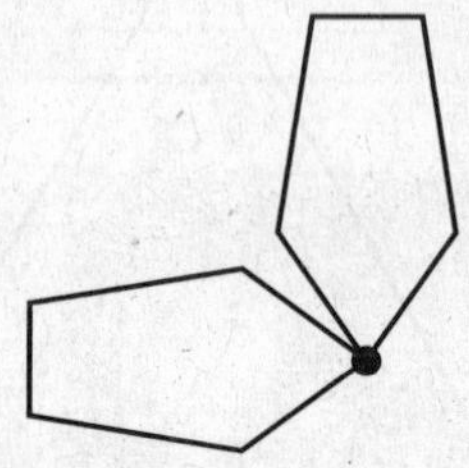

____

Problem Solving

7. Eva made a pattern. What should the next arrow in Eva's pattern look like? Draw it.

Use with text pages 450–453.

Name ______________________ Date ______________

Homework 16.5

Problem-Solving Application: Visual Thinking

Use each tile design. Circle the letter of the missing piece.

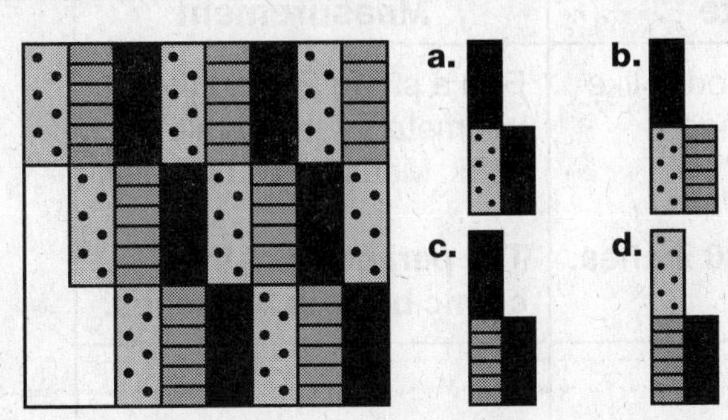

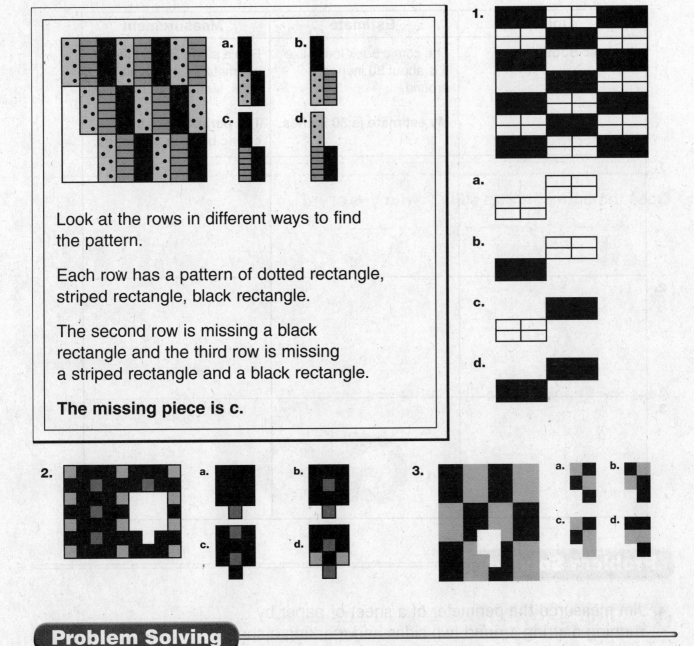

Look at the rows in different ways to find the pattern.

Each row has a pattern of dotted rectangle, striped rectangle, black rectangle.

The second row is missing a black rectangle and the third row is missing a striped rectangle and a black rectangle.

The missing piece is c.

1. 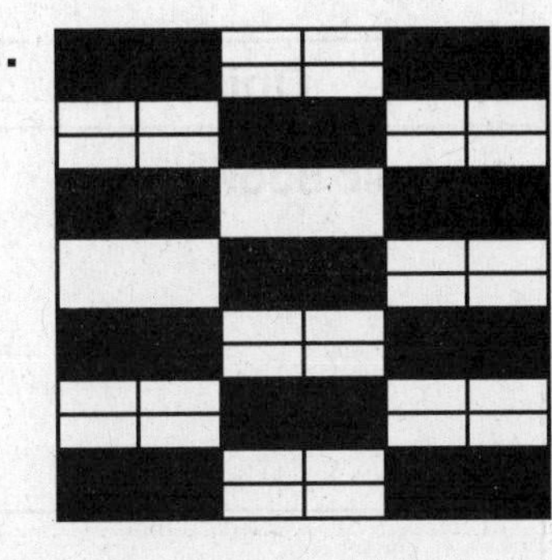

a. 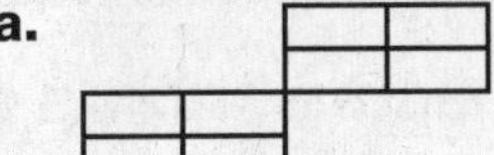

b. 

c. 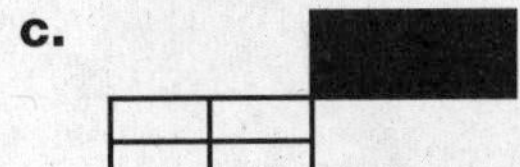

d. 

2. 

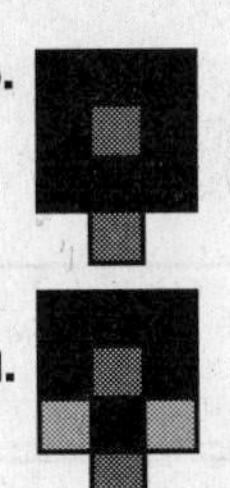

3. 

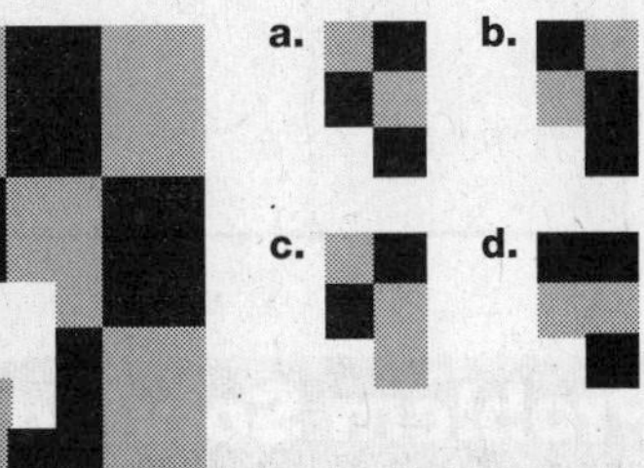

Problem Solving

4. Cindy placed 16 books on 4 shelves. If she placed an equal number of books on each shelf, how many books are on each shelf?

____

Use with text pages 454–456.

Name ______________________ Date ____________

Homework 17.1

Explore Perimeter

Choose three objects in your home. Trace a face of each object. Then estimate the perimeter of the face. Record your estimates. Then measure the perimeter to the nearest inch.

	Object	Estimate	Measurement
	A comic book	The comic book looks like it is about 30 inches around. **My estimate is 30 inches.**	Run a string around the perimeter of the comic book. Measure with a ruler. **The perimeter of the comic book is 32 inches.**
1.			
2.			
3.			

Problem Solving

4. Jim measured the perimeter of a sheet of paper by running a string around two sides and marking a spot at the end. He measured the string. What did he do wrong?

____

____

Use with text pages 462–463.

Name ______________________ Date ____________

Homework 17.2

Find Perimeter

Find the perimeter of each figure.

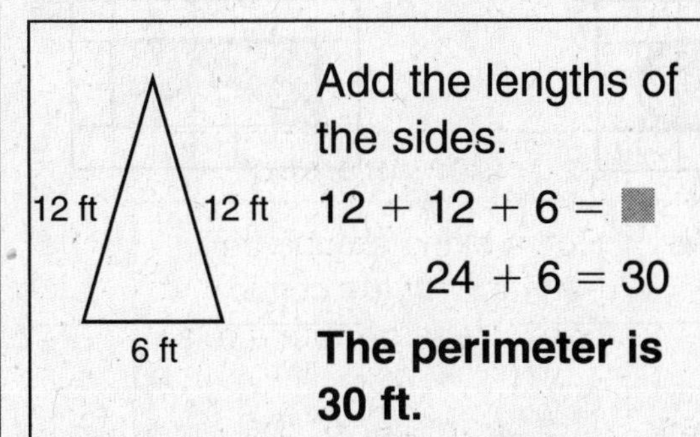

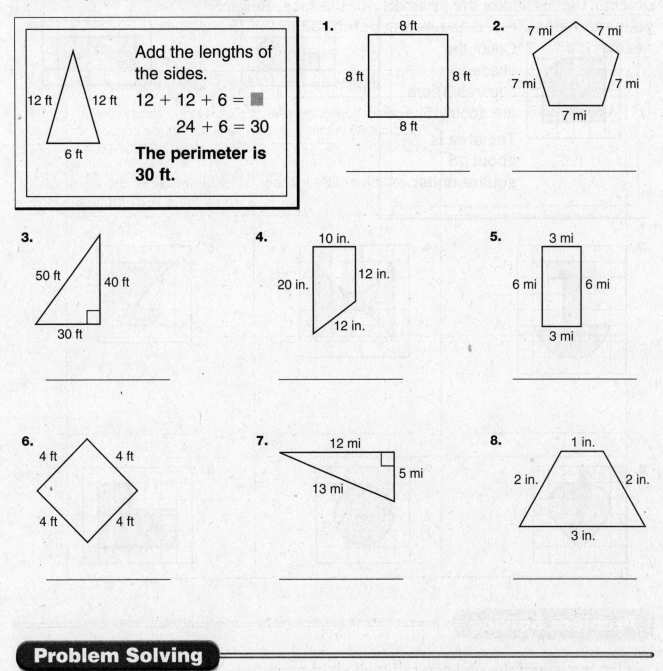

Add the lengths of the sides.

12 + 12 + 6 = ■

24 + 6 = 30

The perimeter is 30 ft.

1. 8 ft, 8 ft, 8 ft, 8 ft

____

2.

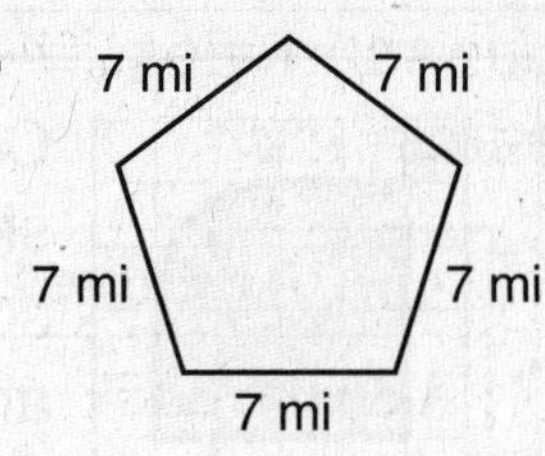

____

3. 50 ft, 40 ft, 30 ft

____

4. 10 in., 12 in., 12 in., 20 in.

____

5. 3 mi, 6 mi, 6 mi, 3 mi

____

6. 4 ft, 4 ft, 4 ft, 4 ft

____

7. 12 mi, 5 mi, 13 mi

____

8. 1 in., 2 in., 2 in., 3 in.

____

Problem Solving

Show your work.

9. The length of one side of a square is 2 feet. What is the perimeter of the square?

____

Use with text pages 464–466.

Name ______________________ Date ____________

Homework 17.3

Explore Area

Estimate the area of each figure. Each □ = 1 square unit.

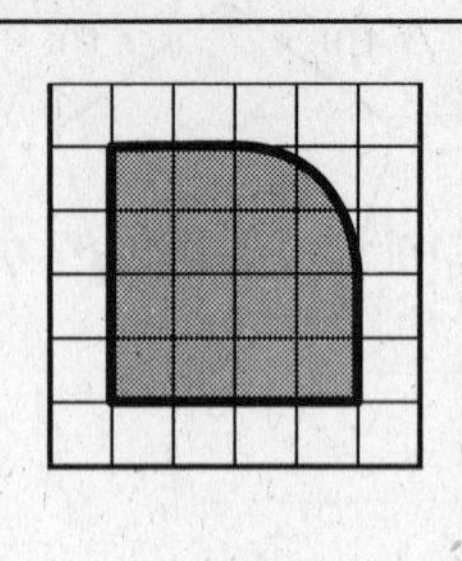

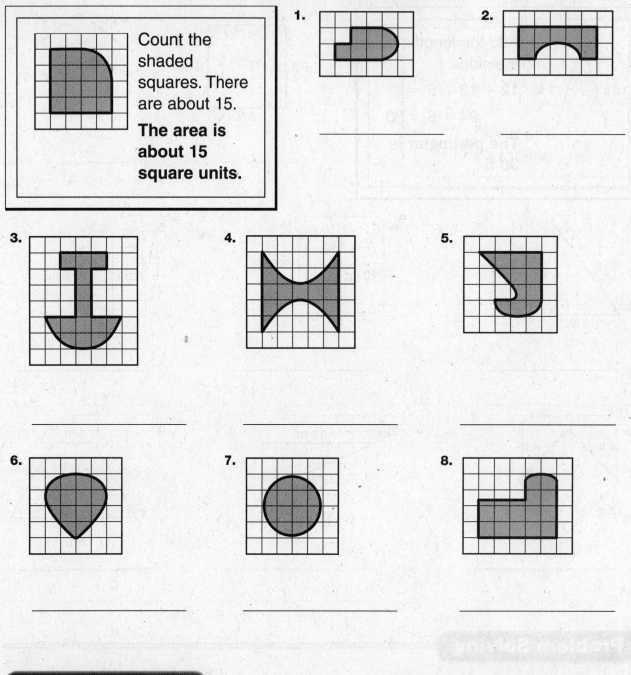

Count the shaded squares. There are about 15.

The area is about 15 square units.

1.  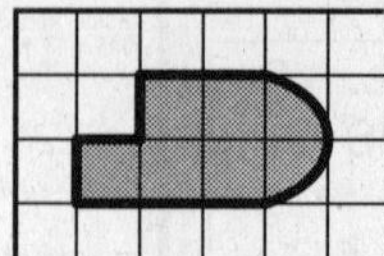

____

2. 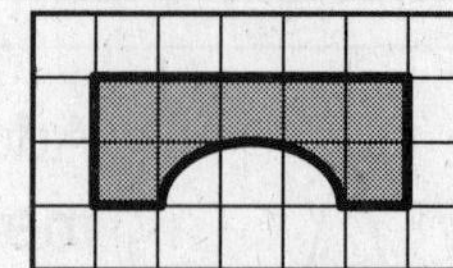

____

3. 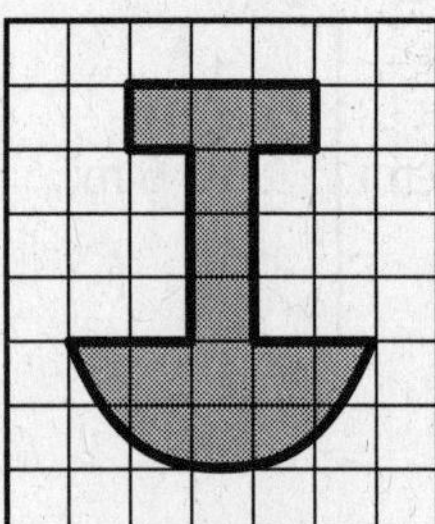

____

4. 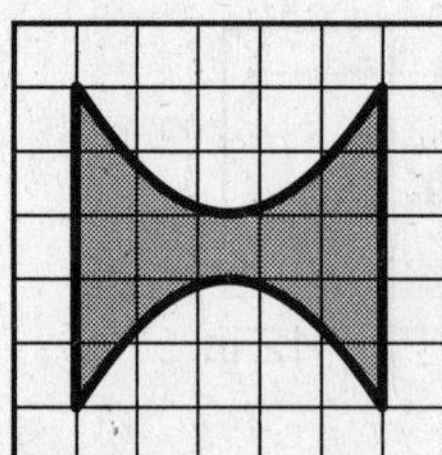

____

5. 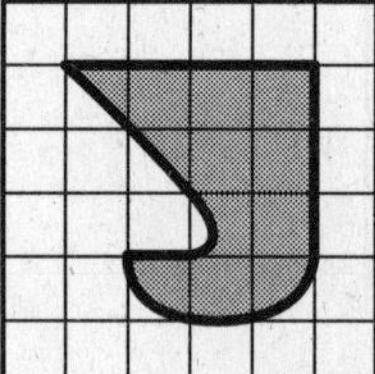

____

6. 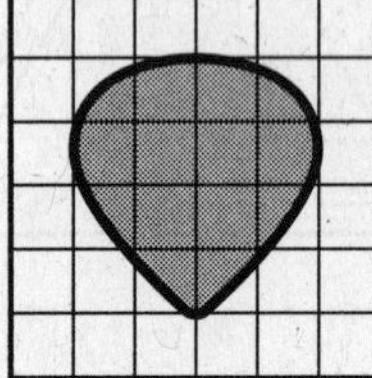

____

7. 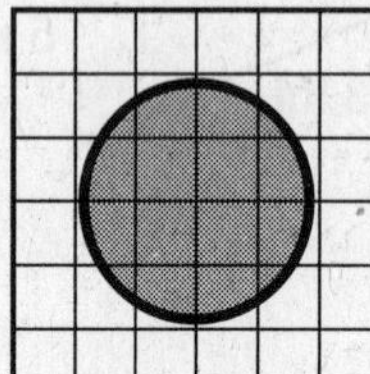

____

8. 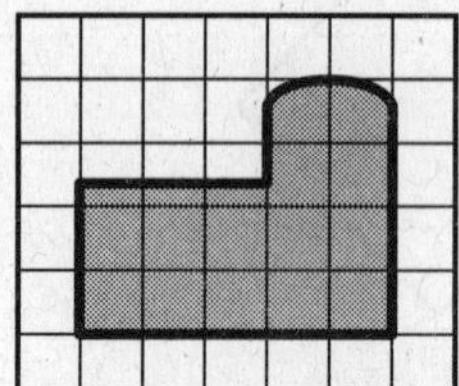

____

Problem Solving

9. The figure that Barry drew has an area of about 4 square units. Draw 2 figures that could be Barry's figure.

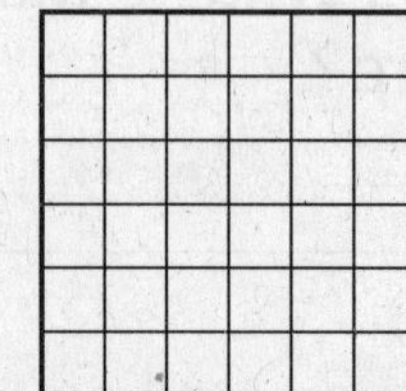

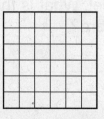

Use with text pages 468–469.

Name ______________________ Date ____________

Homework 17.4

Find Area

Find the area of each figure. Label your answer in square units. Each □ or ⁚⁚ = 1 square unit.

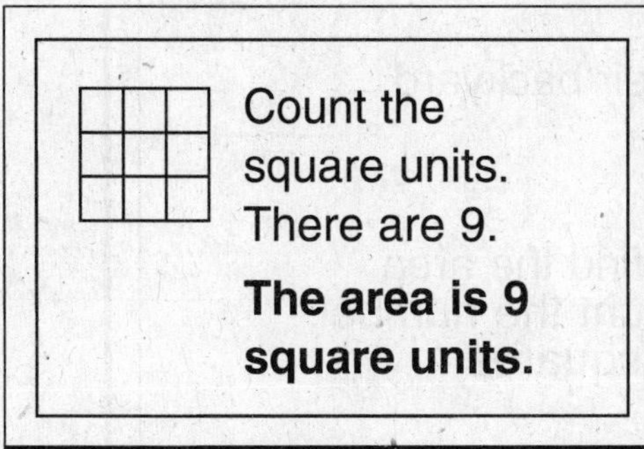

Count the square units.
There are 9.
The area is 9 square units.

1.

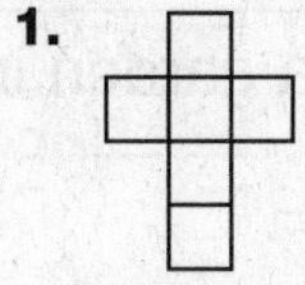

____

2.

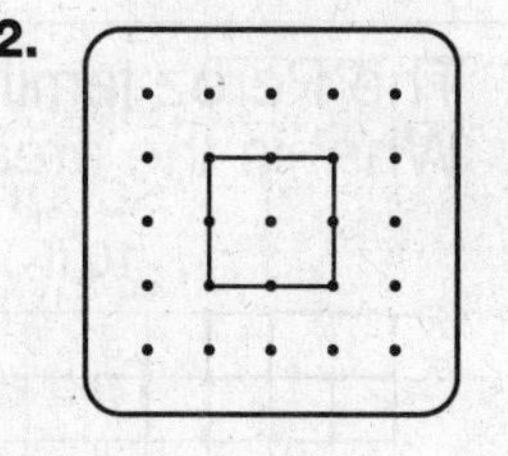

____

3.

____

4.

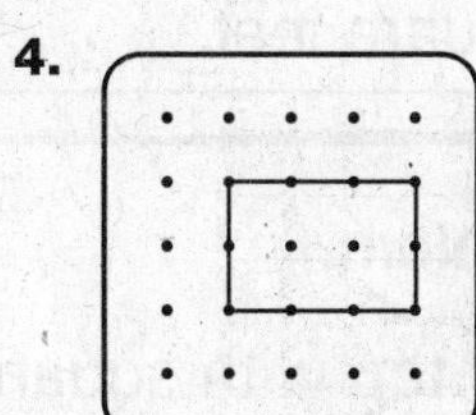

____

5.

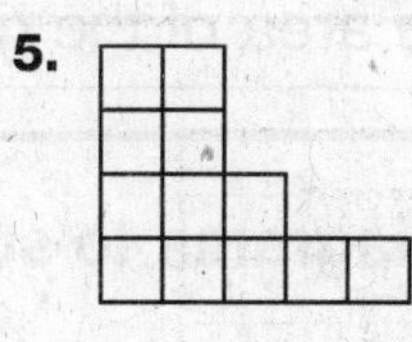

____

6.

____

7.

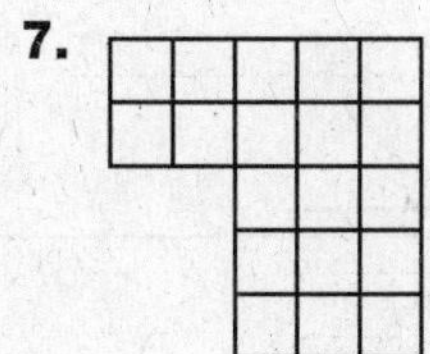

____

8.

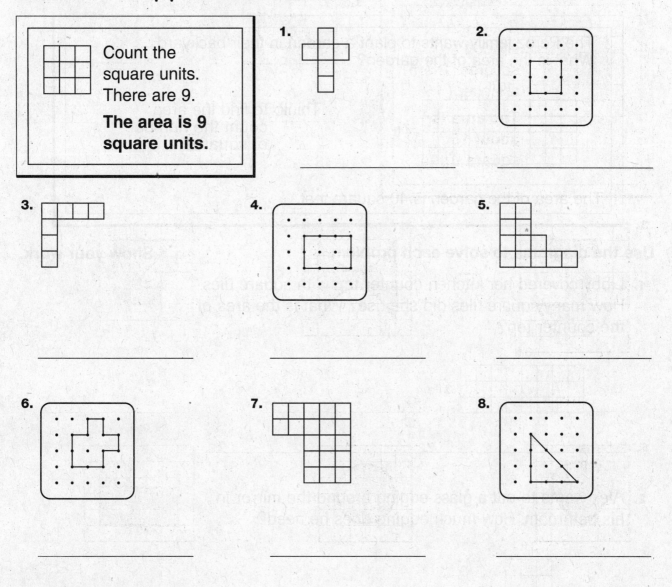

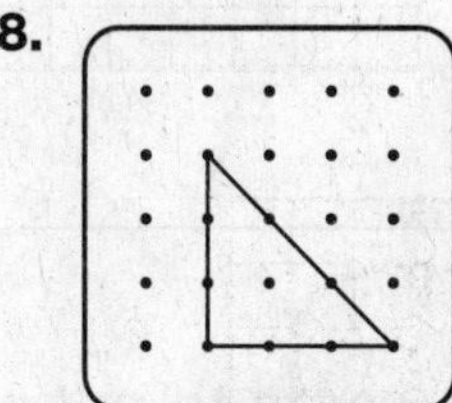

____

Problem Solving

9. Draw a rectangle with an area of 8 square units.

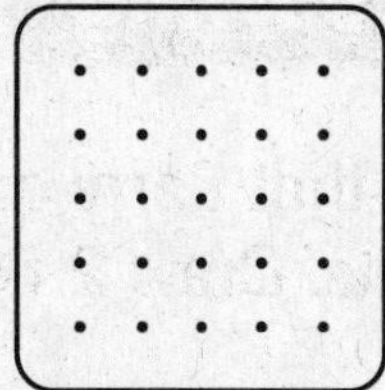

Use with text pages 470–472.

Name ______________________ Date ______________

Homework 17.5

Problem-Solving Application: Use Measurement

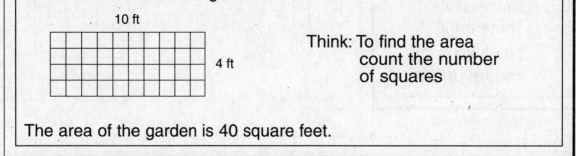

The Perez family wants to plant a garden in their backyard. What is the area of the garden?

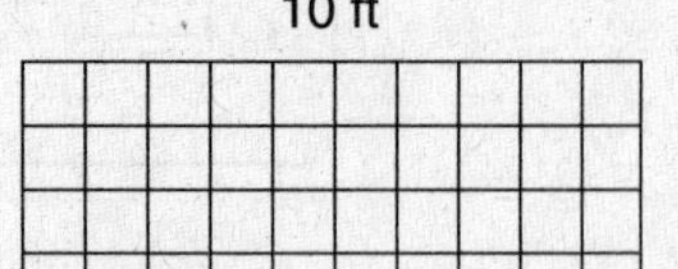

Think: To find the area count the number of squares

The area of the garden is 40 square feet.

Use the diagrams to solve each problem. **Show your work.**

1. Libby covered her kitchen counter top with square tiles. How many square tiles did she use? What is the area of the counter top?

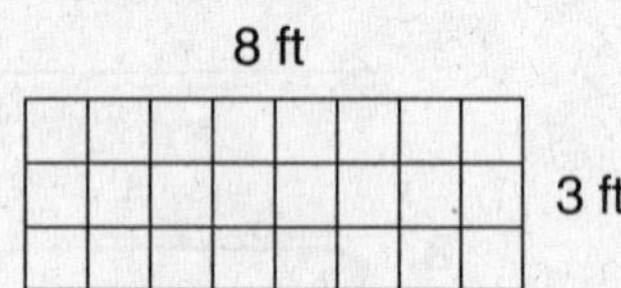

____

2. Alex wants to put a glass edging around the mirror in his bathroom. How much edging does he need?

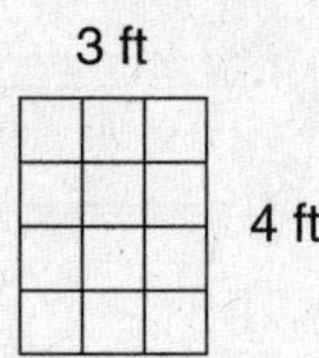

____

Name ______________________ Date ____________

Explore Volume

Estimate the volume of each figure. Then build it with cubes. Write the estimate and the number of cubes you used.

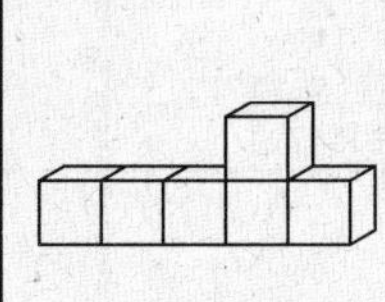

An estimate for the volume is 5 cubic units.

The figure can be made with 6 cubes.

The volume is 6 unit cubes.

1. 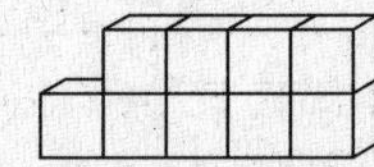

____

____

2. 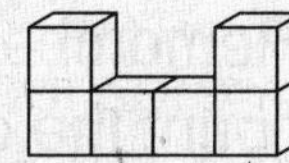

____

____

3. 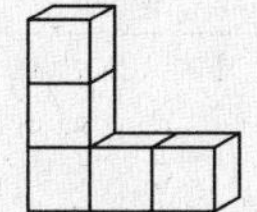

____

____

4. 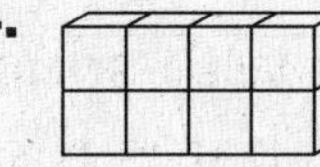

____

____

5. 

____

____

6. 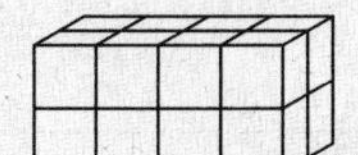

____

____

7. 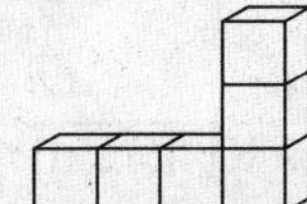

____

____

8. 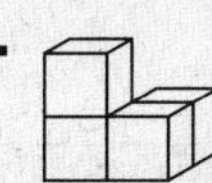

____

____

Problem Solving

9. Josh said the volume of this figure is 12 cubic units. Is he right? Explain.

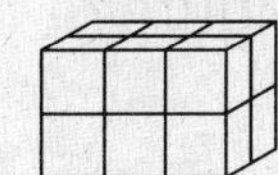

Name ______________________ Date ____________

Homework 17.7

Find Volume

Find the volume of each figure. Each 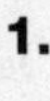 **= 1 cubic unit.**

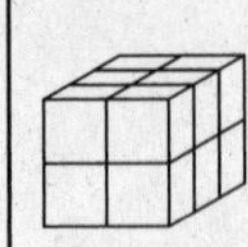

Remember to count the cubes that are hidden.

The volume is 12 cubic units.

1. 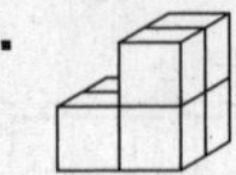

____

2. 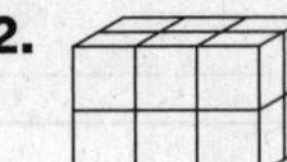

____

3. 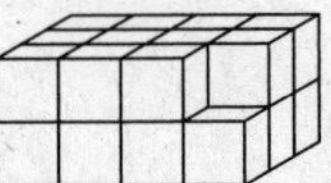

____

4. 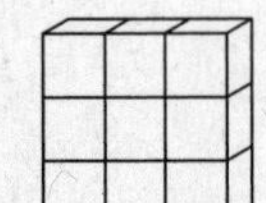

____

5. 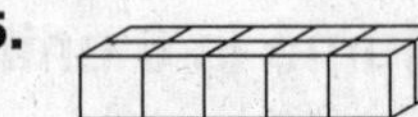

____

6. 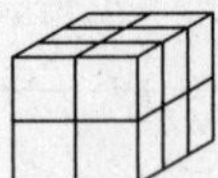

____

7. 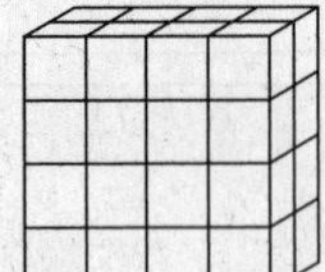

____

8. 

____

Problem Solving

Show your work.

9. A solid figure has 7 cubes in the bottom layer, 5 cubes in the middle layer, and 4 cubes in the top layer. What is the volume of the figure?

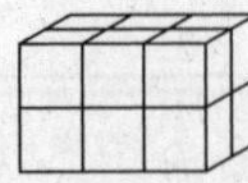

____

Use with text pages 478–480.

Name ______________________ Date ______________

Homework 18.1

Fractions and Regions

Write a fraction for the part that is shaded. Then write a fraction for the part that is not shaded.

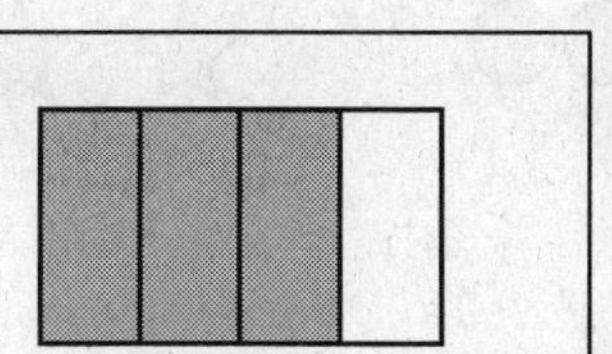

Three fourths or $\frac{3}{4}$ are shaded.

One fourth or $\frac{1}{4}$ is not shaded.

1. 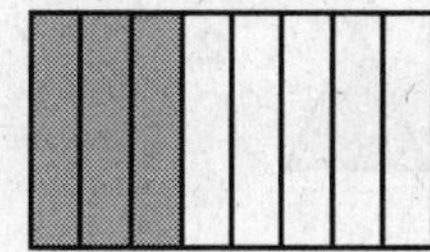

______

______

2. 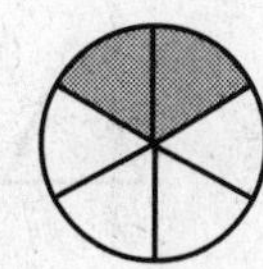

______

______

3. 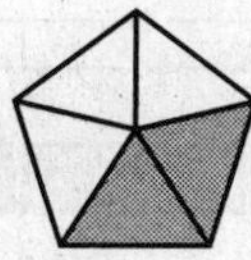

______

______

4. 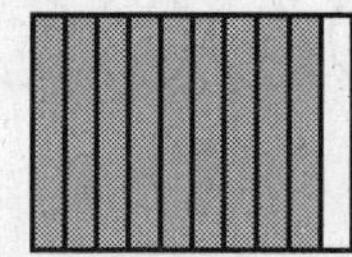

______

______

5. 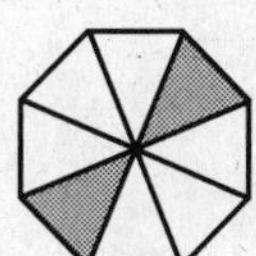

______

______

6. 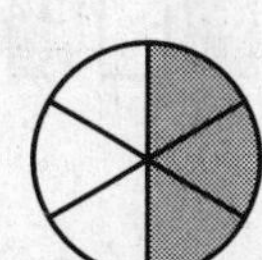

______

______

7. 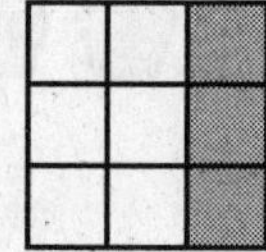

______

______

Draw a picture to show each fraction. Then name the numerator and the denominator.

8. $\frac{4}{5}$ ______

9. $\frac{1}{2}$ ______

10. $\frac{7}{8}$ ______

11. $\frac{6}{6}$ ______

Problem Solving

12. Mick made a pie. He served $\frac{3}{8}$ of the pie to his friends. Draw a picture to show the pie Mick made. Shade the fraction of the pie Mick did not serve to his friends.

____

Name ______________________ Date ______________

Homework 18.2

Fractions and Groups

Write a fraction to name the part of each group that is shaded.

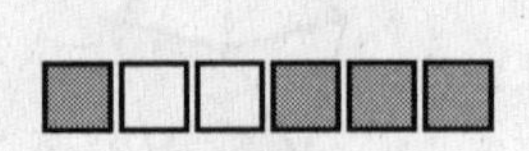

Four out of 6 squares are shaded.

Four sixths or $\frac{4}{6}$ are shaded.

1. 

______

2. 

______

3. 

______

4. 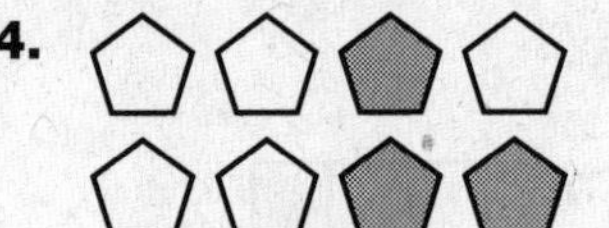

______

5. 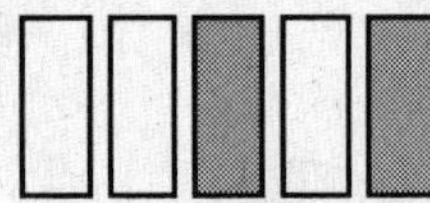

______

6. ♥ ♡ ♡ ♡

______

7. 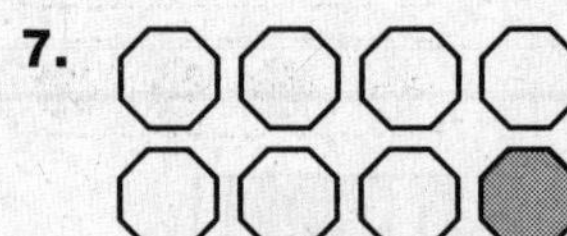

______

Use the picture on the right for Questions 8–9.

8. What fraction of the shapes are triangles?

______

9. Which shape is $\frac{2}{8}$ of the group?

____

Problem Solving

10. Millie has 7 picture frames. She put pictures in 2 of the frames. What fraction of the frames have pictures in them?

____

Name ______________________ Date ______________

Homework 18.3

Fractional Parts of a Group

Use counters to find each answer.

$\frac{3}{4}$ **of 16**

Put 16 counters into 4 groups. Count the number of counters in 3 of the groups.

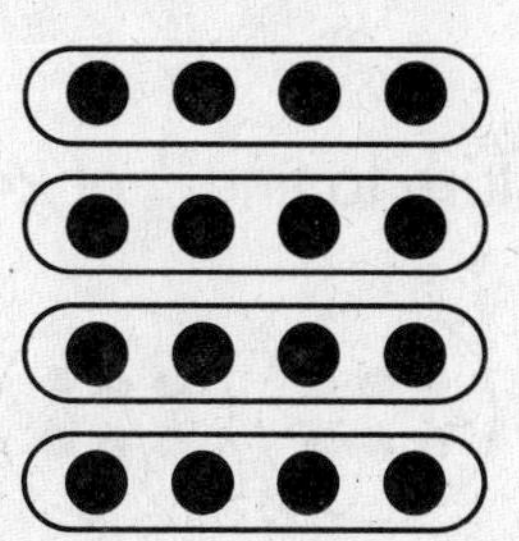

$\frac{3}{4}$ **of 16 = 12**

1. $\frac{1}{3}$ of 6 ______

2. $\frac{1}{4}$ of 12 ______

3. $\frac{2}{3}$ of 12 ______

4. $\frac{2}{4}$ of 16 ______

5. $\frac{1}{5}$ of 20 ______

6. $\frac{1}{6}$ of 12 ______

7. $\frac{2}{3}$ of 9 ______

8. $\frac{3}{8}$ of 8 ______

9. $\frac{2}{5}$ of 10 ______

10. $\frac{1}{3}$ of 18 ______

11. $\frac{3}{10}$ of 20 ______

12. $\frac{1}{6}$ of 24 ______

Problem Solving

13. Nilda has 15 stamps. One fifth of the stamps are stamps of outer space. How many stamps of outer space does Nilda have?

Show your work.

____

Use with text pages 502–504.

Name ______________________ Date ______________

Homework 18.4

Problem-Solving Application: Multistep Problems

Problem Angie bought a package of colored paper to make origami figures. The package had 8 sheets each of red, blue, and green paper. Angie used $\frac{1}{4}$ of the paper she bought to make her origami figures. How many sheets of paper did Angie use?

The problem can be solved using two steps.

Step 1: Find the total number of sheets.

$$\begin{array}{r l} 8 & \leftarrow \text{number of each color} \\ \times 3 & \leftarrow \text{number of colors} \\ \hline 24 & \leftarrow \text{total number of sheets} \end{array}$$

There are 24 sheets in all.

Step 2: Draw a picture to find $\frac{1}{4}$ of 24.

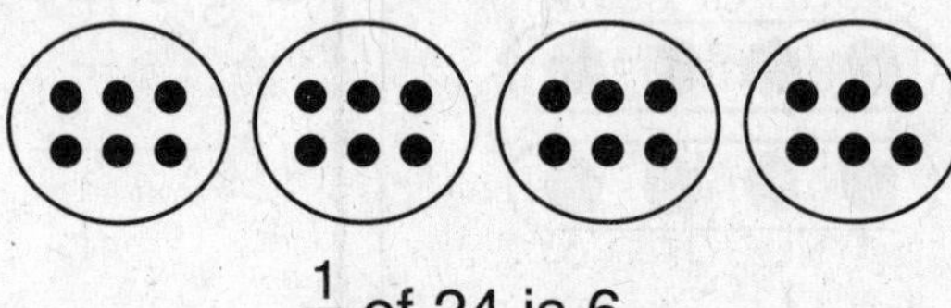

$\frac{1}{4}$ of 24 is 6.

Solution: Angie used 6 sheets of paper.

Solve. **Show your work.**

1. At the craft fair, Angie arranged the origami figures she made in 5 rows with 6 figures in each row. She sold $\frac{2}{3}$ of the figures at the fair. How many origami figures did Angie sell at the craft fair?

   ____

2. Thomas bought a package of pencils. There were 5 pencils each of red, yellow, blue, and green. He took $\frac{1}{5}$ of the pencils to school. How many pencils did he take to school?

   ____

Use with text pages 506–507.

Name ______________________ Date ____________

Homework 18.5

Model Equivalent Fractions

Write *equivalent* or *not equivalent* to describe the fractions in each pair.

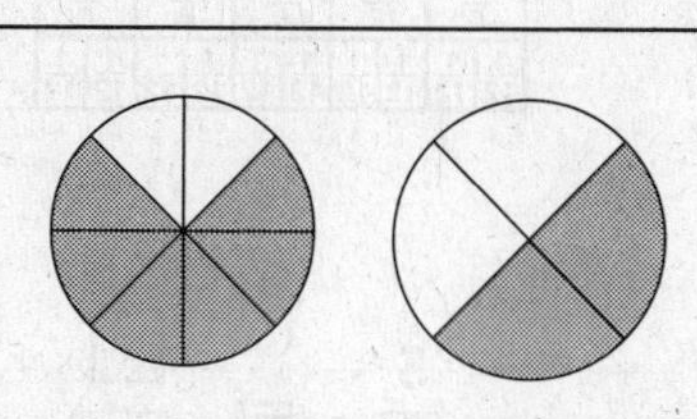

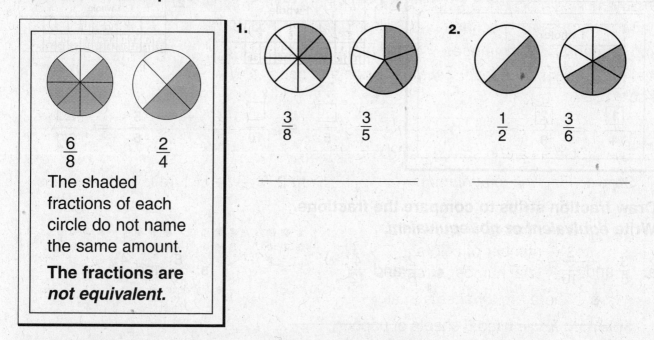

$\frac{6}{8}$ $\frac{2}{4}$

The shaded fractions of each circle do not name the same amount.

The fractions are *not equivalent.*

1.

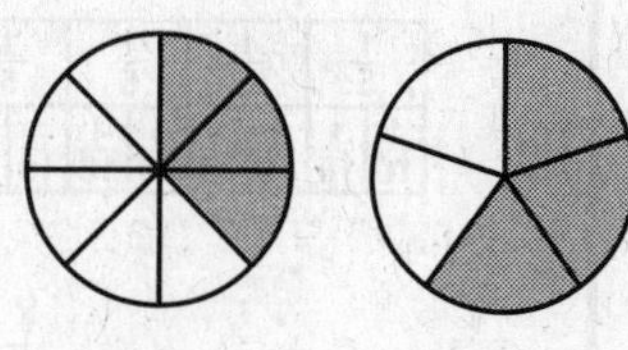

$\frac{3}{8}$ $\frac{3}{5}$

____

2.

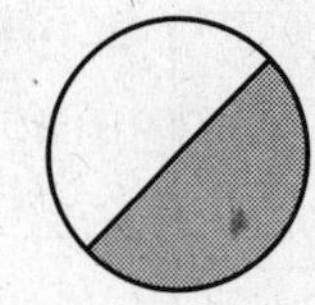

$\frac{1}{2}$ $\frac{3}{6}$

____

Use the circles to complete the equivalent fractions.

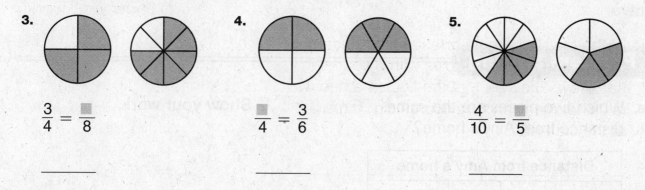

3.

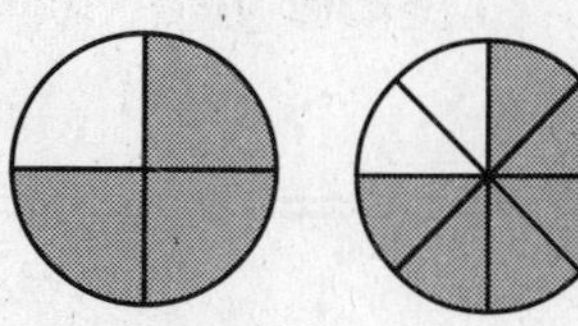

$\frac{3}{4} = \frac{■}{8}$

______

4.

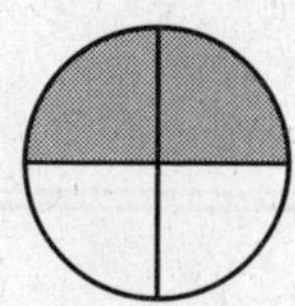

$\frac{■}{4} = \frac{3}{6}$

______

5.

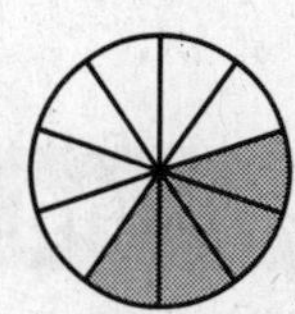

$\frac{4}{10} = \frac{■}{5}$

______

Problem Solving

6. Tyler and Jimmy both order the same size pizza. Tyler cuts his pizza into three equal pieces and eats two of the pieces. Jimmy cuts his pizza into six equal pieces and eats four of the pieces. Have Tyler and Jimmy eaten the same amount of pizza? Explain.

Show your work.

____

Name ______________________ Date ____________

Homework 18.6

Find Equivalent Fractions

Name the equivalent fractions shown.

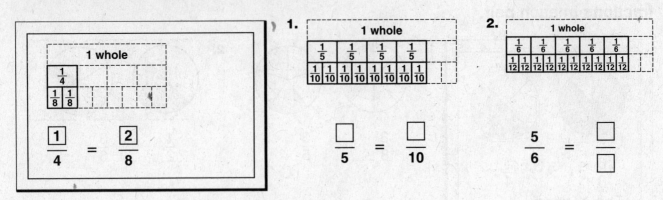

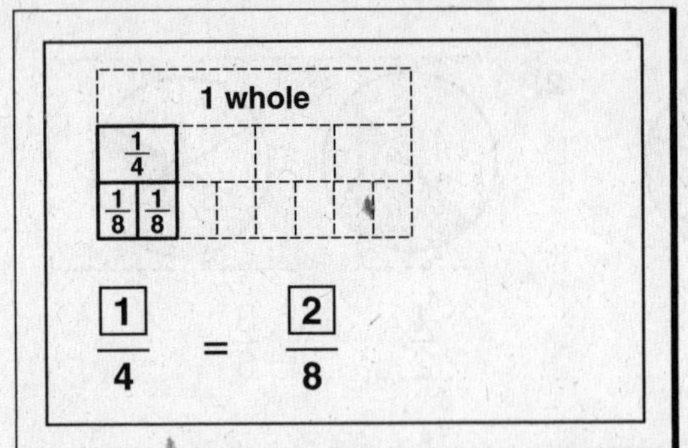

1. 1 whole

$\frac{\square}{5} = \frac{\square}{10}$

2. 1 whole

$\frac{5}{6} = \frac{\square}{\square}$

Draw fraction strips to compare the fractions. Write *equivalent* or *not equivalent*.

3. $\frac{3}{5}$ and $\frac{5}{10}$ ____________

4. $\frac{2}{6}$ and $\frac{4}{12}$ ____________

5. $\frac{8}{10}$ and $\frac{4}{5}$ ____________

Problem Solving

6. Which two places are the same distance from Amy's home?

Show your work.

Distance from Amy's home	
Place	**Distance**
Library	$\frac{2}{5}$ of a mile
Post Office	$\frac{3}{4}$ of a mile
School	$\frac{4}{10}$ of a mile
Store	$\frac{1}{2}$ of a mile

____

Use with text pages 510–511.

Name ______________________ Date ____________

Homework 18.7

Mixed Numbers

Write an improper fraction and a mixed number for the shaded part.

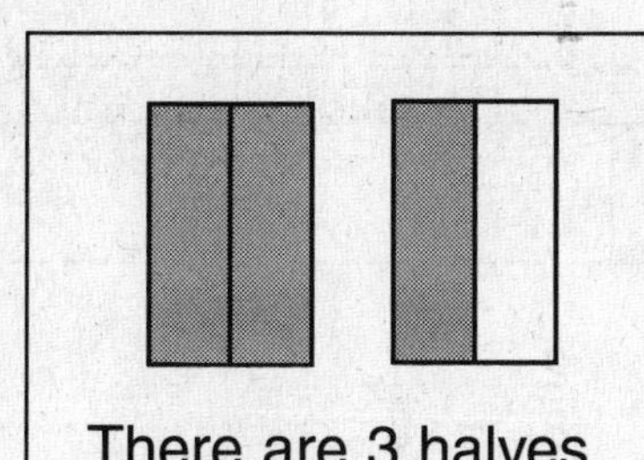

There are 3 halves shaded.

$\frac{3}{2} = 1\frac{1}{2}$

1. 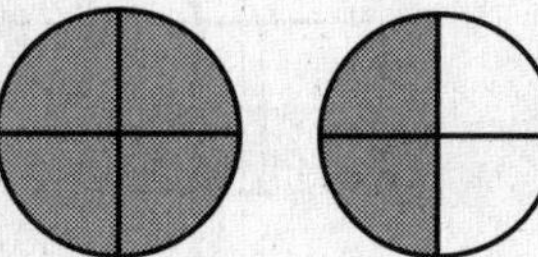

______

2. 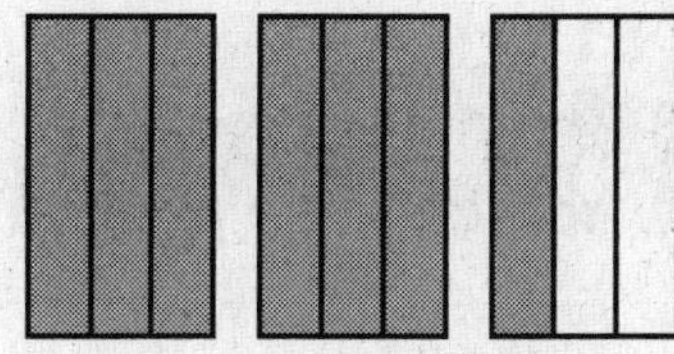

______

Draw a picture to show each improper fraction. Then write a whole number or a mixed number.

3. $\frac{7}{2}$

______

4. $\frac{8}{4}$

______

5. $\frac{5}{3}$

______

Problem Solving

6. Mr. Lam gave each student half a sandwich as a snack. He gave snacks to 9 students. Write a mixed number to represent the number of sandwiches Mr. Lam gave to the students.

____

Use with text pages 512–514.

Name ______________________ Date ____________

Homework 19.1

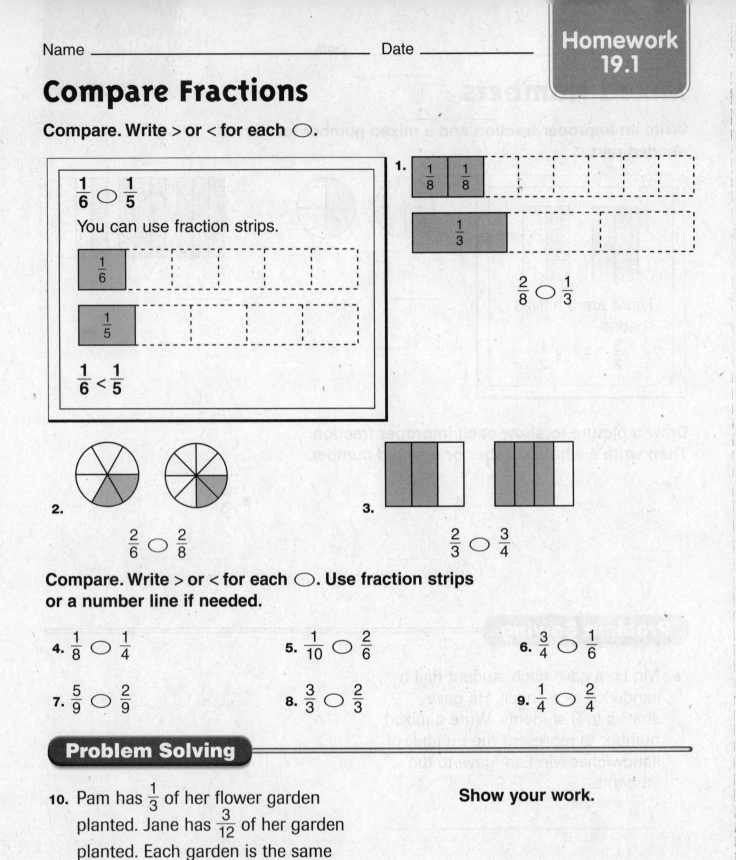

Compare Fractions

Compare. Write > or < for each ◯.

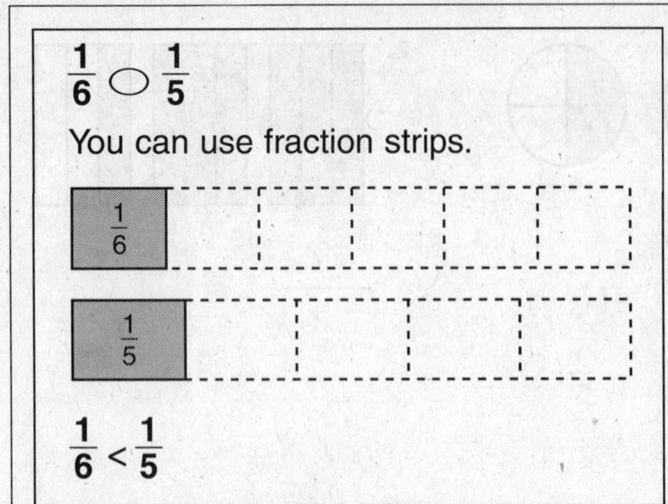
$\frac{1}{6}$ ◯ $\frac{1}{5}$

You can use fraction strips.

$\frac{1}{6} < \frac{1}{5}$

1. $\frac{2}{8}$ ◯ $\frac{1}{3}$

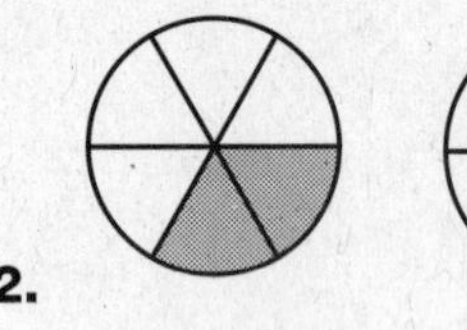
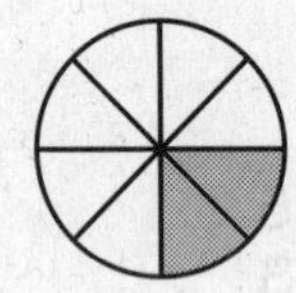

2. $\frac{2}{6}$ ◯ $\frac{2}{8}$

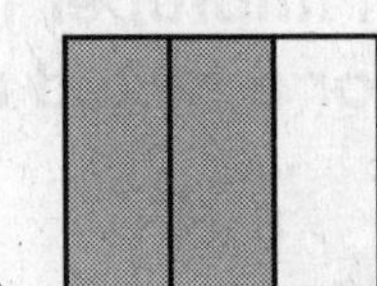
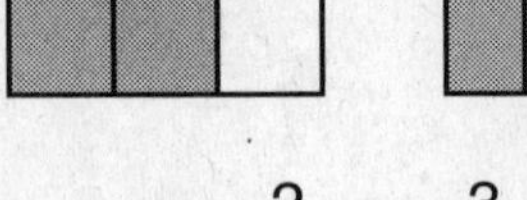

3. $\frac{2}{3}$ ◯ $\frac{3}{4}$

Compare. Write > or < for each ◯. Use fraction strips or a number line if needed.

4. $\frac{1}{8}$ ◯ $\frac{1}{4}$

5. $\frac{1}{10}$ ◯ $\frac{2}{6}$

6. $\frac{3}{4}$ ◯ $\frac{1}{6}$

7. $\frac{5}{9}$ ◯ $\frac{2}{9}$

8. $\frac{3}{3}$ ◯ $\frac{2}{3}$

9. $\frac{1}{4}$ ◯ $\frac{2}{4}$

Problem Solving

10. Pam has $\frac{1}{3}$ of her flower garden planted. Jane has $\frac{3}{12}$ of her garden planted. Each garden is the same size. Who has planted more of her flower garden?

____

Show your work.

Use with text pages 520–521.

Name ______________________ Date ____________

Homework 19.2

Order Fractions

Order the fractions from greatest to least.

$\mathbf{\frac{1}{4}}$ $\mathbf{\frac{1}{8}}$ $\mathbf{\frac{1}{2}}$

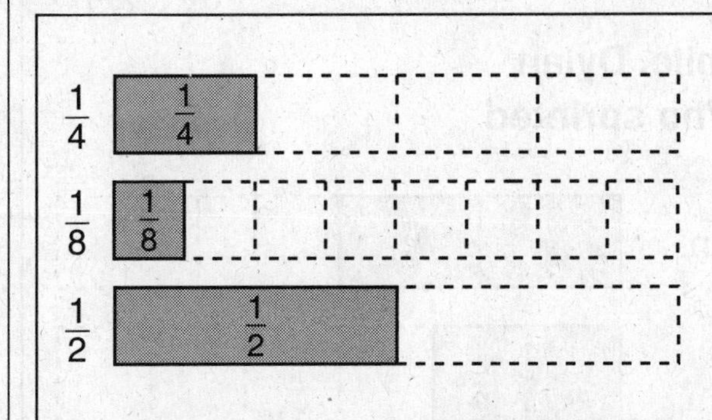

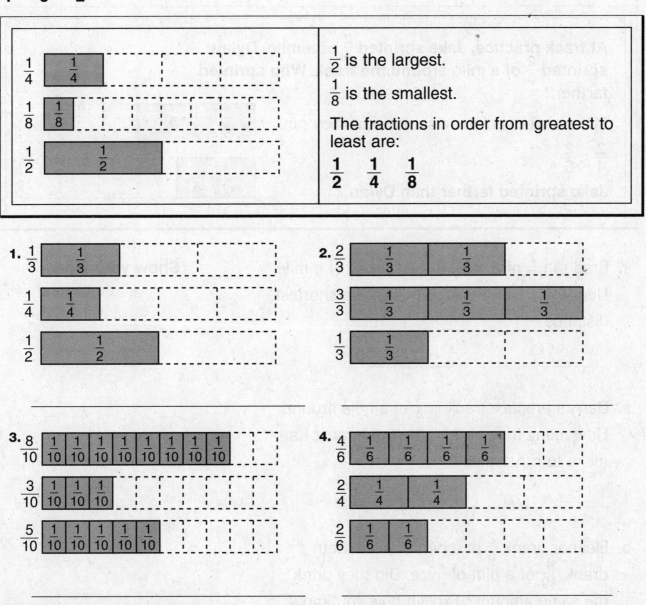

$\frac{1}{2}$ is the largest.

$\frac{1}{8}$ is the smallest.

The fractions in order from greatest to least are:

$\mathbf{\frac{1}{2}}$ $\mathbf{\frac{1}{4}}$ $\mathbf{\frac{1}{8}}$

1. $\frac{1}{3}$, $\frac{1}{4}$, $\frac{1}{2}$

2. $\frac{2}{3}$, $\frac{3}{3}$, $\frac{1}{3}$

______________________ ______________________

3. $\frac{8}{10}$, $\frac{3}{10}$, $\frac{5}{10}$

4. $\frac{4}{6}$, $\frac{2}{4}$, $\frac{2}{6}$

______________________ ______________________

Problem Solving

Show your work.

5. Henry used $\frac{1}{2}$ of the markers.

Kaitlyn used $\frac{1}{3}$ of the markers.

Harriet used $\frac{3}{4}$ of the markers. Who used the most markers?

____

Use with text pages 522–523.

Name ______________________ Date ____________

Homework 19.3

Problem-Solving Strategy: Act It Out

Use models to solve each problem.

At track practice, Jake sprinted $\frac{2}{4}$ of a mile. Dylan sprinted $\frac{2}{6}$ of a mile around the track. Who sprinted farther?

Make a model of the distance each boy ran.

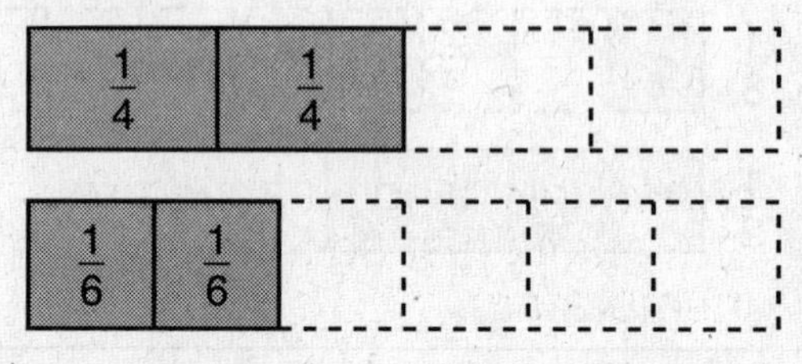

$\frac{2}{4} > \frac{2}{6}$

Jake sprinted farther than Dylan.

Show your work.

1. Brad ran $\frac{7}{8}$ of a mile. Robert ran $\frac{3}{8}$ of a mile. Henry ran $\frac{1}{2}$ of a mile. Who ran the shortest distance?

   ____

2. Gerry's practice track is $\frac{1}{4}$ of a mile around. How many trips around the track must he make to run 1 mile?

   ____

3. Eleanor drank $\frac{2}{5}$ of a pint of juice. Beth drank $\frac{4}{10}$ of a pint of juice. Did they drink the same amount? Explain how you know.

   ____

   ____

   ____

   ____

Use with text pages 524–526.

Name ______________________ Date ____________

Homework 19.4

Add Fractions

Add.

$\frac{1}{4} + \frac{2}{4} =$ ______

$\frac{1}{4}$ | $\frac{1}{4}$ | $\frac{1}{4}$

$\frac{1}{4} + \frac{2}{4} = \frac{3}{4}$

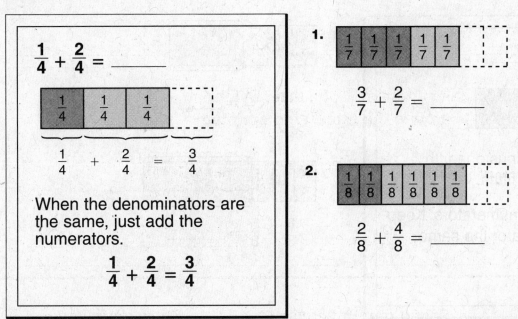

When the denominators are the same, just add the numerators.

$$\frac{1}{4} + \frac{2}{4} = \frac{3}{4}$$

1. $\frac{1}{7}$ | $\frac{1}{7}$ | $\frac{1}{7}$ | $\frac{1}{7}$ | $\frac{1}{7}$

$\frac{3}{7} + \frac{2}{7} =$ ______

2. 

$\frac{2}{8} + \frac{4}{8} =$ ______

Add. Use fractions strips or draw a picture to help you.

3. $\frac{1}{5} + \frac{1}{5} =$ ______

4. $\frac{2}{8} + \frac{2}{8} =$ ______

5. $\frac{5}{12} + \frac{6}{12} =$ ______

Algebra • Variables Find the value of *n*.

6. $\frac{1}{5} + \frac{n}{5} = \frac{3}{5}$ ______

7. $\frac{n}{4} + \frac{2}{4} = \frac{3}{4}$ ______

8. $\frac{2}{10} + \frac{n}{10} = \frac{8}{10}$ ______

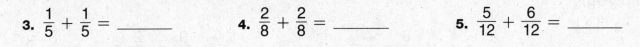

Problem Solving

Show your work.

9. Marcos and Macy ate some pizza. Marcos ate $\frac{4}{8}$ of the pizza. Macy ate $\frac{3}{8}$ of the pizza. What fraction of the pizza did they eat?

____

Use with text pages 528–530.

Name ______________________ Date ____________

Homework 19.5

Subtract Fractions

Subtract.

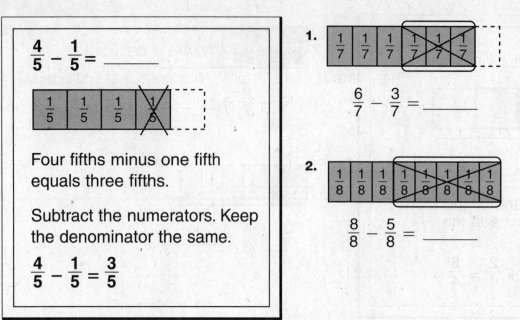

$\frac{4}{5} - \frac{1}{5} =$ ______

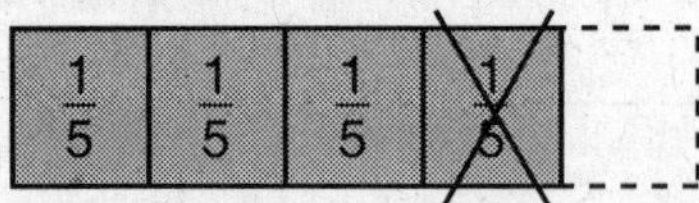

Four fifths minus one fifth equals three fifths.

Subtract the numerators. Keep the denominator the same.

$\frac{4}{5} - \frac{1}{5} = \frac{3}{5}$

1. 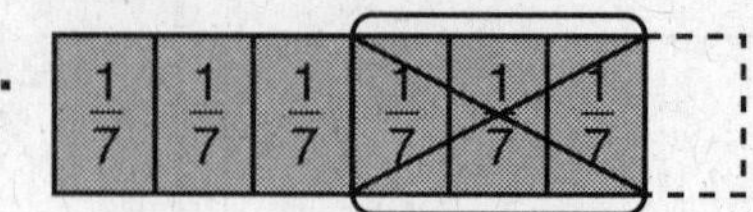

$\frac{6}{7} - \frac{3}{7} =$ ______

2. 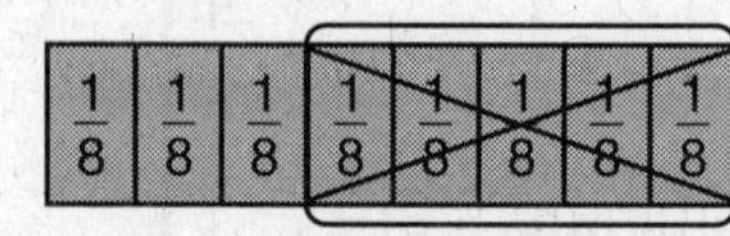

$\frac{8}{8} - \frac{5}{8} =$ ______

Subtract. Use fraction strips or draw a picture to help you.

3. $\frac{2}{7} - \frac{1}{7} =$ ______

4. $\frac{6}{8} - \frac{4}{8} =$ ______

5. $\frac{9}{10} - \frac{2}{10} =$ ______

Algebra • Variables Find the value of *n*.

6. $\frac{7}{10} - \frac{n}{10} = \frac{2}{10}$ ______

7. $\frac{n}{9} - \frac{4}{9} = \frac{4}{9}$ ______

8. $\frac{4}{4} - \frac{n}{4} = \frac{2}{4}$ ______

Problem Solving

Show your work.

9. Phil's mom cut a pie into 8 equal pieces. Phil ate 2 pieces. What fraction of the pie is left?

____

Use with text pages 532–534.

Name ______________________ Date ______________

Homework 20.1

Tenths

Write a fraction and a decimal for the shaded part.

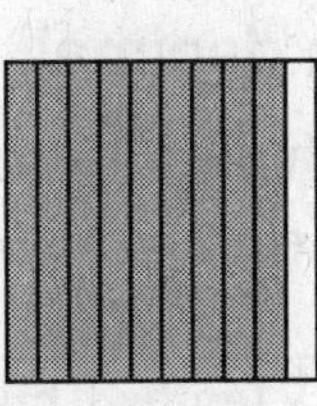

Write a fraction.

There are 10 parts in all. There are 9 shaded parts.

$\frac{9}{10}$

Write a decimal.

Nine tenths are shaded.

ones	.	tenths
0	.	9

1. 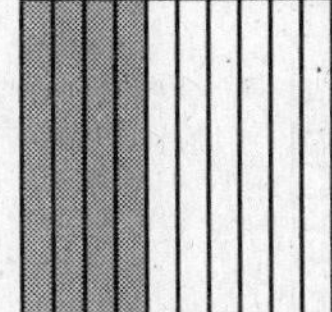

_____

_____

2. 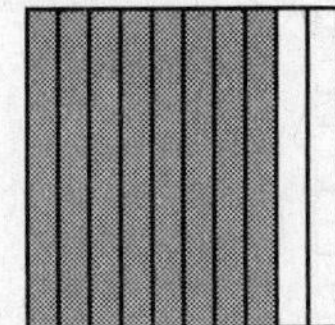

_____

_____

3. 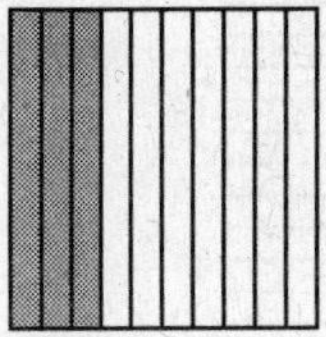

_____

_____

Write each as a decimal.

4. $\frac{1}{10}$ _____

5. $\frac{6}{10}$ _____

6. two tenths _____

7. five tenths _____

Write each as a fraction.

8. 0.7 _____

9. 0.8 _____

10. three tenths _____

11. nine tenths _____

Problem Solving

12. A bird's mass is seven tenths of a kilogram. Write the mass as a decimal.

____

Use with text pages 540–541.

Name ______________________ Date ____________

Homework 20.2

Hundredths

Write a fraction and a decimal for the shaded part.

Write a fraction.

There are 100 parts in all. There are 95 shaded parts.

$\frac{95}{100}$

Write a decimal.

Ninety-five hundredths are shaded.

ones	.	tenths	hundredths
0	.	9	5

1. 

_____

_____

2. 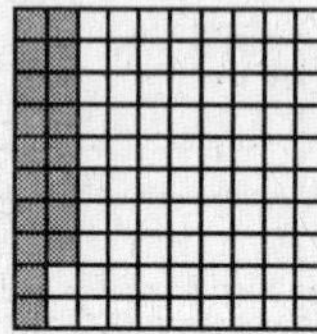

_____

_____

3. 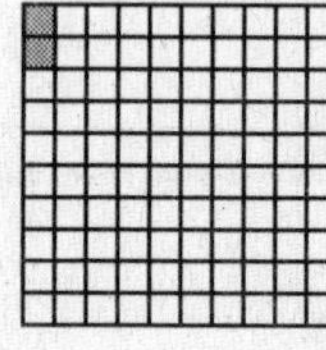

_____

_____

Write each as a decimal.

4. $\frac{23}{100}$ _____

5. $\frac{85}{100}$ _____

6. five hundredths _____

Write each as a fraction.

7. 0.64 _____

8. 0.09 _____

9. seventy hundredths _____

Problem Solving

10. Ben's book has 100 pages. He read 38 pages. Write a decimal that shows the part of the book that Ben read.

____

Name ______________________ Date ____________

Homework 20.3

Decimals Greater Than 1

Write a mixed number and a decimal for the shaded part.

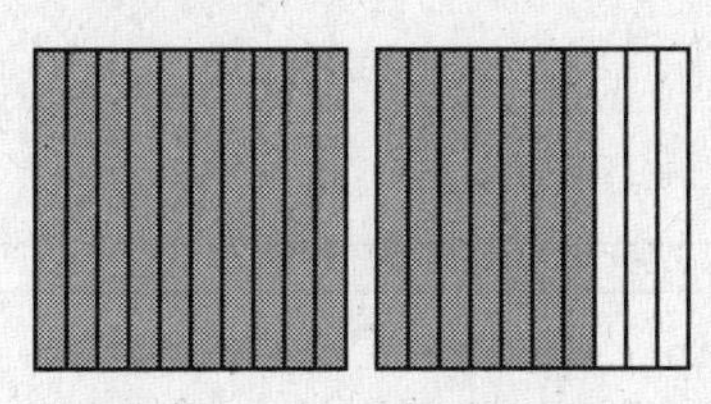

Write a mixed number.

There is one whole rectangle shaded. There are 10 parts in the second rectangle. There are 7 shaded parts.

$1\frac{7}{10}$

Write a decimal.

One and seven tenths are shaded.

ones	.	tenths
1	.	7

1. 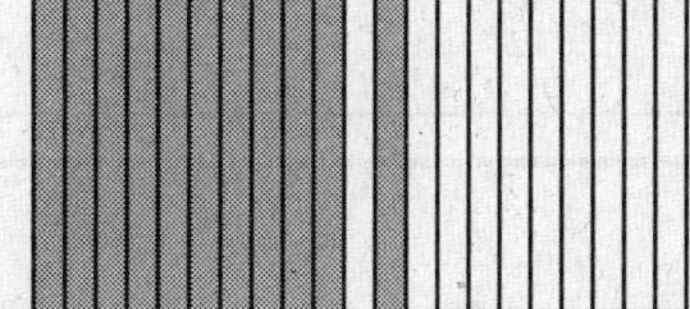

______

______

2. 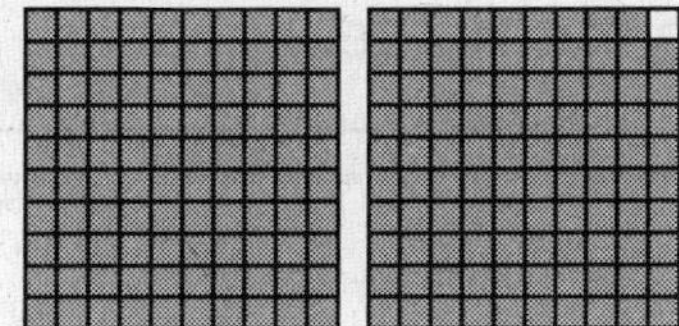

______

______

3. 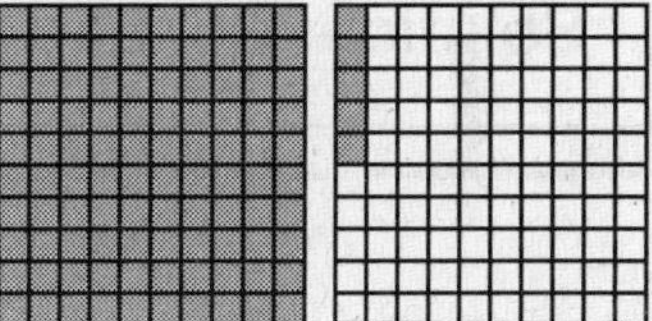

______

______

Write each as a decimal.

4. $5\frac{3}{10}$ ______

5. $2\frac{34}{100}$ ______

6. $6\frac{21}{100}$ ______

7. eight and nine tenths ______

8. nine and five hundredths ______

9. one and seventy-six hundredths ______

Problem Solving

10. Jessica's height is $1\frac{12}{100}$ meters. Write a decimal that shows Jessica's height.

____

Use with text pages 544–545.

Name ______________________ Date ______________

Homework 20.4

Problem-Solving Decision: Reasonable Answers

Problem Ed needs to walk one mile. He walks $\frac{3}{4}$ mile and stops to rest. Then he walks $\frac{1}{4}$ mile more. He thinks he still has $\frac{1}{4}$ mile left to walk. Is this reasonable?

Follow these steps to decide.

Step 1: Find what part of one mile he has walked. $\frac{3}{4} + \frac{1}{4} = \frac{4}{4}$

Step 2: Use what you know about fractions to decide if it is reasonable that $\frac{1}{4}$ mile is left. Since $\frac{4}{4} = 1$, it is not reasonable that $\frac{1}{4}$ mile is left.

Solution: No, Ed's statement is not reasonable.

Solve. Decide whether the answer is reasonable. **Show your work.**

1. Sara used $\frac{1}{5}$ of a box of strawberries on her breakfast cereal. Her brother used $\frac{3}{5}$ of the box on his cereal. She thinks $\frac{2}{5}$ of the box will be left to eat after school. Is this reasonable?

____

2. Callie needs to practice her dance routine for 1 hour. She practices $\frac{1}{6}$ hour in the morning and $\frac{4}{6}$ hour in the afternoon. She said she still needs to practice for $\frac{1}{6}$ hour. Is this reasonable?

____

3. Kurt is putting dirt around the plants in a garden. He made three trips using $\frac{1}{8}$ of the pile of dirt each time. Pablo says that $\frac{4}{8}$ of the pile is left. Is this reasonable?

____

Use with text page 546.

Name ______________________ Date ____________

Homework 20.5

Compare and Order Decimals

Compare. Write >, <, or = for each ◯.

0.4 ◯ 0.6

You can use models.

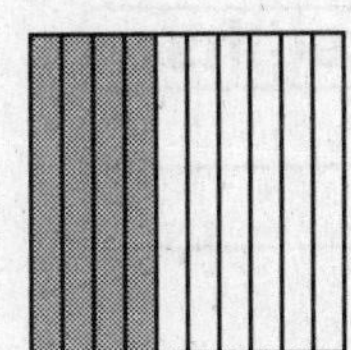

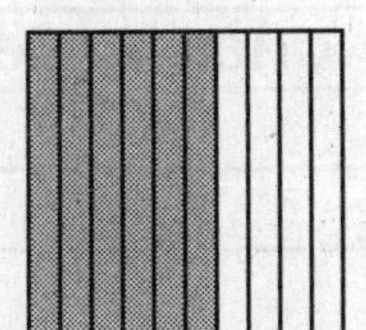

0.4 < 0.6

You can use a place-value chart.

ones	.	tenths
0	.	4
0	.	6

4 is less than 6.

0.4 < 0.6.

1.

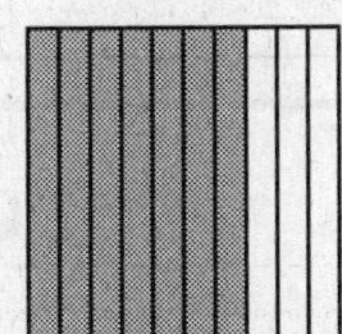

0.9 ◯ 0.7

2.

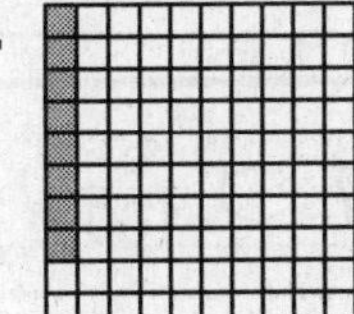

0.08 ◯ 0.11

3. 5.2 ◯ 5.4
4. 0.83 ◯ 0.81
5. 7.6 ◯ 7.60
6. 2.8 ◯ 2.9

7. 0.12 ◯ 0.13
8. 3.01 ◯ 3.10
9. 8.6 ◯ 8.16
10. 3.11 ◯ 2.11

Order the decimals from least to greatest.

11. 0.33 0.32 0.23 ____________

12. 5.6 6.5 5.9 ____________

13. 4.33 5.33 4.34 ____________

Problem Solving

14. The hikers walked 2.2 kilometers in the morning and 3.2 kilometers in the afternoon. Did they walk more in the morning or the afternoon?

____

Use with text pages 548–549.

Name ____________________ Date ____________

Homework 20.6

Compare and Order Fractions and Decimals

Compare. Write >, <, or = for each ◯.

$\frac{13}{100}$ ◯ 0.19

You can use models.

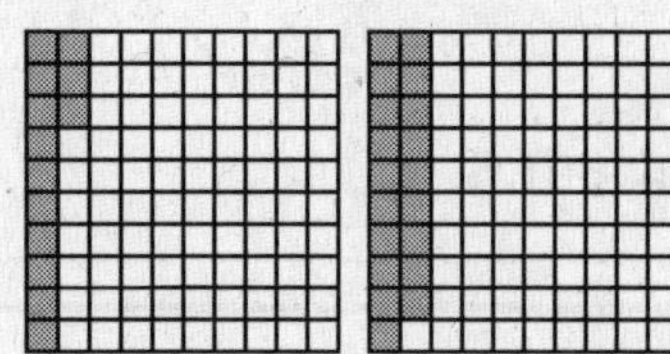

$\frac{13}{100} < 0.19$

You can use a place-value chart.

ones	.	tenths	hundredths
0	.	1	3
0	.	1	9

3 is less than 9.

$\frac{13}{100} < 0.19$

1. $\frac{3}{10}$ ◯ $\frac{5}{10}$
2. 0.07 ◯ $\frac{6}{100}$
3. $\frac{2}{10}$ ◯ 0.1
4. 0.2 ◯ $\frac{8}{10}$
5. $\frac{4}{10}$ ◯ 0. 4
6. 0.09 ◯ $\frac{8}{100}$
7. $\frac{1}{10}$ ◯ 0.3
8. 0.08 ◯ $\frac{7}{100}$
9. 0.33 ◯ $\frac{44}{100}$
10. 0.03 ◯ $\frac{3}{100}$
11. 0.15 ◯ $\frac{11}{100}$
12. 0.09 ◯ $\frac{9}{100}$

Order the numbers from least to greatest.

13. 0.03 0.02 $\frac{6}{100}$ ____________
14. $\frac{8}{10}$ 0.9 $\frac{7}{10}$ ____________
15. 0.24 $\frac{12}{100}$ 0.21 ____________

Problem Solving

16. Issac drank $\frac{3}{10}$ liter of water. Manuel drank 0.5 liter of water. Which boy drank the most water?

____

Use with text pages 550–551.

Name ______________________ Date ____________

Homework 20.7

Relate Decimals, Fractions, and Money

Complete the table below. Use play money to help you.

Coin(s)	Number of Cents	Fraction of a Dollar	Value as a Decimal
1 quarter	A quarter is 25 cents. **25¢**	A dollar is 100 cents. $\frac{25}{100}$	Write the fraction as a decimal. **$0.25**
1. 9 pennies			
2. 5 dimes			
3. 3 quarters			
4. 2 nickels			
5. 2 half-dollars			

Write each amount as a fraction of a dollar.

6. $0.76 = ______ of a dollar

7. $0.33 = ______ of a dollar

8. $0.04 = ______ of a dollar

9. $0.60 = ______ of a dollar

Problem Solving

10. Cliff paid for a carton of milk with the exact change of nine dimes. What is the price of the milk?

____

Use with text pages 552–554.

Name ______________________ Date ______________

Homework 20.8

Add and Subtract Decimals

Add or subtract.

$4.7 + 3.5 =$ ____	$5.15 - 2.32 =$ ____
$\begin{array}{r} \overset{1}{4}.7 \\ +3.5 \\ \hline 8.2 \end{array}$	$\begin{array}{r} \overset{4}{\not5}.\overset{11}{\not1}5 \\ -2.32 \\ \hline 2.83 \end{array}$
Regroup if necessary.	Regroup from larger places if necessary.

1. $\begin{array}{r} 5.2 \\ +3.4 \\ \hline \end{array}$

2. $\begin{array}{r} 6.8 \\ +1.9 \\ \hline \end{array}$

3. $\begin{array}{r} 5.79 \\ +4.11 \\ \hline \end{array}$

4. $\begin{array}{r} 7.94 \\ +1.43 \\ \hline \end{array}$

5. $\begin{array}{r} 6.8 \\ -3.4 \\ \hline \end{array}$

6. $\begin{array}{r} 2.6 \\ -1.8 \\ \hline \end{array}$

7. $\begin{array}{r} 3.17 \\ -2.55 \\ \hline \end{array}$

8. $\begin{array}{r} 3.25 \\ -0.79 \\ \hline \end{array}$

9. 4.30 + 3.41 ______

10. 0.99 + 0.88 ______

11. 8.98 − 5.56 ______

12. 4.01 − 3.40 ______

Problem Solving

13. Trevor is using building blocks to make a castle. The first block is 0.46 feet high. The second block is 0.72 feet high. How high are the blocks when one is stacked on top of the other?

____

Use with text pages 556–558.

Name ______________________ Date ____________

Homework 20.9

Problem-Solving Application: Use Money

Problem Josie goes to Della's Deli for lunch with her friends. She buys a pizza slice and a bottle of fruit juice. She pays with a 5-dollar bill and two 1-dollar bills. How much change should she get?

Step 1:

```
  $3.50  ← cost of pizza slice
 +2.75   ← cost of fruit juice
  $6.25  ← total cost
```

Step 2: $5 + two $1 bills = $7

Step 3:

```
      9
   6 1010
  $7.00
  -6.25
  $0.25
```

Solution: Josie should get $0.25 in change.

Della's Deli

Pizza slice: $3.50 each
Bottled water: $1.29 each
Fruit juice: $2.75 each
Fruit: $0.39 each
Yogurt: $0.85 each
Tuna sandwich: $2.69 each
Sub Sandwich: $3.98 each

Use the prices above to solve each problem. **Show your work.**

1. Rosa buys a sub sandwich and a bottled water. She pays with a 20-dollar bill. How much change should she get back?

____

2. Casey buys 2 pieces of fruit and a tuna sandwich. He pays with four 1-dollar bills. How much change should he get back?

____

3. Karl has a 10-dollar bill. How many pizza slices can he buy?

____

Use with text pages 560–562.

Name ______________________ Date ____________

Homework 21.1

Multiply Multiples of 10, 100 and 1,000

Use a basic fact and patterns to help you find each product.

2 × 8 = ______	Look for a pattern of zeros.	**2 × 8 = 16**
2 × 80 = ______		**2 × 80 = 160**
2 × 800 = ______		**2 × 800 = 1,600**
2 × 8,000 = ______		**2 × 8,000 = 16,000**

1. 3 × 3 ______ **2.** 6 × 3 ______ **3.** 4 × 8 ______

3 × 30 ______ 6 × 30 ______ 4 × 80 ______

3 × 300 ______ 6 × 300 ______ 4 × 800 ______

3 × 3,000 ______ 6 × 3,000 ______ 4 × 8,000 ______

Find each product.

4. 7 × 80 ______ **5.** 3 × 900 ______ **6.** 3 × 2,000 ______ **7.** 4 × 50 ______

8. 3 × 500 ______ **9.** 3 × 400 ______ **10.** 2 × 90 ______ **11.** 8 × 700 ______

Problem Solving

Show your work.

12. Carrie is making 4 beaded necklaces. Each necklace uses 50 beads. How many beads will Carrie need to make the necklaces?

____

Use with text pages 580–581.

Name ______________________ Date ____________

Homework 21.2

Model Multiplication

Use base-ten blocks to help you find each product.

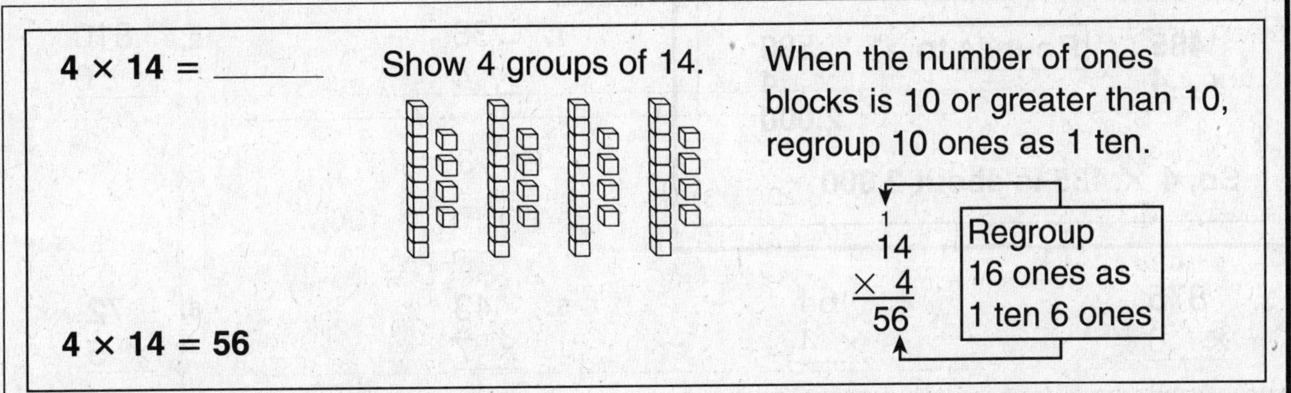

4 × 14 = ____
Show 4 groups of 14.
When the number of ones blocks is 10 or greater than 10, regroup 10 ones as 1 ten.
1
14
× 4
56
Regroup 16 ones as 1 ten 6 ones
4 × 14 = 56

1. 3 × 18 ______
2. 6 × 12 ______
3. 1 × 92 ______
4. 3 × 22 ______
5. 2 × 42 ______
6. 2 × 21 ______
7. 3 × 24 ______
8. 4 × 13 ______
9. 2 × 13 ______
10. 2 × 32 ______
11. 2 × 23 ______
12. 3 × 26 ______

Problem Solving

Show your work.

13. Floyd's mom baked cookies for his class picnic. There are 18 children in the class. She baked enough cookies for each child to have 4. How many cookies did Floyd's mom bake?

____

Use with text pages 582–583.

Name ______________________ Date ______________

Homework 21.3

Estimate Products

Estimate each product.

485 × 4	Rounds to	500 × 4 = 2,000

So, 4 × 485 is about 2,000

1. 38 × 4

2. 810 × 6

3. 875 × 6

4. 64 × 4

5. 43 × 7

6. 72 × 5

7. 8 × 38 ______

8. 5 × 913 ______

9. 4 × 689 ______

10. 9 × 61 ______

Algebra • Symbols Compare. Write >, <, or = for each ◯.

11. 2 × 58 ◯ 2 × 48

12. 3 × 800 ◯ 4 × 600

13. 11 × 33 ◯ 333 × 11

14. 281 × 4 ◯ 412 × 4

Problem Solving

Show your work.

15. The third grade is going on a field trip. There are 48 students on each bus. There are 3 buses. About how many students are going on the field trip?

____

Use with text pages 584–586.

Name ______________________ Date ______________

Multiply 2-Digit Numbers by 1-Digit Numbers

Find each product.

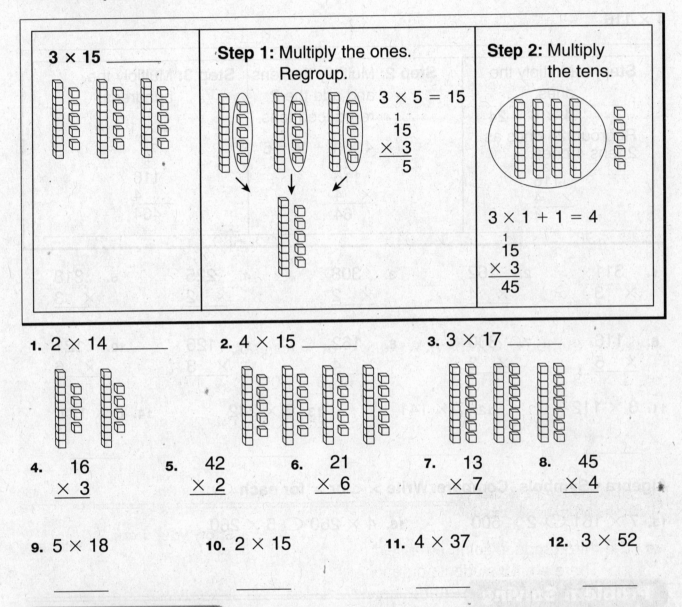

3 × 15 ______

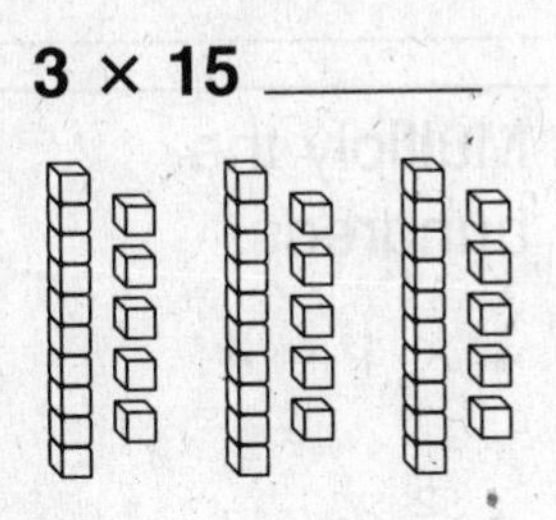

Step 1: Multiply the ones. Regroup.

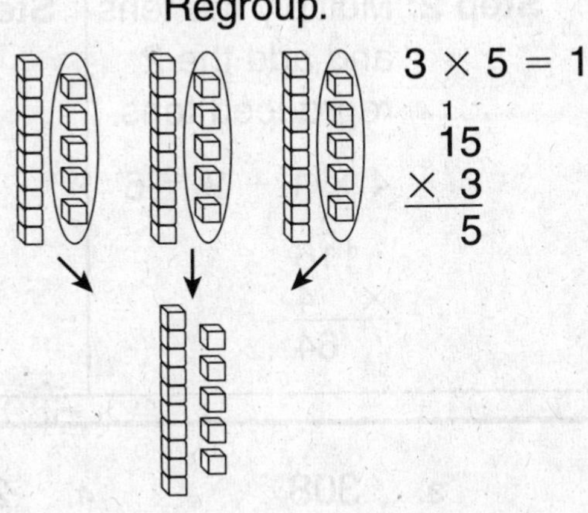

$3 \times 5 = 15$

$$\begin{array}{r} \scriptsize{1} \\ 15 \\ \times\ 3 \\ \hline 5 \end{array}$$

Step 2: Multiply the tens.

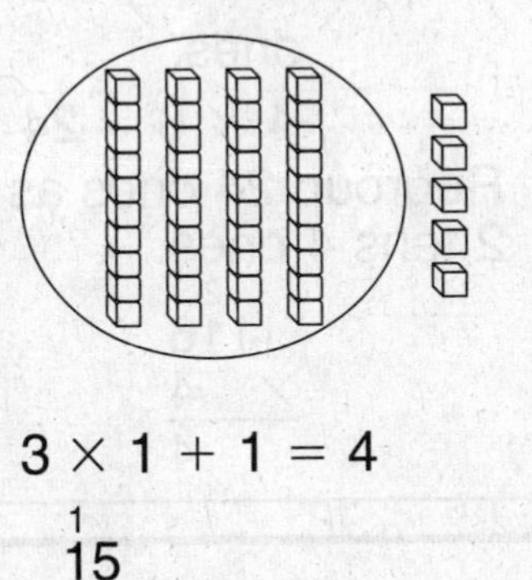

$3 \times 1 + 1 = 4$

$$\begin{array}{r} \scriptsize{1} \\ 15 \\ \times\ 3 \\ \hline 45 \end{array}$$

1. 2 × 14 ______

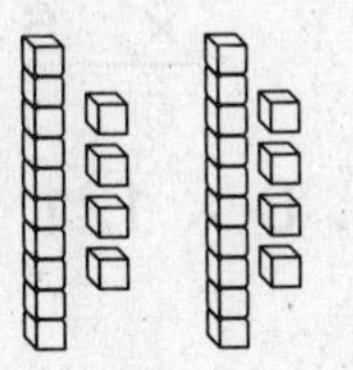

2. 4 × 15 ______

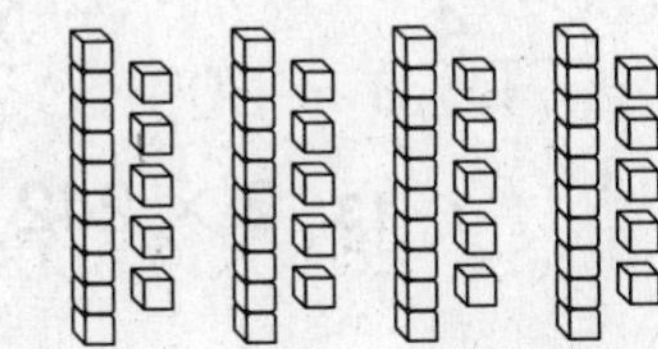

3. 3 × 17 ______

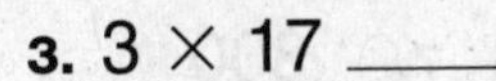

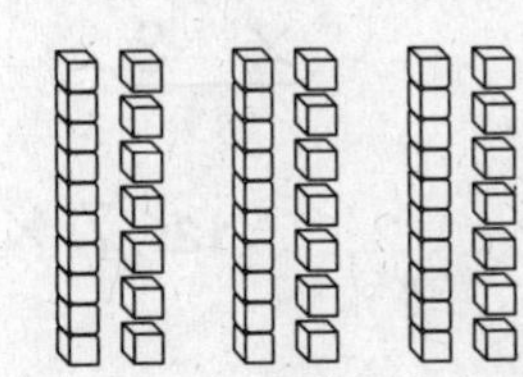

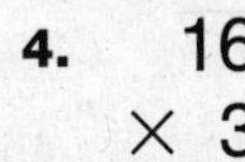

4. $\begin{array}{r} 16 \\ \times\ 3 \\ \hline \end{array}$ **5.** $\begin{array}{r} 42 \\ \times\ 2 \\ \hline \end{array}$ **6.** $\begin{array}{r} 21 \\ \times\ 6 \\ \hline \end{array}$ **7.** $\begin{array}{r} 13 \\ \times\ 7 \\ \hline \end{array}$ **8.** $\begin{array}{r} 45 \\ \times\ 4 \\ \hline \end{array}$

9. 5 × 18 ______ **10.** 2 × 15 ______ **11.** 4 × 37 ______ **12.** 3 × 52 ______

Problem Solving

13. Sheri helped her dad plant strawberries on their farm. They planted 8 rows of strawberry plants with 45 plants in each row. How many plants did they plant in all?

Show your work.

____

Use with text pages 588–590.

Name ____________________ Date ____________

Homework 21.5

Multiply 3-Digit Numbers by 1-Digit Numbers.

Find each product.

4 × 116

Step 1: Multiply the ones.	**Step 2:** Multiply the tens and add the 2 regrouped tens.	**Step 3:** Multiply the hundreds.
4 × 6 = 24 Regroup 24 ones as 2 tens 4 ones. $\begin{array}{r} {}^{2} \\ 116 \\ \times \quad 4 \\ \hline 4 \end{array}$	4 × 1 + 2 = 6 $\begin{array}{r} {}^{2} \\ 116 \\ \times \quad 4 \\ \hline 64 \end{array}$	4 × 1 = 4 $\begin{array}{r} {}^{2} \\ 116 \\ \times \quad 4 \\ \hline 464 \end{array}$

1. $\begin{array}{r} 311 \\ \times \quad 3 \\ \hline \end{array}$
2. $\begin{array}{r} 162 \\ \times \quad 4 \\ \hline \end{array}$
3. $\begin{array}{r} 308 \\ \times \quad 2 \\ \hline \end{array}$
4. $\begin{array}{r} 225 \\ \times \quad 2 \\ \hline \end{array}$
5. $\begin{array}{r} 318 \\ \times \quad 3 \\ \hline \end{array}$
6. $\begin{array}{r} 116 \\ \times \quad 5 \\ \hline \end{array}$
7. $\begin{array}{r} 300 \\ \times \quad 3 \\ \hline \end{array}$
8. $\begin{array}{r} 162 \\ \times \quad 4 \\ \hline \end{array}$
9. $\begin{array}{r} 126 \\ \times \quad 3 \\ \hline \end{array}$
10. $\begin{array}{r} 121 \\ \times \quad 6 \\ \hline \end{array}$
11. 3 × 112 ______
12. 7 × 141 ______
13. 3 × 242 ______
14. 8 × 121 ______

Algebra • Symbols Compare. Write >, <, or = for each ◯.

15. 7 × 161 ◯ 2 × 500
16. 4 × 260 ◯ 5 × 260

Problem Solving

17. The Science Club presented astronomy shows on Friday, Saturday, and Sunday. There were 150 people at each show. How many people saw the astronomy show?

Show your work.

____

Use with text pages 592–593.

Name ________________________ Date ______________

Homework 21.6

Problem-Solving Strategy: Solve a Simpler Problem

Use easier numbers to help you solve each problem.

Inez bought 5 sheets of poster board. The first store charges 69¢ per sheet of poster board. The second store charges 39¢ per sheet of poster board. How much did Inez save buying the poster board at the second store?

Step 1: Choose smaller numbers and think about how to solve.

Multiply.
$$\begin{array}{r} 6 \\ \times 5 \\ \hline 30 \end{array}$$

Multiply.
$$\begin{array}{r} 3 \\ \times 5 \\ \hline 15 \end{array}$$

Find the difference.
$$\begin{array}{r} 30 \\ -15 \\ \hline 15 \end{array}$$

Step 2: Reread the problem. Solve using the original numbers.

Multiply.
$$\begin{array}{r} 69 \\ \times\ 5 \\ \hline 345 \end{array}$$

Multiply.
$$\begin{array}{r} 39 \\ \times\ 5 \\ \hline 195 \end{array}$$

Find the difference.
$$\begin{array}{r} 345 \\ -195 \\ \hline 150 \end{array}$$

Inez saved 150¢ or $1.50 buying poster board at the second store.

Show your work.

1. Allen is walking to Karl's house and back. They live 2 miles from each other. It takes Allen 14 minutes to walk each mile. How long will it take him to walk to Karl's house and come back?

____

2. Patrick's family intends to drive 358 miles each day for 3 days and 439 miles each day for 2 days. How many miles will they drive in all?

____

Name ________________________ Date ____________

Homework 21.7

Regrouping Twice

Multiply. Regroup if needed.

6 × 163

Step 1: Multiply ones.	**Step 2:** Multiply tens.	**Step 3:** Multiply hundreds.
6 × 3 = 18 Regroup 18 ones as 1 ten 8 ones. $\begin{array}{r} {}^{1} \\ 163 \\ \times\ \ 6 \\ \hline 8 \end{array}$	6 × 6 = 36 Add the 1 regrouped 10. 36 + 1 = 37 $\begin{array}{r} {}^{3\,1} \\ 163 \\ \times\ \ 6 \\ \hline 78 \end{array}$ Regroup 37 tens as 3 hundreds 7 tens.	6 × 1 = 6 Add the 3 regrouped hundreds. 6 + 3 = 9 $\begin{array}{r} {}^{3\,1} \\ 163 \\ \times\ \ 6 \\ \hline 978 \end{array}$

1. $\begin{array}{r} 134 \\ \times\ \ 4 \\ \hline \end{array}$ **2.** $\begin{array}{r} 214 \\ \times\ \ 6 \\ \hline \end{array}$ **3.** $\begin{array}{r} 431 \\ \times\ \ 5 \\ \hline \end{array}$ **4.** $\begin{array}{r} 248 \\ \times\ \ 2 \\ \hline \end{array}$ **5.** $\begin{array}{r} 531 \\ \times\ \ 3 \\ \hline \end{array}$

6. $\begin{array}{r} 2{,}116 \\ \times\ \ 5 \\ \hline \end{array}$ **7.** $\begin{array}{r} 1{,}187 \\ \times\ \ 3 \\ \hline \end{array}$ **8.** $\begin{array}{r} 2{,}083 \\ \times\ \ 4 \\ \hline \end{array}$ **9.** $\begin{array}{r} 5{,}210 \\ \times\ \ 9 \\ \hline \end{array}$ **10.** $\begin{array}{r} 9{,}711 \\ \times\ \ 7 \\ \hline \end{array}$

11. 8 × 534 ______ **12.** 4 × 123 ______ **13.** 5 × 4,152 ______ **14.** 2 × 3,081 ______

Algebra • Symbols Compare the products. Write >, <, or = for each ○.

15. 3 × 538 ○ 4 × 367 **16.** 5 × 153 ○ 6 × 154

Problem Solving

Show your work.

17. Mario traveled from his home to Washington, D.C. and back. Washington, D.C. is 1,237 miles from his home. How many miles did he travel in all?

____

Use with text pages 598–600.

Name ________________________ Date ______________

Homework 21.8

Multiply Money

Estimate, then multiply.

	Round to the nearest dollar.	Find the product.
$3.29 × 3	$3.29 → $3 × 3 → × 3 $9	$\overset{2}{\$3.29}$ × 3 $9.87 Place decimal point between dollars and cents. **$3.29 × 3 = $9.87**

1. $1.73 × 2

2. $2.88 × 3

3. $3.66 × 2

4. $1.29 × 4

5. $4.29 × 4

6. $3.15 × 5

7. $2.68 × 8

8. $4.01 × 6

9. 9 × $1.11 ______

10. 5 × $3.16 ______

11. 4 × $2.03 ______

12. 6 × $1.32 ______

13. 5 × $4.61 ______

14. 7 × $1.68 ______

Problem Solving

Show your work.

15. Tim bought 4 burritos. The burritos cost $1.69 each. How much did Tim spend?

____

Name ______________________ Date ____________

Homework 22.1

Use Mental Math to Divide

Use a basic fact and patterns to find each quotient.

9 ÷ 3 = ______ 90 ÷ 3 = ______ 900 ÷ 3 = ______ 9,000 ÷ 3 = ______	Look for a pattern of zeros.	**9 ÷ 3 = 3** **9<u>0</u> ÷ 3 = 3<u>0</u>** **9<u>00</u> ÷ 3 = 3<u>00</u>** **9,<u>000</u> ÷ 3 = 3,<u>000</u>**

1. 6 ÷ 1 = ______
60 ÷ 1 = ______
600 ÷ 1 = ______
6,000 ÷ 1 = ______

2. 4 ÷ 2 = ______
40 ÷ 2 = ______
400 ÷ 2 = ______
4,000 ÷ 2 = ______

3. 21 ÷ 3 = ______
210 ÷ 3 = ______
2,100 ÷ 3 = ______

4. 18 ÷ 6 = ______
180 ÷ 6 = ______
1,800 ÷ 6 = ______

5. 27 ÷ 3 = ______
270 ÷ 3 = ______
2,700 ÷ 3 = ______

6. 42 ÷ 6 = ______
420 ÷ 6 = ______
4,200 ÷ 6 = ______

Divide.

7. 350 ÷ 5 ______

8. 540 ÷ 9 ______

9. 80 ÷ 4 ______

10. 70 ÷ 7 ______

11. 1,800 ÷ 3 ______

12. 3,000 ÷ 6 ______

13. 3,200 ÷ 8 ______

14. 1,600 ÷ 8 ______

Problem Solving

Show your work.

15. Ms. Billow's class is 60 minutes long. She wants to divide it into 3 equal periods. How long will each period be?

____

Use with text pages 610–611.

Name ______________________ Date ______________

Homework 22.2

Model Division with Remainders

Use the picture to divide.

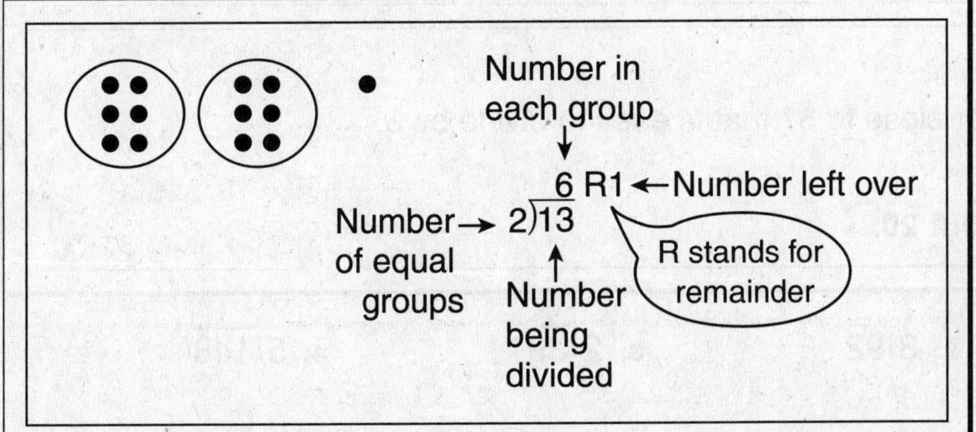

1. ______________________

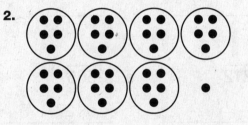

2. ______________________

Divide. Use counters and repeated subtraction to help you.

3. 36 ÷ 9 ________

4. 64 ÷ 8 ________

5. 62 ÷ 8 ________

6. 41 ÷ 5 ________

7. 56 ÷ 7 ________

8. 36 ÷ 5 ________

9. 26 ÷ 8 ________

10. 15 ÷ 3 ________

Problem Solving

Show your work.

11. Hector had 39 stickers. He placed them into 6 equal piles. How many stickers did he have left over?

____

Use with text pages 612–614.

Name ______________________ Date ____________

Homework 22.3

Estimate Quotients

Estimate. Write the compatible numbers you used.

$3\overline{)57}$

Think of a number close to 57 that is easy to divide by 3.

$60 \div 3 = 20$

So 57 ÷ 3 is about 20.

1. $7\overline{)45}$
2. $3\overline{)92}$
3. $2\overline{)39}$
4. $5\overline{)148}$
5. $7\overline{)212}$
6. $8\overline{)565}$
7. $4\overline{)159}$
8. $2\overline{)179}$
9. $536 \div 9$
10. $321 \div 8$
11. $220 \div 4$
12. $121 \div 6$

Problem Solving

Show your work.

13. There are 179 students attending the field trip. A chaperone is required for every 9 students. About how many chaperones are attending the field trip?

Use with text pages 616–618.

Name ______________________ Date ____________

Homework 22.4

Two-Digit Quotients

Use base-ten blocks to help you divide.

$3\overline{)35}$

Step 1. Divide the tens into 3 equal groups.

$$\begin{array}{r} 1 \\ 3\overline{)35} \\ -3 \\ \hline 0 \end{array}$$

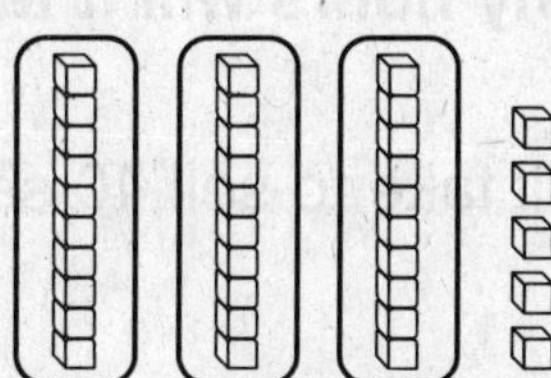

There are 3 groups of 1 ten each with 1 ten left over. Regroup the 1 ten as 10 ones.

Step 2. Divide the ones into 3 equal groups.

$$\begin{array}{r} 11 \\ 3\overline{)35} \\ -3 \\ \hline 05 \\ -3 \\ \hline 2 \end{array}$$

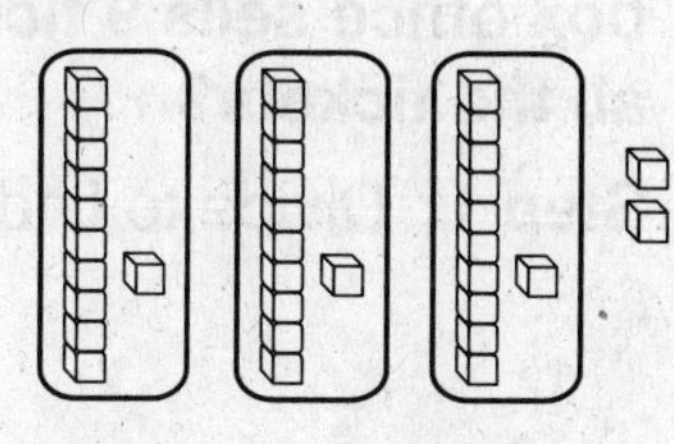

There are 3 groups of 3 ones each with 2 ones left over.

35 ÷ 3 = 11 R2

1. $5\overline{)59}$ **2.** $5\overline{)50}$ **3.** $4\overline{)82}$ **4.** $2\overline{)49}$ **5.** $4\overline{)46}$

6. $7\overline{)71}$ **7.** $5\overline{)58}$ **8.** $3\overline{)64}$ **9.** $5\overline{)57}$ **10.** $3\overline{)67}$

11. 94 ÷ 3 ________ **12.** 83 ÷ 2 ________ **13.** 66 ÷ 6 ________ **14.** 49 ÷ 4 ________

Problem Solving

15. Josie planted 36 plants. She planted them equally in 3 rows. How many plants did she place in each row?

Show your work.

____

Use with text pages 620–621.

Name ______________________ Date ______________

Homework 22.5

Problem-Solving Application: Interpret Remainders

Solve.

There are 40 seats available at the Aquarium for the dolphin show. The box office sells 9 tickets each hour. How many hours will it take to sell all the tickets?

Step 1: Divide to find out how many hours it will take to sell 40 seats.

$$\begin{array}{r} 4 \text{ R4} \\ 9\overline{)40} \\ -36 \\ \hline 4 \end{array}$$

Step 2: Interpret the remainder.

The tickets will take longer than 4 hours to be sold.

It will take 5 hours to sell all the tickets.

Show your work.

1. There are 33 trained dolphins at the Aquarium. Each dolphin performs once each day. There are 5 shows each day. If an equal number of dolphins perform at each show, what is the largest number of dolphins that will perform at one show?

____

2. Each dolphin learns 3 new tricks each month. How many months will it take a dolphin to learn 23 new tricks?

____

Use with text pages 622–623.

Name ______________________ Date ____________

Homework 22.6

Three-Digit Quotients

Divide and check.

$3\overline{)379}$

Step 1. Divide the hundreds.	**Step 2.** Bring down the tens. Divide the tens.	**Step 3.** Regroup leftover tens as ones.	**Step 4.** Divide the ones.
$\begin{array}{r} 1 \\ 3\overline{)379} \\ -3 \\ \hline 0 \end{array}$	$\begin{array}{r} 12 \\ 3\overline{)379} \\ -3\downarrow \\ \hline 07 \\ -\ 6 \\ \hline 1 \end{array}$	$\begin{array}{r} 12 \\ 3\overline{)379} \\ -3 \\ \hline 07 \\ -\ 6\downarrow \\ \hline 19 \end{array}$	$\begin{array}{r} 126\text{ R1} \\ 3\overline{)379} \\ -3 \\ \hline 07 \\ -6 \\ \hline 19 \\ -18 \\ \hline 1 \end{array}$
			379 ÷ 3 → 126 R1

1. $3\overline{)681}$ **2.** $4\overline{)496}$ **3.** $2\overline{)232}$ **4.** $5\overline{)567}$ **5.** $6\overline{)684}$

6. $6\overline{)643}$ **7.** $4\overline{)848}$ **8.** $3\overline{)639}$ **9.** $3\overline{)377}$ **10.** $4\overline{)884}$

11. 595 ÷ 5 ________ **12.** 856 ÷ 4 ________ **13.** 672 ÷ 2 ________ **14.** 834 ÷ 2 ________

Problem Solving

15. Manuella is planning a trip to New York. She lives 975 miles away. She plans to drive the same distance each day for 3 days to get there. How many miles should she plan to drive each day?

Show your work.

____

Name ______________________ Date ____________

Homework 22.7

Place the First Digit

Divide. Check your answers.

$6\overline{)246}$ **Step 1.** Divide the hundreds. $2 < 6$ There are not enough hundreds to divide. Go to the tens place.	**Step 2.** Divide the tens. $\begin{array}{r} 4 \\ 6\overline{)246} \\ -24 \\ \hline 0 \end{array}$	**Step 3.** Bring down the ones. Divide the ones. $\begin{array}{r} 41 \\ 6\overline{)246} \\ -24\downarrow \\ \hline 06 \\ -\ 6 \\ \hline 0 \end{array}$	**Step 4.** Check. $\begin{array}{r} 41 \\ \times\ 6 \\ \hline 246 \end{array}$ **246 ÷ 6 = 41**

1. $5\overline{)445}$ 2. $6\overline{)312}$ 3. $9\overline{)558}$ 4. $3\overline{)177}$ 5. $2\overline{)196}$

6. 116 ÷ 2 ________ 7. 581 ÷ 7 ________ 8. 546 ÷ 6 ________ 9. 340 ÷ 5 ________

Algebra • Equations Solve for *n*.

10. $488 \div 2 = n$; $488 \div 4 = n$; $488 \div 8 = n$ ________

11. $56 \div 2 = n$; $56 \div 4 = n$; $56 \div 8 = n$ ________

12. $272 \div 2 = n$; $272 \div 4 = n$; $272 \div 8 = n$ ________

13. $256 \div 2 = n$; $256 \div 4 = n$; $256 \div 8 = n$ ________

Problem Solving

Show your work.

14. Harry's mom is making tamales. She has to make 819 tamales. If she plans to make an equal number of tamales each day for 9 days, how many should she make each day?

____

Use with text pages 626–627.

Name ______________________ Date ____________

Homework 22.8

Divide Money

Divide. Model with coins and bills if you wish.

$3\overline{)\$6.48}$

Step 1. Divide the dollars. Place the dollar sign in the quotient.

$$\begin{array}{r} \$2 \\ 3\overline{)\$6.48} \\ \underline{-6} \\ 0 \end{array}$$

Step 2. Divide the dimes. Use a decimal point to separate the dollars and cents.

$$\begin{array}{r} \$2.1 \\ 3\overline{)\$6.48} \\ \underline{-6} \\ 04 \\ \underline{-\ 3} \\ 1 \end{array}$$

Step 3. Divide the pennies.

$$\begin{array}{r} \$2.16 \\ 3\overline{)\$6.48} \\ \underline{-6} \\ 04 \\ \underline{-\ 3} \\ 18 \\ \underline{-18} \\ 0 \end{array}$$

$6.48 ÷ 3 = $2.16

1. $2\overline{)\$8.54}$
2. $2\overline{)\$4.78}$
3. $5\overline{)\$9.95}$
4. $3\overline{)\$9.57}$

5. $4.96 ÷ 4 ________
6. $9.81 ÷ 3 ________
7. $6.76 ÷ 2 ________
8. $5.85 ÷ 5 ________

Algebra • Equations Solve for *n*.

9. $n \div 3 = \$2.43$ ________
10. $\$8.36 \div 4 = n$ ________
11. $\$2.13 = n \div 3$ ________

Problem Solving

Show your work.

12. Monique bought 3 pairs of scissors. Her bill was $3.78. How much did each pair of scissors cost?

____

Use with text pages 628–630.

ARGOOD OIL AND GAS CORPORATION
402 Hales Building
Phone 7-3771
OKLAHOMA CITY, OKLA.

AN INSTITUTION DEVOTED TO THE PROFITABLE DEVELOPMENT OF OIL

OWNERS & OPERATORS OF
KEENE-OKLA OHIO NO. 1
CATALINA NO. 1
CATALINA NO. 2
IN OKLAHOMA CITY GUSHER FIELD

USED 1/7/37

April-24-34 MAN-DRINKS UP

Mr Ripley
Dear Sir-
I am sending you a Picture of my self of drinking up-not down on a step ladder I did the act 26 yrs ago in Denver Colo on a Bet of 25.00 that I could drink a Bottle of Soda or Beer with out drop going down my throat as you see in the Picture. its going up.

you Can have the answer in the Paper the Next day if you wish

I Conceived the Idea of two mules drinking water from a Brook of 45 Per Grade down a steep Bank; after they drank 4 or 6 Swallow they would throw there heads to one side or the other, & Kept on repeating untill there thirst was Satisfied. I was 16 yrs old at the

PAGE 144

Sligh and Tyrrell
INCORPORATED
MUSIC • ENTERTAINMENT • STAGE UNITS
140 NORTH DEARBORN STREET • CHICAGO • PHONE STATE 2860

CABLE ADDRESS: SLITEL

Feb. 1, 1938.

Mr. Bob Ripley,
% W M A Q,
Chicago, Ill.

Dear Bob:

BELIEVE IT OR NOT ---

JACKIE DEL RIO, not only chews his steak, but he chews the table as well! Not only his own table, but the next table and all the chairs! Yes, TWO TABLES AND SIX CHAIRS all in one mouthful! The enclosed photograph is no fake.

To prove it, Jackie will appear on your radio program - and do his stuff in full view of your studio audience, and to the delight of your millions of listeners - many of whom have been so hungry at some time or other, that they could "eat the table" themselves!

If this intrigues your interest, as it does ours, we will gladly arrange the details immediately. As an added attraction, Jackie, who is only "five feet in height" weighing 115 pounds, and young, will actually pick you up in his teeth and carry you around the microphone seated in your chair!

Yours very truly,
Fred Joyce
FRED JOYCE, PRESS AGENT
SLIGH & TYRRELL, INC.

FJ/L

NEW YORK • CLEVELAND • DETROIT • LOS ANGELES

PAGE 39

NATIONAL BUSINESS COLLEGE BUILDING

E. M. COULTER, PRESIDENT
ESTABLISHED 1886
M. A. SMYTHE, VICE PRES. AND GEN'L MGR.

Roanoke National Business College

BUSINESS MEN FURNISHED BOOK KEEPERS AND STENOGRAPHERS
GRADUATES ASSISTED TO POSITIONS

ROANOKE, VIRGINIA
March 30, 1936

USED 2/5/37

NAMES

FILE No.

Mr. Robert L. Ripley,
c/o King's Syndicate,
235 East 45th Street,
New York City.

My dear Mr. Ripley:

Enclosed is a photograph which we believe will be of interest to you.

The small man on the right is E. E. East of West Virginia. The larger man on the left is E. E. West of east Virginia. These two men met recently at the National Business College in Roanoke, Virginia. Mr. East is a student this year at this school, and Mr. West was a student in former years and is now Assistant Cashier of the First National Exchange Bank of Roanoke.

Each of these gentlemen has given me permission to pass this information along to you.

Sincerely yours,
M. C. Townsend
Personnel Director

MCT:Ea
Enc.

The Emblem of the Efficient School

ROBERT FERN DALLAS TEXAS MAR 1933

CAN BALANCE A QUARTER ON ITS EDGE ON HIS NOSE

BY BEARING DOWN COIN HARD - HE MAKES CREASE ON NOSE -

WHILE MAKING CREASE - HE SHAKES HEAD IN "YES" MOTION - RELEASING COIN OCCASSIONALLY TO SEE IF COIN WILL STAND ALONE -

WHEN COIN STANDS ALONE - HE RELEASES FINGERS - THEN SLIGHTLY, BUT QUICKLY SHAKES HEAD IN "NO" MOTION -

SIMPLE TO WATCH IT - - IT'S NOTHING MORE THAN MOMENTUM -

TAKES HIM ABOUT 3 MINUTES TO GET CONTROLL OF COIN -

CAN HOLD IT FOR ONLY APPROXIMATELY 25 SECONDS -

I HAD TO USE A BLACK BACK GROUND TO SHOW COIN - HAVE SPOILED SEVERALS PICTURES - HAVING HAD DIFFICULTY IN SHOWING COIN AGAINST OTHER THAN BLACK BACK GROUND -

FERN IS LEAVING FOR SAN ANTONIO MAR. 13 - IF EXCEPTED - DESIGNATE DALLAS - (HE ASKS)

Robert Fern

W. L. MONTGOMERY
116 E 104 ST
CHICAGO

Dear Mr. Ripley

A Compendium of Curioddities from the Believe It or Not! Archives

In Celebration of the 100th Anniversary of Robert Ripley's Birth

Dear Mr. Ripley

A Compendium of Curiodditites from the Believe It or Not! Archives

Compiled and edited by
Mark Sloan, Roger Manley, and Michelle Van Parys

A Bulfinch Press Book
Little, Brown and Company
Boston Toronto London

A META Museum Project

First Edition
Library of Congress Cataloging-in-Publication Data
Dear Mr. Ripley : a compendium of curioddities from the Believe It or Not! archives / compiled and edited by Mark Sloan, Roger Manley, and Michelle Van Parys. –1st ed.
p. cm.
"In celebration of the 100th anniversary of Robert Ripley's birth."
"A Bulfinch Press book."
ISBN 0-8212-1968-5
1. Curiosities and wonders. I.Sloan, Mark. II. Manley, Roger.
III. Van Parys, Michelle. IV. Ripley, Robert LeRoy, 1893–1949.
V. Title: Dear Mister Ripley.
AG243.D47 1993
031.02–dc20 92-23246

Book design by Eric Baker Design Associates Inc, NY
Cover airbrushed by Ron Bertuzzi, NY

Bulfinch Press is an imprint and trademark of
Little, Brown and Company (Inc.)
Published simultaneously in Canada by
Little, Brown & Company (Canada) Limited

Printed in the United States of America

This book is dedicated to the memory of

ROBERT LEROY RIPLEY

1893–1949

R.I.P.

Contents

Notes to the Reader. All of the photographs in this book came from the immense Believe It or Not! Archives. The majority of these materials **have never been published before.** This is the backup documentation that Ripley required for his cartoons. Each caption is followed by the date that the cartoon appeared. Some of the photographs have visible pencil marks on them, which were likely applied by Ripley himself as he used the original photographs as the basis for his cartoon drawings. **None of the photographs in this book is the result of trick photography.** There are occasional examples of hand-applied modifications, but these additions are obvious.

If you know of an unbelievable fact or unusual item you think should be in our next book, please send it to Ripley's Believe It or Not! Museum,
19 San Marco Avenue, St. Augustine, Florida 32084.

Albert J. Smith of Dedham, Massachusetts, was billed as The Busiest Man in the World: A One-Armed Paper Hanger with Hives.

Ripley
Believe it or not!

PREFACE: PROSPECTORS OF THE PECULIAR

When we met in the middle after starting from both ends of the 300-foot-long files of the Ripley's Believe It or Not! Archives, we may have felt like driving a golden spike or cracking a champagne bottle, but instead stumbled to a trio of massage therapists to get the kinks worked out of our backs. The arduous task of tunneling through the millions of letters and drawings and photographs sent in to Robert Ripley over the decades of his worklife—ourselves hunched over, straining our eyes in narrow passageways between the ranks of file shelves, sifting through the Strata of the Strange (as we affectionately called it)—might faintly compare with working a mine, but the sense of discovery, the excitement we felt each time we pulled some new nugget of weirdness from the already enriched ore, sustained us through the whole long job. We had entered a realm of outlandish frontiers and alternate realities that had been discovered in otherwise ordinary neighborhoods and farms scattered across the continent. We were miners working the Mother Lode of Oddity; we had become prospectors roaming through the territory of the unusual.

DR. A. BOINKER of Jersey City, New Jersey, demonstrates his unusual specialty of being able to jump from a train going 20 miles per hour—backwards! (June 23, 1932)

Our first encounter with the Ripley Archives occurred in 1988, while we were working on a book called *Hoaxes, Humbugs, and Spectacles: Astonishing Photographs of Smelt Wrestlers, Human Projectiles, Giant Hailstones, Contortionists, Elephant Impersonators, and Much, Much More!* Under the aegis of the META Museum (a conceptual, unincorporated creative collaboration founded by the authors in 1985), we had visited nearly a hundred state and local historical societies, archives, and photographic collections throughout the United States and Canada, hunting for visual records of "human spectacle." At our first eyeball-to-emulsion encounter with only a few of the many hundreds of thousands of never-before-published images in the holdings of Ripley's Believe It or Not! we knew right away we had another book to do, this time concentrating only on this one great collection.

The enormity of the task nearly overwhelmed us at first. Robert Ripley, and later his staff, had filed correspondence relating to the cartoon chronologically week by week for more than half a century. We decided to narrow our focus by concentrating primarily on the three decades of Ripley's worklife, and even that left more than sixteen hundred weeks of correspondence to sort through, most of it handwritten on everything from banana leaves to aluminum foil. It would have been a huge undertaking to read mail received by any well-known person over a thirty-year period, but this was Ripley, who received more mail than anyone in history, and the job seemed nearly impossible.

After the first few achingly long days we were dismayed with our progress: we had proceeded toward each other only a matter of inches, and it looked as if we would grow old before we even came within sight of each other working from opposite ends of Ripley's career. But as our skills at sorting slowly developed, the speed picked up. For instance, if while flipping through a file our eyes fell on the words scrawled in pencil across the top of a sheet of foolscap

"Dear Mr. Ripley, I'm the eleventh . . ."

we'd learned to flip immediately to the next letter, because the writer is about to say, "I'm the eleventh son of the eleventh son born at eleven o'clock on November 11, 1911," like scores of others who excitedly contemplated their own numerological uniqueness and wrote Robert Ripley to say almost exactly the same thing. A *little* fascinating, maybe, if mainly for the way they kept turning up in the files, but these finds weren't particularly visual, and photographic imagery was our quarry. We could also skip any letter that didn't include a photo, although most did.

The next file might open to a yellowed snapshot of a man gingerly presenting a shaving brush with only a few bristles still attached to the handle, and again we'd come to know it was safe to keep flipping: this is the ninth or tenth time this day we'd run across a shaving brush that miraculously served its owner for decades, finally entering the realm of almost unbelievable longevity—or not, as we'd quickly decide, and go on ahead.

The Marshall Brothers Dry Creek Holstein Ranch in Cheboygan, Michigan, produced a bull (through artificial breeding) that displayed an upside-down map of the lower peninsula of Michigan on its side! (December 11, 1953)

Often the letters sent in to Ripley would include poignant descriptions of the sender's financial plight, along with instructions detailing how much money was to be sent, under the mistaken impression that Ripley or his newspaper syndicate paid huge rewards for each entry. Belief in this rumor, so widely held it nearly constituted a folk legend, was undoubtedly fueled by the highly publicized Ripley contests in which amazing prizes (cars, airplanes, etc.) actually were given away. Most senders were content to receive the customary *Ripley's Believe It or Not!* book for their efforts. A great many people sent in their suggestions hoping to become famous, and indeed anyone who actually appeared in the cartoon *was* famous across the nation, albeit briefly. This was such a momentous occasion to many that they left word it should be mentioned in their obituaries!

After tickling through file after endless file, we began to suspect that oddity, like the universe itself, might be finite. Only Ripley's Believe It or Not! had amassed enough raw data on oddity to make such a conclusion possible.

This isn't to say we became jaded. Quite the opposite: we saw so much weirdness, so many odd things in such a compressed time, that the commonplace now seemed the exception. We'd wonder, Why is it that when we crack an egg to make breakfast, there's only one yolk inside? We'd come to feel shortchanged with any egg in the Ripley Archives that had only two yolks.

So many armless guitar players turned up in the files that we began to marvel at anyone who strummed an instrument with mere hands. "What's wrong with that guy?" we'd find ourselves asking. "Why isn't he at least playing it upside down or underwater?"

No, when we say oddity is finite—and this is a realization come to after looking at millions upon millions of the oddest things in the world—we mean that a taxonomy presented itself, and a pattern something like a Peri-ODD-ic Table began to emerge. The ordinary world—the chaotic everyday world that includes simple one-yolk eggs and musicians with all their extremities—might form only one section of such a table. All the other columns on our Peri-ODD-ic Table would be filled with the kinds of things people submitted to Robert Ripley.

Sequences and repetitions (like the "elevens" mentioned above) began to form a category that might also include people who named all their children alphabetically or alliteratively (as in "Dwight, Dwayne, Dwanda, Dworkin, and Dwella Dwindle of Dwyer, Delaware").

Dozens and dozens of duck-shaped sweet potatoes, hand-shaped carrots, dogs with heart-shaped spots, and cows with sevens on their forehead markings began to fall not only into their individual categories, but into a larger column of symbolic subjects that also included cross-shaped trees, snow, cacti, corn, cracks in mountains, and markings on fish. We couldn't resist the Holstein cow with the upside-down map of the Lower Peninsula of Michigan on its side, or the turtle Travis Robison found near Naples, Texas, whose shell looked like the face of a Chinese man.

A turtle marked with the face of a Chinaman, caught in Texarkana by TRAVIS ROBISON in 1933.

Another heading could include all the ironic submissions describing hens that insisted on laying their eggs in frying pans, all the turkeys that flew through butcher shop windows to rest their heads on chopping blocks, as well as all the ironic occupations like deaf phone operators, blind bowlers, bearded barbers, illiterate postmen, teetotaling barkeeps, swimming coaches who couldn't swim, and vegetarian hamburger cooks who had never tasted their own hamburgers. We didn't keep the Vegetarian Party presidential candidate, even though at eighty-six he was the oldest nominee ever to run.

A column of longevity items on the Peri-ODD-ic Table would list not only the folks who had smoked cigars all day every day since childhood and the shaving brushes that had given years of service, but razors and razor strops, hairbrushes, can openers, rolling pins, hairpins, collar buttons, socks, pens and pencils that all survived decades of such hard and constant use by their owners that they now provided them with incessant amazement. Wilbur Wilson of Tulsa sent Ripley a photo of a bicycle inner tube with 119 patches—and still holding air!

Readers would often hedge their bets when they sent items in for Ripley's consideration. "Not only do I have a razor blade that has served me faithfully for more than 52 years and never once been sharpened," wrote one anxious correspondent, "but also I have never gone a single day since age 14 without a carnation in my lapel."

Ripley fans sent in photos or descriptions of enough pocket watches found inside beef hearts, missing diamond rings discovered inside eggs, and lost keys that turned up inside Irish potatoes to set up an improbable Lost and Found Office. But they were run-of-the-mill Ripley correspondence fare, and we rarely set them aside. However, when Clinton Blume went swimming at Manhattan Beach in Brooklyn and bumped into his own monogrammed hairbrush floating in the surf—a hairbrush lost at sea when his ship was sunk by a German U-boat in 1918—now *that* was worth a pause to read the submission right through and a "Hey, come have a look at this!" to each other. Blume won the Grand Prize: an airplane and flying lessons in the 1932 Ripley's Contest with that entry. It didn't have a very exciting photograph, though, so back into the file it went, along with the letter from the man who scratched his initials onto a coin in California and had the same coin turn up in change in New York City five years later. . . .

There's often a fine line between the mundane and the truly miraculous, and whenever possible we opted for the latter—unless, of course, things were somehow miraculously mundane. Drinking a lot of water may not be miraculous in

16

and of itself, but when Edd Woolf downed almost six gallons and *still had room for a malt and sandwich* (see page 163), he crossed that line.

It was fun to think about a beer stein falling from the window of a third-floor tavern and landing on the sidewalk below without spilling a drop (or killing a passerby), but somehow the incident lacked that certain *je ne sais quoi* we were after for this book. If, say, it had dropped into the hands of a determined Prohibitionist and a photographer had captured the surprised and disgusted look, we might have included it here. Whenever possible, we wanted our lilies gilded!

The Ones That Got Away

A great deal of oddity failed to make it into this book because tastes, habits, social mores, and civil rights have changed since the heyday of Ripleymania. In the 1990s, for instance, when everyday wearing of hats is an exception rather than the norm, it's hard to share the thrill of all those who wrote Ripley to make the bold claim that they had gone more than a year without donning a cap, or else had traveled from Philadelphia to San Francisco *"without once putting on headgear!"* And even though Bub McKnight and Bill Shumacher thought their feat amazing enough to submit to Ripley, we weren't so impressed: they drove from Statesville, North Carolina, to Los Angeles *without a license plate* on their Model-A Ford! But this was back when there weren't so many patrolmen stalking the highways, either.

We drew other lines at racially or socially insensitive submissions, even though they might reflect in their own way the spirit of the times. We felt that kind of history should be studied, but not repeated. We'll admit to a wistful moment, though, when we considered using a photo of Methodist minister Hugh Williams of Ladora, Iowa, lifting his two-year-old daughter by the hair, but only because she was smiling. . . .

ELMER WILSON of Gorham, New Hampshire hedged his bets when sending in a photo to Ripley. On the one hand he is displaying a shaving brush which gave him 61 years of service. On the other hand he holds a potato that was "raised with only the sprout–no piece of potato was used."(November 19, 1947)

With few exceptions we have not included human or animal "freaks" in this book, though the files bulge with this type of material. For now, we decided to draw the line at Weng, the Human Unicorn, and Lentini, the Three-Legged Man, leaving other such human oddities for future prospectors to uncover and publish, and to limit the images of objects to a few weirdly animalized vegetables unless there happened to be people in the picture too.

A good portion of the Ripley Archives material is more verbal than visual, and because this is primarily a photo book we only hint at the riches with the inclusion of a selection of unusual names. It's enough, for instance, to state that the most expensive brand of perfume sold in the Soviet Union in 1952 was called "Stalin's Breath" without actually having to show you the bottle. We liked the picture of the sign outside the Washington, Indiana, cemetery that said

ANY THING
SO UNIVERSAL
AS DEATH
MUST BE
A BLESSING

and the wonderfully succinct epitaph cut into a rough gravestone that marked the spot where some unknown cowboy lay:

HE CALLED
BILL SMITH
A LIAR

But even though there were perfectly good pictures of these and thousands of other similar items, we left them aside here because as images they lacked that certain intersection of moment and event that makes the rest of the photographs in the book so memorable. We were after *show* as well as *tell.*

Any number of other books could have been done, and perhaps will be, by other workers who might come up with their own Taxonomy of the Odd. Ours is only a single core-sample extracted from an immense and vastly rich deposit, and the veins we worked would be extracted differently by others coming at them from different directions. Though our selection is unabashedly personal, we think our discoveries nevertheless hint at a precious and resilient spirit of human imagination that formed during hard times of economic and international struggle—a spirit still more valuable than gold.

What follows are some of the wonderful nuggets we found.

ROBERT RIPLEY: THE MAN AND THE PHENOMENON

In an era marked by two world wars and the Great Depression, Robert Ripley's *Believe It or Not!* cartoons, books, and radio and television programs provided the public with a much-needed diversion from their daily routine. At the height of his extraordinary career, each installment of the daily cartoon was eagerly awaited by up to 80 million readers. The feature was syndicated in 300 newspapers and was translated into seventeen different languages. Additionally, his two books were best-sellers and his radio and television broadcasts were the most popular of the era. He received more mail than any other individual in history and earned the title of The Modern Marco Polo for his incessant globe-trotting. All this does not begin to describe the phenomenon Ripley created when, in 1918, he penned his first *Believe It or Not!* cartoon.

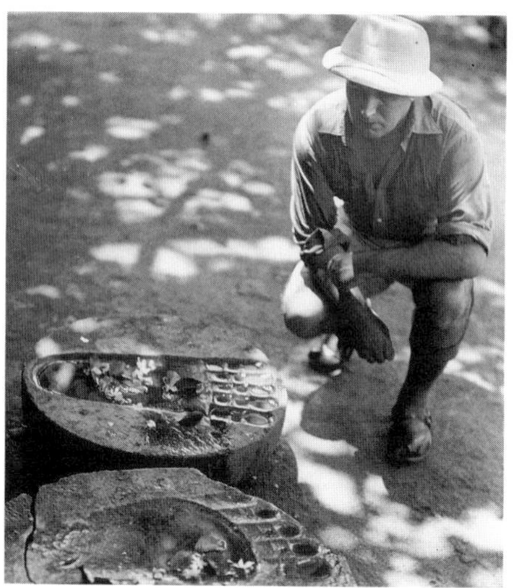

RIPLEY at the Temple of Maha Bodhi inspecting Buddha's footprints, 1936–37.

The Early Years

Robert LeRoy Ripley was born to parents of modest means in Santa Rosa, California, on Christmas Day in 1893. LeRoy, as he was then known, was always interested in drawing and in sports, particularly baseball. A self-taught artist, he published his first cartoon, entitled "The Village Belles Were Slowly Wringing," in *Life* magazine in 1908. The $8 check he received was enough to convince him that his future was in illustration. Ripley was an average student in high school but managed to persuade his teachers to allow him to illustrate the essays that other students were required to write. Young LeRoy Ripley also pitched baseball and achieved some local notoriety until an elbow injury put a stop to that ambition. Luckily Ripley's skills as an artist were very much intact. Through the efforts of a family friend, the fifteen-year-old Ripley landed a sports cartoonist job on the *San Francisco Bulletin* for $18 a week.

After a few successful years there, he managed to land a better-paying job at the prestigious *San Francisco Chronicle*. During his four years in the City by the Bay, Ripley met Jack London and many other luminaries of the literary world and indulged his lifelong fascination with Chinese culture in Chinatown. In 1913 he asked for a slight raise from the *Chronicle* and was promptly fired. Undaunted, Ripley gathered his belongings and moved to New York with no job and little money.

RIPLEY'S **first cartoon. December 19, 1918.**

The New York of 1913 was a thriving metropolis. Ripley was instantly hired as a sports cartoonist for the *New York Globe* at $100 a week, which allowed him to send money back to his ailing mother in Santa Rosa until her death in 1915. Ripley gravitated to the numerous San Francisco transplants now working in New York. Restless after a year at his new job, the young cartoonist took his first trip abroad in 1914, with London, Paris, and Rome on the itinerary. There he visited the world's great museums and exposed himself to many new ideas.

Birth of *Believe It or Not!*

One day Ripley had a fast–approaching deadline but few ideas for his next day's cartoon. He had collected stories of unusual sports feats for quite some time with no particular idea of what to do with them. This time he grouped a selection of these sports oddities for his cartoon and at the top of the drawing lettered the words "Champs and Chumps." Upon seeing the cartoon, Ripley's editor said, "I like this idea, but these guys aren't really champs or chumps." Ripley then looked down at the pad, drew a line through the title, and wrote "Believe It or Not." His life was not to be the same after this cartoon appeared in the December 19, 1918, issue of the *Globe*.

Suddenly *Believe It or Not!* was a hit with the readers and there was a demand for more of these sports oddities. First it was a weekly, then a daily feature, then suddenly his little cartoon was syndicated in more than two dozen newspapers in the greater New York area. After nine more years with the *Globe* Ripley signed on with the *New York Evening Post*.

Ripley in the Book World

Though Ripley had begun his career as a sports cartoonist, he soon realized that believe-it-or-nots could be found in all walks of life. The cartoon garnered scores of admirers, among them Max Schuster of the publishing firm Simon & Schuster, who tried to convince Ripley to put some of his most interesting *Believe It or Not*s between the covers of a book. Schuster even went so far as to dig up a few incredible items and send them to Ripley, but he shrugged off the idea and told Schuster that he was just a "two-cent man," the cost of a daily newspaper. Somehow, Schuster managed to cajole Ripley into assembling some of his personal favorites, and in 1929 the first *Ripley's Believe It or Not!* book was released to rave reviews. A second book followed a few years later, then a third, omnibus edition, which was a combination of the first two books, was released in 1934. Millions of copies sold even though they were released during the dark years of the Depression.

RIPLEY'S contest submission (with cross-eyed cat).

The Hearst Connection

With his books climbing the best-seller charts, Ripley was on the way to becoming an institution. During the late 1920s, the newspaper business was dominated by King Features Syndicate, presided over by William Randolph Hearst. After seeing a copy of Ripley's first book, Hearst sent a two-word telegram to Joe Connoly, one of his operatives in New York: HIRE RIPLEY. Ripley was then in the enviable position of having several offers from rival syndicates, but after discussing the proposition with several of his associates, he decided to go with Hearst and signed with King Features Syndicate on July 9, 1929.

RIPLEY with local residents in Serrinia del Sabo, Panama, 1940.

King Features Syndicate brought *Believe It or Not!* into millions of households every day. Through an ingenious series of locally run contests, Ripley's cartoon began to generate huge mountains of correspondence. Everyone wanted in on the act. Ripley received more than 3,500 letters per day, or a million letters per year, during the thirties and forties. During one contest Ripley received 2,500,000 letters in fourteen days! This explosion of interest forced Ripley to hire a team of secretaries just to sort and edit the incoming mail. Now that the feature was being carried in dozens of foreign newspapers as well, Ripley had to hire translators to help him reach his worldwide audience. The colossal distribution network of King Features Syndicate newspapers was one of the key ingredients to Ripley's success.

The Modern Marco Polo

Ripley stayed close to home during World War I but in 1920 took his first trip to South America. He returned there in 1924 and wrote a column for the *New York Post* called "Rambles 'Round South America." After his first encounter with the Orient in 1923, China became his adopted country. A dedicated Orientalist, for a brief period he even signed his cartoons "Rip Li." The cartoonist had already made many trips, but after he signed with King Features Syndicate and became known as The Modern Marco Polo (a phrase attributed to the Duke of Windsor), all of his travels were highly publicized.

While his newspaper feature was fast becoming one of the most popular of the era, Ripley took advantage of the

Human unicorn. (June 10, 1945)

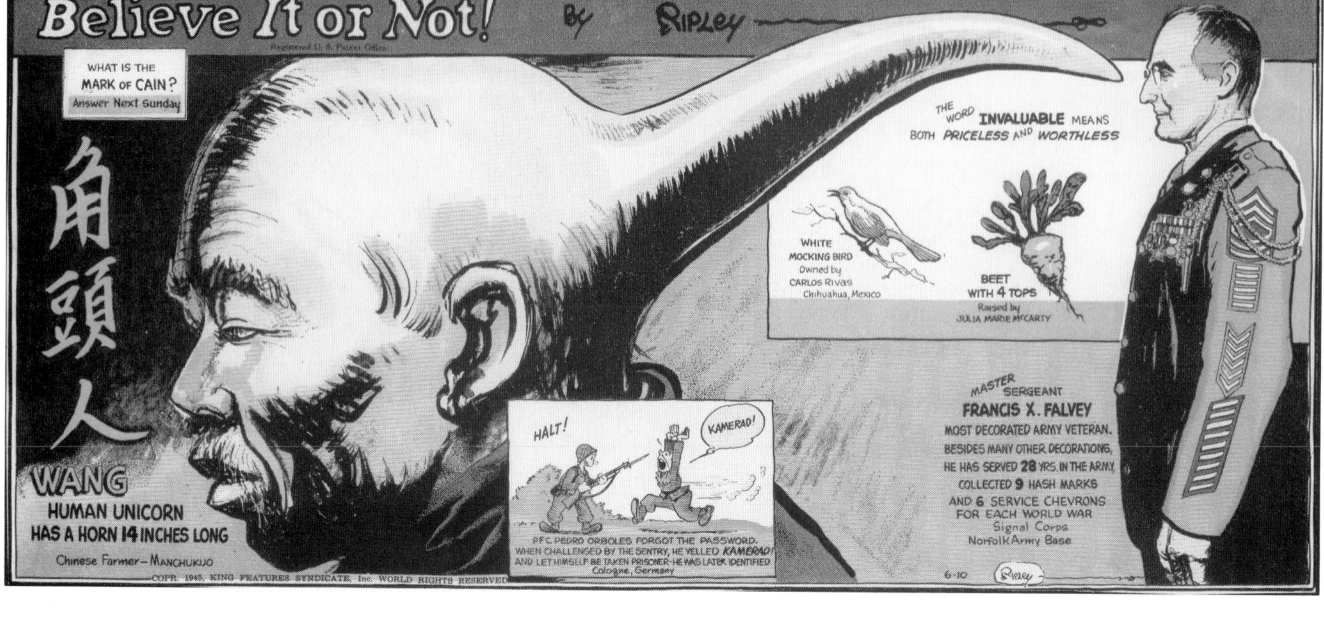

opportunity to travel in search of adventure—and, of course, to hunt for new material for the cartoon. Travel thereafter dominated Ripley's life, and with his passport stamped by 198 countries, he became the most widely traveled man of his time. As befitted a man of his celebrity, he traveled by luxury steamer and airplanes, but, as a connoisseur of the unusual, he also straddled camels and donkeys and floated by gufa boat. Because of his association with Hearst, Ripley had virtually unlimited wealth at his disposal. He traveled to some of the most primitive and remote corners of the globe in search of ever stranger wonders and curiosities. The more remote and inaccessible the location, the more Ripley enjoyed going there.

Many of his comings and goings were celebrated with lavish feasts and parties. Fifteen hundred people attended one soiree at the Waldorf-Astoria ballroom, where the dinner menu was penned in fifteen different languages.

Despite the economic hardships pounding the United States during the 1930s, Ripley weathered the Depression with an annual income of approximately $500,000. However, his success had not blinded him to the disparity between rich and poor. After his visit to the Soviet Union in 1934, Ripley wrote a scathing indictment of the Communist government and called the country "a great poorhouse," where thousands of citizens were starving and the living conditions were unbearable. Since his columns were carried by the largest newspaper syndicate in the world, the Communist government branded Ripley *persona non grata,* forbidding his return. Ripley, always a fierce patriot, donated his time freely to worthy causes—selling war bonds or raising morale at home after the outbreak of World War II.

Famous for his constant globe-trotting, Ripley became a member of the Circumnavigator's Club, and the Royal Geographic Society made him a Fellow. To commemorate his obsession with travel he had a giant compass embedded in the floor of his Mamaroneck home that indicated the mileage to various faraway destinations. In his thirty-five years on the road Ripley traversed a distance equal to eighteen revolutions around the planet. On one expedition he crossed two continents and covered over 24,000 miles from New York to Cairo and back. The modes of travel for this journey included 15,000 miles by air, 8,000 by ship, and over 1,000 miles by camel, donkey, and horse.

RIPLEY cartoon with Charles Schulz illustration.

Anvil lifter. (October 27, 1946)

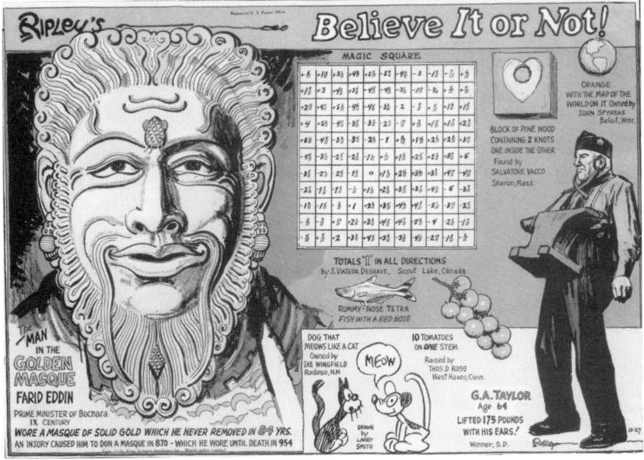

Evolution of the Cartoon

Ripley's bold style of cartooning spurred many imitators. None, however, ever got very far. In Ripley's case it was not only the drawings that captivated viewers, but the stories behind them as well. One gigantic advantage Ripley had over his competition was that his readers kept him supplied with more material than he could possibly use. Readers were constantly trying to one-up a feat they had seen in the cartoon, and in this sense it was not merely a reflection of the society, it actually fed on itself. An example would be the case of a waiter named Mr. Hugo (page 44), who could carry eleven cups of coffee with one hand. After seeing this feat chronicled in the Ripley cartoon, Charles Russell (page 45) carried twelve cups of coffee in one hand while holding his sister over his head with the other. While he was wearing ice skates. This kind of sportsmanship was part and parcel of Ripleymania.

Ripley's admirers and cartoon hopefuls sent him all kinds of documentary evidence of their particular claims to fame, but Ripley preferred photographs over all other forms of proof. Most of his cartoons were drawn directly from these photographs. In the days before the photocopier, Ripley lightly covered the back of the photograph with graphite from a pencil. He would then flip the print over, lay it on a sheet of paper, and firmly outline the figure directly on the surface of the picture. When he lifted up the photo, there would be a faint outline traced by the graphite on the blank paper below for him to use as the basis for the cartoon. As a commercial illustrator Ripley depended on photographic documentation, both as evidence and as visual catalyst.

Occasionally, Ripley fans would send in one of their own drawings to entice the master. Fledgling cartoonist Charles Schulz, who later created *Charlie Brown* and *Peanuts,* first appeared in print in a 1937 Ripley cartoon. Schulz, who submitted a drawing of his dog, was twelve years old at the time. The dog was the model for the now famous Snoopy character in Schulz's wildly successful cartoon.

Color postcard
from the Chicago Odditorium, 1933.

24

FRANÇOIS RUSSELL, **removes nails with his teeth.**

Odditoriums

At the 1933 Century of Progress World's Fair in Chicago Ripley unveiled his first Odditorium. This landmark exhibition contained posters of *Believe It or Not!* cartoons, shrunken heads, instruments of torture, medieval chastity belts, and other strange artifacts from around the world. Living performers served as proof of some of his more colorful cartoon personalities. This type of museum was a direct descendant of P. T. Barnum's American Museum in New York City of the 1840s. One of P. T. Barnum's most famous and celebrated hoaxes involved the Fiji Mermaid, wherein prospective museum-goers saw an artist's rendition of the beautiful, buxom maiden-fish of legend and lore, yet upon entering found a monkey's head clumsily joined to the body of a fish. The gambit netted Barnum a national reputation as a showman and an ace promoter, along with boosting the coffers of the American Museum. When Robert Ripley purchased a Fiji Mermaid that was said to have once been owned by P. T. Barnum, the historical links and natural affinities between these two born showmen were clearly demonstrated.

RIPLEY and friend with the Fiji Mermaid, New York Odditorium, 1939.

Visitors fainted by the dozens at the Chicago Odditorium, yet it was one of the most heavily visited of all of the World's Fair attractions during the two-year run of the Century of Progress. More than two million people passed through the Odditorium doors in 1933. Inside they witnessed contortionists, fireproof people, razor blade eaters, sword swallowers, magicians, eye poppers, and other live attractions. Ripley disdained the term *freaks* and insisted his employees refer to unusual people instead as *oddities*. The showing in Chicago was so successful, Ripley soon opened other Odditoriums in Cleveland, Dallas, San Diego, San Francisco, and New York. By the time his New York Odditorium opened on Broadway in 1939, Ripley had toned down some of the more extreme acts from the Chicago days. Fewer people fainted anyway.

26

Joe Laurello, Head Turner.

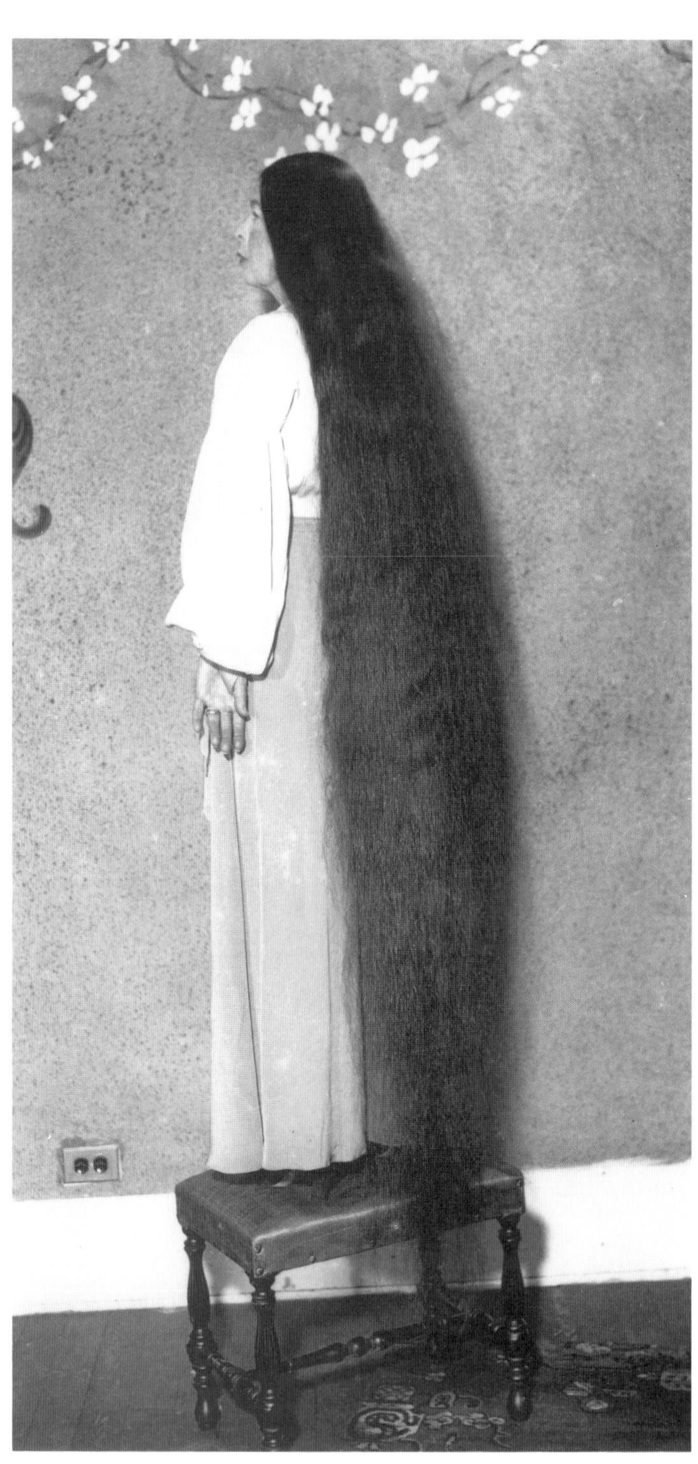

Lydia McPherson,
The Longest Red Hair in the World.

SINGLEE, The Fireproof Hindu.

THE GREAT OMI, The World's Most Heavily Tattooed Person.

HABU KOLLER, The Iron Tongue Man.

ANCIENT TORTURE DEVICES...SEE MUMMIFIED HUMAN HEADS...SEE ACTUAL REINCARNATION OF THE "FORBIDDEN CITY"...SEE WEAPONS OF THE CANNIBALS...SEE JESSE JAMES' FIRST GUN...SEE THE CROWN OF NAPOLEON...

The Biggest Entertainment BOMBSHELL That Ever Stunned New York!

Ripley

Believe It or Not!

"ODDITORIUM"

The Greatest ODDITY Show On Earth!

...under one roof!

STEP INTO A FANTASTIC WORLD
OF WONDERS AND HORRORS!

YOU WON'T BELIEVE YOUR EYES!

YOU WON'T STOP TALKING ABOUT IT!

**New York's Fabulous House of Wonders...
With Sights That Will Amaze...
Bedazzle...Educate!**

Thousands Upon Thousands of Awesome,
Unforgettable Curiosities!

- A Spine-Tingling Tableau of Terror!
- Timeless Horrors Ripped From The Forgotten Corners of the Earth!
- A Dazzling Display of Weird Sights and Lost Treasure! and More...More.

Ripley

Believe It or Not!

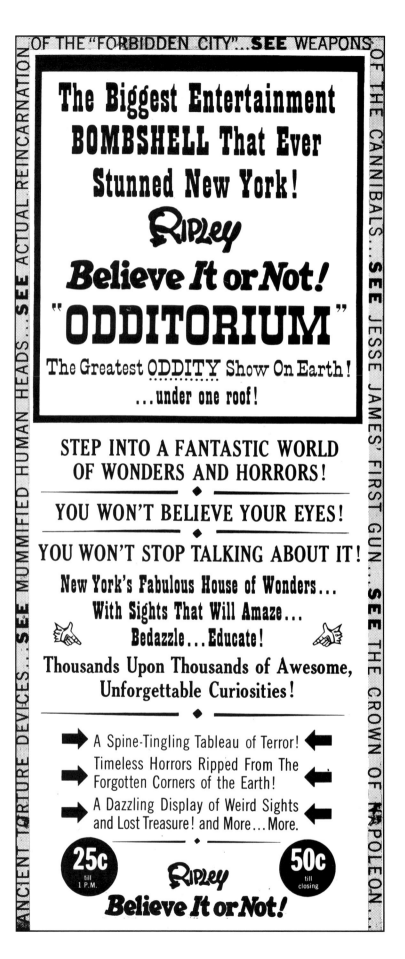

Handbill from New York Odditorium.

Ripley, the Unlikely Broadcast Pioneer

Surprisingly shy in public and afflicted with a slight stutter, Robert Ripley nevertheless became a pioneer in the field of radio and television broadcasting. His first radio broadcast was in 1930 when he delivered a few believe-it-or-nots on a show called the *Collier Hour.* Three years later and with several modifications, the radio version of *Believe It or Not!* expanded to include guest stars and featured a live band. Ripley had been strenuously coached in diction by his producer/director Doug Storer. The *Believe It or Not!* broadcasts were among the most popular of their day, attracting numerous sponsors eager to take advantage of Ripley's popularity. The radio program produced a number of scoops during a time before instantaneous news. One of these was the story of "Wrong Way" Corrigan. This fearless young East Coast pilot wanted to fly across the Atlantic but knew that the authorities would never grant him permission. Corrigan filed a flight plan stating the West Coast as his final destination, yet he ended up in Dublin, Ireland, where Ripley interviewed him: "A fellow can't help it if he gets mixed up, can he?"

Some of the other remote pickups were remarkable for their rarity and for the technological accomplishments they illustrated. For example, one radio program set up a two-way link with parachutist Jack Huber, who gave a blow-by-blow description of a two-mile free-fall plunge before opening his parachute. Other unusual broadcasting locations included the North Pole, the Cave of the Winds under Niagara Falls, Carlsbad Caverns in New Mexico, and Nassau in the Bahamas, where the Duke of Windsor gave his first Western Hemisphere radio interview. One of the broadcasts originated from a twelve-foot canvas boat shooting the rapids of the Colorado River at night. Oddly enough, the announcer on board was a Phoenix-based department store owner named Barry Goldwater.

ROBERT RIPLEY, Birmingham, Alabama, 1948 (with radio equipment).

Earlier Ripley radio programs originated from a small studio where Ripley and his producer dramatized a *believe-it-or-not!* and brought to life the incredible stories behind some of the cartoons. The programs often featured Odditorium performers who were brought into the studio for interviews. In 1940, *Radio Guide* magazine rated Ripley's program as "consistently the most interesting and thrilling on the air."

In 1931 and 1932, Ripley contracted to make a series of twenty-six short talking movie features with Warner Brothers–Vitaphone. In these brief film clips, presented along with newsreels and previews in movie theaters across the United States, Ripley interviewed some of his *Believe It or Not!* personalities or explained some of the more elaborate stories behind his cartoons. Today, these shorts seem amateurish and contrived, but at the time they were among the most popular entertainments available. One of Ripley's favorite ploys was to challenge a popularly held notion. One such *believe-it-or-not!* rested on a rather spurious distinction, but Ripley was correct when he claimed that "Buffalo Bill never shot a buffalo in his life." The animal that roamed the American plains was the bison.

Ripley insured his place in history books when he proclaimed in a 1929 cartoon that the United States did not have an official national anthem. Thousands of readers wrote in response, and Ripley referred their letters to Congress. As a result of the cartoon, "The Star-Spangled Banner" was officially adopted as the national anthem of the United States.

In the early 1940s Ripley also participated in the embryonic days of television. At the time there were only a few thousand television sets in New York City, and the primitive Nielsen-type rating system was conducted with postcards. The war effort drew attention away from this new entertainment technology, but when peace returned Ripley jumped back into television with both feet. The *Believe It or Not!*

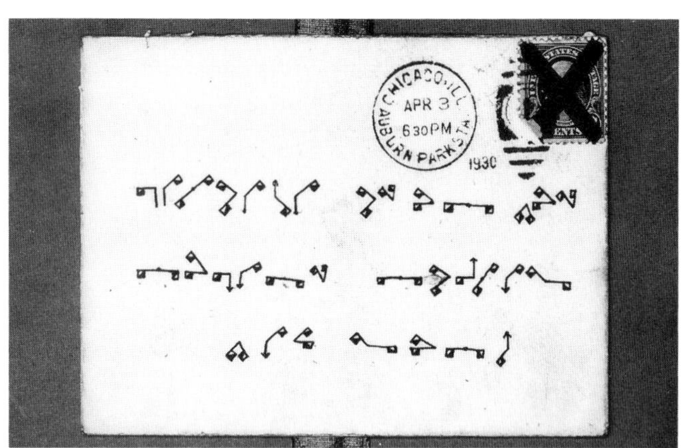

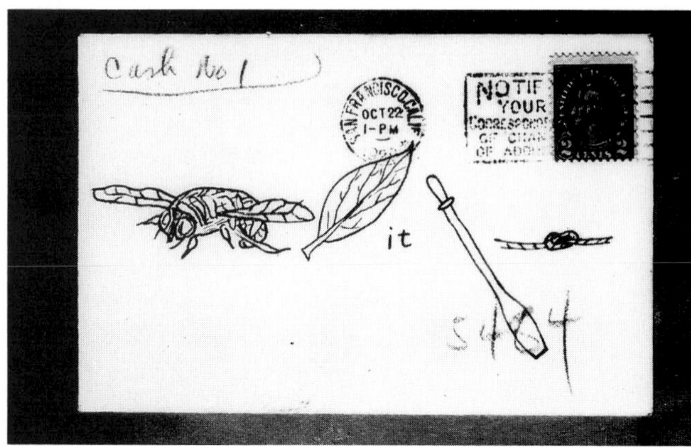

A selection of RIPLEY'S mail.

television series was also one of the most popular of the era, covering much the same ground as his radio broadcasts.

The highlights of Ripley's broadcasting career include several firsts: he was the first to send a cartoon by radio (from London to the *New York Tribune* in 1927); the first to send a drawing by telephone (from Chicago to New York in 1927); the first to broadcast to a nationwide network from mid-ocean (in 1931); the first to broadcast from Australia to New York, from aboard the *Mariposa* (in 1932); the first to broadcast from Buenos Aires to New York (in 1933); and the first to broadcast to every nation in the world simultaneously, assisted by a corps of linguists who translated his message into various tongues (in 1934).

Ripley's Mailbag

Ripley maintained that he would furnish proof of any of his claims if the doubter would send in a stamped envelope. Some of his voluminous mail was from people eager to prove him wrong, but most of it contained suggestions for future cartoons. People sent Ripley photographs, maps, charts, drawings, notarized napkins, and sworn affidavits pertaining to all manner of subjects, attempting to provide conclusive proof of items that would pique the cartoonist's curious mind. Some people went to extremes to provide iron-clad evidence. Many of the verification forms in the Ripley Archives were signed by police chiefs, judges, clergy, or, when absolute proof was required, by bartenders.

The *Believe It or Not!* phenomenon spawned its own fads. One of these was to see who could come up with the most obscure address on their envelope and still have Ripley receive it. There were some truly spectacular examples, including those addressed to him in Braille, wigwag, Morse code, semaphore, and in backwards, upside-down English. Sometimes the envelope would be addressed simply to the World's Biggest Liar. Many had only a squiggly (ripply) line drawn on the front, or there were those who put a photograph or drawing of Ripley on the envelope. One of Ripley's favorite specimens in the unusual mail category was a stamp from Yokohama, Japan, with only the word *Ripley* written on the back, which arrived despite its lack of an envelope.

The *Mon Lei*—an original watercolor by RIPLEY himself.

So prevalent was this fad that the U.S. Postmaster General Walter F. Brown issued a decree on April 30, 1930:

Mail to Robert Ripley will not be delivered if the address is incomplete or indecipherable. Such letters hereafter will be either returned to the sender or sent to the dead letter office. Postal clerks have had to devote too much time recently deciphering freak letters intended for Ripley.

Wayne Harbour of Bedford, Iowa, became so obsessed by the *Believe It or Not!* craze that he spent all his spare time trying to disprove Ripley. For twenty-six years this persnickety postmaster wrote a letter a day challenging at least one claim in the daily cartoon. As of 1970, he had written 22,708 letters to people highlighted in the cartoon and had received 10,363 replies. None of the responses Harbour received contradicted Ripley's claims.

Obsessive Collector

Ripley surrounded himself with objects of his liking. Whether he was at his palatial home in Mamaroneck, New York, called BION (the acronym for Believe It or Not), his sumptuous apartment on Central Park, or his beach estate called Hi-Mount in Palm Beach, Florida, Ripley's personal collection of "curioddities" were in abundance everywhere. His biographer, Bob Considine, claimed that Ripley confused "tonnage with taste" when it came to outfitting his houses. There did seem to be a great many massive objects in all of Ripley's homes. Without question, Ripley's most prized possession was a Chinese junk called the *Mon Lei*, a Foochow riverboat that had been confiscated by the Japanese when they invaded China in the 1930s. In typical Ripley fashion, the ship was modified with a gigantic engine that worked at cross-purposes with the wind-filled sails. There were a number of other vessels in the Ripley fleet: an Alaskan kayak, a gufa boat made of woven reeds in the shape of a giant round basket, a Seminole Indian dugout canoe, and an assortment of more conventional rowboats, but the *Mon Lei* was the skipper's pride. Ripley used the ship both for relaxing and as a floating advertisement. He could be seen sailing this unusual craft near his home on Long Island Sound and occasionally up the Hudson River. The *Mon Lei* was one of Ripley's favorite places to entertain his many guests. He

32

greeted statesmen, celebrities, and common folk aboard this floating anachronism. And what better way to announce the arrival of the creator of *Believe It or Not!*

Besides boats and houses, Ripley had dozens of other interests as a collector. In the 1930s it was still possible for a person of means to travel to distant lands and bring back cultural treasures, which Ripley did, self-consciously living out the myth of the Great White Explorer. He had collections of money from around the globe, Fijian war clubs, Tibetan altar bowls made from the skulls of Buddhist saints, Japanese armor, Samurai swords, and Jivaro shrunken heads, to list but a few of his holdings. Many of these objects later found their way into the Odditoriums, but some stayed in his personal collections at home. One of his favorite conversation starters at BION was his stein and tankard collection, which numbered in the hundreds and included one that was made from the tooth socket of a walrus! Ripley delighted in showing his possessions to visitors, whether in his own homes or in the Odditoriums. No matter how consumed he was in tending to his sprawling enterprise, he could still sparkle as he wondered aloud whether the hair on the shrunken heads continued to grow *after* he acquired them.

RIPLEY with giant cigar, Brazil, 1923.

The Legacy

Robert LeRoy Ripley died of a heart attack on May 27, 1949, at the age of fifty-five, but his legacy is still very much with us. The expression "believe it or not!" has entered the language and has a universally understood meaning, and an organization that bears his name is still in existence and continues to publish the books and cartoon features he created. There is a Ripley Memorial in his hometown of Santa Rosa, California, in a church made entirely out of a single giant redwood tree. He is buried in the Odd Fellows Cemetery.

ALEXANDRE PATTY descending a staircase by cranial hopping. (February 15, 1931)

The golden age of Robert Ripley was during the 1930s and '40s, when his popularity was unrivaled and the phrase "There's one for Rip" was on everyone's lips. Ripley succeeded in creating an American institution that celebrated the uniqueness and diversity of the human spirit. He employed every medium available to tell of the unusual people he had met, places he had seen, and phenomena he had witnessed. King Features Syndicate kept the cartoon going in the style of the master for many years, and today it is produced in-house by Ripley's Believe It or Not! It continues to appear regularly in nearly two hundred newspapers. The Ripley's organization is active and thriving, with new museums opening each year. The collection of over 8,000 objects that Ripley amassed has been dispersed to the various Believe It or Not! museums throughout the world, which continue to attract millions of new fans annually. That the interest in the life and activities of Robert Ripley continues speaks of the universal appeal of the phenomenon he created. Today there are numerous popular television shows that mine the same mother lode that Ripley did, while many of the so-called tabloid newspapers now present items that would fall into the "or not" rather than the "believe it" column.

One of the most enduring legacies left by Robert Ripley is his insistence on the authenticity and verification of the facts presented in the cartoon. His chief of research, Norbert Pearlroth, worked six days a week for fifty-two years at the New York Public Library checking and double-checking the source materials for accuracy. The man who was frequently called the World's Biggest Liar was in fact a stickler for details. The hallmark of the *Believe It or Not!* phenomenon was that the basic outline of these outrageous claims was true, and that Ripley could invariably furnish some sort of proof, frequently in the form of an actual photograph of the oddity he described. More often than not, seeing is believing.

A Delicate Balance

"Etiquette requires us to
admire the human race."

Mark Twain

Joe Horowitz could balance an 18-pound saber on his nose. Billed as the Man with the Iron Nose, Horowitz performed his spectacular act in theaters near his native Los Angeles. **(December 21, 1934)**

Empire

Gravity seemed to be no obstacle for Hurley, Wisconsin's **Eli Vicellio,** who **could lift a table and chair** weighing 70 pounds **with his teeth. (March 25, 1947)**

Five- and seven-year-old **Patricia and Geraldine Ellert** of Baltimore, Maryland, **perform an outstanding feat of agility and strength.** Geraldine is the "understander" and Patricia is the top mount. **(September 4, 1941)**

Twenty-one-year-old **Alice Penfold lifts her sister Mary** on a stool **by her teeth only.** The sisters were from Bury, England. **(December 21, 1953)**

ADRIAN C. FOX of Park River, NORTH DAKOTA, shown here **lifting a 145-pound mandolinist** in a chair supported by his head and mouth. **(July 5, 1936)**

JACKIE DEL RIO chewed not only his steak but the table as well! And not only his own table but the next table and all the chairs! **Two tables and six chairs altogether.** Aside from merely lifting ordinary furniture by his molars, the five-foot-tall Chicagoan was also able to lift a person seated in a chair. **(February 17, 1938)**

Lawn mower hoister **ROBERT DOTZAUER** of Lisbon, IOWA, although crippled in one leg, **could balance three heavy iron mowers on his chin.** Total weight of lawn mowers: 150 pounds. Total weight of Dotzauer: 145 pounds. **(November 12, 1953)**

James Paul, The Greek Titan of Brooklyn, New York, **could lift six persons totaling 735 pounds with his teeth.** He claimed to have had a "weak condition" of the teeth for three years for which he visited a quack doctor in Cypress, Greece, who gave him a special preparation paste that had dramatic results. Favorite foods: cabbage heads and carrots. Height five foot six, weight 140 pounds. **(August 14, 1951)**

South Chicago "Y" physical instructor **Charles Russell lifted two ukelele-playing belles** to prove that music could tame but not weaken the savage beast. **(May 18, 1939)**

CALUMET STUDIO.
CHARLES C. RUSSELL
Y.M.C.A.
ICE SKATING AND BARBELL INSTRUCTOR
LIFTING 265 LB'S.

Squad of men standing on a Douglas fir plywood board at the Elliott Bay Mill Company in SEATTLE. **Only a quarter-inch thick, the plyboard supported their combined weight of 1,833 pounds** without splitting. **(November 1, 1931)**

A magnetic pulley holds a man by the iron nails in his shoes (with co-workers dangling from an iron bar) at Dings Magnetic Separator Company in MILWAUKEE. **(May 4, 1937)**

MR. HUGO, an employee of Brown's Restaurant in NEW YORK CITY, here shown **carrying eight cups of coffee with one hand.** Hugo later topped his own feat by toting ten cups in one hand. He was also able to take orders for twenty-five sandwiches at one time without writing them down and serve them all correctly. **(August 13, 1931)**

Clayton's Café in Tyler, TEXAS, boasted that waitress **BLANCHE LOWE** could **carry twenty-three coffee cups in one hand. (April 9, 1940)**

"PHYSICAL PERFECTIONIST" **CHARLES RUSSELL** received quite a bit of mail after his appearance in Ripley's cartoon on May 18, 1939, prompting him to try even harder for another claim to fame. Russell saw the BION cartoon about Mr. Hugo, who was able to carry eight cups of coffee with one hand, and figured if he **hoisted his sister in one hand and twelve cups of coffee in the other—on ice skates—**he, too, could achieve another entry in Ripley's feature. His logic proved infallible. **(February 21, 1942)**

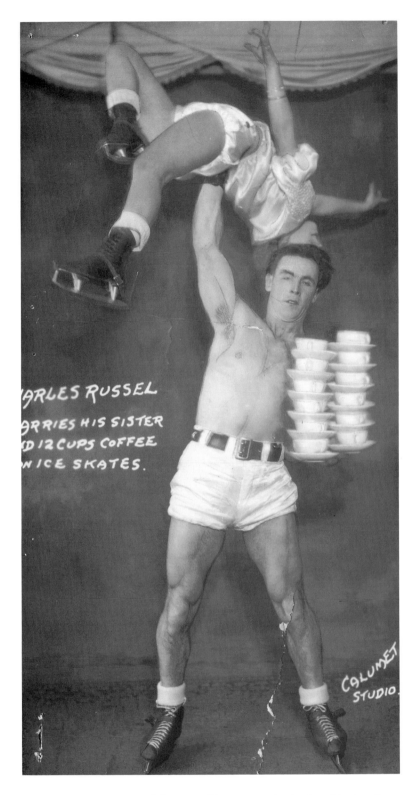

Jeannette, Pa;
June 9, 1931.

Mr. Ripley-: If the feat of Charles Gordon (Holding 17 tennis balls) is worthy of your Believe It Or Not Column Compare it to the two photographs I submit to you.

I am still watching and waiting for results, concerning the two submissions made by Harold Cook, Dec. 27, 1930. The picking up and holding of 18 regulation sized base balls, or 9 in each hand, held with palms down. Also the picking up and holding of 20 pocket billiard balls, or 10 in each hand, held with palms down.

Respectfully Yours,
(The World's Champion)
?

Julius B. Shuster,
#700 Magee Ave.

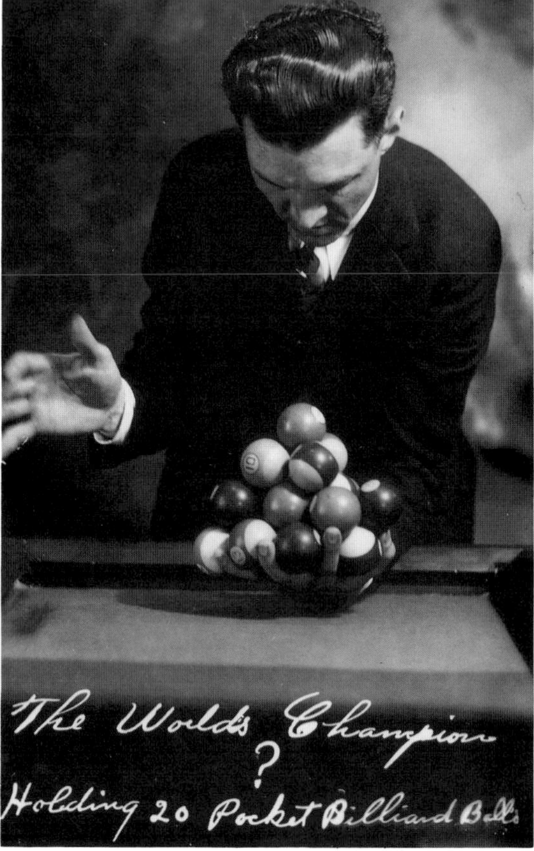

Julius B. Schuster, card sharp and world's champion "Pickup Artist," **held twenty billiard balls in one hand** in Jeanette, Pennsylvania. Schuster was one of Ripley's favorite Odditorium performers, and Ripley frequently featured his manual dexterity skills not only in the cartoon, but also on *Believe It or Not!* radio and television programs. Other stunts included picking up and **holding twenty-five tennis balls and twenty baseballs,** and most difficult of all, picking up from a flat surface and holding ten billiard balls in each hand in such a way that the hands could be turned **in any position, even upside down. (July 6, 1931)**

Joseph E. Wiedenmayer, Jr., of Bloomfield, New Jersey, developed the unique specialty of **lifting eight full quarts of milk with one hand. (September 14, 1932)**

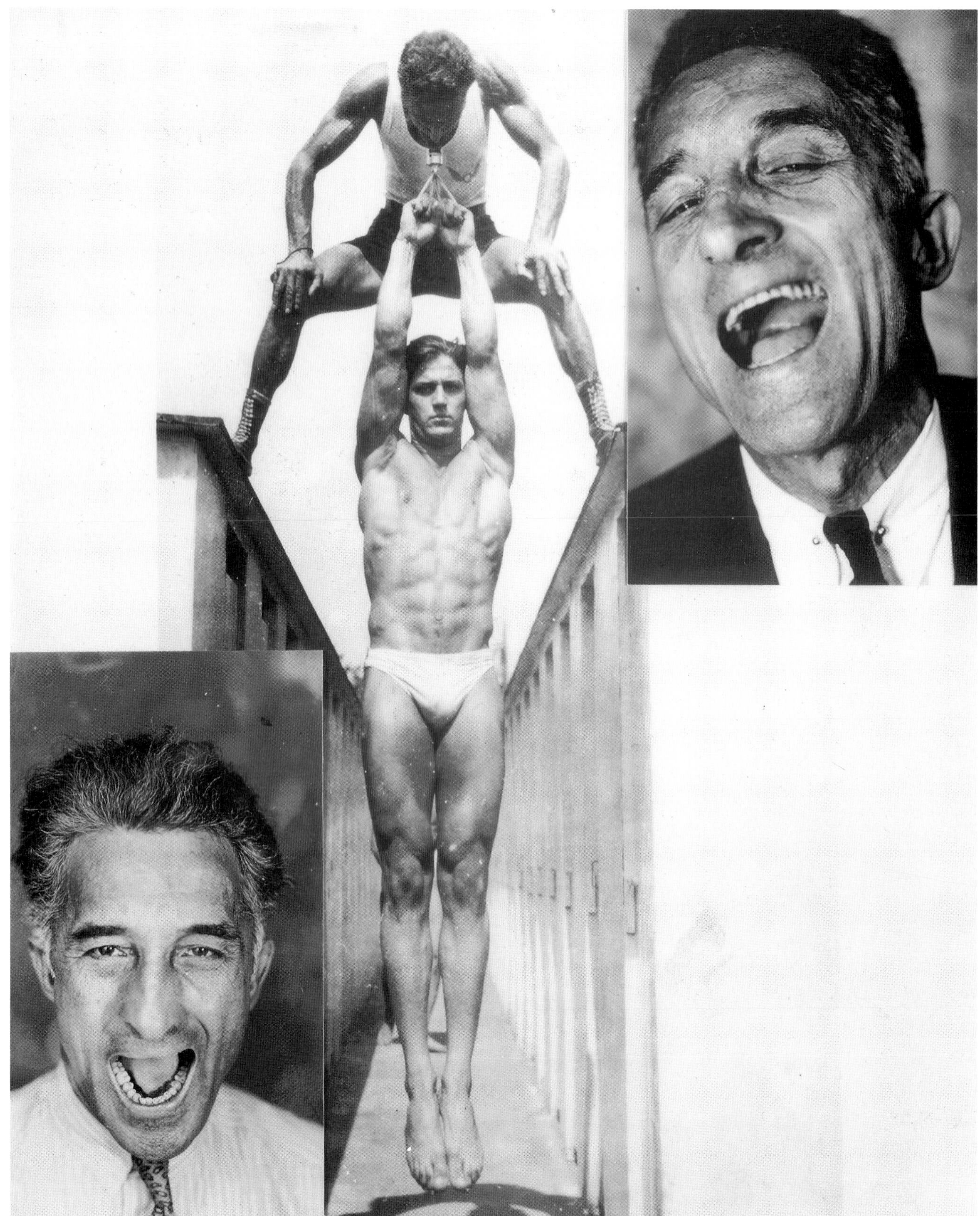

48

For a man who had not used a toothbrush, toothpaste, or tooth powder in over twenty years, **John M. Hernic** sure had good teeth. Here he is shown **lifting a 180-pound man** with little effort. **(December 8, 1935)**

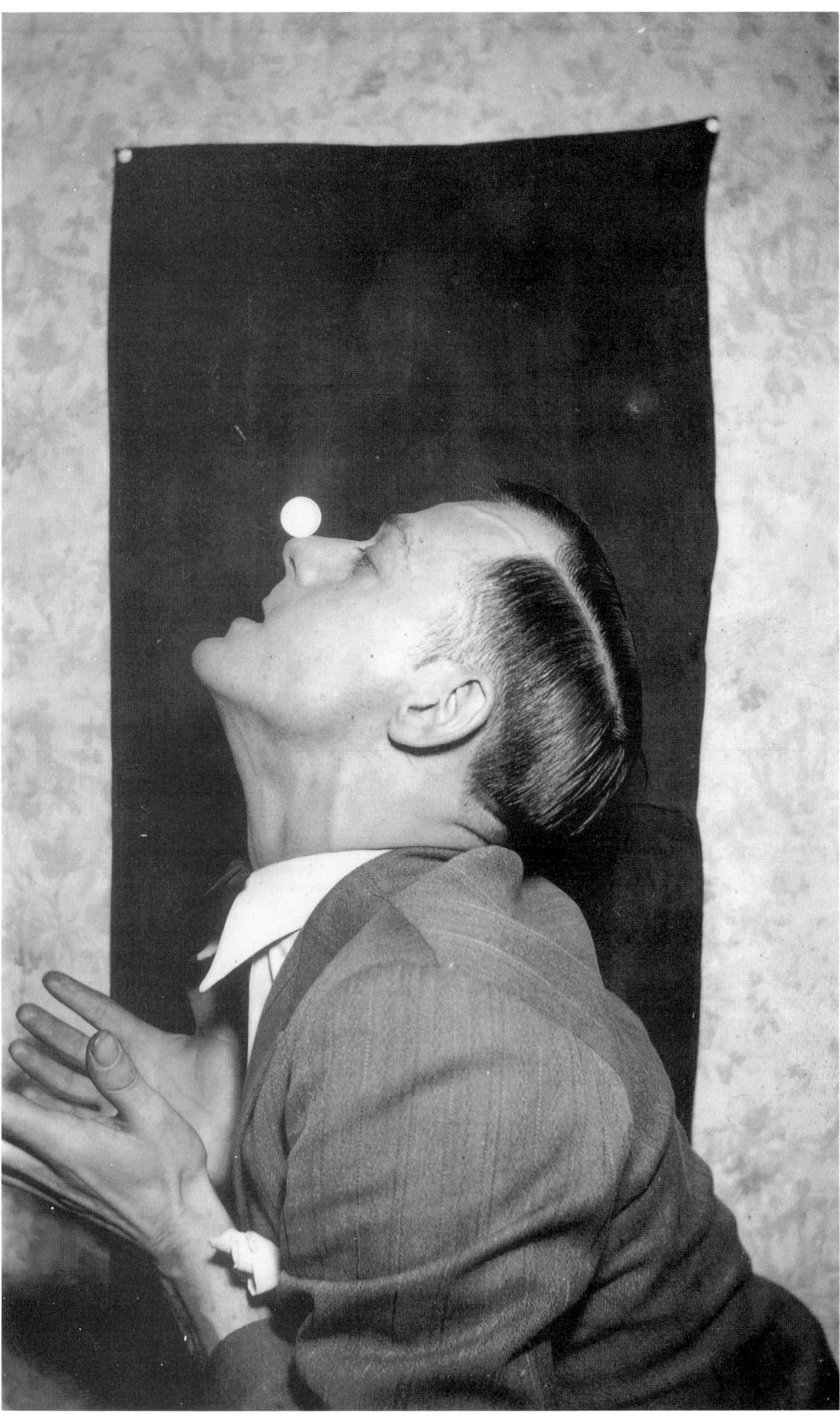

Robert Fern of Dallas, Texas, could **balance a quarter on his nose for half a minute. (June 28, 1933)**

Dislocationists, Contortionists, and Elastic People

"Anatomy is destiny."

Sigmund Freud

Henry D. Lewis, the oldest person in St. Augustine, Florida (itself the oldest city in the United States), **at age ninety-five proved he was still spry.** He said his ability spoke well for the Florida climate, where he had wintered for the last twenty-nine years. **(June 3, 1936)**

HENRY D. LEWIS
95 YEARS YOUNG

Hats off to acrobat **Dad A. T. Brown, who climbed a forty-foot pole** in Grand Junction, Colorado, **on his eightieth birthday.** As if that weren't enough, he lowered himself down headfirst! **(August 7, 1934)**

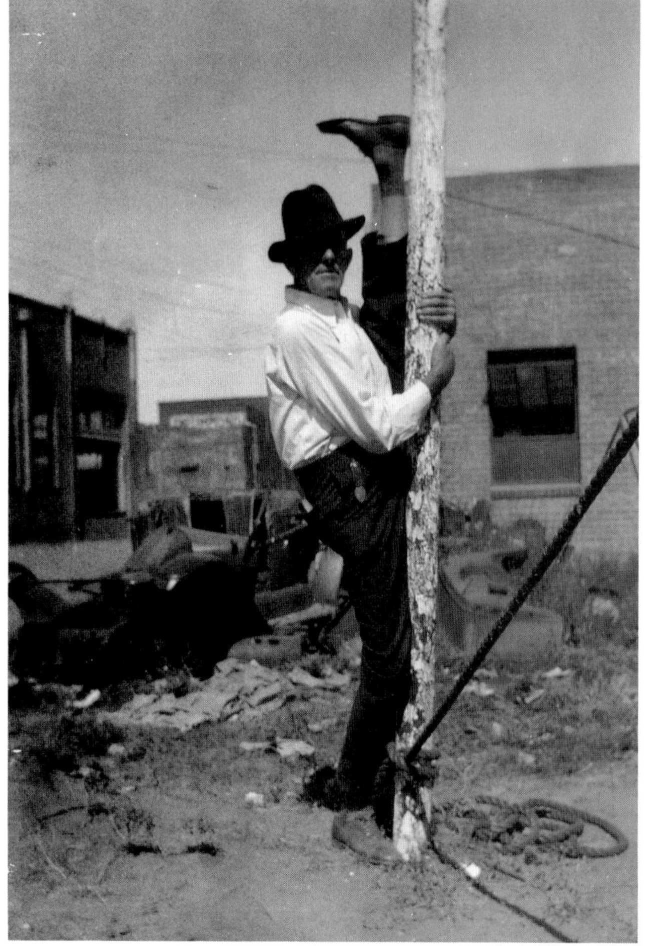

Perry L. Biddle of DeFuniack Springs, Florida, **hoists himself up into a Human Flag** position on his **ninetieth birthday. (October 30, 1936)**

Sixty-four-year-old Ed Thardo performed this contortion feat in Handley, Texas. He was the contortionist for the Harley Sadler Traveling Show for many years. **(March 4, 1934)**

Champion of the Freearm Planche, **sixty-five-year-old W. H. Mering challenged anyone else in the world** to perform this stunt. Mr. Mering taught a hand-balancing class at the Hollywood Y.M.C.A. **(October 11, 1938)**

Robert Aitken of San Francisco could **take off his hat with a doubled-back arm. (November 22, 1938)**

F. Velez Campos, dislocationist, strikes a peculiar pose in Fortuna, Puerto Rico. **(September 23, 1933)**

Is he coming or going? DEMETRIO ORITZ of LOS ANGELES performs the unusual feat of **twisting his body 180 degrees. (August 12, 1932)**

Due to a strange **twist** of fate, **AVERY TUDOR** of NEW YORK CITY was able to **turn his feet around backwards. (December 15, 1936)**

MAY RUTH BASS of Jacksonville, FLORIDA, said, **"I have been kissing the floor, kicking my forehead with either foot, and shaking my hips** [independently of other body parts] **all my life."** What's more, she wrote Ripley to say she could sing a song while kissing the floor, change flat tires and fan belts, and drive a stick shift. **(November 23, 1937)**

WILLIAM D'ANDREA
Contortionist

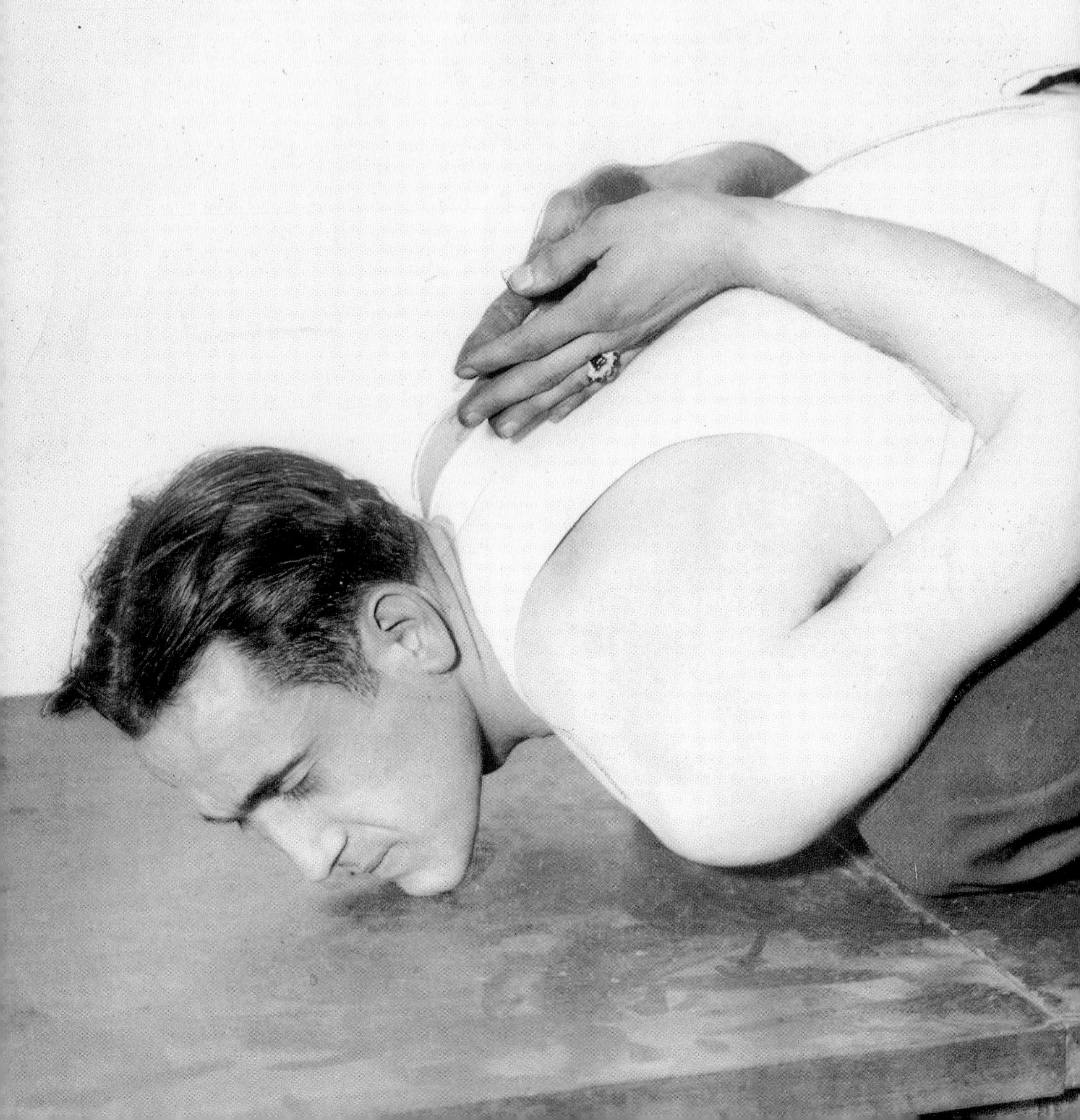

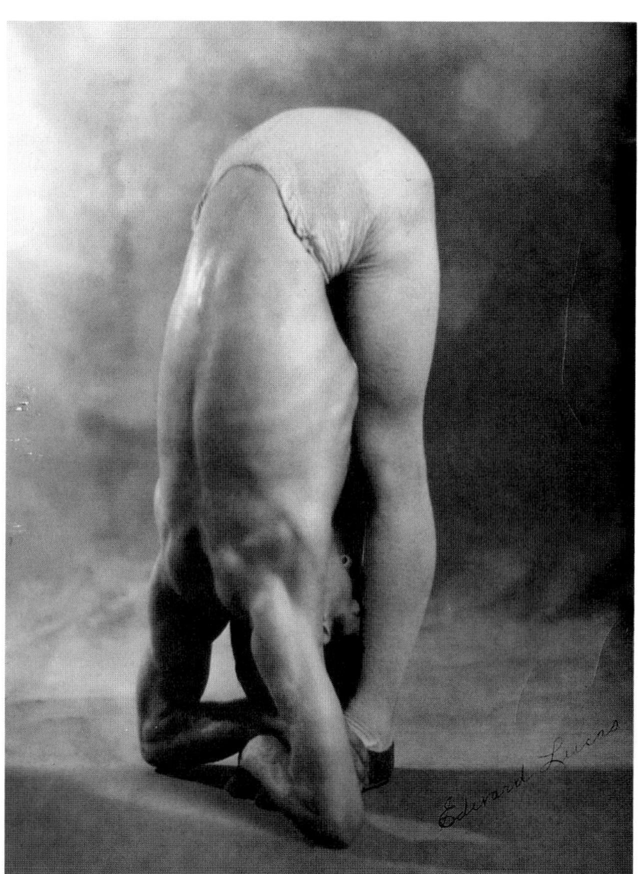

Contortionist **Edward Lucas** of Chico, California, **takes a deep bow.** The young dancer attributed his ability to "loose hips and extremely stretched muscles." **(January 9, 1934)**

William D'Andrea, contortionist of Waterbury, Connecticut, could put his feet in his pockets while standing, in addition to his **unusual praying position. (February 14, 1935)**

60

THE ONLY MAN IN THE WORLD WHO CAN SIT ON A GLASS $2\frac{1}{2}$ INCHES ACROSS THE TOP

THE GREAT JOHNSON, a.k.a. THE SILENT ENTERTAINER, was able to **balance himself on an ordinary 2 1/2-inch-wide drinking tumbler** in addition to performing countless other contortionist poses to dazzle the masses. **(November 6, 1940)**

LOS ANGELES dancer **MISS RENÉE DELUE** and her partner, **RUBY DALE,** demonstrate their version of **a Human Belt.** Appreciative audiences put them **on a pedestal** for many years. **(August 29, 1946)**

MOYNE MULLIN of Berkeley, CALIFORNIA, worked for five years to perfect this **funny-bone balance.** Her entire weight is supported by her elbows. **(January 25, 1948)**

A direct descendant of the Chevalier Troupe of acrobats, **LORRAIN CHEVALIER** of Philadelphia, PENNSYLVANIA, **was actually able to sit on her own head!** The family claims that in 200 years only one person per generation of Chevaliers was suited to this type of work. **(October 24, 1937)**

Jacqueline Terry of Montgomery, Alabama, performing her **unusual jaw-balancing act** at age seventeen in Philadelphia. Rumor had it that her father was an orthodontist. **(October 5, 1948)**

Alma Ynclan, child contortionist of Tampa, FLORIDA, appeared in Ripley cartoons several times, performing such stunts as The Living Cross, **standing on her own back,** and the like. **(April 5, 1937)**

Hammers, Nails, Needles, and Pins

"Democracy is based on the conviction that there are extraordinary possibilities in ordinary people."

Harry Emerson Fosdick

Leo Kongee of Pittsburgh **could drive 60-penny nails into his nose** and stick hatpins into his body without discomfort. He traveled around the country for twenty-three years performing his Painless Wonder act in mud shows before joining the Odditorium Show in 1933. He also **held his socks up with tacks driven into his legs** or with safety pins and thread sewn through his flesh. He sewed buttons onto his arms and tongue and put skewers through his cheeks and nose.
His friends called him Professor Kongee or sometimes Professor Nesbitt. **(September 2, 1934)**

Richmond, VIRGINIA'S own Peruvian fakir, **JOSÉ FERNANDEZ,** could swallow safety razor blades and **drive a 20-penny nail into his head up to the hilt** (if nails have hilts). This feat was witnessed by the *Richmond News Leader* staff and was submitted as their entry in a national Ripley contest.
(July 9, 1932)

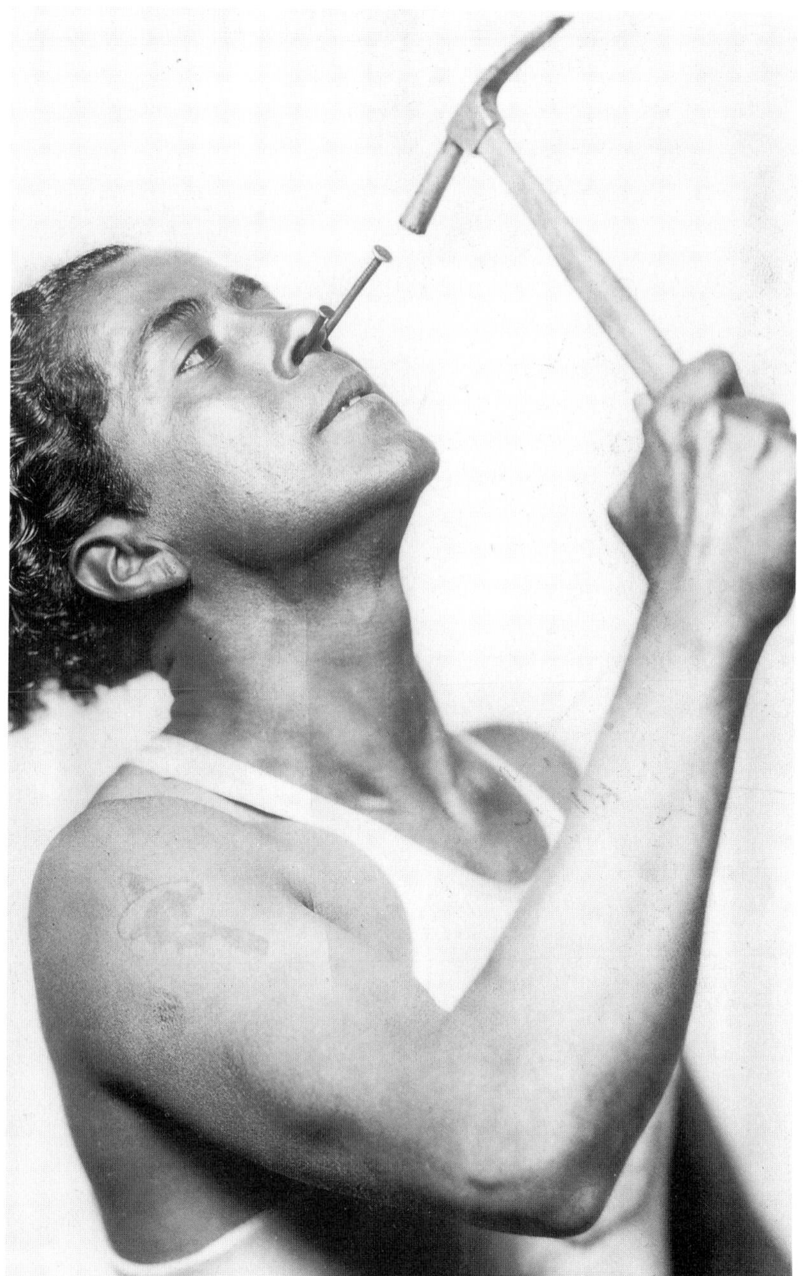

AUGUST L. SCHMOLT of SAN FRANCISCO **banged his biceps with a four-pound hammer daily for forty years** without ever bruising or blackening his skin. No reason was given for this unique pastime, but Schmolt said that he was a "performer" in his youth.
(August 15, 1944)

MRS. JAKE HAMON of Ardmore, OKLAHOMA, had her husband's diamond cuff links made into **a pin that she wore pierced through her throat.** She wore it this way continuously while, presumably, Mr. Hamon's cuffs went linkless.
(December 15, 1933)

CORDELIA STEWART of San Jose, CALIFORNIA, **swallowed a needle as a young woman.** Several years later, **her firstborn child, Julia, produced the same needle from her thigh at six months of age.** The biggest question in this mystery of the migrating needle is how it got swallowed in the first place. **(March 17, 1941)**

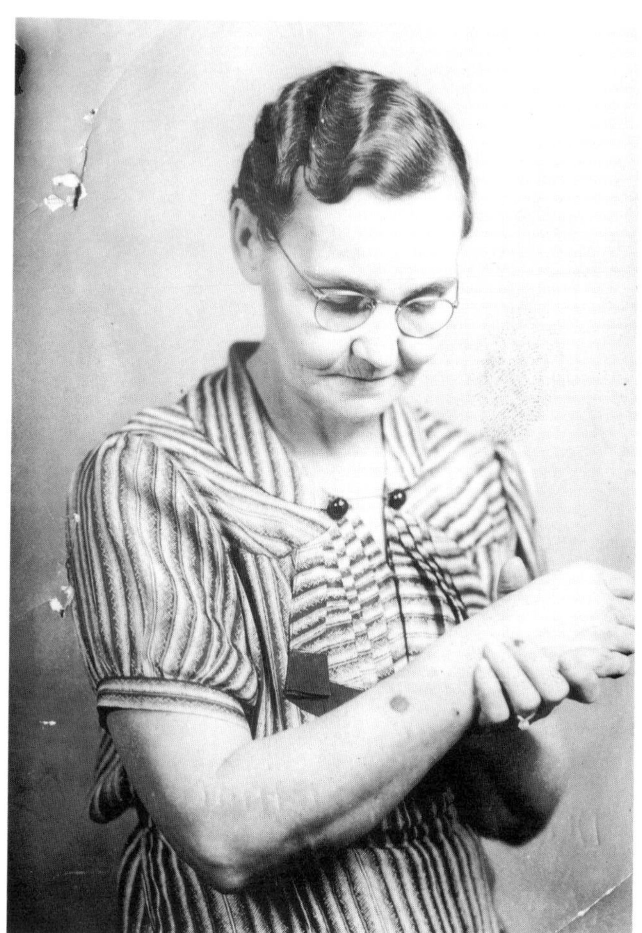

Suffering from an intense pain in her right arm, **MARION LINDLEY** of Springdale, ARKANSAS, went to a doctor who removed a steel needle an inch and a quarter in length from between the bones above her wrist. Mrs. Lindley eventually remembered that she had swallowed a needle when she was a young girl "running and looking up at some bluebirds." **The needle was in her body for thirty-six years. (February 11, 1935)**

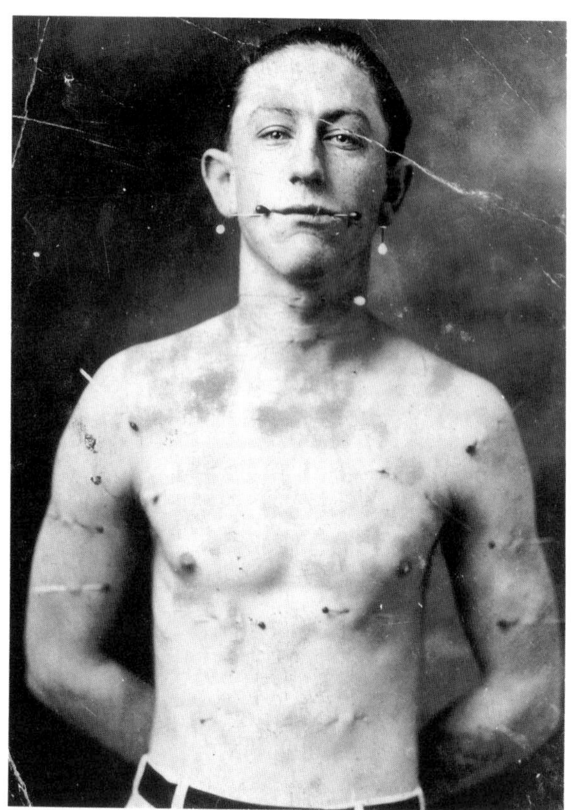

B. A. BRYANT of Waco, TEXAS, could stick as many as a **hundred pins and needles in his body at the same time.** This human pincushion claimed that he felt no pain while doing this. Mr. Bryant performed at the Dallas Odditorium in 1937 to the amazement of thousands. **(May 26, 1937)**

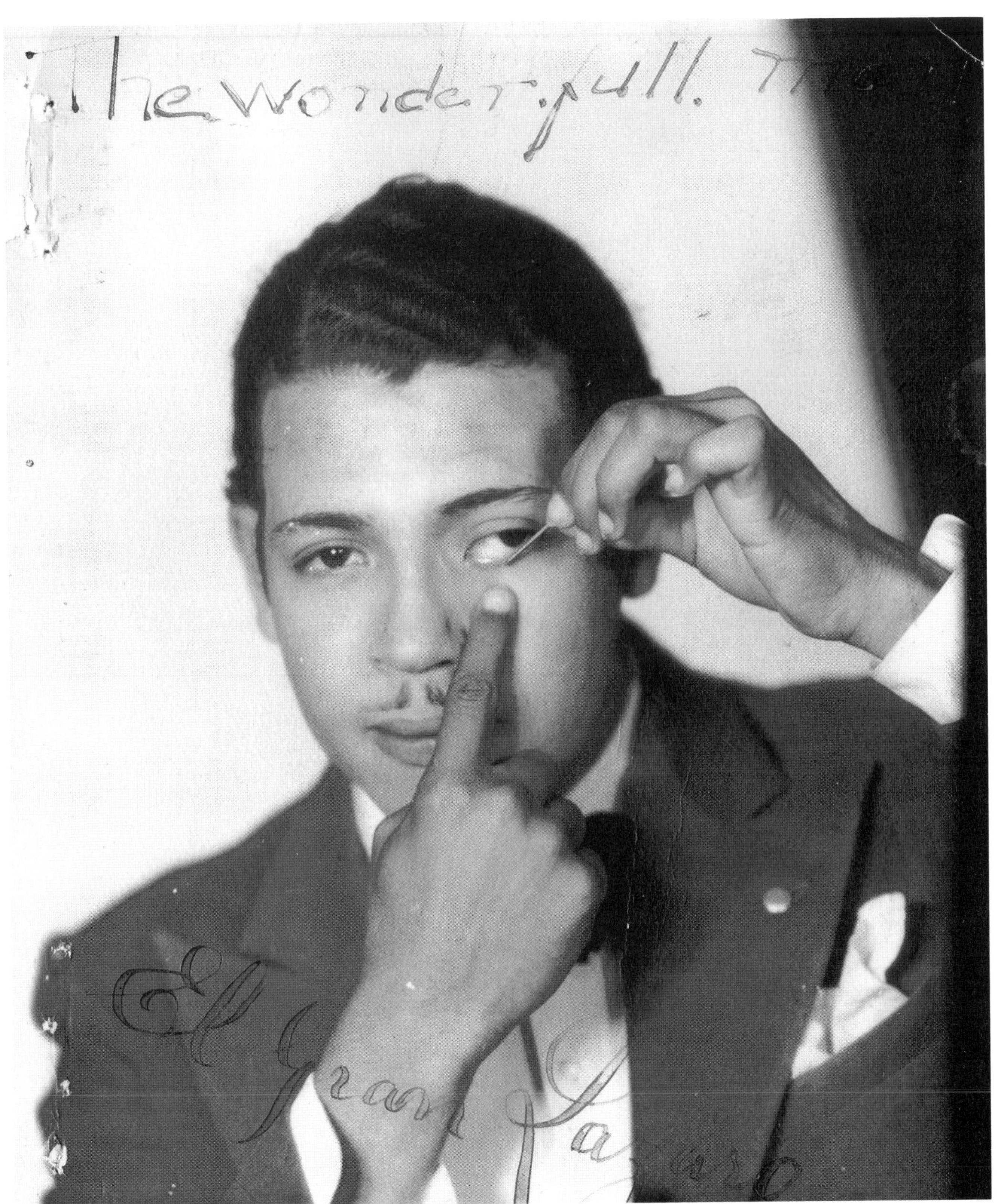

We have all heard that needles have eyes, but **El Gran Lazaro,** El Indio de Baracoa of Havana, could **put a needle in his eye socket and pull it out of his mouth! (February 21, 1935)**

Face Facts

"God has given you one face,
and you make yourselves another."

William Shakespeare

Jimmy Durante's celebrated **schnozzola was insured for $100,000 by Lloyd's of London,** at considerably less than face value. **(November 4, 1932)**

Jackie Gross of Boston could **whistle harmony while playing harmonica with his nose. (August 16, 1947)**

H. C. Harris, Sr., played harmonica with his nose while whistling, in Jackson, Mississippi. All of the dozens of Ripley contestants who submitted their simultaneous whistling and harmonica-playing talents believed theirs was a unique skill. **(March 11, 1933)**

PHONE 62

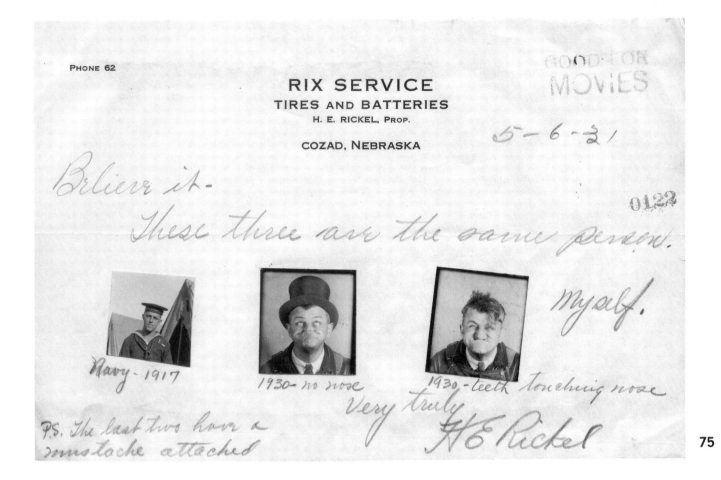

RIX SERVICE
TIRES AND BATTERIES
H. E. RICKEL, PROP.

COZAD, NEBRASKA

GOOD FOR
MOVIES

5-6-31

Believe it-

0122

These three are the same person.

myself.

Navy-1917

1930- no nose

1930-teeth touching nose

Very truly
H E Rickel

P.S. The last two have a mustache attached

H. E. Rickel could **touch his nose with his teeth,** in Cozad, Nebraska. **(November 1, 1931)**

J. T. Saylors of Villa Rica, Georgia, **had a face that could launch a thousand ships. (September 8, 1933)**

76

Claude R. Overholt of Marietta, Ohio, claimed he **could make over a hundred different faces.** He was declared a champion "Acrobatic Facemaker" in New York City by those in the know. **(May 7, 1931)**

James Aagaard of Ord, Nebraska, **had a voice that could be heard over a distance of six miles.** He traveled the Midwest and Canada in the early 1930s presenting his "physical voice culture" theories and singing popular opera numbers. Arriving for one such performance at Plaster Rock, New Brunswick, in 1931, he discovered that there had been a mix-up in the advance publicity, and no one knew of the concert. Aagaard stepped outside the hall and sang two incredibly loud tenor solos, and within an hour people from throughout the county were lined up to attend the show! Aagaard was also said to be the best game shot in Nebraska. **(October 1, 1932)**

Bob Ryan, owner of the Park Restaurant in Hudson, New York, had **his front teeth replaced with seven gold ones set with a diamond in each.** After his restaurant folded he depended on welfare relief for support, refusing to disturb his teeth to retrieve the money they cost. **(June 20, 1938)**

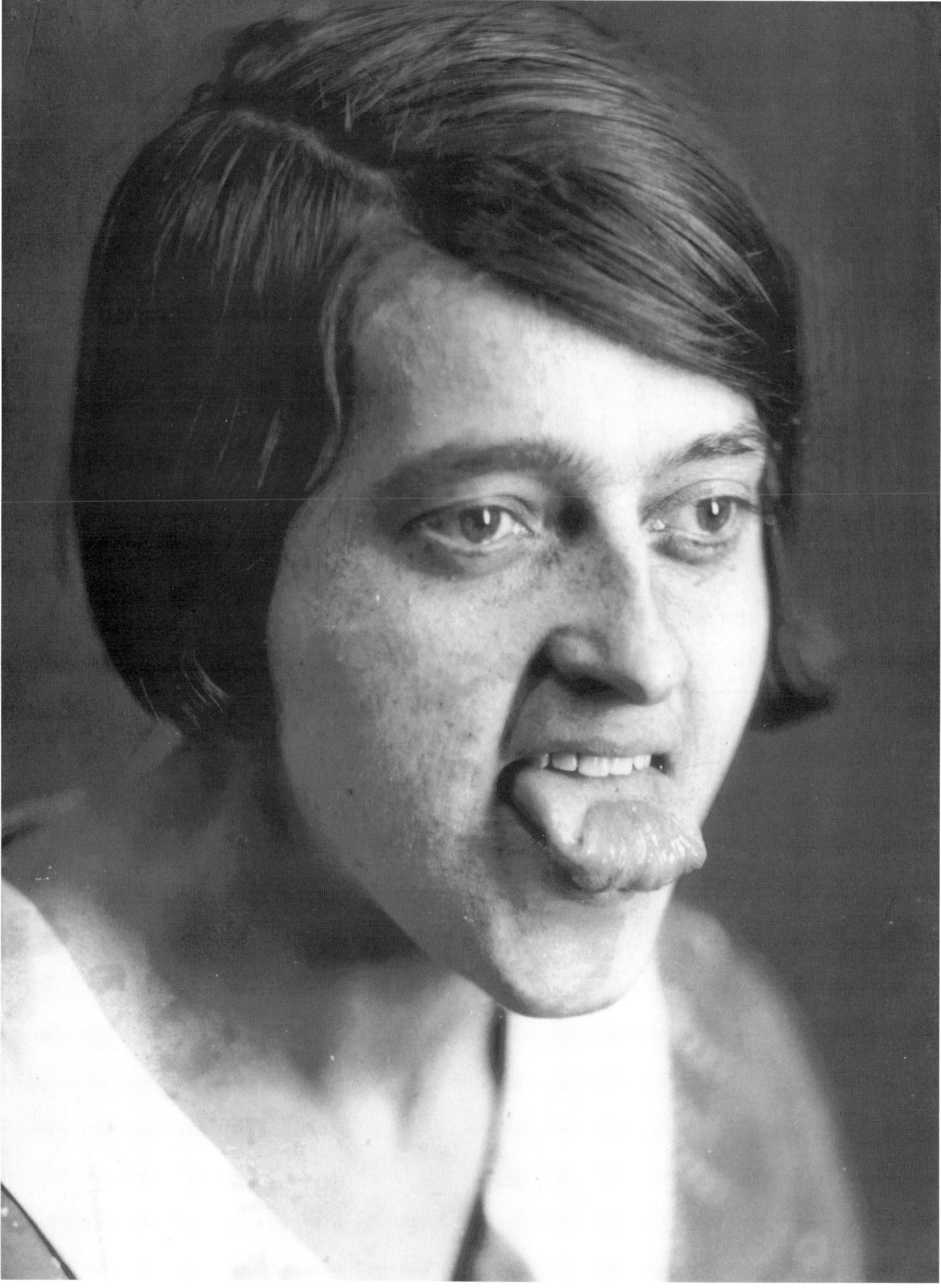

CHICAGO'S **SAUL BROWN blew saliva bubbles with smoke inside.** When they landed they popped like smoke bombs. **(May 30, 1935)**

Tongue-lapper **MARGUERITE ROSSELL** of Burlington, NEW JERSEY, **could fold her tongue at will. (May 6, 1933)**

W. V. Meadows of West Point, Georgia, was shot in the eye at the battle of Vicksburg on July 1, 1863. **Fifty-eight years later he unexpectedly coughed up the Civil War slug** (shown). **(July 21, 1932)**

'Most Sixty Years Ago Bullet Entered Eye; Coughed It Up Today

1921

West Point, Ga., March 21.—(Special.)—After carrying in his head for fifty-eight years, a bullet with which he was wounded in the eye at the battle of Vicksburg, July 1, 1863, W. V. Meadows today coughed up the bullet at his home here, and is feeling all right. Mr. Meadows, who was a member of G company, 37th Alabama infantry, was blinded in one eye by the bullet which he coughed up today.

EASTMAN SMILEY of Hartford, CONNECTICUT, had **a mustache twenty-five inches long. (October 10, 1948)**

Shown here is **BERTHA HOWARD** of Prairie City, OREGON, who **could stand straight up on her five-foot-five-inch-long hair. (September 25, 1946)**

82

Mrs. E. E. Smith of Dallas, Texas, **grew her own hat.** Her Easter bonnet was crocheted out of the hair from her own head, which she had saved for eight years. A spiritualist, Mrs. Smith never allowed her hair to be cut and trusted in a regimen of facial calisthenics rather than allow herself the use of cosmetics. **(May 26, 1938)**

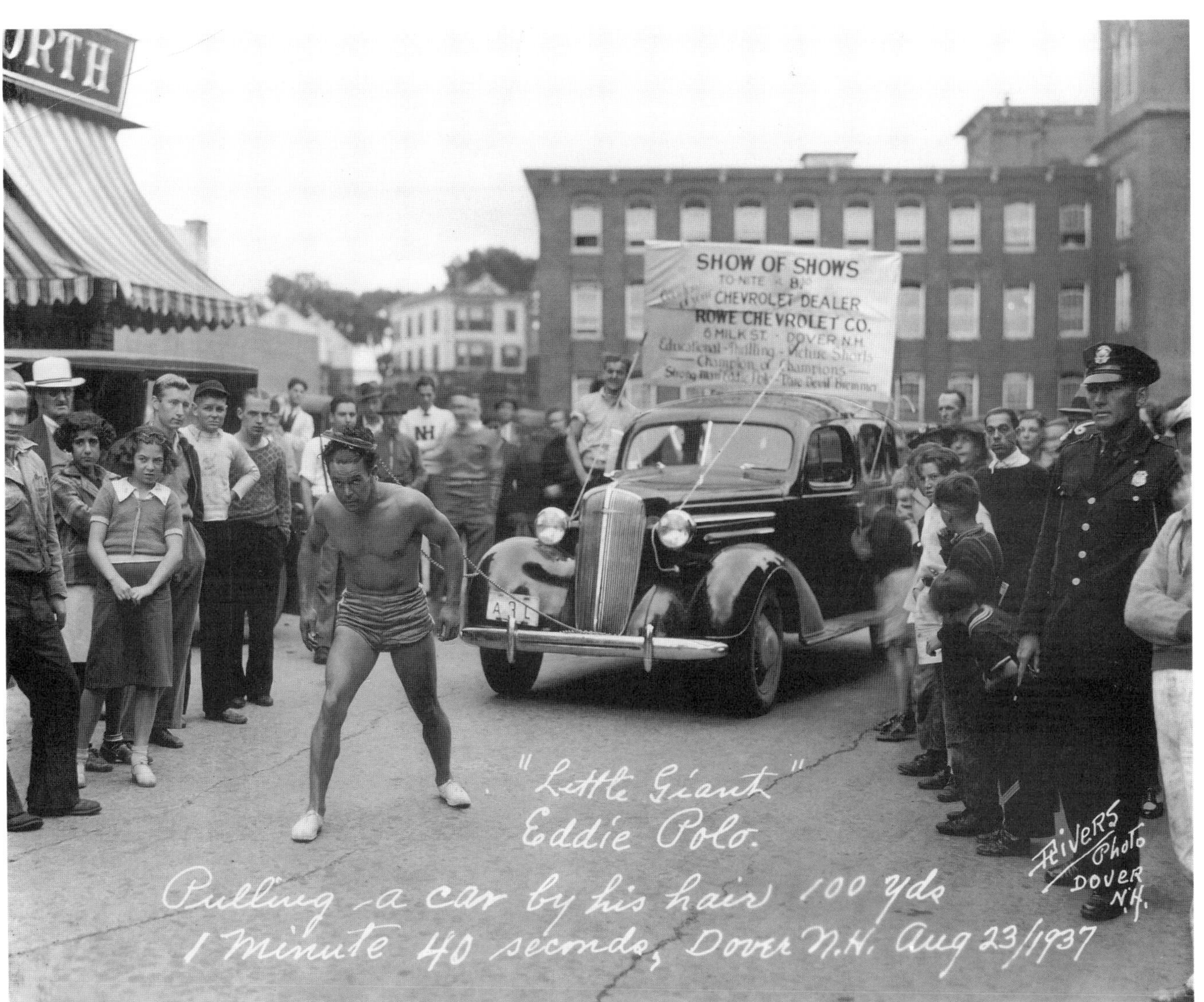

One-hundred-thirty-five-pound "Little Giant" **Eddie Polo pulled a car with his hair** in Dover, New Hampshire. Later that evening he broke heavy chains with his chest, bent steel bars and horseshoes, and successfully challenged eight men to pull together against him in a tug of war. **(October 4, 1937)**

LEONA YOUNG, of Norwich, NEW YORK, **applies a blowtorch to her tongue.** A colleague of Professor Kongee, The Painless Wonder, Young called herself THE DEVIL'S DAUGHTER and **performed with hot lead, volcanic explosions,** and a regulation plumber's torch, which she **passed over her exposed flesh. (March 3, 1938)**

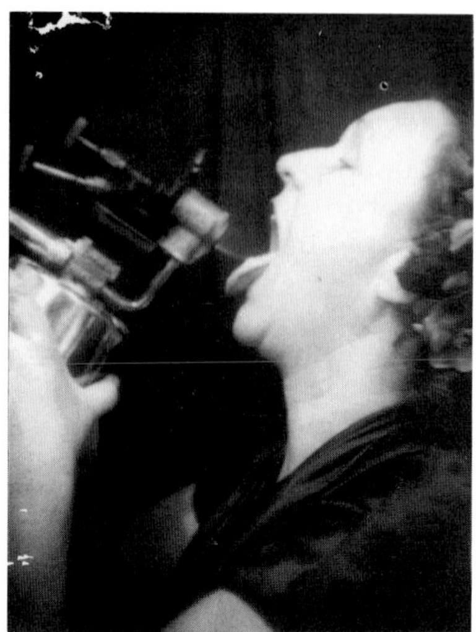

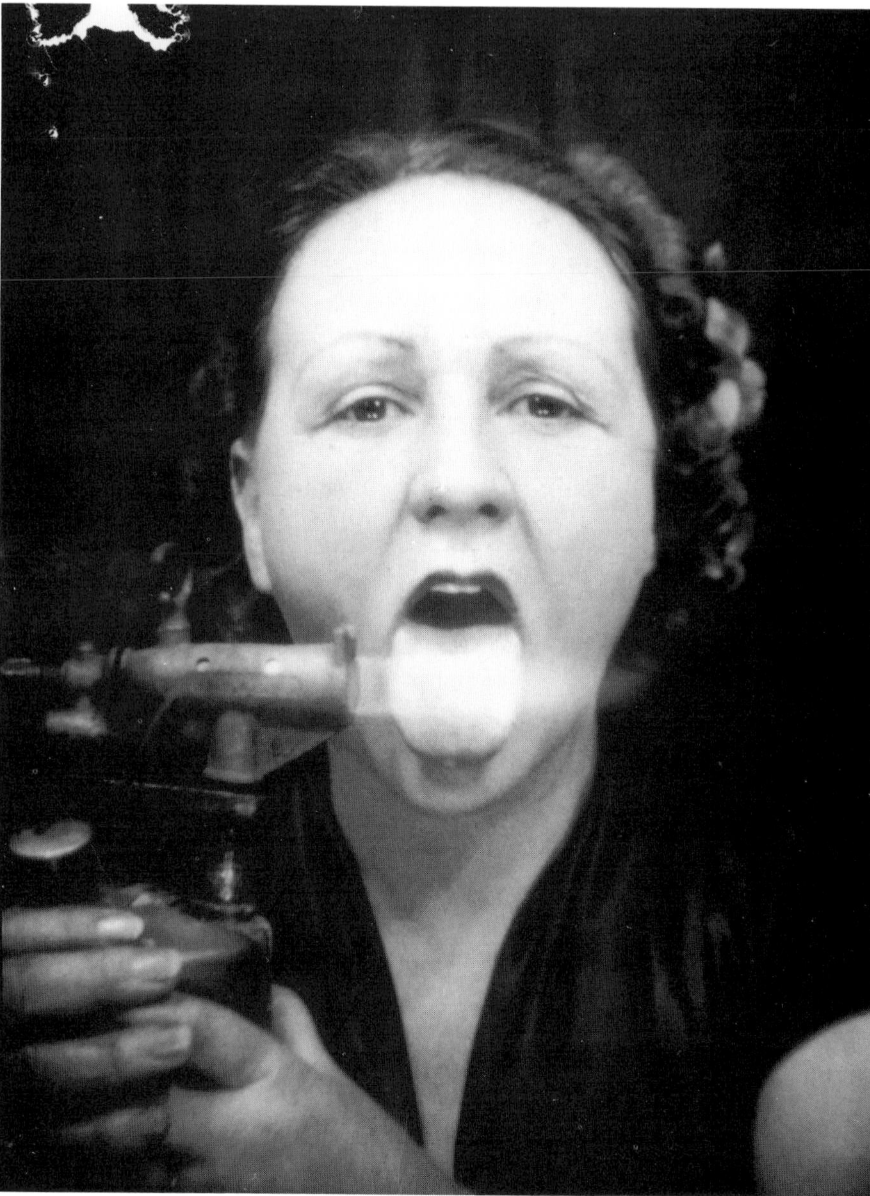

THEODORE KAUFMAN licks a hot soldering iron in Astoria, LONG ISLAND. He could also pour molten lead into his cupped palm, after washing his hands with soap and water for fifteen minutes. **(June 26, 1953)**

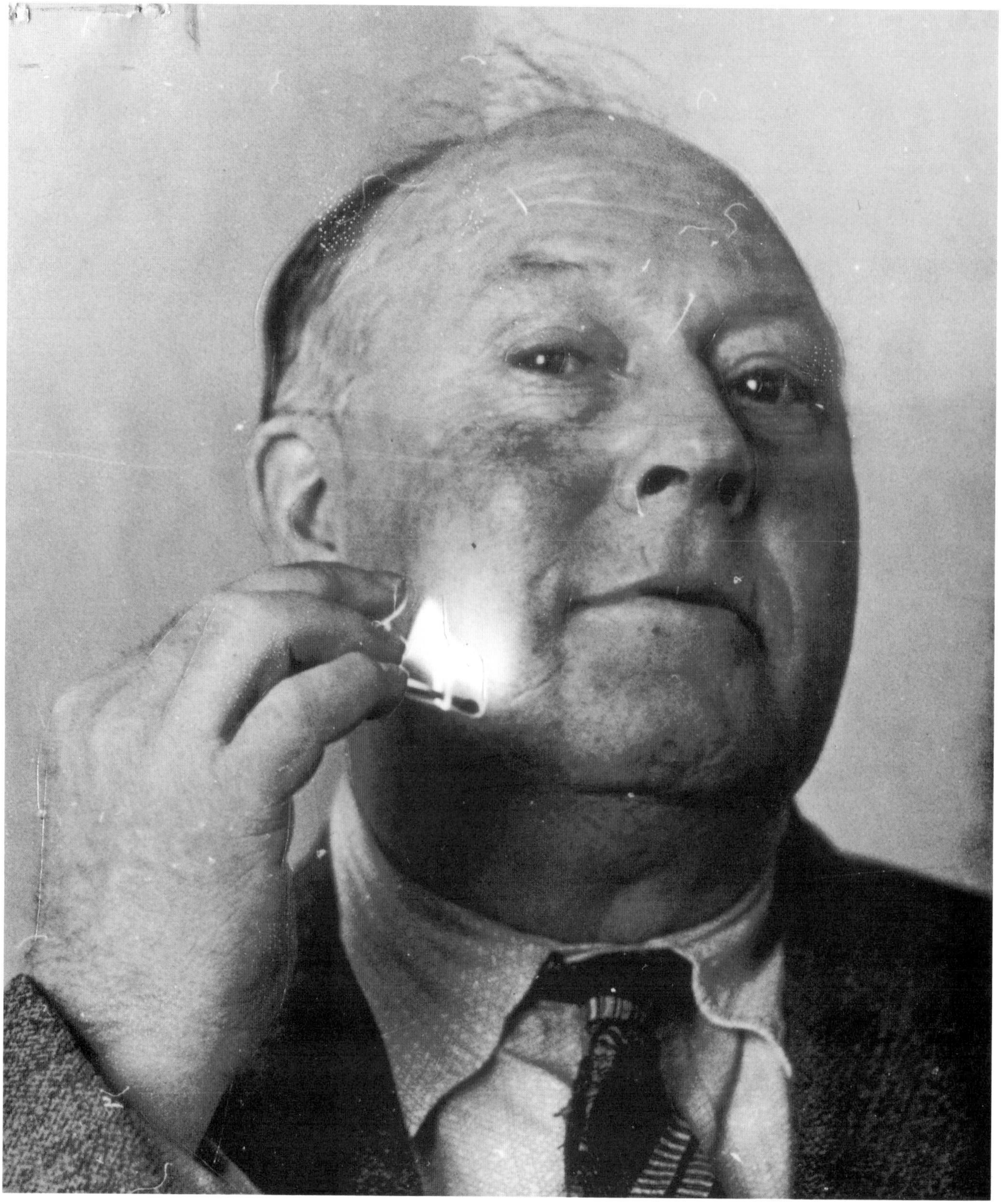

Edmonton, Alberta, boasted a citizen with "Asbestos Skin." It seems a **Mr. H. H. Getty** walked into the editorial offices of the *Edmonton Bulletin* and proceeded to prove his fire-resisting abilities to a bug-eyed staff. Mr. Getty could **hold a lighted match close to the skin on various parts of his body** without any blistering or pain. **(May 20, 1940)**

Back at the beach just six weeks after giving birth, **ALICE RENO** of Allerton, MASSACHUSETTS, noticed that **a perfect portrait of her newborn had appeared on both her knees. (June 4, 1940)**

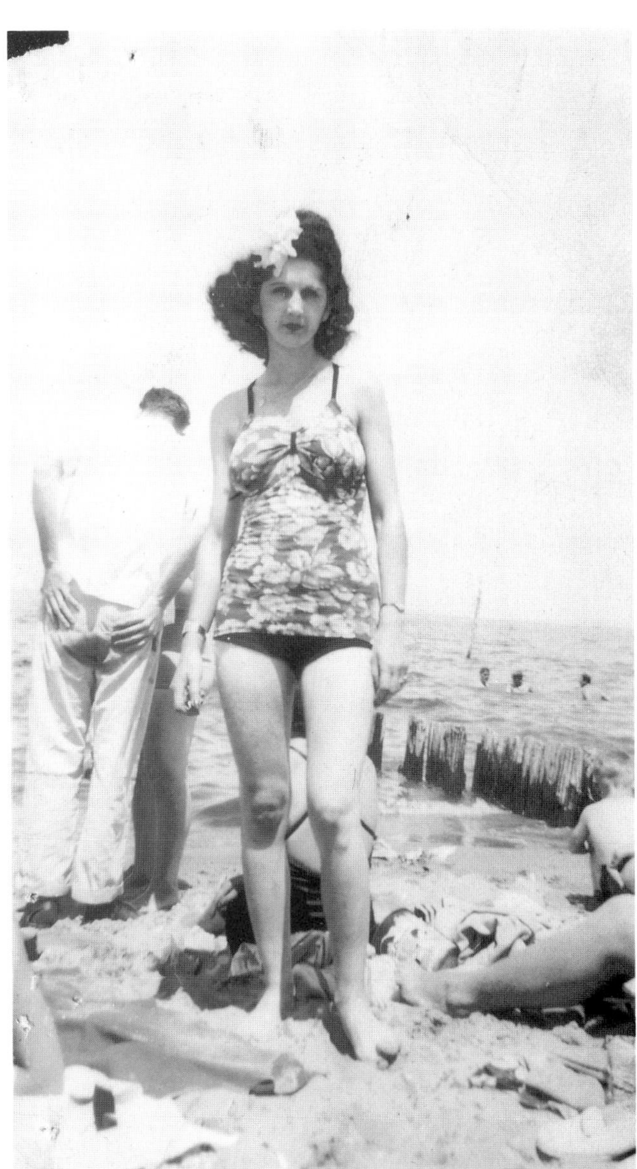

MARY SALZANO of North Bergen, NEW JERSEY, had a perfect **Cupid's face on her right knee. (February 14, 1950)**

HOLD EVERYTHING

"An idea that is not dangerous is unworthy of being called an idea at all."

OSCAR WILDE

Here is a man who could do many things well, and simultaneously! JAMES J. WEIR of Weirton, WEST VIRGINIA, could hold a half-dollar in his eye, a pencil between his upper lip and nose, another pencil between his lower lip and chin, and a cigar between his teeth all while moving his scalp back and forth and singing. He claimed he had crossed the country twenty-nine times and asked upwards of 30,000 people to match his trick, but no one succeeded in duplicating the performance. **(June 18, 1932)**

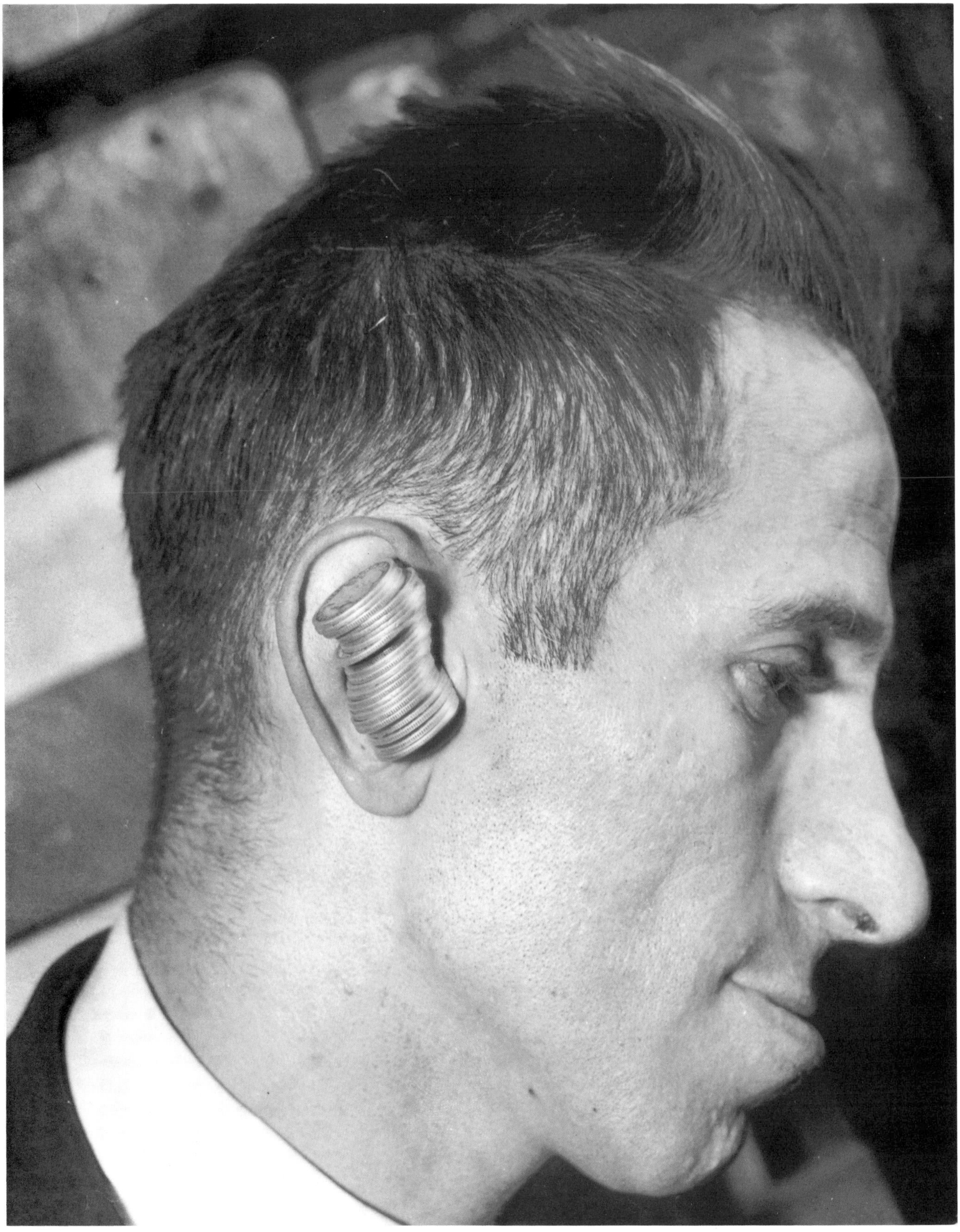

BROOKLYN'S **MAX CALVIN** never needed to fish for change. He could **hold twenty-five quarters in his ear! (July 15, 1933)**

Mt. Elliot Recreation employee **Bill Wausman** of Detroit insisted on **carrying a pencil** under, instead of above, his ear. Lobe and behold! **(February 2, 1942)**

Henry Gibbs lifts a whiskey bottle with his shoulder blades in Old Fort, North Carolina. This stunt won him third prize in an Asheville, North Carolina, Believe It or Not! contest. **(October 28, 1931)**

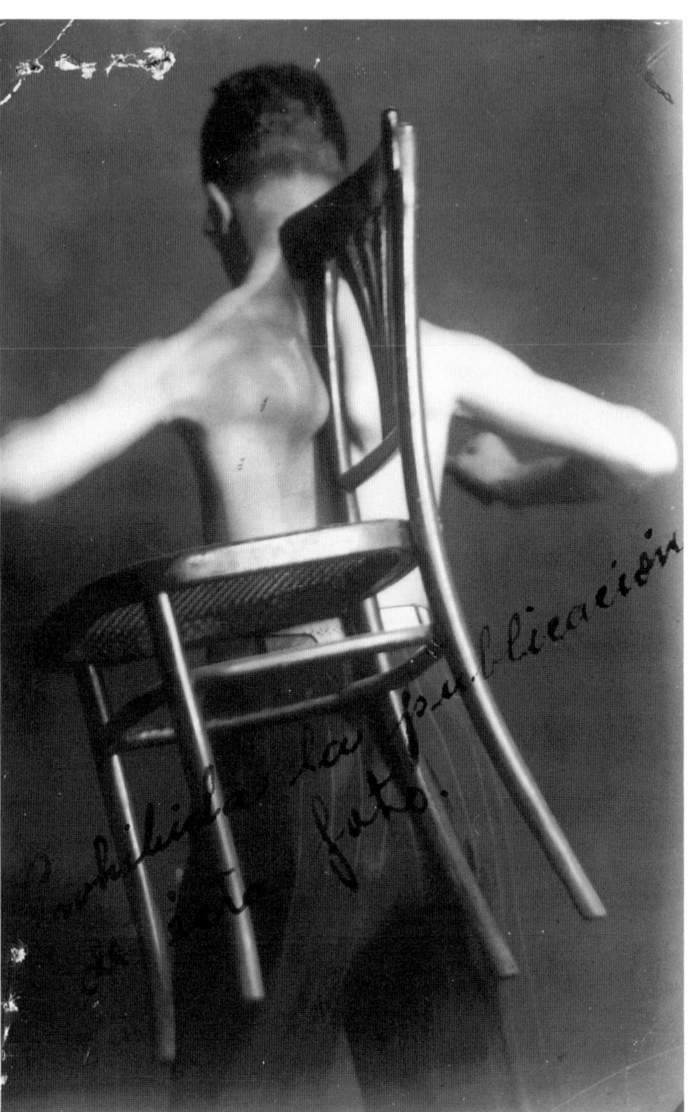

Feria Mundial lifts a chair with his shoulder blades in Mexico City. **(September 4, 1947)**

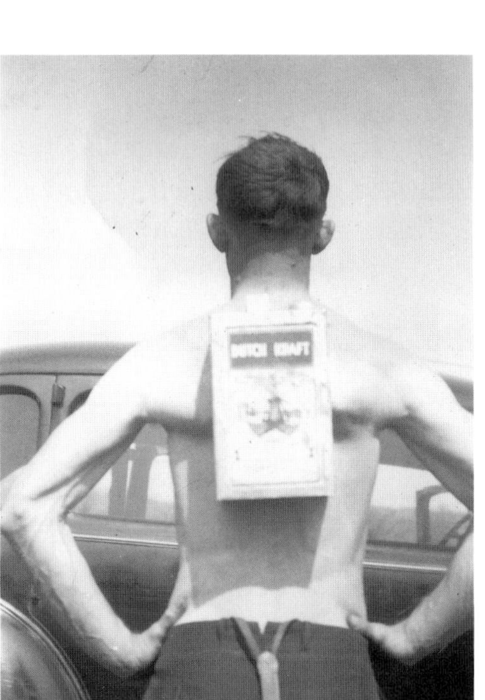

Grand Rapids native son **Joe Jirgles** could **hold a one-gallon varnish can between his shoulder blades.** He claimed he could attach himself to a fence this way so firmly that he could hang in place. **(March 14, 1945)**

Eleven-month-old **Judith Elayne Entine** of Philadelphia, Pennsylvania, **performing a one-foot feat. (September 17, 1947)**

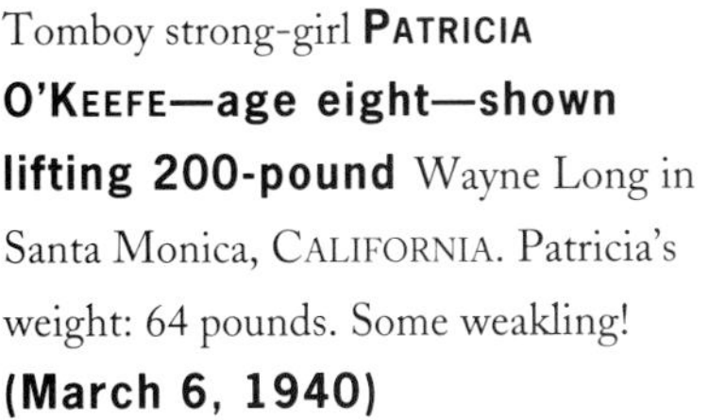

Tomboy strong-girl **Patricia O'Keefe—age eight—shown lifting 200-pound** Wayne Long in Santa Monica, California. Patricia's weight: 64 pounds. Some weakling! **(March 6, 1940)**

City team championship player **ALICE HUMBARGER palms two basketballs** in Houston, TEXAS. The six-foot-four-inch jewelry salesperson could also reach two octaves on a piano with one hand, but she could not carry a tune. Item submitted by Miss Frances Short. **(September 6, 1931)**

Triple view of Master Engineer Junior Grade **GARDNER A. TAYLOR lifting a 155-pound anvil with his ears,** at the Pheasant Hunters Banquet in Winner, SOUTH DAKOTA. Later the sixty-four-year-old war veteran broke his own record by adding a 20-pound weight to the same anvil at the Peacock Café. Sixteen years later he was still going strong, lifting a 110-pound anvil with his ears on his eightieth birthday. **(March 10, 1944)**

Mental Marvels, Wizards, and Prodigies

"What you don't know would make a great book."

Sydney Smith

Mr. George Bove of the Bronx demonstrated a unique and curious ability in the Believe It or Not! office in 1933. **By suspending a key on a silk thread and dangling it over a specimen of handwriting he was able to tell the sex of the person who wrote it.** The staff at Ripley's gave him dozens of examples, and he never failed to come up with the correct response. Baffled by this demonstration, Ripley sent a query over to Bellevue Hospital in New York to see if anyone there could shed any light on the phenomenon. A Dr. Brooke seemed to think this might be the first true case of **"sexographia"** on record. Bove maintained that he could sense the electricity of people through their handwriting, and that men have a different "wattage" than women. Simple. **(September 25, 1933)**

MISS CECIL EDNA KING of LOS ANGELES could **read a book just as fast holding it upside down** as right side up. **(November 3, 1941)**

OSCAR SPURGEON of Salem, INDIANA, could **read newspapers and books upside down** or at any other angle. **(December 31, 1935)**

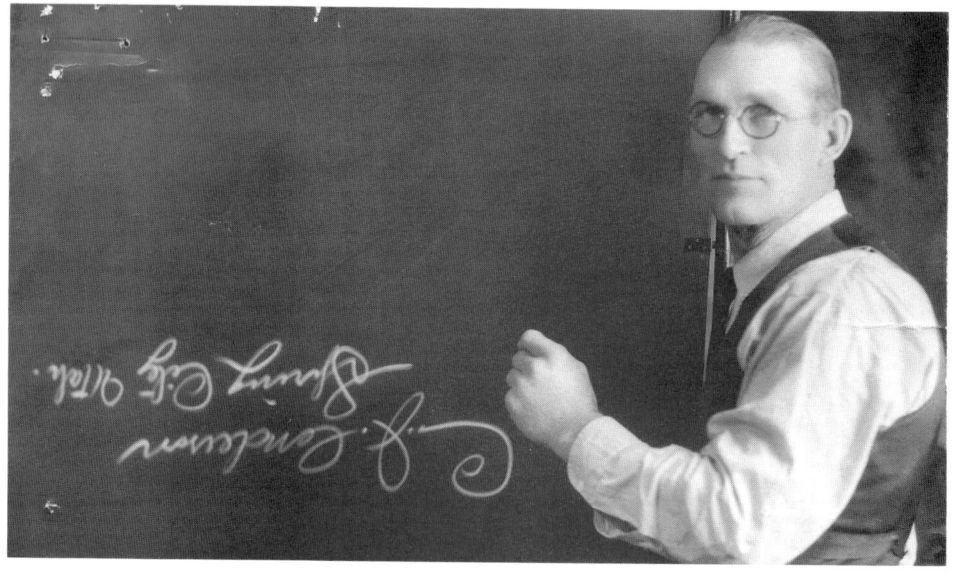

C. J. ANDERSON of Spring City, UTAH, **wrote all correspondence upside down and backwards. (July 11, 1938)**

Miss Zelma George of Canton, Ohio, **could write forwards, backwards, upside down, and upside down backwards,** and also write a different sentence with each hand in any combination of upside down, backwards, etc., simultaneously. Whew! **(January 5, 1948)**

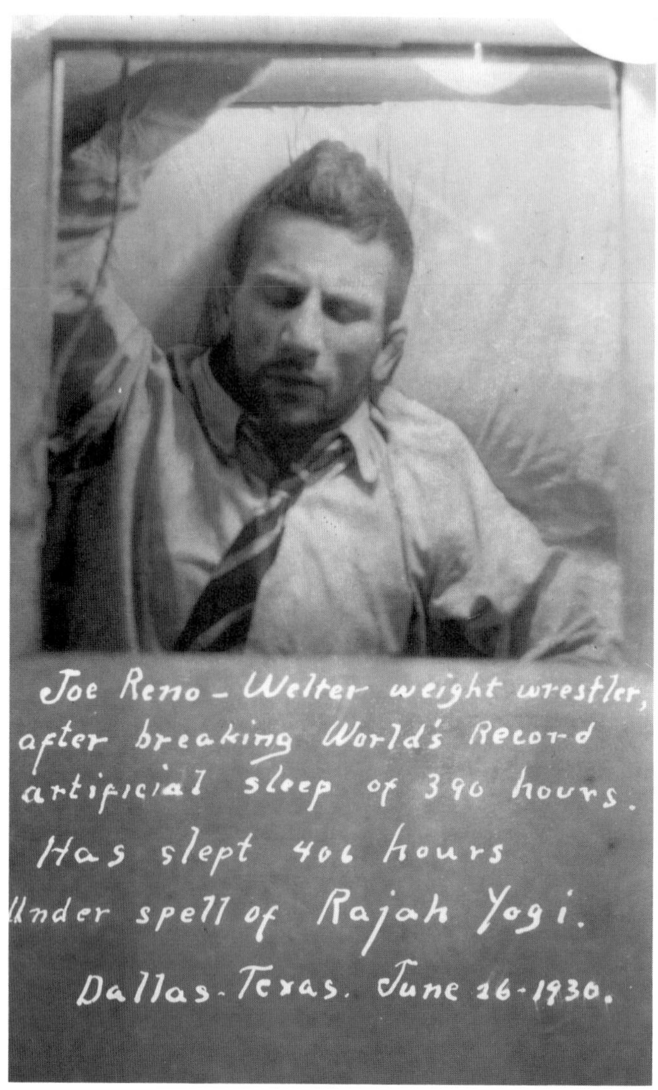

Joe Reno - Welter weight wrestler,
after breaking World's Record
artificial sleep of 390 hours.
Has slept 406 hours
Under spell of Rajah Yogi.
Dallas-Texas. June 26-1930.

U.S. Navy wrestling champion **Joe Reno,** hypnotized by **Rajah Yogi** in Dallas, Texas, **slept buried in a coffin for nearly seventeen days in June 1930 without food or water** to set a new world record for hypnotic sleep. Within fifteen minutes after being reawakened by Rajah Yogi, Reno wrestled Shreveport, Louisiana, middleweight champion Red Lindsay to a ten-minute draw! **(February 3, 1931)**

Eastern mystic and hypnotic trance man **Rajah Yogi** of Oklahoma autographed this promotional photograph for presentation to Ripley **after waking Joe Reno from his record-breaking slumber. (December 11, 1934)**

Beleive it or not, to Mr Robert L. Ripley;
with my admiration and gratitude.
Rajah Yogi.
march 22-1933.

NATURE'S WHIMS

"There is nothing so powerful as truth–and often nothing so strange."

DANIEL WEBSTER

MISS MARIE IDAH BRUNOZZY of Wanamie, PENNSYLVANIA, **spent three years and eight months growing these attractive fingernails** —the longest of which was 5 3/8 inches. Employed in a children's toy store, she claimed the children admired her nails and would stop in the shop just to see how things were growing. **(June 29, 1953)**

An unknown patient at the Soochow Hospital in CHINA here displays his world-record fingernails. He had a **thirty-three-inch fingernail that took forty-four years to grow,** and his "little" fingernail was fifteen inches long. **(January 15, 1935)**

WENG, THE HUMAN UNICORN, a Chinese farmer **with a thirteen-inch horn growing out of his head,** briefly exhibited himself in the early 1930s among a company of Chinese fakirs in Fuchiatien, MANCHURIA, where this snapshot was taken by a Russian employee of the National City Bank of New York. For years Ripley offered large rewards to anyone who could find him again and bring him to America for an Odditorium appearance. **(May 11, 1930)**

This horned rooster was the Pride of the White Owl Café, owned by **JESSE T. PARKER** of DeQueen, ARKANSAS. **(December 23, 1931)**

ROOSTER OWNED BY
JESSE T. PARKER
PRIDE OF THE
WHITE OWL CAFE"

FRANCESCO LENTINI of SICILY **was born with three legs.** He used two legs for walking and the third as a chair to sit on. He was for many years a part of Buffalo Bill's Wild West Show and an ace soccer player.

NASIB N.Y.

William H. Rainey of Fort Worth, Texas, holds his **four-foot-eleven-inch Snake Cucumber. (April 14, 1930)**

A. B. Tyler found an edible **21-pound 14-ounce giant puffball fungus** near his home in Cattaraugus County, New York. It briefly held the record for the biggest reported in a season of unusually large puffballs, broken only a few weeks later when B. H. Kippenstein brought a 28-pound 8-ounce monster to the Manitou, Manitoba, post office for a weigh-in. Puffballs are near cousins to mushrooms. **(October 24, 1931)**

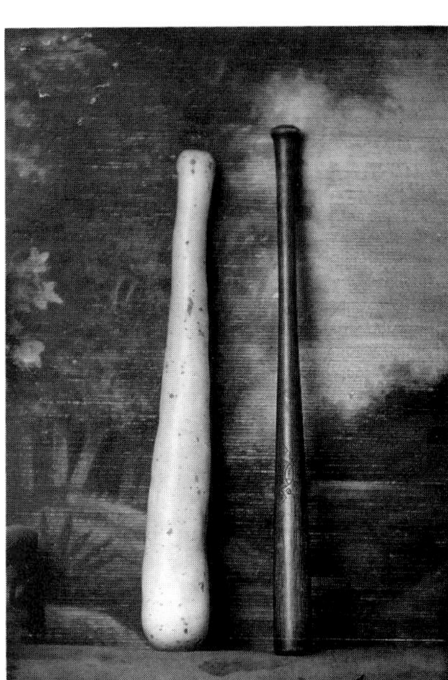

A gourd in the shape of a baseball bat was grown near Ft. Worth, Texas, by **Miller Daniel** on the Glenn Brothers Ranch. This variety, sometimes called a dishrag gourd, rarely grows to the whopping dimensions of this 32-inch slugger. **(November 20, 1945)**

Carrot hand found by **TOMMY ANDREWS** at the Palace Café, Redlands, CALIFORNIA. **(May 11, 1935)**

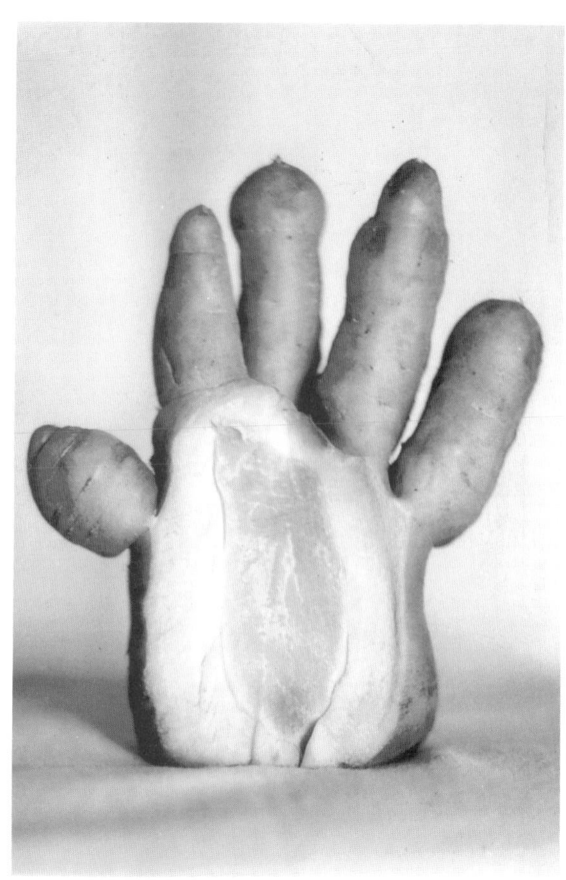

Carrot hand grown by **M. L. LITTLE** of Bellingham, WASHINGTON. **(January 10, 1932)**

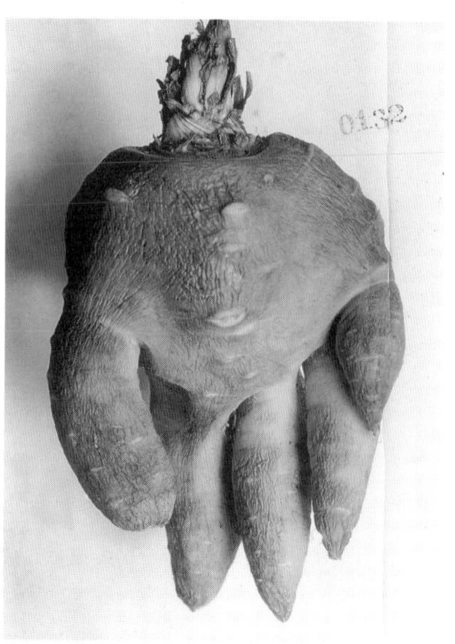

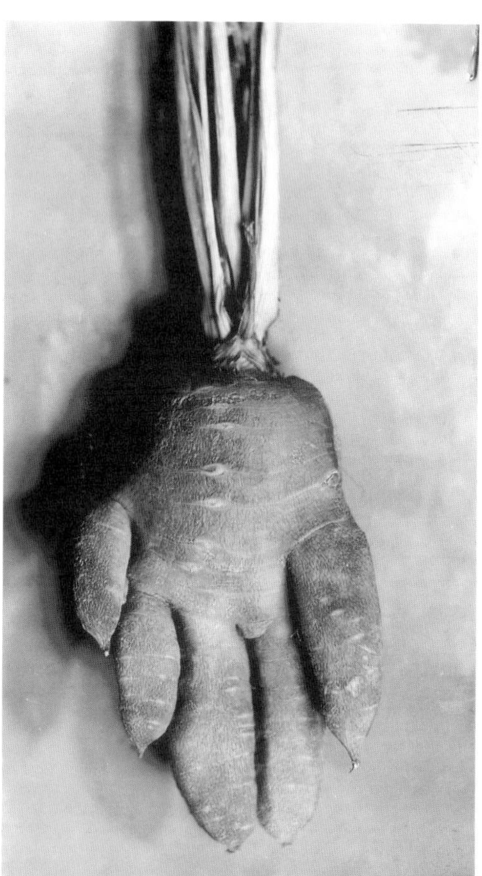

Carrot hand grown by **ALEXANDER MOE** of Brainerd, MINNESOTA. **(December 12, 1932)**

Carrot hand grown by **HARRY SIMS**, Grand Prairie, ALBERTA, CANADA. **(November 5, 1940)**

Singing and playing piano were just two of the extraordinary talents of toy shepherd **LADY TRILLING** of Hollywood, CALIFORNIA. Her trainer, **MRS. ADELA FOWLER,** could not play a note. **(November 23, 1947)**

A nearsighted rock cod was caught sporting spectacles in the waters off Bellingham, WASHINGTON. As if that were not enough, the glasses were identified by **IRA D. ERLING,** salesman, as his own. It seems his glasses went overboard while he was out trolling for salmon in the same area where the fish was caught. **(April 9, 1940)**

This vaudeville roller-skating dog was owned and trained by **FRANK JACOBS** of New Castle, MAINE. Although Jacobs occasionally presented the dog in local theater performances, his Riverview Restaurant business kept him too busy to make a career out of his sensational skating canine. **(August 4, 1931)**

TEX, part bulldog and part bird dog, was only 22 inches tall but 44 inches around and weighed 120 pounds! His owner, **IRMA FAREK** of Hockley, TEXAS, says his favorite food was lemon snaps, which he is holding in the picture. **(August 22, 1932)**

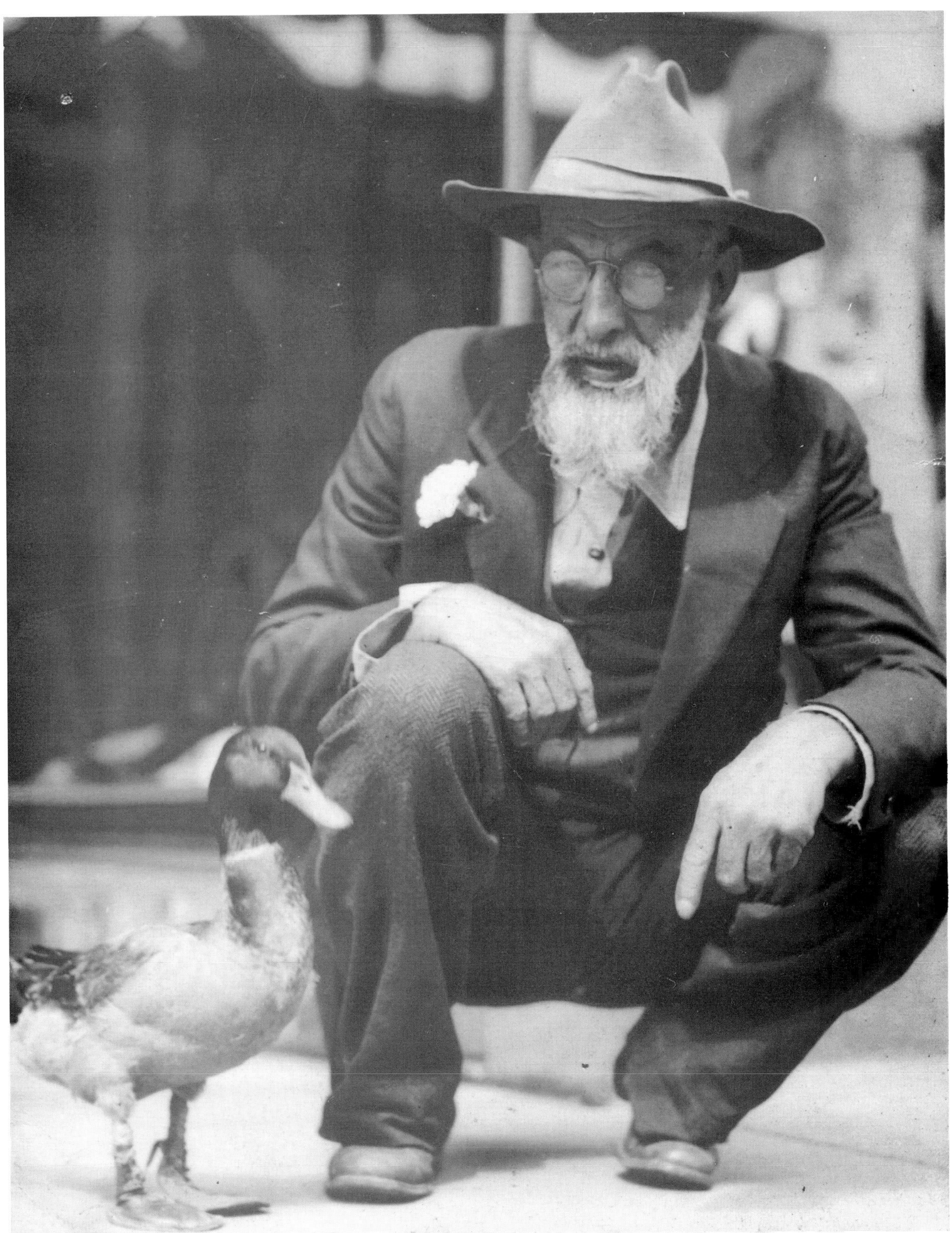

The Wild Duck with the Human Mind was owned by **F. G. CLARK** of CHICAGO. Shown here out for a walk with Clark, it could distinguish between coins, and it is said to have displayed signs of patriotism. **(September 21, 1933)**

Craigsville, VIRGINIA, could boast **a horse with a perfect Indian head on it.** This horse was born on August 15, 1935, to owners **R. L. ANDERSON and J. F. DANIEL. (June 14, 1940)**

Up in Port Townsend, WASHINGTON, **trout were trained to jump through a hoop.** Item submitted by **W. R. RAMSEY. (July 10, 1931)**

EIN ZEICHEN DER ZEIT ALS NATURWUNDER!
geb. 22.10.33 zu Wrist in Holstein
beim Landmann Max Granzow

Translation: A Sign of the Times—calf born October 22, 1933, at Wrist-Holstein, GERMANY, **with a Nazi cross on its forehead.** Farmer/owner **MAX GRANZOW** was stunned by this amazing coincidence. **(April 10, 1934)**

Cow with "7," born on July 7, 1937, on **CHRIS WATTENBERG'S** farm in Brighton, COLORADO. **(August 2, 1938)**

Calf with a perfect "7" on its head. Submitted by **CARL MARTINSEN** of Bellingham, WASHINGTON. **(December 5, 1955)**

Heifer with a perfect "7" on its head. Owned by **CLETUS BUECHNER** of Convoy, OHIO. **(July 15, 1952)**

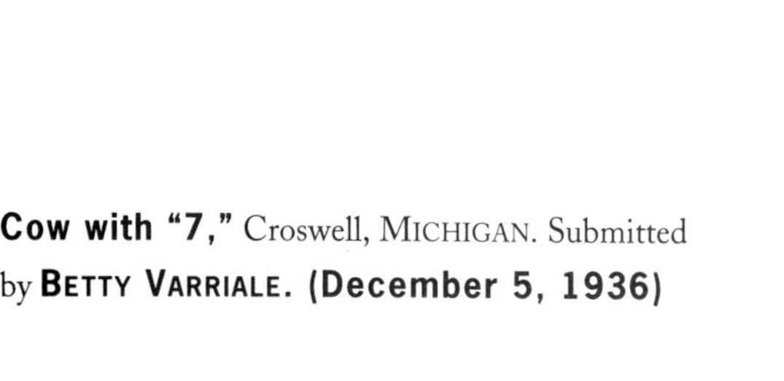

Cow with "7," Croswell, MICHIGAN. Submitted by **BETTY VARRIALE. (December 5, 1936)**

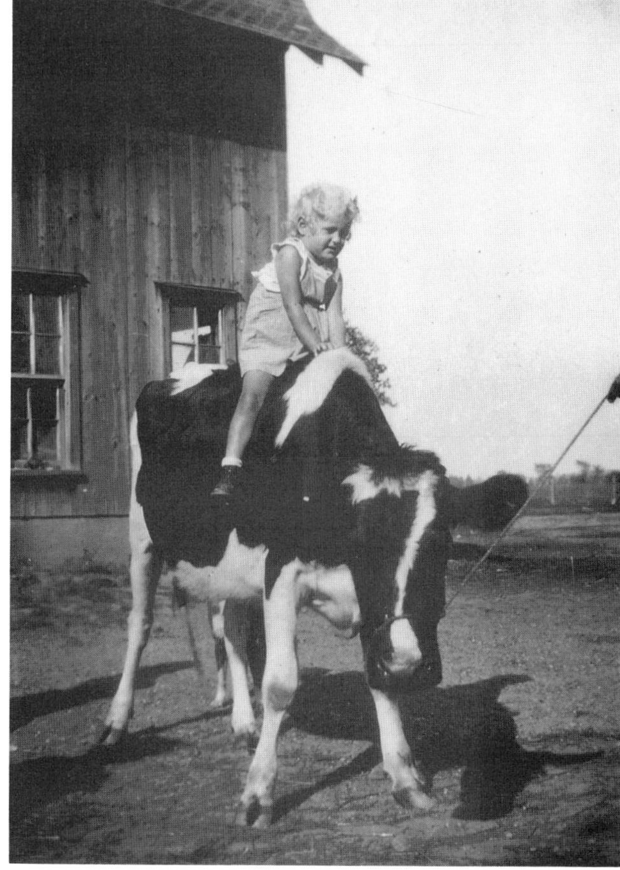

This pup has a chicken on his hindquarters. His name and that of his owner are lost to history, but **MR. V. K. BIGALKE** of CHICAGO sent in this snap for Ripley's approval. **(February 9, 1931)**

Patches, a dog with two hearts, owned by **JACK RIMOL** of Casa Grande, ARIZONA, was fond of mint-flavored chewing gum and wore cowboy outfits on special occasions. She earned an A-1 Credit Rating at the local Pioneer Meat Market. **(October 24, 1939)**

Sweetheart, **a horse with two hearts,** owned by **MRS. WEAVER BLAKE** of Humboldt, KANSAS, was blind and had prosthetic eyes made of glass. **(May 7, 1939)**

This **black bear with a white heart** lived near Beckley, WEST VIRGINIA. Submitted by **CHARLES DE SPAIN. (July 28, 1939)**

Ginger, a ten-month-old **fox terrier with two hearts,** was owned by **Edna Markham** of Hollywood, CALIFORNIA. **(May 30, 1936)**

Cow with a perfect heart, born on Valentine's Day. Submitted by **Mrs. L. E. Kirby** of Florence, South Carolina. **(February 14, 1952)**

This lamb **with a perfect heart on its shoulders,** (also) born on Valentine's Day, was owned by **Lee Epperson** of Edina, Missouri. **(May 6, 1938)**

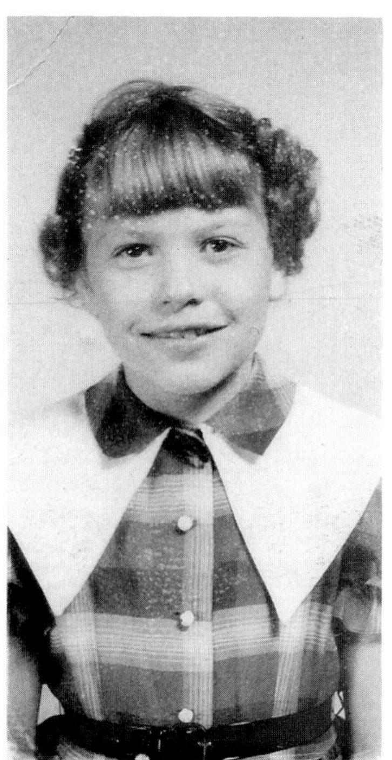

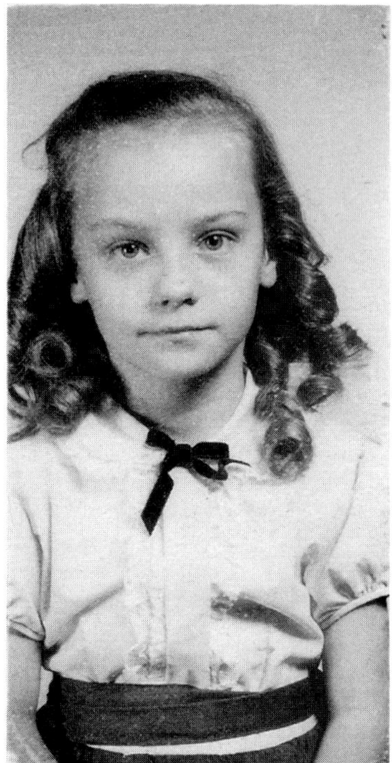

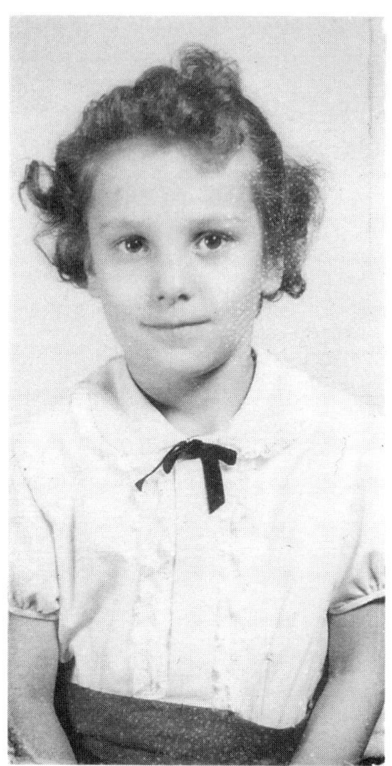

Two sets of twins both named Loretta and Lorraine Szymanski attended the same school, were in the same classroom, and lived just a few doors apart on the same street in Pittsburgh, but were not related! Their teacher was the first to discover the amazing coincidence. **(July 20, 1955)**

After fifteen years of regularly being mistaken for another woman in the same city, Vivian Weiss finally met her double, Mrs. Joseph Pepper. Both, as it turned out, had the same birthday, the same wedding anniversary, the same stomach ailments, the same food likes and dislikes, and both had three children almost exactly the same ages. They met one night at a party in Omaha, Nebraska, after discovering that both had hurt their legs in the same way at the same place on the same day. **(July 2, 1939)**

Identical twins Max and Bernard Friedman bought identical coats without the knowledge of the other brother in stores 350 miles apart. Bernard lived in East Chicago, Indiana, and Max lived in Des Moines, Iowa, but both purchased light plaid topcoats with the serial number 17343, only discovering the coincidence months later. **(March 28, 1943)**

NEVER/ALWAYS

"Most people would succeed in small things if they were not troubled with great ambitions."

HENRY WADSWORTH LONGFELLOW

This brother-and-sister **duo had twenty-two years of perfect attendance between them.** At Alachua High School in Alachua, FLORIDA, student **EUNICE COX** completed twelve years of schooling in ten years without being absent or tardy. When her baby brother was an infant, their mother whispered into young **JOHN COX, JR.'s** ear that she hoped that he too might be 100 percent loyal to his school. Sure enough, he graduated from the same school without being absent or tardy for twelve years. Submitted by **H. L. ROCKWOOD,** former principal of the school. **(October 25, 1936)**

Never-Never Man **Simon P. Crone** of Brunswick, Maryland, age seventy-five, **had never done many things.** Among the things he had never done: shot a gun, read a novel, used tobacco or liquor, been married or had a sweetheart, crossed a river, or been out of the county where he was born. He also used the same pencil for fifty years. The cost of the pencil was one penny. **(September 15, 1935)**

Can you top this? **At age thirty-six, ROY ROBERT SMITH** of Denver, COLORADO, had never tasted an ice cream soda, Coca-Cola, ginger ale, wine, beer, or whiskey; never used tobacco in any form, never dipped snuff; **never gone swimming,** hunting, fishing, hiking, or ice-skating; never played football, billiards, poker, cards, baseball, basketball, tennis, golf, hockey, or polo; **never pitched a horseshoe;** never driven a car or ridden a bicycle, motorcycle, or horse; never seen an earthquake, flood, or tornado, nor **witnessed a fatal accident;** never seen a race of any kind; never been inside a saloon or speakeasy; never been struck or stunned by lightning or bitten by any kind of animal, reptile, or poisonous insect; never had a surgical operation; never shot a gun, pistol, rifle, or cannon; never been robbed or burglarized; never participated in a fight; never gambled nor bet; never been aboard a steamship or yacht; never ridden in a balloon or airplane; **never milked a cow or goat; never** been **underground in a cave** or mine; never joined a club, lodge, church, or organization; never seen a bullfight or duel; never harnessed a horse; never attended a rodeo; never been in a lumber camp, sawmill, granary, or foundry; never studied a foreign language; never been outside the United States; never been convicted of a crime; **never fainted;** never been inside a penitentiary, nor **been a patient in a hospital or sanatorium;** never kissed a girl; and never been engaged to marry. **(March 18, 1934)**

DENNIS CULLEN of Galesburg, ILLINOIS, **at seventy years of age had never tasted chicken.** What's more, Mr. Cullen had been a locomotive fireman for the C. B. and Q. Railroad for thirty years and claimed he had not had a drink of water in forty years. **(May 1, 1932)**

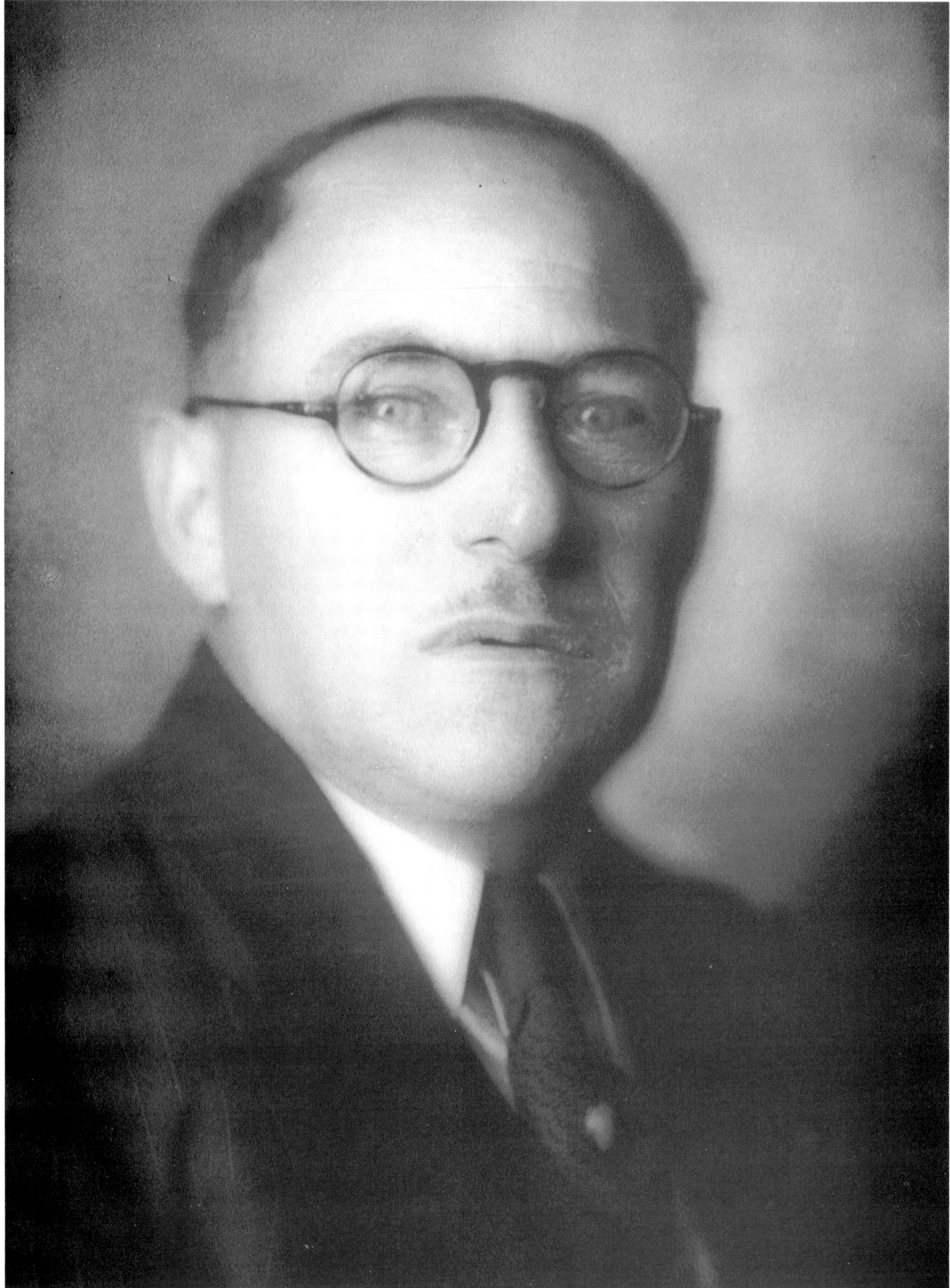

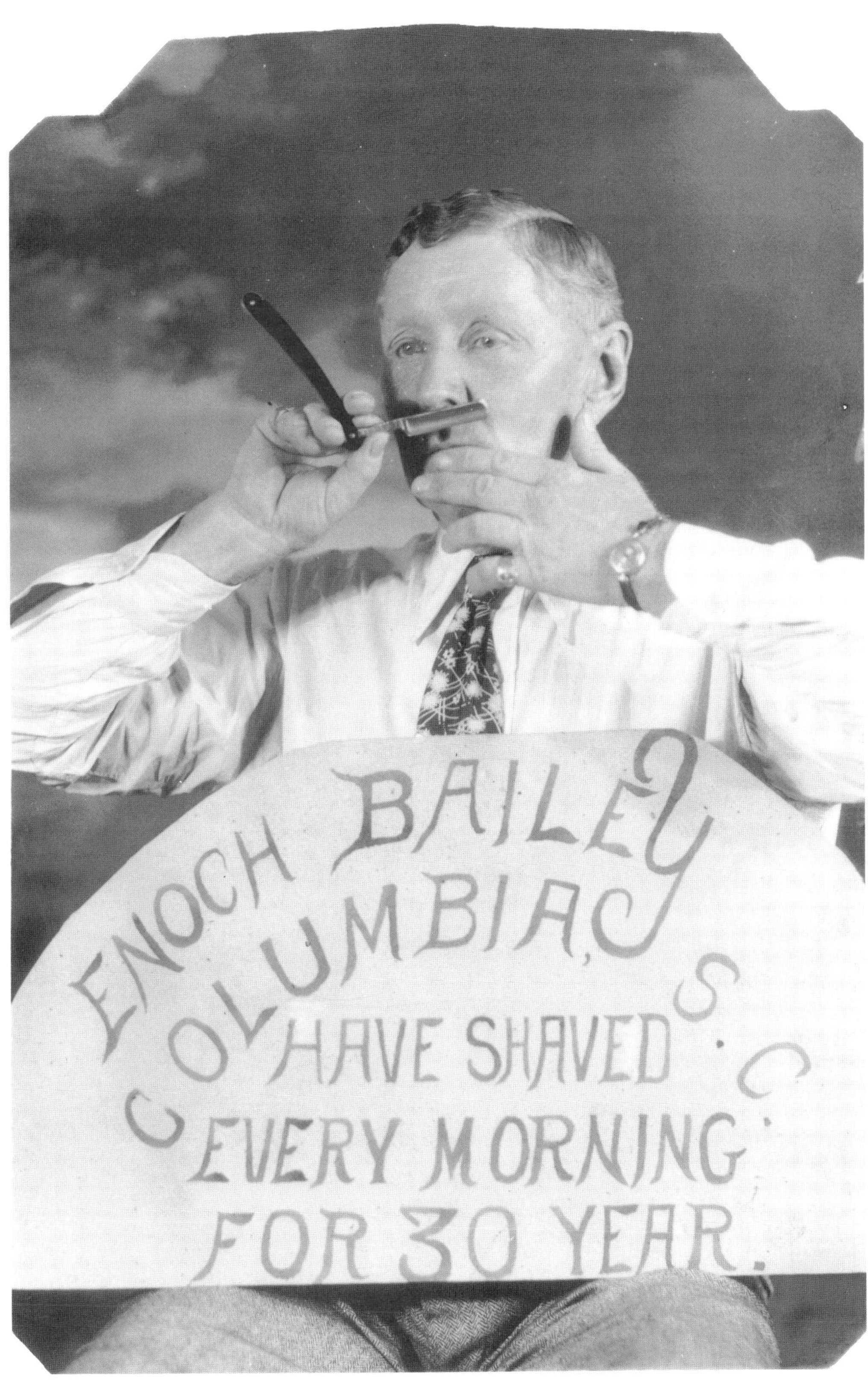

Ben Seiff, the Barber of Venice, California, **had a headache for twenty-six years** but never missed a day's work. Seiff lived on Ozone Street. **(September 22, 1932)**

Enoch Bailey, of Columbia, South Carolina, actually **shaved every morning for thirty years!** You could say he made it into immortality by a close shave. **(May 2, 1935)**

The fact that he was not a winner at fishing made **O. H. L. Bell** of Chillicothe, Texas, all the more appealing for a Ripley cartoon. It seems that Bell fished often and in areas where others fishing beside him were bringing in good fish, but he never managed to even get a nibble at his bait. **He fished for six years** with both live bait and artificial lures **without ever once feeling the quiver of a fish. (February 15, 1935)**

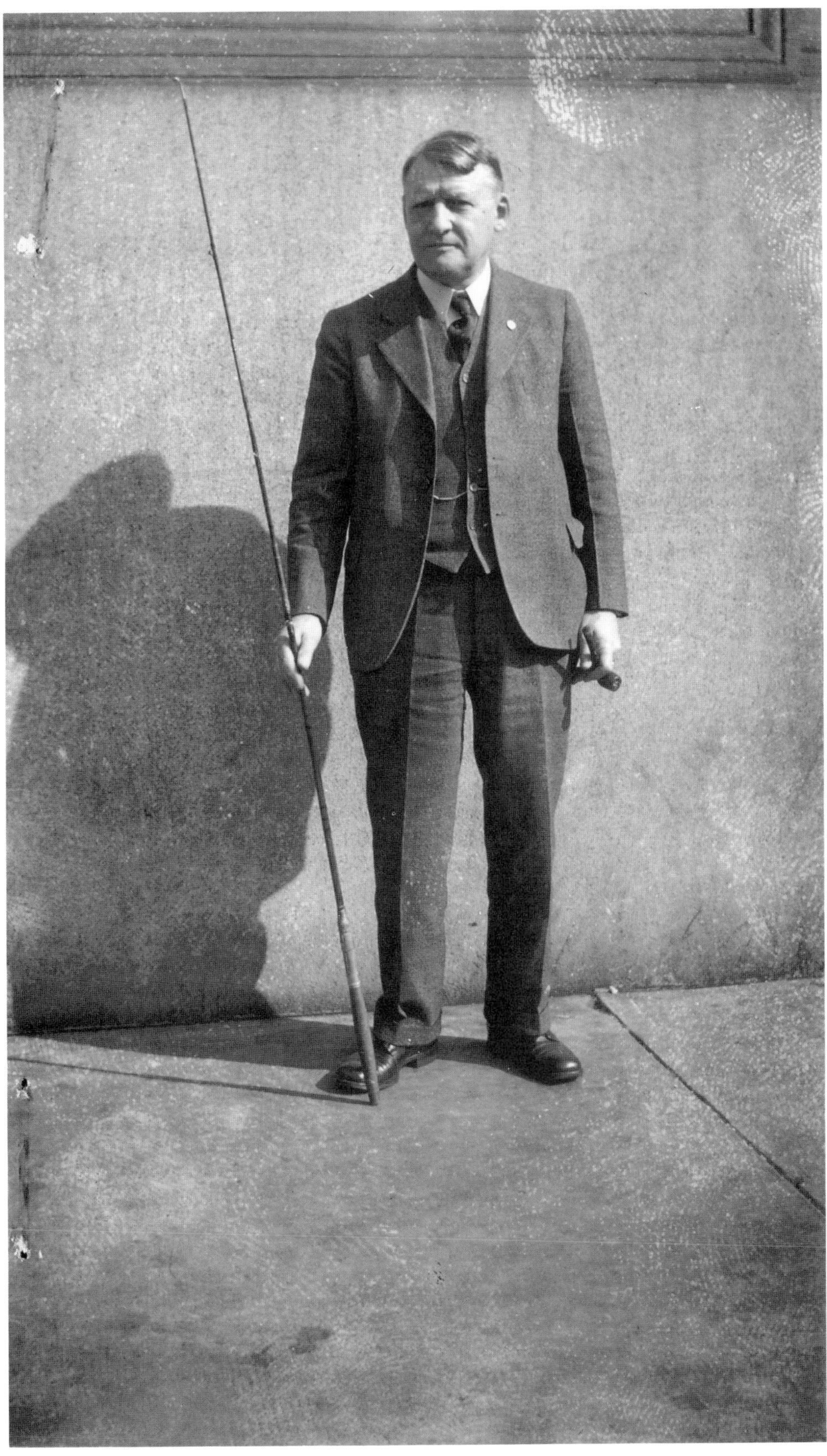

Audacious angler **F. D. HILL,** Treasurer of the Life Insurance Company of VIRGINIA, **caught 30,578 fish in forty years with the same rod.** Item submitted by M. M. Gregory. **(March 13, 1935)**

Where There's Smoke

"It is easier to suppress the first desire than to satisfy all that follow it."

Benjamin Franklin

Shown here is **two-year-old Leslie Louis Young,** of Nicholasville, Kentucky, **relaxed with his pipe** and tobacco after a tough afternoon playing in the sandbox. **(August 17, 1931)**

W. J. EVANS of Poteau, OKALAHOMA, **could hold a dime between his chin and nose,** while smoking. **(April 9, 1948)**

MRS. BELLE RYANS of Savannah, GEORGIA, **smoked a pipe every day for more than a hundred years,** but she didn't approve of young flappers smoking cigarettes. She far outlived her sons, who died fighting for the Confederacy, but never realized her ambition of flying in an airplane. She was 109 years old in this photograph and lived to the ripe old age of 119! **(March 10, 1931)**

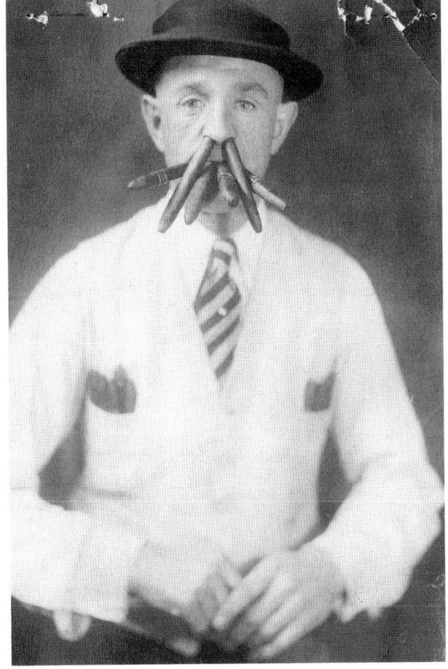

By the time **he was three, JOHN MULLICAN, JR., had been smoking for more than two years.** The McAlester, OKLAHOMA, youngster started with a pipe but soon switched to smoking two White Owl cigars a day and the occasional store-bought cigarette. He didn't care much for candy and refused to chew anything but Brown Mule Tobacco in between smokes. When this picture was taken, Johnny was described as "healthy in every way," seldom suffering from nervous attack or common colds despite the fact that he insisted "on going 'round with very little clothes even in the winter time." **(July 18, 1935)**

JOHNNY "CIGAR" CONNORS of Roxbury, MASSACHUSETTS, held the record for **smoking 600 cigars in forty-eight hours** without eating, drinking, or sleeping. **(February 25, 1933)**

The only dog
in the world
who actually
smokes!
The dog has no
hat on!

= Hello = Good-friend =
Bill Sharples
& Artur
Paramount K.N
Hollywood

George Kohan, of Smithers, West Virginia, had a three-year-old dog named Briddle, who **not only smoked a pipe and cigarettes but could tell the time of day,** day of the week, date of the month, and perform all four functions of arithmetic. **(October 24, 1931)**

Here's **Bill Sharples** with Artur, **the only dog in the world who took up the smoking habit,** in Hollywood. **(February 14, 1932)**

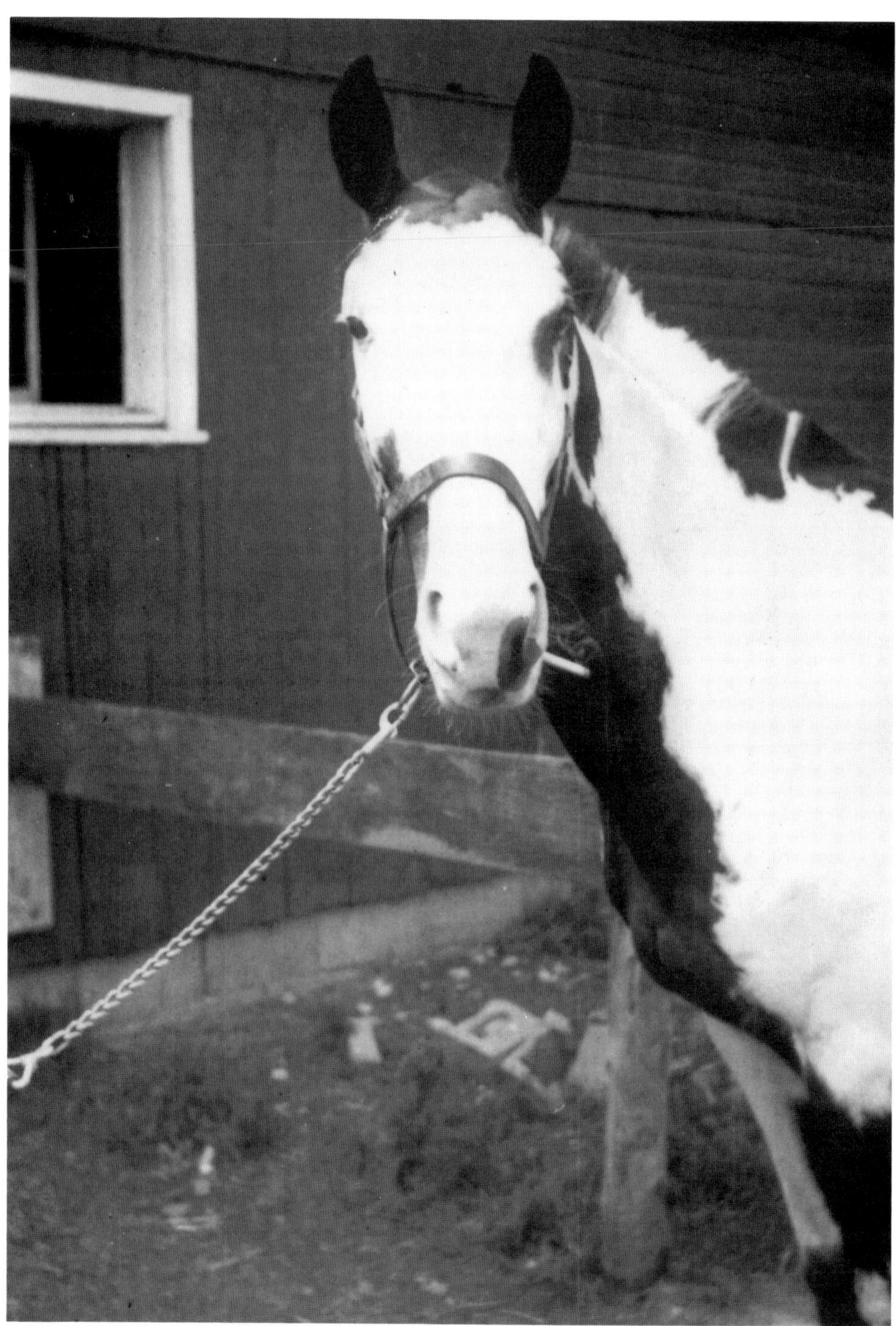

Out behind the stables **HANS STEINMETZ** of Durand, MICHIGAN, **taught his horse to smoke and inhale cigarettes. (November 2, 1950)**

A white Australorp rooster belonging to the Woodside Poultry Farm of Neenah, WISCONSIN, **gazed contentedly at his prize ribbons while enjoying a smoke. (May 28, 1934)**

SUSPENDED ANIMATION

"No knowledge can be more satisfactory to a man than that of his own frame, its parts, their functions and actions."

THOMAS JEFFERSON

Milkman **HENRY O. DARKEN** and his seven-year-old daughter, **NANCY JOYCE DARKEN,** tripped the light fantastic as an **upside-down trumpet-playing and tap-dancing duo.** They performed their novelty act in the Chicago suburb of Elmwood Park, ILLINOIS. **(October 9, 1938)**

Theatrical
CHICAGO

Cornish immigrant **Uncle Billy Hooper,** shown in front of his farmhouse in Lebanon, Kansas, **could still stand on his head at the age of eighty-six. (March 12, 1935)**

SALT LAKE CITY letter carrier **FRANK OLSEN** did the **can-can on his hands while playing his own accompaniment on the harmonica. (May 2, 1935)**

55

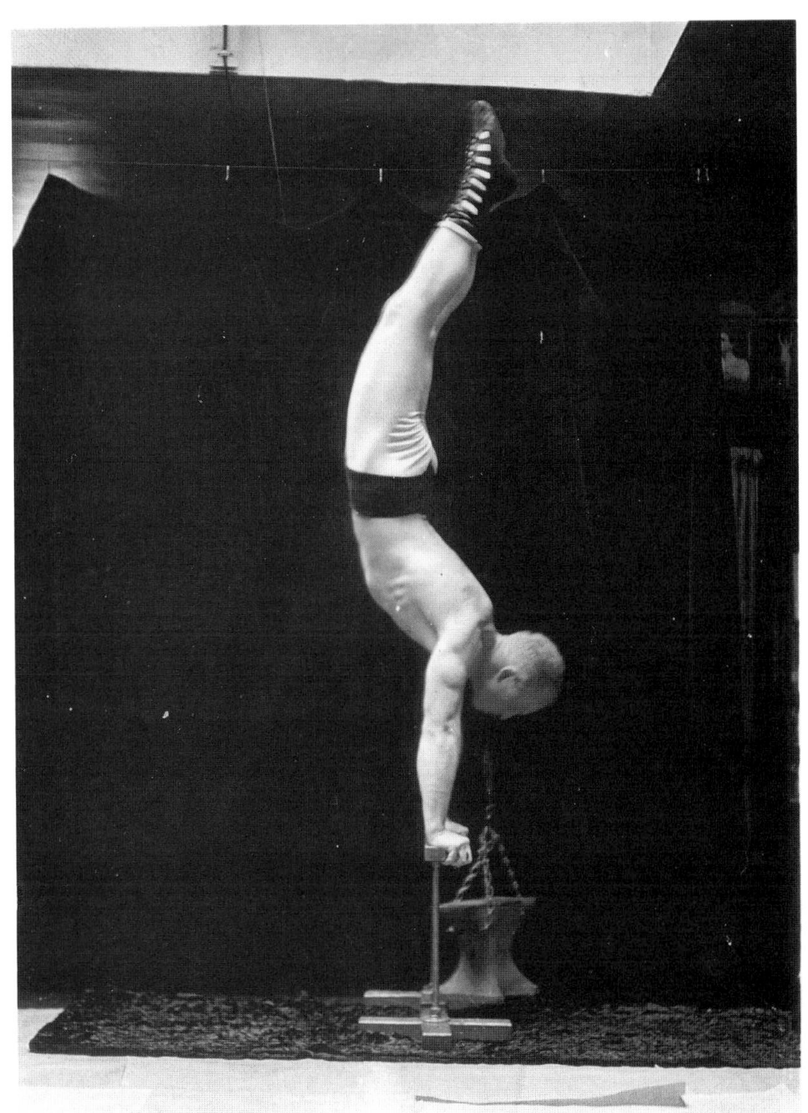

BROOKLYN strong man **RAYMOND VAN CLEEF could lift a 110-pound anvil with his teeth while doing a handstand.** Van Cleef's stationery proclaims his membership in the New York Society of Graduate Medical Gymnasts & Masseurs. **(March 25, 1934)**

SIEGMUND KLEIN could do five sets of ten dips or vertical pushups (fifty in all) without having to pause for a rest. Due to his mastery of unusual physical abilities, Ripley frequently consulted with Klein on items submitted that required specialized knowledge of the capabilities of the human body. **(November 8, 1941)**

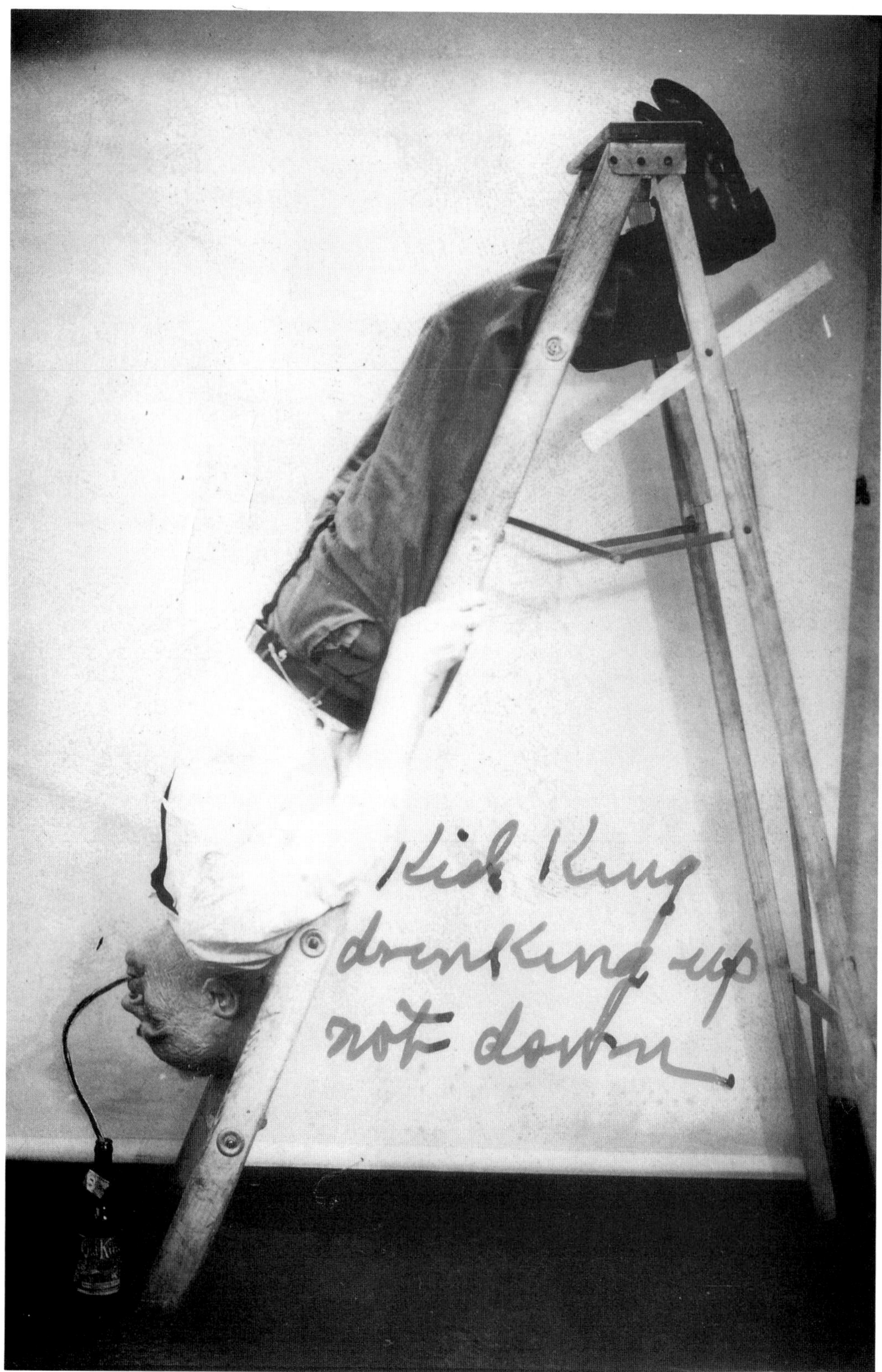

OKLAHOMA CITY foot racer **F. W. S. "KID" KING** saw two mules leaning down a steep embankment to quench their thirsts at a waterfall and **concocted the idea of teaching himself to drink upside down.** He perfected the skill after a few practice tries and won $25 in a DENVER bar a few years later by betting another man that he could drink a bottle of beer without a drop going down his throat. Twenty-six years later (at age seventy-three) he repeated the stunt for Ripley. **(January 7, 1937)**

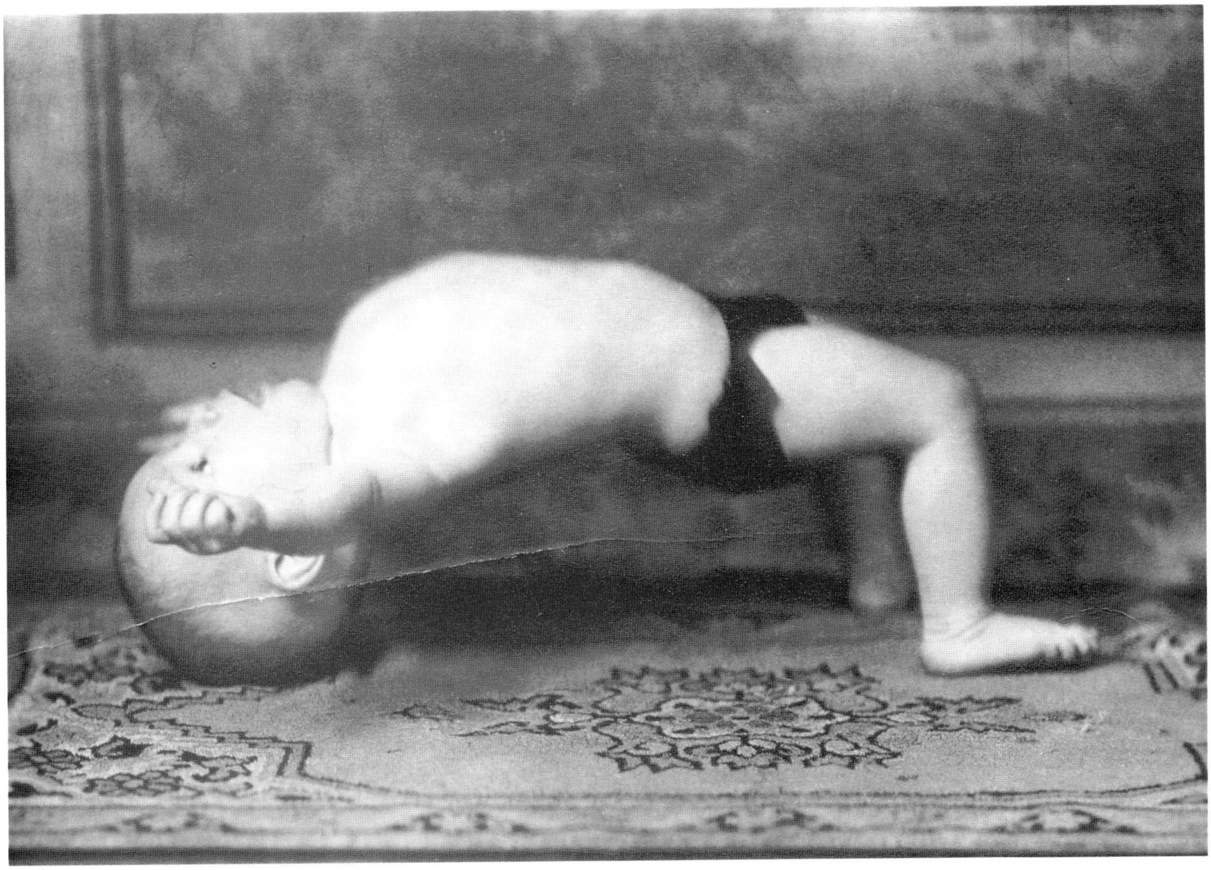

Ralph Roland Dowell did his first **perfect "wrestler's bridge"** in Grand Junction, Colorado, **at the age of two and a half months.** By the time he was six months old he could hold the position for more than two minutes. **(January 9, 1932)**

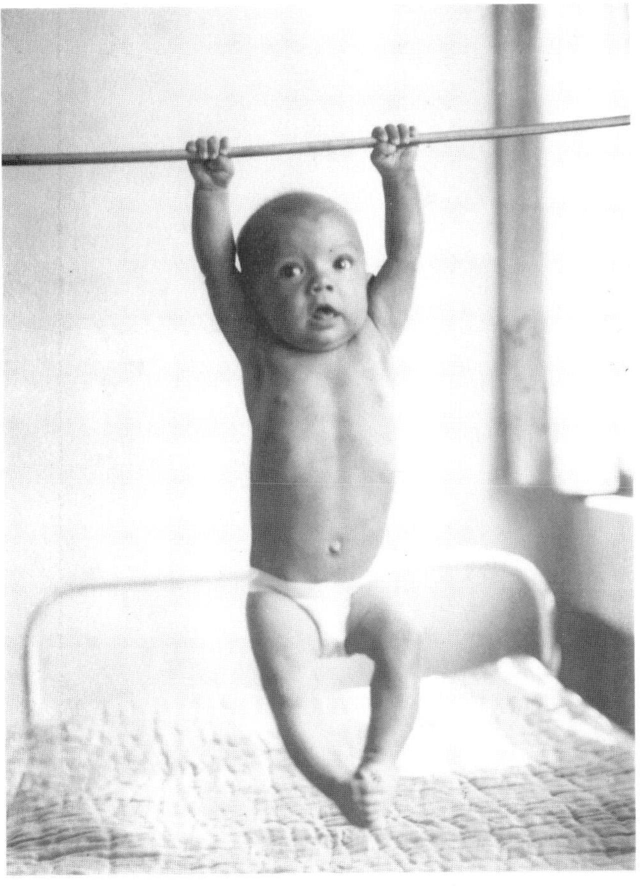

Ted Elbert Carmack, at three and a half months old, could lift his own weight on a chin-up bar. His father, an Army officer stationed in Denver, began young Ted's physical conditioning when the boy was three weeks old. **(December 19, 1934)**

At seventy-four years of age, MRS. F. M. IRWIN of Raleigh, NORTH CAROLINA, could still do more work than the average woman of twenty, **run as fast as the average girl of sixteen,** and still do chin-ups. **(June 9, 1940)**

THE ONE AND ONLY HUMAN CORK, **ALAN COOKE** of BALTIMORE **could eat, drink, and sleep while floating on the water.** To prove that he couldn't (or wouldn't ?) sink, he was thrown tied, taped, and bound into Lake Michigan, numerous rivers and indoor pools, and into the Chesapeake Bay fifteen times. *Believe It or Not!* radio program guest, 1940.

THE HUMAN CORK, steel-mill worker **W. C. CAVENDER** of Pueblo, COLORADO, **relaxed for hours each day afloat while drinking soda pop,** reading a newspaper, and smoking a cigar. He enjoyed demonstrating his unusual buoyancy by allowing himself to be bound hand and foot and thrown into the pool, or as shown here, by balancing tumblers of water on his chest, forehead, and both palms. Coincidentally, Mr. Cavender **died the day the cartoon appeared. (February 11, 1953)**

Four-year-old **Billy Crawford jumped over the Cleveland Municipal Building wearing a harness attached to a balloon** that barely held him aloft! When this picture was taken, Billy had spent more than four solo hours aloft, leaping around the city. **(June 1, 1934)**

TATTOO TALENT

"Good sense is the body of poetic genius, fancy its drapery, motion its life, and imagination the soul."

SAMUEL TAYLOR COLERIDGE

"PROFESSOR" **WILLIAM LUCAS,** of St. Paul, MINNESOTA, had **his wife's name tattooed inside his mouth.** He also had stars tattooed on his earlobes, the words *Holy Ghost* tattooed on his fingers, and most of the rest of his body heavily tattooed.
(December 19, 1936)

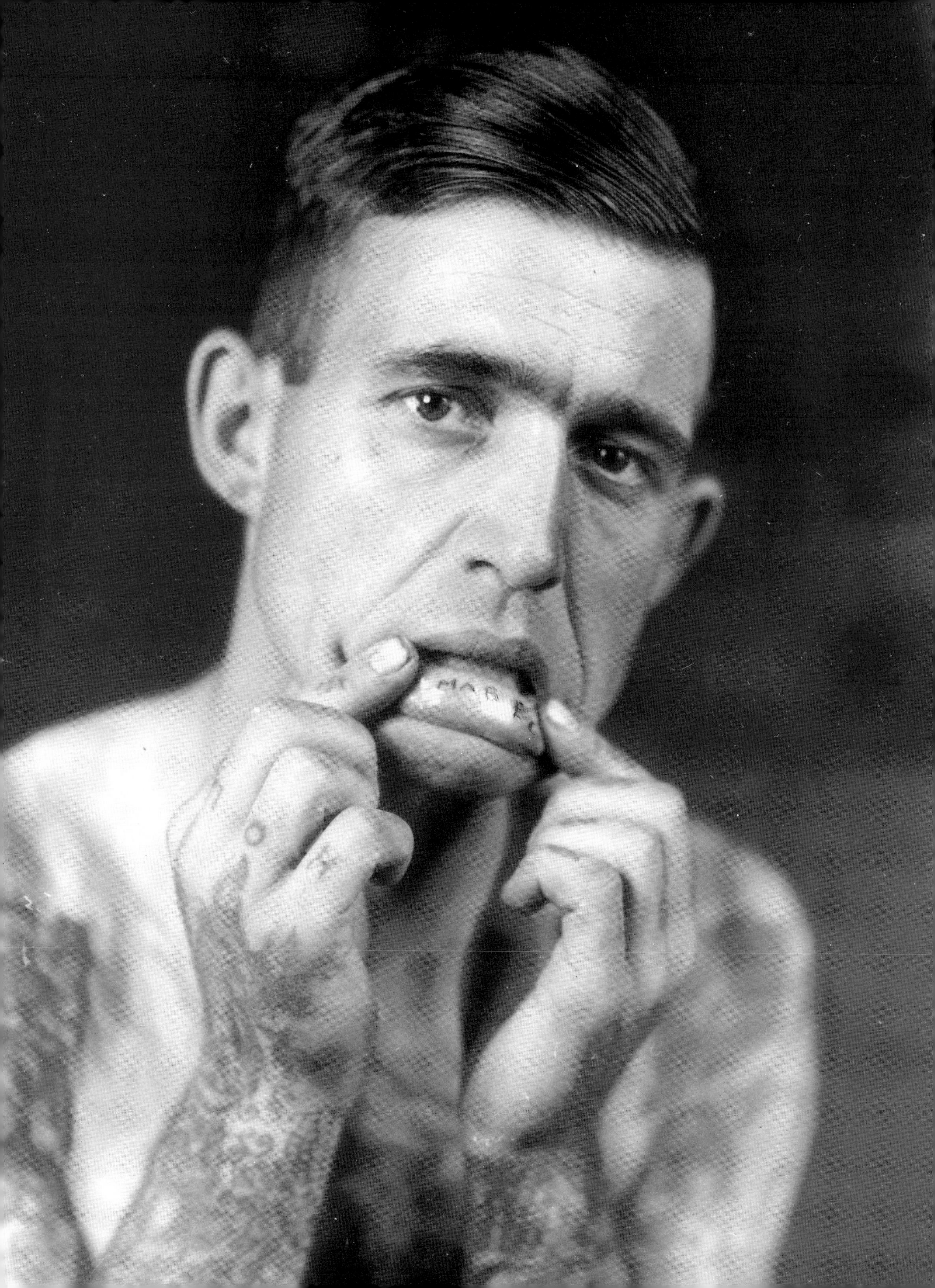

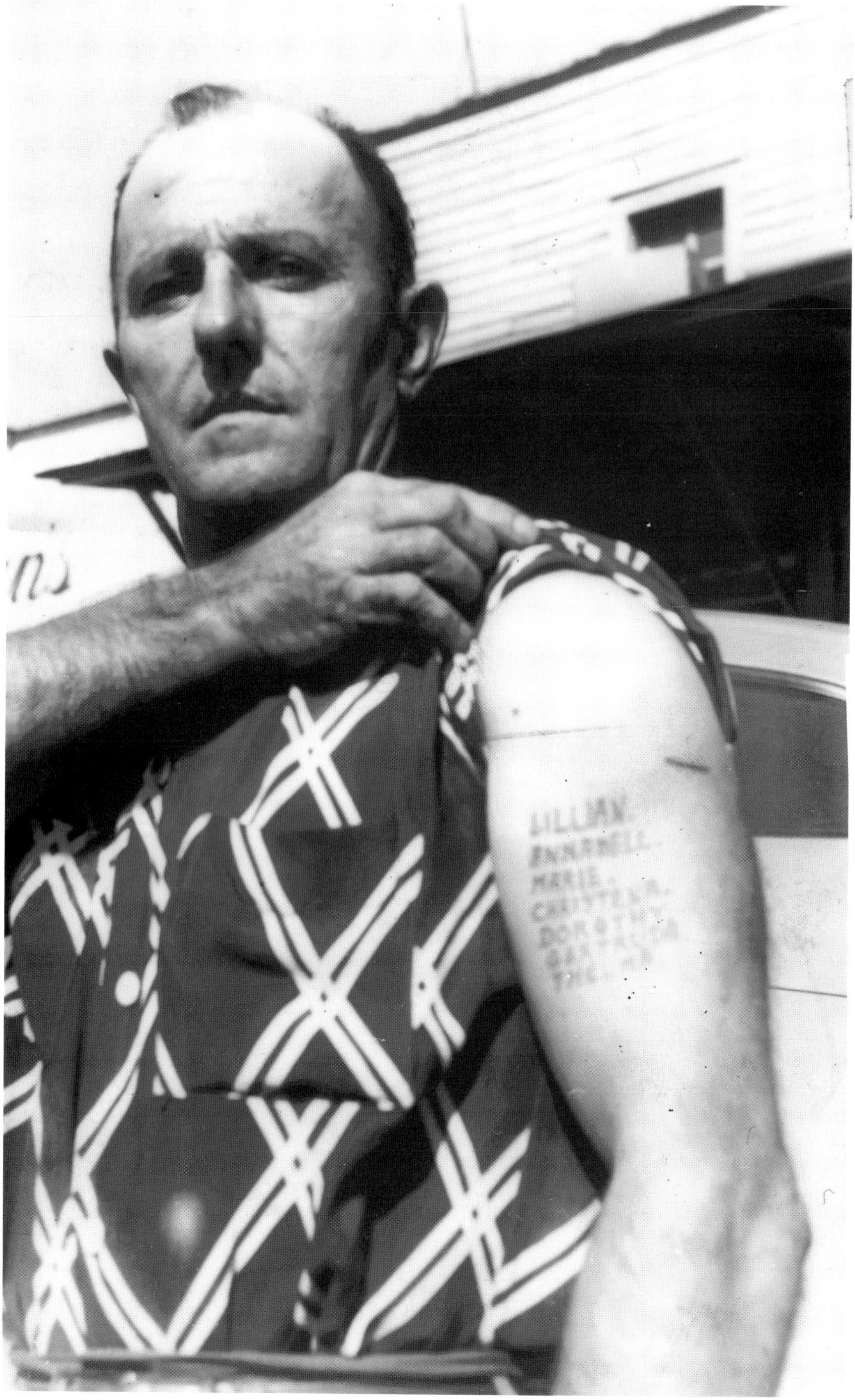

Cleston Jenkins of Kuttawa, Kentucky, had **the first names of each of his seven divorced wives tattooed on his arm. (February 27, 1953)**

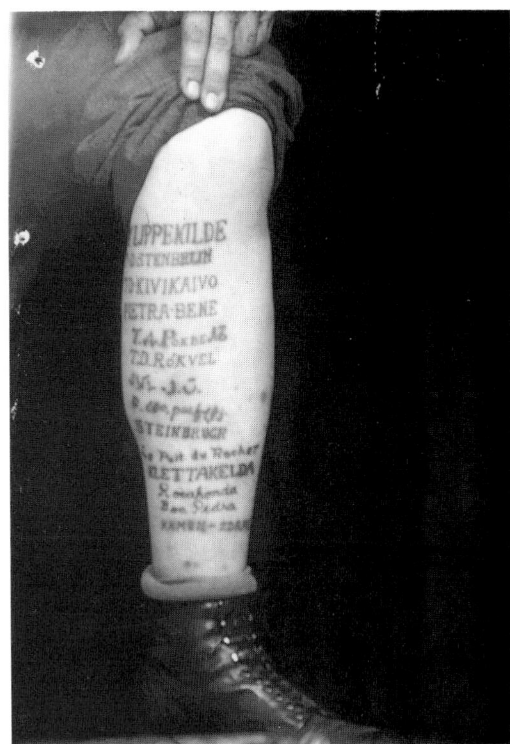

San Francisco razor blade salesman **T. D. Rockwell,** The Man Who Couldn't Get Lost, **had his name and address tattooed on his body in Chinese, Japanese, English,** Hebrew, Palestinian, Greek, Danish, Swedish, Finnish, Italian, Russian, Hungarian, Arabic, Persian, Turkish, Armenian, German, French, Spanish, Portuguese, Bohemian, Polish, Gaelic, Icelandic, Morse code, Gregg shorthand, and semaphore. He originally did it, he said, **"for ease in cashing checks,"** since not only was his own address rendered on his legs but also the address of his bank! **(January 13, 1937)**

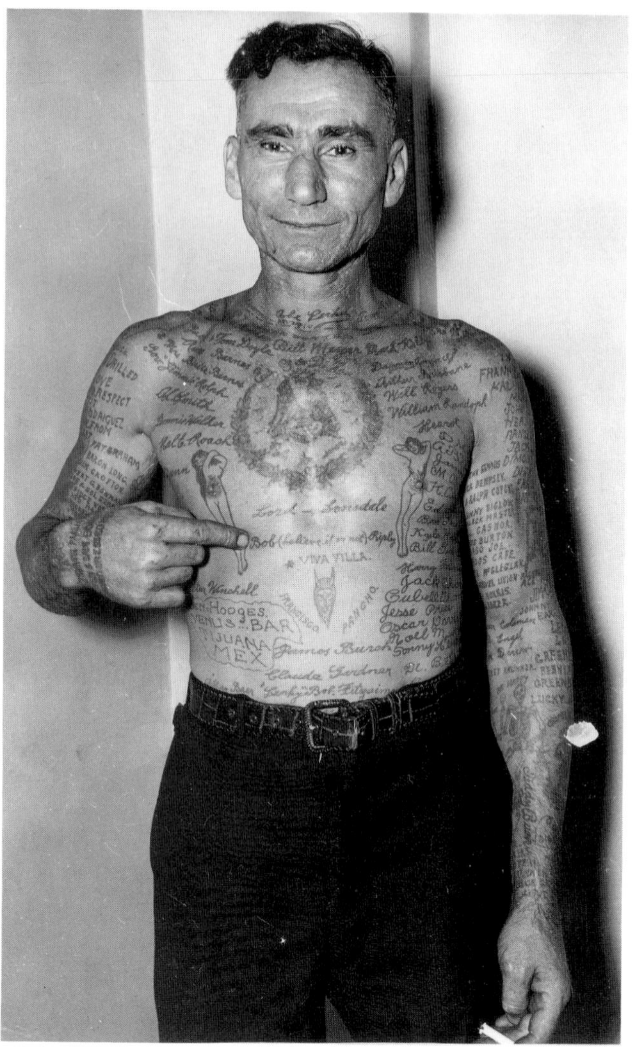

Former boxer **Dick Hyland,** the Human Autograph Album, **was tattooed from head to foot with the names of more than six hundred friends,** celebrities, and chance acquaintances. Here Hyman points at the signature of Bob (*Believe It or Not!*) Ripley, just above a dedication to Pancho Villa. Ripley's sponsor, William Randolph Hearst, was also a "signee." Hyland was a 1939 New York Odditorium performer. **(July 12, 1939)**

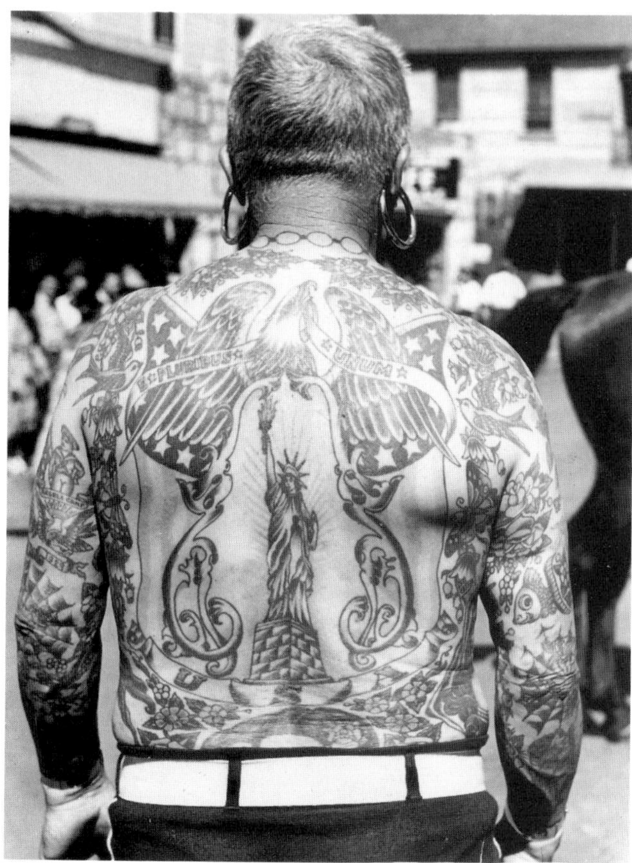

Rasmus Nielsen (above and at right) of Angel's Camp, California, **lifts a 200-pound anvil with a metal bar pierced through his nipples.** He could also lift a 115-pound rock by one nipple, and 10-pound hammers from rings through his ears. His extensive tattoos depicted giant sequoia trees and patriotic scenes, among other things. **(July 16, 1938)**

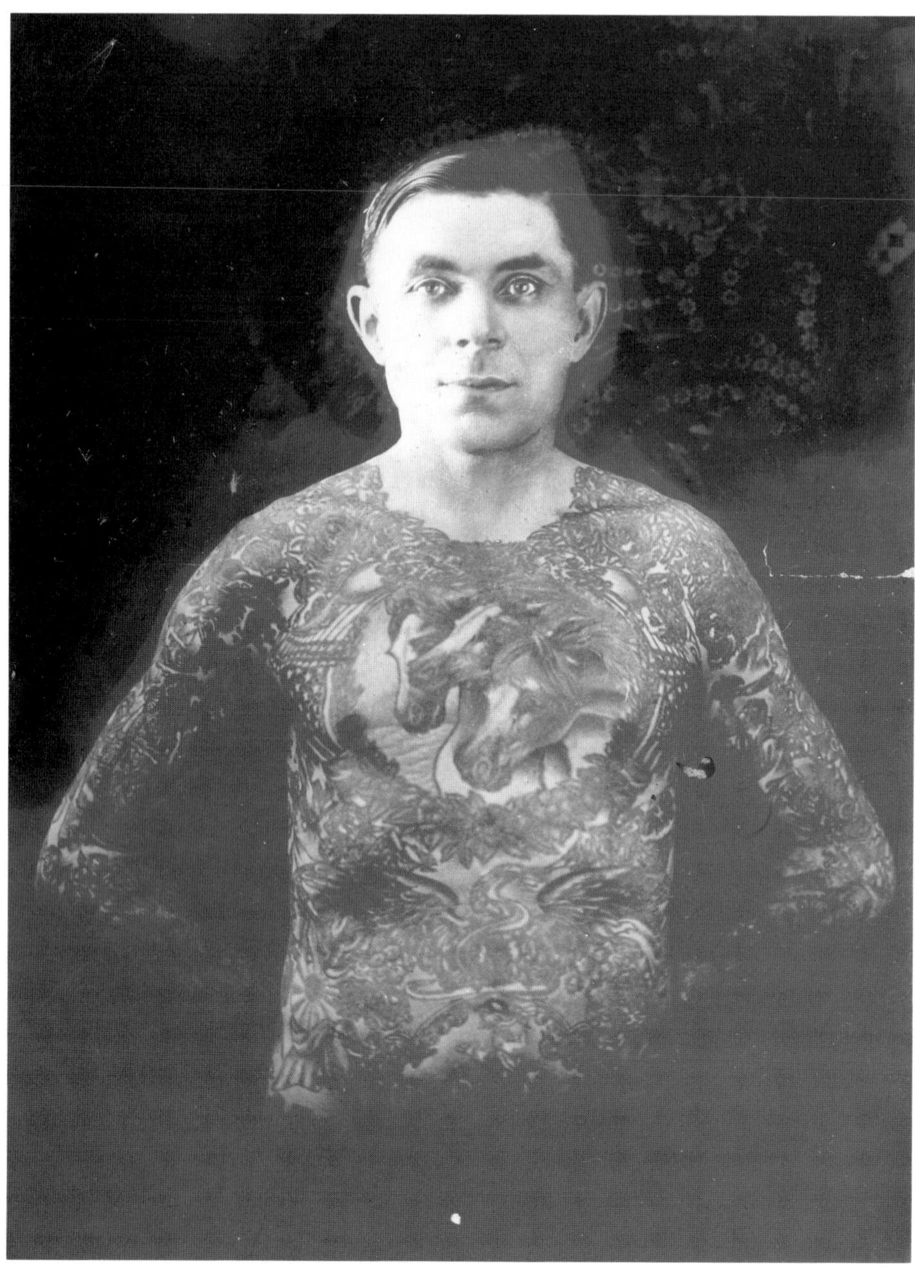

"PROFESSOR" **CHARLES WAGNER** claimed to be "one of the most artistic of tattooed people." **His back depicted a scene entitled "Child Christ and a Trip to Mars (in an airplane)."**

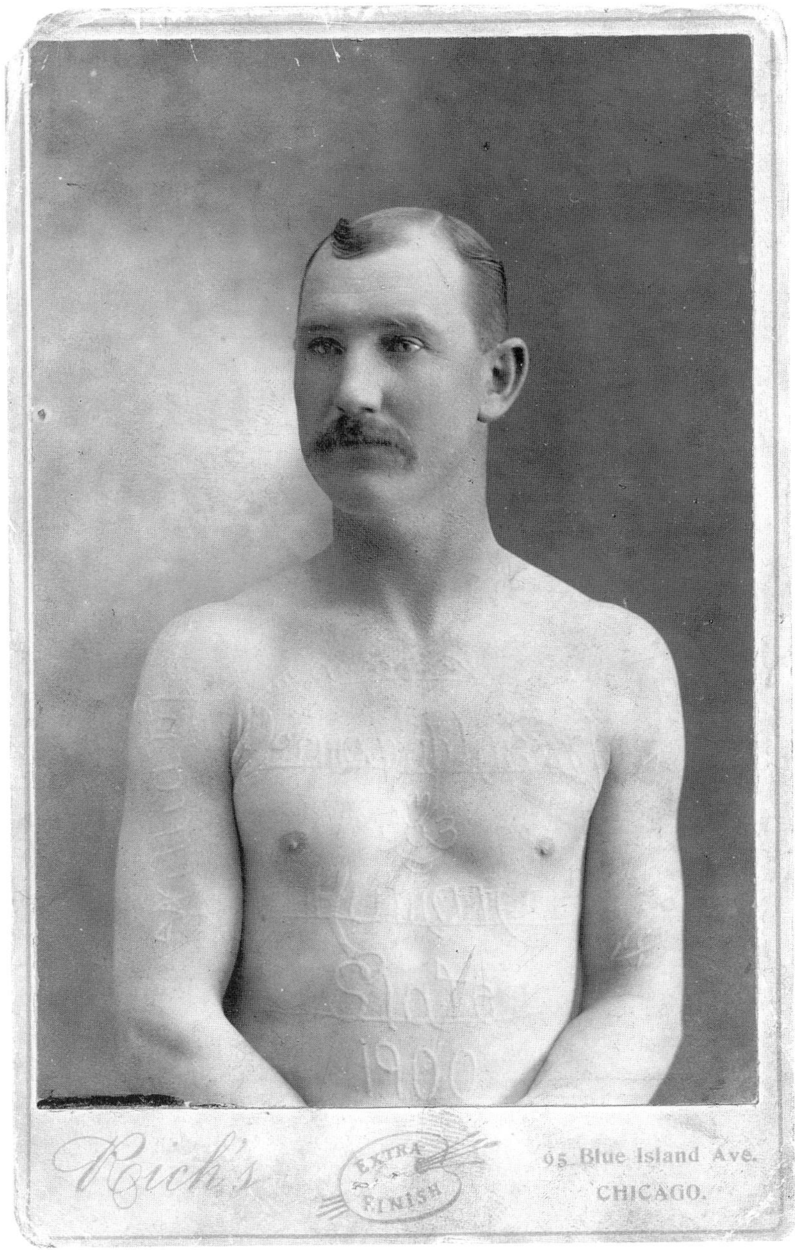

William H. Fiekling of Cambridge, Illinois, was known as the Human Slate because **his skin raised temporary welts when touched with a blunt instrument.** Apparently it all began one very hot afternoon as he was putting up hay. After each load he would jump into a cold spring to cool off. The next day he became very sick and since that time was unable to perspire except on his head and hands. Not long after that he discovered that his "lithographic skin" would swell in response to rubbing or scratching. **(November 26, 1932)**

WORLD CHAMPIONS

"He was a bold man who first swallowed an oyster."

KING JAMES I OF ENGLAND

FRANK ANTONIEVICH won a bronze medal, a diploma, and a ten-dollar gold piece when he **cooked 100 pancakes in 22 1/2 minutes** at the Grand Central Palace in NEW YORK. He was as fancy as he was productive, tossing the flapjacks in six different pans behind him from between his legs and catching them in the same pans in front of him. **(September 10, 1945)**

Mrs. W. E. UpdeGraff could cook sixty pies in forty-five minutes. A team of witnesses in Vinita, Oklahoma, reported that they each tasted excellent. **(July 10, 1933)**

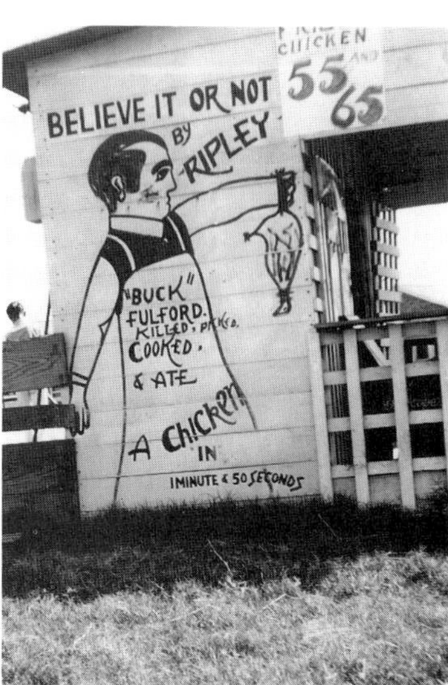

World-champion chicken picker **"Buck" Fulford** of Port Arthur, Texas, **could kill, pick clean, cut up, cook, and eat a chicken in one minute and fifty seconds.** Elaborating on his technique, he explained that it took forty seconds to cut off the chicken's head and allow it to die, ten seconds for scalding, three or four seconds to pick and clean the chicken, three seconds to cut it into four portions and drop it into boiling grease, thirty seconds to cook it, followed by cooling in cracked ice, and the rest of the time was for savoring and eating the fowl. Fulford's other accomplishments included plucking and picking as many as twelve chickens in one minute. **(April 30, 1935)**

BELIEVE *IT* OR *NOT* INFORMATION BLANK

5/4/38

From: John Strocco
6107 Bway
Woodside L.I.

To: *B*elieve *It* or *N*ot, Inc.

*B*ELIEVE *IT* OR *NOT*:

I can smash, with one snap of the finger as shown in above photograph, Hazel Pecan & Walnuts. In the thirty-five years that I have been doing this I have got

He did this in office it look very goo

Cracks mits b flippi his fing on them

VERIFICATION: (Give names of witnesses, book reference, or other source of information, and *include photographs* if possible).

I have seen Mr. Strocco break nuts with his finger
G. L. McIntosh c/o United Shoe Machine Corp. of America. N.Y.C.
Mr. John Strocco has performed before me as described above. I. D. Mechaneck M.D. 41-25-70th St. Woodside, L.I.
Witnessed by. Mr. Robert Ripley in Believe it or not. office

I hereby grant to Robert Ripley and *B*elieve *It* or *N*ot, Inc. permission to make use of this material.

Signed John Strocco
NAME
6107 Broadway
STREET
Woodside L.I. New York C
CITY

Date Jan 16, 1938

KINDLY RETURN IN STAMPED ADDRESSED ENVELOPE

Eighteen-year-old **Edd Woolf drank five gallons and thirty ounces of water,** then had a sandwich and a malt at Cheque's Confectionery in Duncan, Oklahoma. All this **in less than thirty minutes!** Woolf performed this amazing feat to win six dollars. **(November 7, 1935)**

Ed Kottwitz, four times world-champion sweet corn eater, **gnawed fifty ears of corn** at the Third Annual Ortonville (Minnesota) Sweet Corn Festival. Kottwitz was a forty-year-old South Dakota farmer. **(February 26, 1935)**

John Strocco of Woodside, Long Island, **cracked hazelnuts,** pecans, and walnuts **by smashing them with his finger. (May 4, 1938)**

LORENZO LECLET rode 3,465 miles around the circumference of the island of PUERTO RICO in three days on a borrowed bicycle, without eating or sleeping! The trip only cost a nickel: three cents for a pack of matches and two cents for a candle to light his way after dark. **(June 13, 1931)**

In an era of nonstop ballroom dancing and flagpole sitting, **ice-sitting** was a little-known avenue for competition. **Gus Simmons** (arrow) **sat for twenty-seven hours and ten minutes before being disqualified** for running a 102 degree fever (!) at this contest held at CHICAGO'S White City Casino. **(October 17, 1933)**

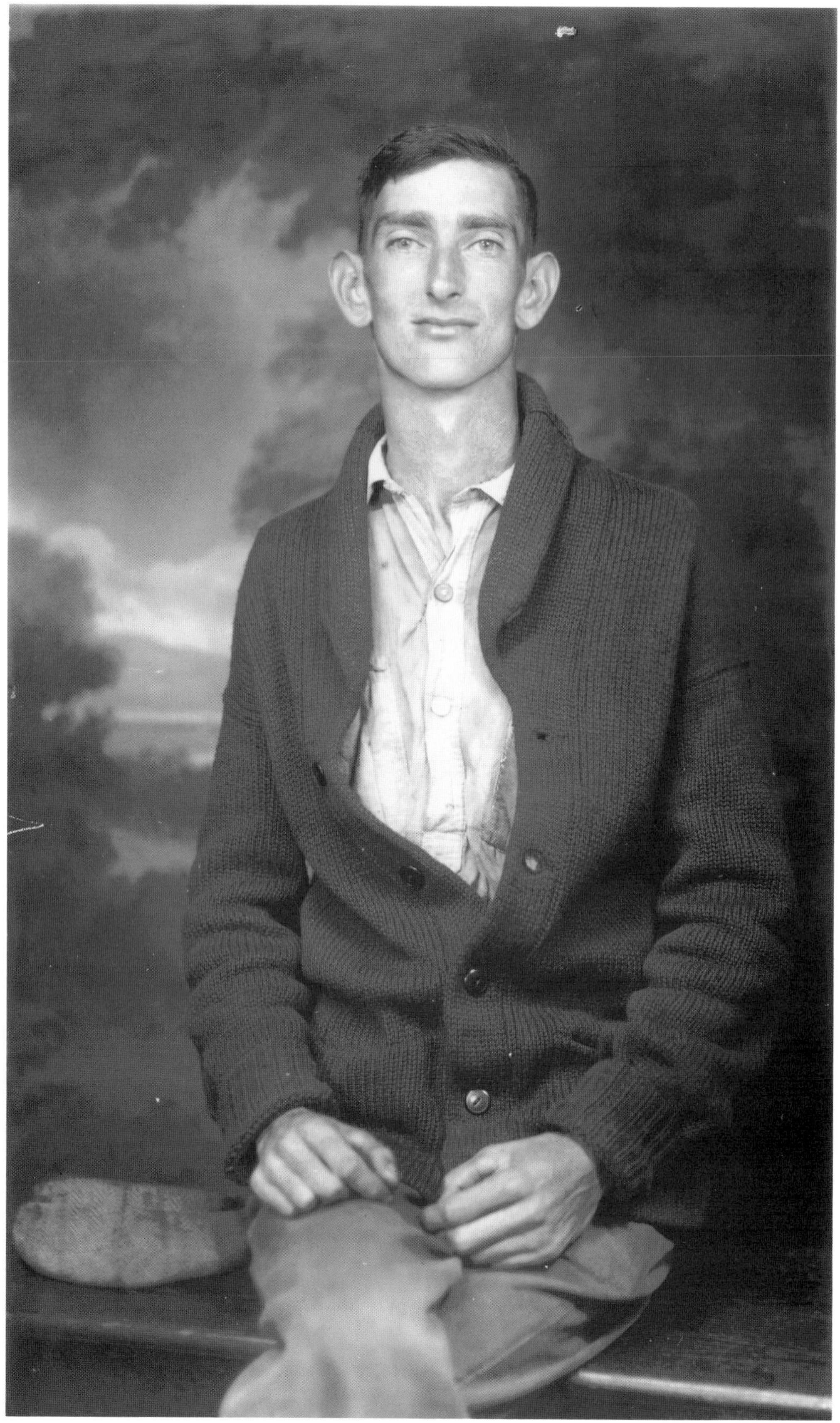

ISRAEL "LUCKY SLIM" BRESSNER, BALTIMORE street cleaner, **found a penny each day for fourteen days! (March 3, 1932)**

CHICAGO'S **PAULO GIGANTI** claimed to be the only **full-blooded Italian who had never eaten spaghetti** or macaroni in his life. His mother served it every day for years, but he never touched a bite. **(December 16, 1937)**

FORREST YANKEY lassoed a house-fly with a length of cotton thread in Grand Rapids, MICHIGAN. The momentous event was witnessed by his immediate family. Astoundingly, the fly lived through the unsettling experience. **(December 4, 1934)**

Hawaiian swimmer **Tommy Kaeo caught a four-pound white sea bass** off Steel Pier at Atlantic City, New Jersey, with his bare hands **after swimming a quarter mile. (July 13, 1935)**

"Sharpshooter Supreme" **Edna Alee** of Detroit, Michigan, **cut a card edgewise at a distance of sixty-three feet with her .22 caliber revolver** held as shown. She cut another card edgewise twice in succession at seventy-five feet with a .38 caliber revolver that same afternoon. **(April 13, 1938)**

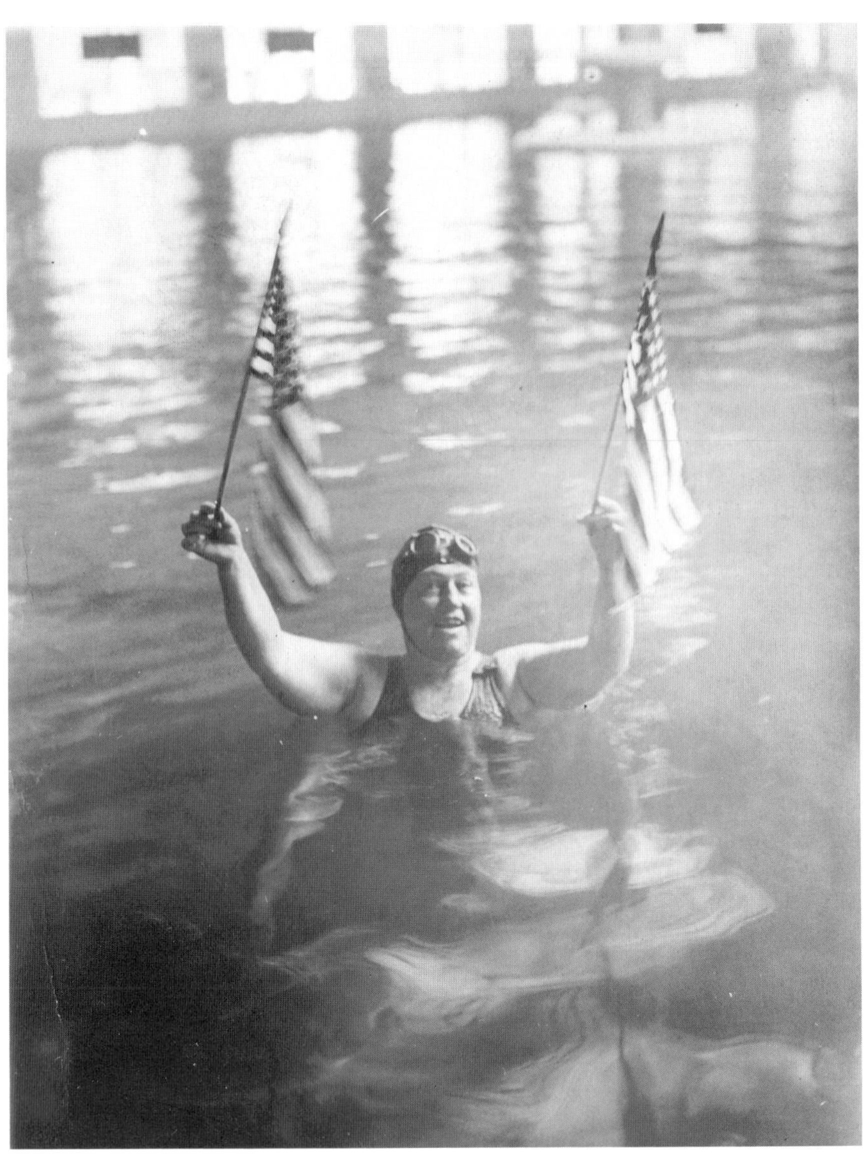

MRS. ANNA E. VAN SKIKE of Santa Monica, CALIFORNIA, **swam over 3,000 miles *after* her sixtieth birthday.** She marked her seventieth birthday with a twenty-mile swim in the Pacific Ocean, and her seventy-second birthday by swimming around the Rainbow Pier at Long Beach singing "The Holy City" and "The Star-Spangled Banner" while holding aloft a flag in each hand. **(December 1, 1933)**

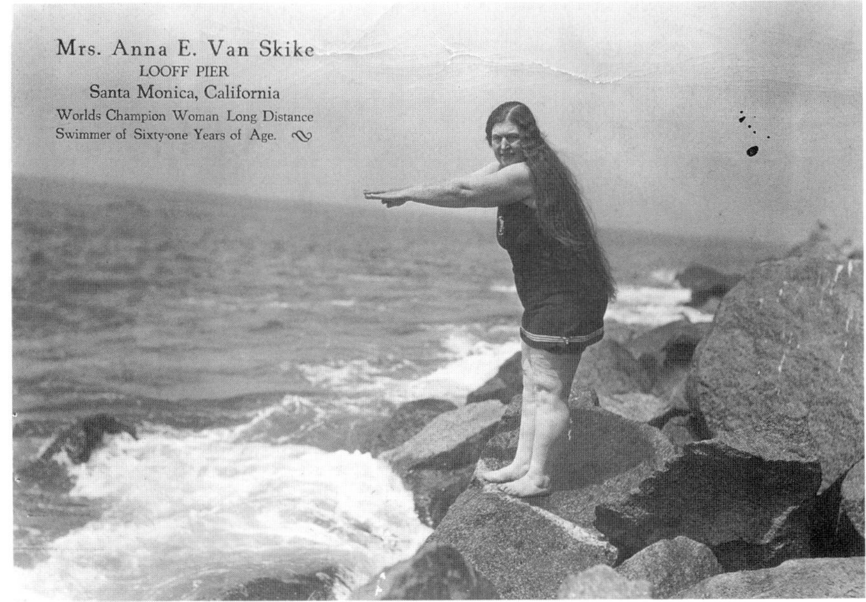

Mrs. Anna E. Van Skike
LOOFF PIER
Santa Monica, California
Worlds Champion Woman Long Distance
Swimmer of Sixty-one Years of Age.

Long-distance swimmer **Fred Newton** of Clinton, Oklahoma, **swam the Mississippi River from Minneapolis to New Orleans**—a distance of approximately 2,300 miles. Newton spent a total of 742 hours in the river and claims to have gained ten pounds in the process. **His first bathing suit wore out** after 1,700 miles. He painted signs at night along the way to finance the swim. **(June 10, 1931)**

What's in a Name?

"This generation of Americans has a rendezvous with destiny."

Franklin Delano Roosevelt

SAM HELLER, a "Ham Seller" of Richmond, Virginia, shown here with the Smithfield ham he presented in person to President Coolidge. **(March 30, 1931)**

RICHMOND GROCERY CO.
RICHMOND, VIRGINIA
Hon. Calvin Coolidge
The White House
Washington, D.C.
SAM HELLER BRAND
GENUINE
SMITHFIELD HAM
DISTRIBUTED BY
RICHMOND GROCERY COMPANY
INCORPORATED
RICHMOND, VIRGINIA
NET WEIGHT WHEN PACKED
LBS. OZ.

Teller's Photograph

NAME Mr. I.Teller, Information Clerk

STREET ADDRESS Hudson Terminal Post Office

CITY AND STATE New York City

USED 3/9/35

BELIEVE IT OR NOT: I. Teller — quite an appropriate name for the information man

Rip:

I. TELLER IS THE NAME OF AN INFORMATION CLERK AT THE HUDSON TERMINAL P.O. NYC. JM Bunnell

BELGIAN LINE
New York, 10 PEARL ST., Tel. Bowling Green 8960-4
COMPAGNIE MARITIME BELGE S. A.
(LLOYD ROYAL)
See Blotter on Back for Sailing Dates and Steamers
NEW YORK—ANTWERP DIRECT

VERIFICATION: Mr M. G. Knowles
410 Van Buren St
Bklyn N.Y.

I. TELLER was an information clerk at the Hudson Terminal Post Office in NEW YORK CITY. **(March 9, 1935)**

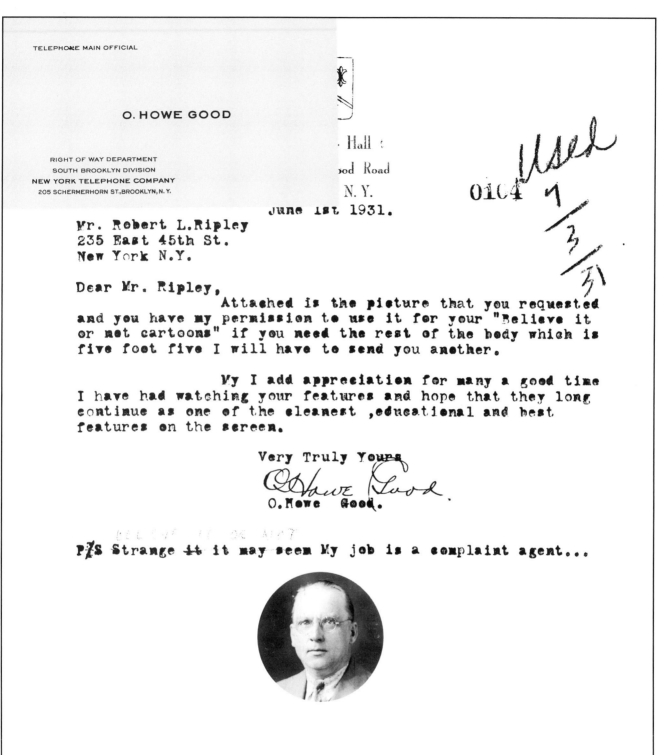

TELEPHONE MAIN OFFICIAL

O. HOWE GOOD

RIGHT OF WAY DEPARTMENT
SOUTH BROOKLYN DIVISION
NEW YORK TELEPHONE COMPANY
205 SCHERMERHORN ST., BROOKLYN, N. Y.

Hall
ood Road
N. Y.

0104 Used 7/3/31

June 1st 1931.

Mr. Robert L.Ripley
235 East 45th St.
New York N.Y.

Dear Mr. Ripley,

Attached is the picture that you requested and you have my permission to use it for your "Believe it or not cartoons" if you need the rest of the body which is five foot five I will have to send you another.

My I add appreciation for many a good time I have had watching your features and hope that they long continue as one of the cleanest ,educational and best features on the screen.

Very Truly Yours

O. Howe Good

O.Howe Good.

P/S Strange ~~it~~ it may seem My job is a complaint agent...

O. HOWE GOOD was a complaint agent for the New York Telephone Company in BROOKLYN. **(July 3, 1931)**

Smith A L
Camino las Cerros Athertn . Palo Alto-4445
Santa Rita Av . . Palo Alto-6683
Smith A R L r 139 . . . . Sn Mateo-5696-M
Mill Vly-83-M
Smith A W r King Richmnd-771-W
Smith A W Mrs r 801 Standard . . . . Palo Alto-22400
Smith Adelaide r 627 Bryant . . . Palo Alto-4740
Lytton Av . Palo Alto-8193
Main Centrvl-76
Smith Albert r 971 Addison . . . . . . Palo Alto-8193
Smith Alfred H r BaywoodAv Ross . Sn Anslmo-2086-W
Smith Alfred J r 1220 Quince . . . . Sn Mateo-1589
Smith Another r 1017BayswaterAv . Sn Mateo-5516-W
Smith Antique Shop Highway Menlo Pk . Palo Alto-6715
Smith Arthur A r 130 Byron . . . . . . Palo Alto-6649
Smith Arthur H r 413 Hazel . . . . . . Sn Bruno-982-J
Smith Arthur Hedderly r
424 Midway Rd . Sn Mateo-2371
. . . . Hayward-123-J
Smith B K r Main . . . . Palo Alto-5450
Smith B M Mrs r 428 Ruthven . . . . . Sn Mateo-2854-J
Smith Bert r 551 S Grant Redwood-1207
Smith Bertha osteopathic phys
D R Stafford Bldg . Redwood-366-J
If no answer call . . . . Sn Mateo-1066-J
Smith Bertha F r 217 Villa Ter . . Sn Mateo-1066-J
Smith Bettie r
Central N Palo Alto . Palo Alto-7440
1010-3rd . . Sn Rafel-653
Palo Alto-4264

176

Newspaperman **ANOTHER SMITH,** who **signed his friendly letters "Just Another,"** was manager of Wide World Photos for the *New York Times*. **(August 29, 1932)**

Two radio repairmen both working at the same time at Rabeck Music Company in Olympia, WASHINGTON, **were named LES COOL and LES HOT. (July 28, 1953)**

LES' COOL

LES' HOT

TWO RADIO REPAIR MEN
EMPLOYED AT SAME TIME
BY RABECK MUSIC CO.
OLYMPIA, WASH.

U. S. WALKER was a mail carrier in Kansas City, MISSOURI. **(May 26, 1933)**

East met West when **MR. E. E. EAST** of West Virginia met **MR. E. E. WEST** of east Virginia at the National Business College in Roanoke, VIRGINIA. Imagine the odds! **(February 5, 1937)**

JACK FROST sold refrigerators in WASHINGTON, D.C. **(February 12, 1931)**

WASHINGTON, D.C., milkman **I. M. WISER** was married to **MAY B. WISER. Their child was "a little Wiser." (May 2, 1941)**

A. C. CURRENT was an electrical contractor in Tontogany, OHIO. His son's name was **D. C. CURRENT. (December 16, 1931)**

MR. PINK DUCK was a janitor in Jackson, Mississippi. **(November 27, 1933)**

MISS BIRDIE SNYDER married **MR. C. CANARY** to become **BIRDIE CANARY. (January 6, 1938)**

Native Alabaman **LEGAL TENDER FAIRCLOTH** claimed to be **the only person in the world named for currency. (October 16, 1939)**

IONA FIDDLE of St. Paul, MINNESOTA, **never owned or played a fiddle. (February 23, 1935)**

WILLIAM WILLIAMS lived on **Williams Street in Williamsburg,** KANSAS. **(May 13, 1936)**

ATTA ATTA, an immigrant **from Ata, in Attica,** GREECE. **(March 21, 1940)**

VIRGINIA HIGHT was the librarian for the **Virginia Heights** School in ROANOKE. **(September 20, 1941)**

An eye specialist in Hillsboro, OHIO, was named **C. SITES. (February 28, 1935)**

H. M. BALMER

FUNERAL DIRECTOR

To Serve Humanity Better

Day and Night LADY ASSISTANT 208 Remington

Fort Collins, Colo.

Phone 372-W

WILLIS I. BROOKS

ASSOCIATE

Phone 372-J

AMBULANCE SERVICE

H. M. BALMER was a **funeral director** in Fort Collins, COLORADO. **(November 8, 1934)**

NINA CLOCK passed her time in St. Paul, MINNESOTA. **(June 3, 1931)**

THE CLIPPER BROTHERS were barbers in Bakersfield, CALIFORNIA. **(November 9, 1951)**

GEORGE KOPMAN was a police officer in SAN FRANCISCO for more than thirty years. **(April 22, 1935)**

MR. AB C DEFGHI lived in Villa Park, ILLINOIS, **with his alphabetic name. (May 28, 1935)**

MISS ANNIE RAINER SHINE grew banana plants in Luverne, ALABAMA. **(March 3, 1933)**

HANNAH LABAL married **BOB OTTO** on November (the eleventh month) 22, and lived at 1991 33rd Drive in the BRONX. **All the names and numbers associated with their wedding and address could be read backwards and forwards. (October 30, 1947)**

MR. SANTA C. KLAUS paid $225.50 cash to the Tennessee Electric Power Company for a DeLuxe 837 Frigidaire in Chattanooga, TENNESSEE, **seventeen days before Christmas. (December 21, 1944)**

MR. A. BALL PITCHER of Melrose Park, ILLINOIS, **never threw a ball** in the seventy years of his life. **(September 23, 1933)**

MISS HELEN FERNAL was a peace-loving girl from Portland, OREGON. **(May 21, 1930)**

MISS MERRY CHRISTMAS DAY was born on December 25, 1903, in Bellingham, WASHINGTON. In submitting her daughter's name and picture to Ripley, Merry's mother asked it not appear "alongside a three-legged calf or some other monstrosity." **(December 25, 1932)**

When her name appeared in the Ripley's cartoon, **DINA MIGHT was just a young girl** from Flint, MICHIGAN. **(September 22, 1932)**

CALIFORNIA POPPE lived in Inglewood, **CALIFORNIA. (July 8, 1933)**

MISS CALI FORNIA lived in San Pedro, **CALIFORNIA. (October 28, 1931)**

MRS. ALMA MATER was a housewife in Tulsa, OKLAHOMA. **(January 31, 1933)**

DOCTOR LAWYER was mayor of Ironwood, MICHIGAN. **(August 6, 1947)**

ICCOLO MICCOLO played a piccolo for the LOS ANGELES Philharmonic Orchestra. **(July 26, 1935)**

DEEP C. FISHER hated fishing because he didn't like to hurt animals of any kind. Instead, he sold real estate in SAN FRANCISCO. **(February 7, 1939)**

MISS NELLIE MAY FLY married an aviator who worked for Richfield Oil in Fresno, CALIFORNIA. **(February 4, 1936)**

TWINKLE STARR came to Ripley's attention when she was struck by a car in Portland, OREGON. She recovered from her injuries. **(June 26, 1931)**

B. A. CRANK may have turned things around on his farm in Waldo, ARKANSAS, but was reported in the local paper to have **"plenty of mental calibre" nonetheless. (December 27, 1932)**

In Charleston, WEST VIRGINIA, **an automobile frame and axle repair shop was run by FRANK FRAME and JOE AXLE. (March 30, 1943)**

PARSON B. R. PARSONS lived in the **parsonage** on **Parsons Street** in Saranac, MICHIGAN. **(October 13, 1935)**

A. FISH was in charge of fish distribution in OREGON. **(November 20, 1932)**

The school dentist for the Burlington, IOWA, Independent School District was **DR. H. A. TOOTHACRE. (November 30, 1932)**

BARBER SAUL of NEW YORK was **the seventh son of a seventh son,** and he and every other male in his family for the previous three generations were barbers. **(March 2, 1942)**

JOHN PAINTER was a painter and paperhanger in Centralia, ILLINOIS. **(February 17, 1955)**

NOVEL IDEAS

"Imagination is more important than knowledge."

ALBERT EINSTEIN

Shown here is **the biggest broom ever made. It was thirteen feet across the base and forty feet tall.** Made in Deshler, NEBRASKA, at the Deshler Broom Factory (at the time the largest broom factory in the world), the giant broom was made to celebrate the fiftieth anniversary of the factory. Standing in front are the town mayor and the president of the factory. Later the broom was dismantled and recycled to make 1,440 standard-sized brooms. **(November 14, 1940)**

GOLDEN 1940
SITTLER
DRUG
CO.
RITZ
DRUG STORE
Coca-Cola
DRUGS

The World's Largest Strawberry Shortcake was a nineteen-year tradition at the time of this photograph in 1954. Lebanon, OREGON, was the site of this whopping dessert, which, with toppings, weighed in at over 5,000 pounds and **served a modest 12,000 persons. (September 21, 1954)**

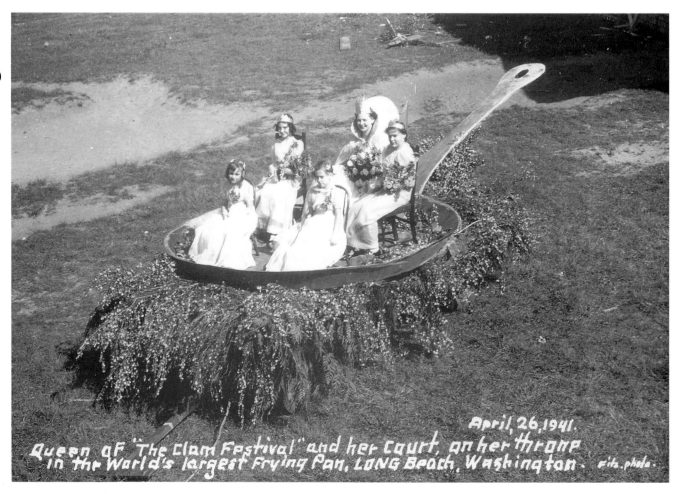

April, 26, 1941.
Queen of "The Clam Festival" and her court, on her throne in the World's largest Frying Pan, LONG Beach, Washington.

QUEEN OF THE CLAM FESTIVAL AND HER COURT ON HER THRONE in **the World's Largest Frying Pan** in Long Beach, WASHINGTON, in 1941. **(December 2, 1948)**

Here CHICAGO auto mechanic **JOSEPH STEINLAUF** is shown posed with two of his bicycle inventions: **a bedroom bicycle and a sewing machine bike.** Steinlauf's ingenious bikes, including one built with guns (in firing condition), appeared in the Ripley's cartoon feature a number of times. The gun bike weighed 350 pounds and carried fifteen different antique guns ranging from a 1780 Chinese flintlock to a Springfield repeating rifle used in the Indian Wars. **(April 30, 1939)** (bedroom bike) and **(October 23, 1939)** (sewing machine bike)

Former farmer **Roy Gardner** of Mason City, Illinois, was a star attraction at Ripley's Chicago Odditorium in 1934. He had **eighty pipes and strings** in his set and claimed to have spent three hours per day just tuning up. Both hands, both feet, and even his head got in on the act while **he played all of these instruments simultaneously.**

Although blind, **Anton Pagani could simultaneously whistle and play the accordion and the cello,** frequently entertaining crowds at theaters and Shrine Temples within range of his home in LaSalle, Illinois. **(April 29, 1940)**

In Bristol, VERMONT, a farmer named **HOWARD HASELTINE had a set of musical wood** on which he could play tunes with a hammer. Over the years he tuned them by sawing or splitting off pieces to raise the pitch until they were perfectly tuned. **(May 27, 1935)**

After ten years' practice, **ARTHUR SCHULTZ** of Hamtramck, MICHIGAN, taught himself to **play the song "Black Eyes" on the piano with both his hands upside down. (March 29, 1939)**

Evangelist **CLYDE VAN PATTEN** attracted crowds to hear his sermons by promising to **perform musical numbers with his nose.** Based in Highland Park, MICHIGAN, Van Patten attended revival meetings throughout the upper Midwest. **(March 16, 1934)**

Mrs. Willis N. Ward and **Mrs. John Hoppemath,** regular winter tourists visiting in Mount Dora, Florida, often sported "Eskimo-style" **clothing made from *Florida Times Union* newspapers.** They saved winter issues of the paper for seven years to make the costumes, each of which required 700 yards of thread to assemble. **(August 17, 1936)**

Josephine-Joseph, born half-man, half-woman. He/she had a traveling show called the Josephine-Joseph show, which featured a number of unusual people. **Circa 1930s.**

John Pecinovsky, Lime Springs, Iowa's **Half-and-Half Man,** was **of Bohemian descent** and ran a tavern in Bonair, four miles northwest of Cresco, in Howard County. He dressed in **different colors** on both sides and cut his hair and **shaved differently** on each side. **(May 22, 1940)**

Six hundred Colorado sales tax tokens—with a combined value of $1.20—went into making the ski costume **AUDREY TWITCHELL** wore when she showed up to schuss down the Broadmoor–Glen Cove ski course on Pike's Peak. **(July 4, 1938)**

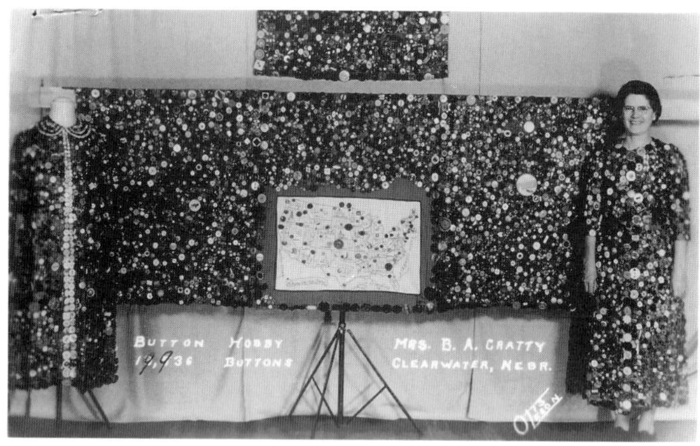

MRS. B. A. CRATLY of Clearwater, NEBRASKA, for many years collected buttons, but only if she could get them without paying for them. Through trading and exchanging, she had **gathered 19,922 different kinds of buttons from thirty-seven different countries** at the time this picture was taken. **(December 12, 1945)**

Bachelor **OWEN TOTTEN** of Mt. Erie, ILLINOIS, wore a button suit he **covered with 5,600 buttons, "no two alike." (March 31, 1946)**

200

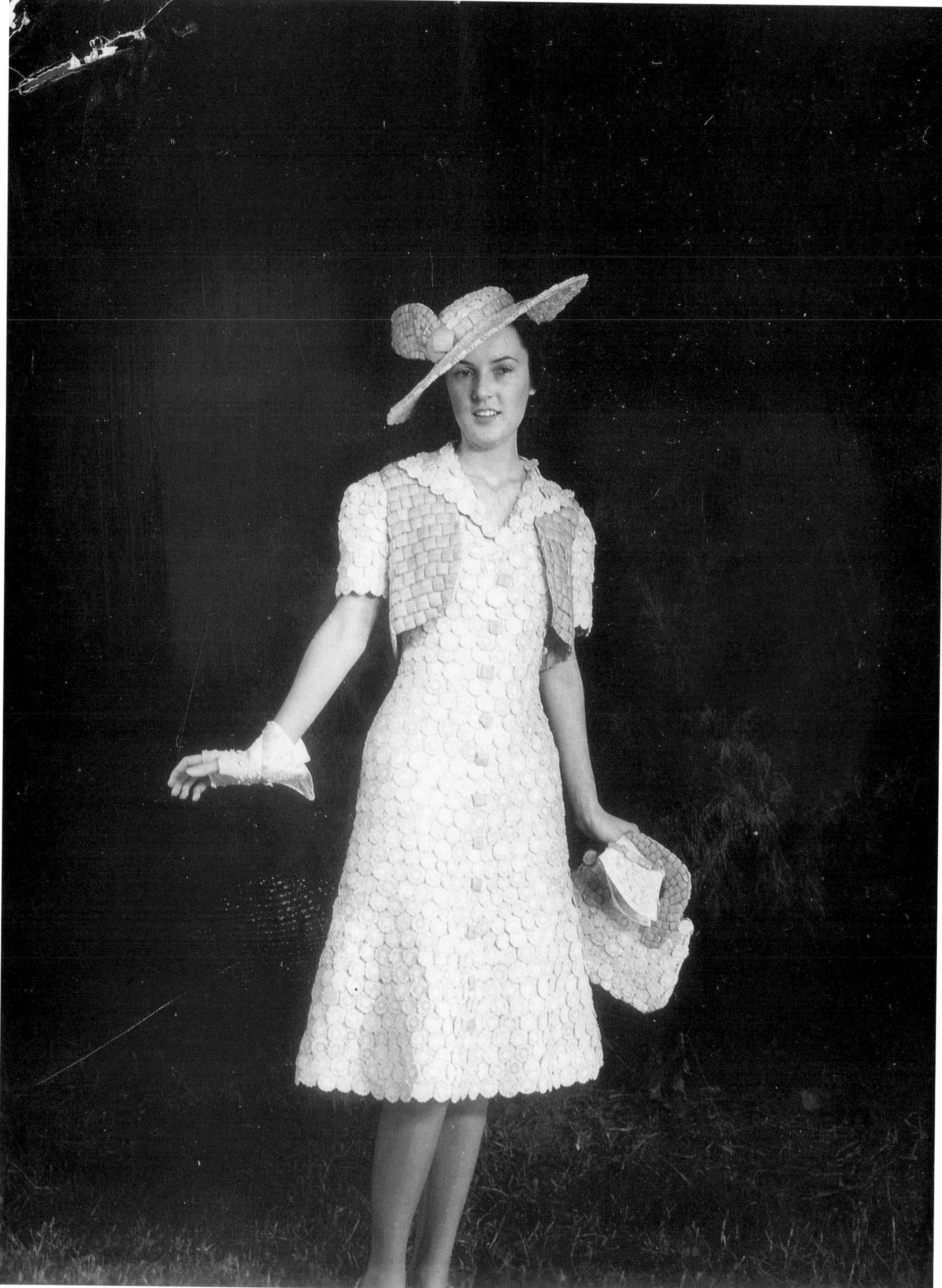

Mission, TEXAS, the self-proclaimed "Home of the Grapefruit," was also home to **WILMA BETH SHULKE,** who decorated this **dress with cross-sections of corn cobs trimmed with orange peels. (May 23, 1940)**

Not to be outdone by her rivals elsewhere in Texas, **VIRGINIA WINN** of Mercedes, TEXAS, modeled a **forty-pound evening dress covered with nearly 60,000 grains of corn** stitched to the material one at a time. **(February 11, 1940)**

In order to push new uses for turkey products, the Chamber of Commerce of Cuero, TEXAS, in 1947 sponsored a fashion show for turkey feather attire. **BEVERLY BELL** spent five hours making this entry, which included **shoes made from the quill ends of the feathers. (August 4, 1947)**

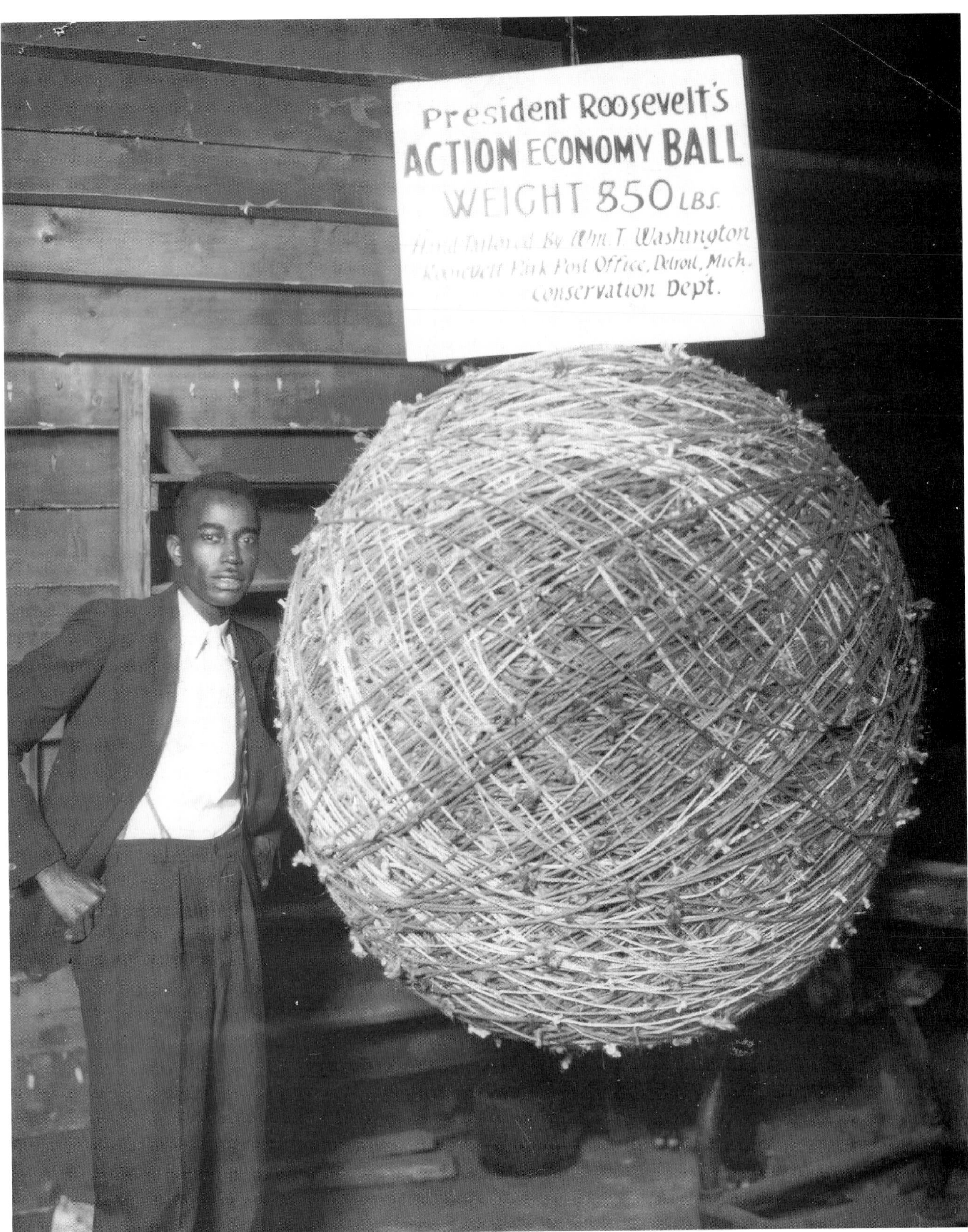

In 1933, **William T. Washington "hand tailored" an 850-pound ball of string during lunch hours** while at the Conservation Department at a DETROIT post office. The ball was six feet in diameter. In a letter dated March 13, 1940, Ripley tried unsuccessfully to obtain the string ball for the Odditorium in New York City.

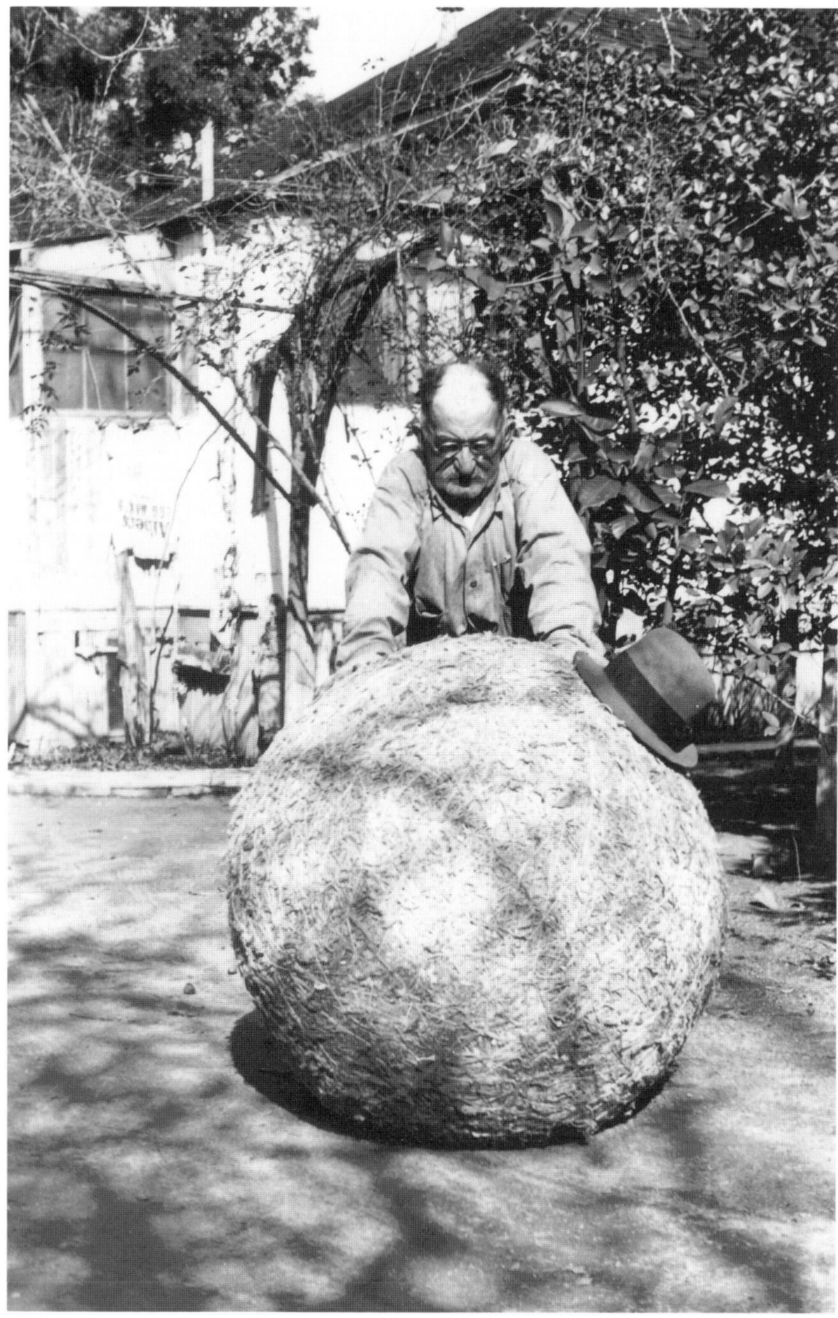

A recluse named **S. S. STAMBAUGH** for several years collected **eight-inch lengths of string** from a local flour mill in Tulare, CALIFORNIA, and by knotting and winding the pieces was able to build a three-foot-diameter twine ball in less than two years. Upon seeing the huge creation a friendly visitor calculated that **Stambaugh had tied 463,040 knots in nearly 132 miles of twine to make the 320-pound ball. (March 22, 1938)**

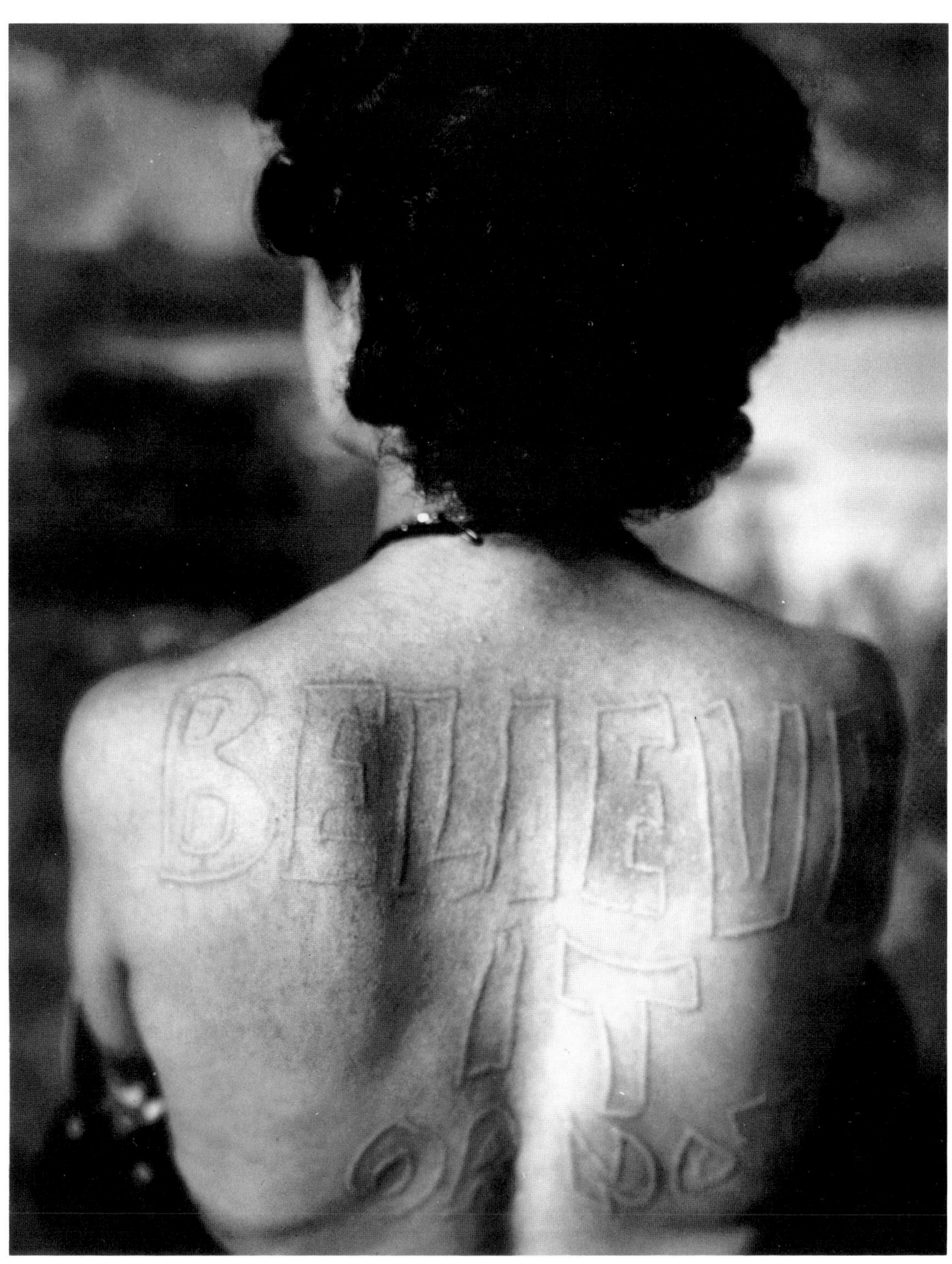

Rosa Barthelme—The Human Slate.

Museums

Ripley's Believe It or Not! Museum
4960 Clifton Hill
Niagara Falls, Ontario L2G 3N4
Canada
(416) 356-2238

Ripley's Believe It or Not! Museum
Cranberry Village
Cavendish, P.E.I. C0A 1N0
Canada
(902) 963-3444

Ripley's Believe It or Not! Museum
7850 Beach Boulevard
Buena Park, California 90620
(714) 522-1155

Ripley's Believe It or Not! Museum
175 Jefferson Street
San Francisco, California 94133
(415) 771-6188

Ripley's Believe It or Not! Museum
19 San Marco Avenue
St. Augustine, Florida 32084
(904) 824-1606

Ripley's Believe It or Not! Museum
250 S.W. Bay Boulevard
Mariner Square
Newport, Oregon 97365
(503) 265-2206

Ripley's Believe It or Not! Museum
901 North Ocean Boulevard
Myrtle Beach, South Carolina 29578
(803) 448-2331

Ripley's Believe It or Not! Museum
800 Parkway
Gatlinburg, Tennessee 37738
(615) 436-5096

Ripley's Believe It or Not! Museum
301 Alamo Plaza (across from the Alamo)
San Antonio, Texas 78205
(512) 224-9299

Ripley's Believe It or Not! Museum
601 East Safari Parkway
Grand Prairie, Texas 75050
(214) 263-2391

Ripley's Believe It or Not! Museum
115 Broadway
Wisconsin Dells, Wisconsin 53965
(608) 254-2184

Ripley's Believe It or Not! Museum
P.O. Box B1
Raptis Plaza, Cavill Mall
Surfer's Paradise, Queensland 4217
Australia
(61) 7-592-0040

Ripley's Believe It or Not! Museum
Units 5 and 6
Ocean Boulevard
South Promenade
Blackpool, Lancashire
England FY4 IEZ
(44) 253-41033 x 286

Ripley's Believe It or Not! Museum
Yong-In Farmland
310, Jeonda-Ri, Pogok-Myon
Yongin-Gun, Kyonggi-do, Korea

Ripley's Believe It or Not! Museum
6780 Hollywood Boulevard
Los Angeles, California 90028
(213) 466-6335

Ripley's Believe It or Not! Museum
Radhuspladsen 57
DK-1550 Copenhagen V
Denmark
(45) 33-918991

Ripley's Believe It or Not! Museum
8201 International Drive
Orlando, Florida 32819
(407) 872-3081

Ripley's Believe It or Not! Odditorium
The Windmill
9 Marine Parade
Great Yarmouth, Norfolk
England NR30 3AH
(44) 493-332217

Ripley's Believe It or Not! Museum
Aunque Ud. No Lo Crea de Ripley
Londres No. 4
Col. Juarez
C.P. 06600
Mexico, D.F.
(52) 5546 7670

Cecil E. King

USED 11/3/41

Los Angeles, California
Aug. 25, 1941

Mr. Robert Ripley
c/o King Feature Syndicate.

Dear Mr. Ripley.

A few days ago I read in the Los Angeles Examiner, your cartoon which featured a woman in Chicago who can read a book upside down. I have always been able to do so, as fast and accurate as when book is right side up. I did not think it was an accomplishment to rate sending the fact in to you, altho' my friends have urged me to do so, many times. However, I will be very pleased if you could use this fact; and I'd be very glad to send you a picture, and anyway to prove my statement. I am an amateur poet, having had over one hundred poems published in various newspapers thro'out the United States.

Very Sincerely Yours,

(Miss) Cecil Edna King.
240 W. Santa Barbara Ave.
Los Angeles, Calif.

PAGE 98

Siegmund Klein
PHYSICAL CULTURE STUDIO

USED 11/8/41

717 SEVENTH AVENUE
(AT 48TH STREET)
NEW YORK CITY

Aug.25,1941

Mr. Robert L.Ripley
235 East 45 St.,
New York City

My Dear Mr. Ripley:

It has been a long time since I have mailed you something about myself for publication in your "Believe It Or Not".

I have in the past few weeks made a few experiments in hand-balancing and think that the enclosed picture with the explanatory remarks on the back explain what I have done.

In the event that you use this in your column, I do not know if it would be advisable to let readers know how I timed this or not. I had to find out about the rest periods and how long it takes to do the "dips" through experiment.

Much to my surprise I found that the sets of "five" for 10 times went the easiest, and that "3" dips of 17 sets about the hardest, but think that the 5 sets of 10 "dips", would be the best one to use if you think it worthy of your column.

I also have a picture showing the full hand stand, but thought that the position of the chest touching the bench each time would be more appropiate.

There are many thousands of "hand-balacers" in the country that I know would like to try this, as I hold quite a few records on this type of balancing.

Trusting to hewr from you at your earliest conveniese, and I would appreciate hearing from you if you will use this, the approximate date.

Yours sincerely,

Siegmund Klein

The Studio, Located In The Heart of New York's Theatrical District, Is The Only Gymnasium Of Its Kind In The World

PAGE 143

IVanhoe 1395

Larry Foto Service
PRESS - COMMERCIAL - AERIAL PHOTOGRAPHY
8097 DWYER
DETROIT - MICHIGAN

USED 2/2/42

November 31, 1941

Mr. Robert Ripley
% King Features Syndicate Inc.
235 E. 45th. Street
N.Y. N.Y.

Dear Mr Ripley:

Enclosed is 1-8x10 glossy photograph of Bill Wausmann carrying a pencil under his ear, instead of on his ear. Mr. Wausmann works at the Mt. Elliot Recreation in Detroit.

I am Submitting this photograph for publication at your usual rates.

3rd. class return postage is enclosed should the photograph be unacceptable.

Memo to send both sent to B. McDat Maw- on 1/23/42

Sincerely yours,

L. Jamrisko Jr.
L. Jamrisko Jr.

PAGE 91

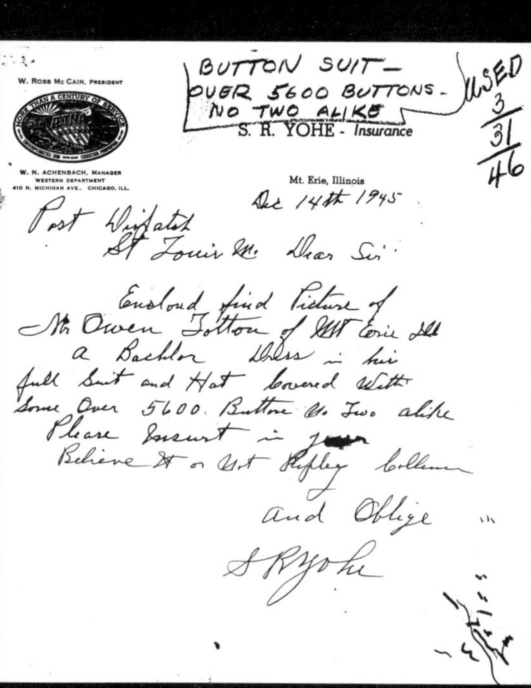

W. Ross McCain, President

W. N. Achenbach, Manager
Western Department
410 N. Michigan Ave., Chicago, Ill.

BUTTON SUIT—
OVER 5600 BUTTONS—
NO TWO ALIKE

S. R. YOHE - Insurance

USED 3/31/46

Mt. Erie, Illinois

Dec 14th 1945

Post Dispatch
St Louis Mo. Dear Sir:

Enclosed find Picture of Mr. Owen Totton of Mt Erie Ill a Bachlor Dress in his full Suit and Hat Covered With Some Over 5600 Buttons No Two alike. Please Insert in your Believe It or Not Ripley Collum

And Oblige

S R Yohe

PAGE 198